GOVERNMENT, BUSINESS, AND THE AMERICAN ECONOMY

Robert Langran
Villanova University

Martin Schnitzer
Virginia Tech

Prentice Hall

UPPER SADDLE RIVER, NEW JERSEY 07458

Library of Congress Cataloging-in-Publication Data

Langran, Robert.
    Government, business, and the American economy/Robert Langran, Martin Schnitzer.
        p. cm.
    Includes bibliographical references and index.
    ISBN 0-13-949132-5
        1. Industrial policy—United States.   2. Trade regulation—United States.   I. Schnitzer,
Martin.   II. Title.

HD3616.U453 L35 2000
338.973—dc21   00-058014

VP, Editorial director: Laura Pearson
Director of marketing: Beth Gillett Mejia
Assistant editor: Brian Prybella
Editorial assistant: Beth Murtha
Editorial/production supervision: Kari Callaghan Mazzola
Prepress and manufacturing buyer: Ben Smith
Electronic page makeup: Kari Callaghan Mazzola and John P. Mazzola
Interior design: John P. Mazzola
Cover director: Jayne Conte
Cover design: Bruce Kenselaar
Cover photos: Left and top right: Laimute E. Druskis; Bottom right: Jane Latta

This book was set in 10/12 Meridien by Big Sky Composition
and was printed and bound by Courier Companies, Inc.
The cover was printed by Phoenix Color Corp.

© 2001 by Prentice-Hall, Inc.
A Division of Pearson Education
Upper Saddle River, New Jersey 07458

Printed in the United States of America
10   9   8   7   6   5   4   3   2   1

ISBN 0-13-949132-5

PRENTICE-HALL INTERNATIONAL (UK) LIMITED, *London*
PRENTICE-HALL OF AUSTRALIA PTY. LIMITED, *Sydney*
PRENTICE-HALL CANADA INC., *Toronto*
PRENTICE-HALL HISPANOAMERICANA, S.A., *Mexico*
PRENTICE-HALL OF INDIA PRIVATE LIMITED, *New Delhi*
PRENTICE-HALL OF JAPAN, INC., *Tokyo*
PEARSON EDUCATION ASIA PTE. LTD., *Singapore*
EDITORA PRENTICE-HALL DO BRASIL, LTDA., *Rio de Janeiro*

CONTENTS

PART III SOCIAL REGULATION OF BUSINESS 117

CHAPTER 7 GOVERNMENT AND THE CONSUMER 117

CHAPTER 8 EMPLOYMENT POLICY 144

CHAPTER 9 ENVIRONMENTAL PROTECTION 173

PREFACE

The purpose of *Government, Business, and the American Economy* is to integrate economics, business, and U.S. politics into a unified whole. Most Americans cite the economy as their major concern. When times are good, as they have been in recent years, Americans are satisfied, and this bodes well for politicians on election day; when times are bad, Americans are not satisfied, and this means trouble for politicians. Business is the centerpiece of the American economy, and private enterprise employs the great majority of American workers. Moreover, American business firms operate all over the world. Government is important to the economy and business in several ways: It regulates the functions of business, such as foreign trade, consumer product safety, labor relations, and competition. It also purchases many kinds of goods and services, and is a major employer of workers. Finally, it affects the American economy through taxation and expenditures.

This book also covers some of the major developments of the past century and extends them into the twenty-first century. Probably the most important development is the creation of the European Union, which represents the economic and political integration of most of the countries of Europe. A common currency unit called the Euro has also been created. In the Western hemisphere, two major trading blocs have been created: Canada, Mexico, and the United States signed a free trade agreement called NAFTA, which is designed to promote the flow of trade among these countries. In South America, a customs union called MERCOSUR includes Argentina, Brazil, Bolivia, Chile, Paraguay, and Uruguay. Economic integration is also occurring in other parts of the world.

A cross-disciplined approach gives the book a flexibility that will broaden its appeal. It is adaptable to many courses. It can be used in courses taken by public administration and pre-law majors. It also can be used in government and business courses that are normally taught in business schools and in introductory courses in colleges where economics and political science may be integrated. The book's strength is that it is topical and it covers a wide range of events that are relevant to the twenty-first century.

The book utilizes cases that are related to topical events. An example involves sexual harassment at Mitsubishi, a Japanese conglomerate with plants in the United States. Other cases involve product liability lawsuits, with the tobacco industry serving as the most visible example. Another very important case involves the federal government's antitrust lawsuit against Microsoft. At the end of each chapter there are "Questions for Discussion," which can be used to stimulate class participation or as examination questions. A list of "Recommended Readings" is also presented at the end of each chapter.

ABOUT THE AUTHORS

Robert Langran is professor of political science at Villanova University. His area of expertise is American constitutional law, and he also teaches a course on Government and Business. He has won the Lindback Award for Distinguished Teaching and the Faculty Service Award. He has published a book on the Supreme Court, which is in its fourth edition, plus numerous articles.

Martin Schnitzer is a professor of international management at Virginia Tech. He has taught economics at the University of Arkansas, the University of Florida, and Virginia Tech. He has published many books, including *Comparative Economic Systems*, which is in its eighth edition, and has served as a consultant to the Joint Economic Committee of the U.S. Congress and the House Ways and Means Committee. He is a former editor of the *Virginia Social Science Journal*.

ACKNOWLEDGMENTS

Many people have contributed to the preparation of this book: We are deeply indebted to other authors who have informed us, and, where appropriate, we have cited their works. We thank Michael Brown of the University of California, Santa Cruz, and Neil Mitchell of the University of New Mexico for reviewing the manuscript. We also thank Kari Callaghan Mazzola of Big Sky Composition. Martin Schnitzer thanks his wife, Joan, and his secretary, Melissa Kessinger, for their invaluable assistance in putting together his part of the book. He also thanks Larry Thompson of Refugees International, who has traveled extensively in Africa and East Asia; Dr. Harrison Fox, former aide to Senator John Danforth, who provided the information on special interest groups; and his graduate students from France and Spain, who wrote about the impact of the European Union on their countries. Robert Langran thanks his wife, Eleanor, for her patience and support during the writing of this book, and the people at Prentice Hall for their encouragement throughout this endeavor.

CHAPTER 1

THE STATE IN A CHANGING WORLD

The role of the state has changed throughout history. From earliest times people have grouped together into larger associations, starting with clans and extending to the modern state of today. States have come in various forms, depending on a mix of factors including culture, natural endowments, and geographical location. Athens developed as a state because its location provided it opportunities for trade.[1] Its economic underpinning was based on slave ownership. Rome developed on a much larger scale. Its success was based on its coercive power, as represented by its legions, over all individuals and organizations within its territories. Its wealth was based on the spoils of war, and its legal system gave it authority in key areas such as commerce.[2] The city-state of Venice developed as a maritime power because of its location on the Adriatic Sea. It was ruled by an oligarchy that provided goods and services to the people in return for their support.[3]

By the end of the fifteenth century, the balance of economic and political power had begun to shift away from Venice, Genoa, and other city-states to the maritime countries of Spain and Portugal. Spain had become a nation-state with a consolidated territory and population. Authority was centralized and encompassed separate judicial, legislative, and executive functions. State intervention played a vital role in the development of Spanish colonies and markets in North America and South America. Mercantilism involved a major state role in the promotion of trade. The proponents of mercantilism were concerned with national wealth because they perceived national power as resting on an economic foundation. They believed that government ought to undertake actively to guide the activities of its citizens along those lines that were conducive to national well-being.[4]

Notions of the role of the state began to change in the eighteenth and nineteenth centuries, largely as a result of the Industrial Revolution. It consisted mainly of the application of machinery to manufacturing, mining, transportation, and agriculture. The factory system replaced the traditional method of small-scale production in the home, and a new class of industrial capitalists was created. It was they who shaped the course of economic development by reinvesting their earnings in new enterprises. It was the individual, not the state, who created wealth, and it was generally recognized that the market was the best instrument for allocating resources.[5] The state was best held to certain core functions—providing public goods such as defense, educating its citizens, and enforcing contracts—deemed essential for the market to flourish. Redistribution of income came mainly through private charity and other actions.

The twentieth century changed the role of the state in several ways. World War I ended the monarchies in Germany, the Austro-Hungarian empire, and Russia.[6] The Russian Revolution of 1917 led to the rise of a new political and economic system by which private property ownership was abolished, the state was put in control of resource allocation through central planning, and the Communist Party ruled. The Depression of the 1930s caused economic and social devastation in the Western world. The role of government in the United States, Canada, and Western Europe expanded. This role took several forms. The first was the use of fiscal and monetary policies to stimulate economic activity in order to create jobs.[7] The second was the provision of welfare benefits to provide assistance for those who were unemployed and for those who were too old to work.

But as Table 1-1 indicates, the role of government increased significantly during the period after the end of World War II up to the present. The war destroyed most of Europe and government expenditures, supported by Marshall Plan aid from the United States, were necessary to rebuild it. Fear of a return to the mass unemployment of the Depression led governments to adopt a policy to promote full employment through the use of Keynesian economic policies designed to promote consumption through government expenditures. The welfare state expanded through the transfer of income from the public sector to the private sector. The role of the state, as measured by expenditures, doubled between 1960 and 1996. Sweden, the consummate example of the welfare state, increased its expenditures relative to Gross National Product (GNP) by 800 percent from 1937 to 1996.

THE ROLE OF GOVERNMENT IN THE AMERICAN ECONOMY

For the purpose of organization, government intervention and participation in the American economy can be divided into four areas that provide the subject matter of the remainder of this chapter. First, there is the area of public finance, in which government is a purchaser of goods and services as well as a tax collector. Government economic stabilization policies can be considered a part of this area. Second, government regulation and control prescribe specific conditions under which private economic activity can and cannot take place. It may interpose itself in employer-employee relations by prescribing rules of

TABLE 1-1 GOVERNMENT EXPENDITURES AS A PERCENT OF GDP, 1913–1996

COUNTRY	1913	1920	1937	1960	1980	1996
Canada	—	13.3	18.6	28.6	38.8	44.7
France	17.0	27.6	29.0	34.6	46.1	54.5
Germany	14.8	25.0	42.4	32.4	45.1	49.0
Italy	11.1	22.5	24.5	30.1	41.9	52.9
Japan	8.3	14.8	25.4	17.5	32.0	36.2
Netherlands	9.0	13.5	19.0	33.7	55.2	49.9
Norway	8.3	13.7	—	29.9	37.5	45.5
Spain	8.3	9.3	18.4	18.8	32.2	43.3
Sweden	6.3	8.1	10.4	31.0	60.1	64.7
Switzerland	2.7	4.6	6.1	17.2	32.8	37.6
United Kingdom	12.7	26.2	30.0	32.2	43.0	41.9
United States	1.8	7.0	8.6	27.0	31.8	33.3
Average	**9.1**	**15.4**	**19.4**	**27.7**	**46.4**	**46.1**

Source: "A Survey of the World Economy: The Future of the State," *The Economist* (London, England: September 20, 1997), p. 8.

employment. It may also influence business operations both directly and indirectly through antitrust and other laws. Third, government is the single largest employer in the U.S. economy and, as such, competes directly with private industry for labor. Fourth, government is a major provider of credit.

PUBLIC FINANCE

Public finance involves the spending and taxing activities of government. Government spending for goods and services divert resources from the private to the public sector of the economy. Taxes give the government control over an economy's resources and also affect the distribution of income among groups of people. The public sector of an economy differs from the private sector because the state has the sovereign power to compel individuals to make financial contributions and to accept certain services. Another difference is the nonmaterial and general welfare character of most government activities. Unlike private business, government is not always expected to yield financial returns. Moreover, if financial returns are expected from a given government activity, the returns need not be immediate and may be adjusted to a cost basis rather than a profit basis.

FEDERAL GOVERNMENT BUDGET

The importance of the federal government's budget to the American economy cannot be minimized. It exerts an influence on the economy in terms of the level of revenues and taxes, of whether or not it is balanced, and of the specific expenditures it authorizes. It is the focal point for the presentation and implementation of the government's economic policy. It is often used as a means of publicizing government policies toward particular sectors, groups of people, or industries, either in an attempt to improve the chances of success for the proposed measures or, at times, as a substitute for any specific measure. Finally, through the implementation of fiscal policy, the budget can be used to raise or lower the level of national income.

Resources   The budget of the federal government is financed from two income sources—taxes and borrowing. As Table 1-2 and Figure 1-1 indicate, the two most important tax sources of federal government revenues are the personal income tax and payroll taxes, which accounted for 74 percent of total revenue for the fiscal year 2000. The corporate income tax, which was once the most important source of federal government revenue, is of little importance today, accounting for 11 percent of total revenue. Excise taxes are a minor source of government revenue, accounting for 4 percent in 2000. Excise taxes are consumption-based taxes and are levied on the sale of a particular commodity. Excises are levied on the consumption of gasoline, alcohol, tobacco,[8] and other products. They can be employed as "user charges" to collect part or all of the cost of services enjoyed by specific taxpayers.

Payroll taxes were introduced into the federal revenue system by the Social Security Act of 1935 and have increased in importance to the point that they are now second to the personal income tax as a source of revenue. Payroll taxes are earmarked through trust funds to finance Social Security programs, of which there are two types. The first type is a federal system of old age, survivors, disability, and health insurance (OASDHI), which is financed by payroll taxes collected from employers and employees in equal amounts. The second type is a federal and state system of unemployment compensation, which is financed mainly by a payroll tax on employers. Payroll taxes constitute a significant part of the tax payments made by lower-income groups.

TABLE 1-2   FEDERAL GOVERNMENT REVENUE BY SOURCES
FOR THE YEAR 2000[1] (BILLIONS OF DOLLARS)

SOURCES	AMOUNT
Individual income taxes	900
Corporate income taxes	189
Payroll taxes	637
Excise taxes	70
Estate and gift taxes	27
Customs duties	18
Miscellaneous receipts	42
Total revenues	**1,883**

[1]Estimate.

Source: Executive Office of the President, Office of Manpower and Budget, *A Citizen's Guide to the Federal Budget, Fiscal Year 2000* (Washington, D.C.: OMB, 1999), p. 8.

FIGURE 1-1   THE FEDERAL GOVERNMENT DOLLAR—WHERE IT COMES FROM

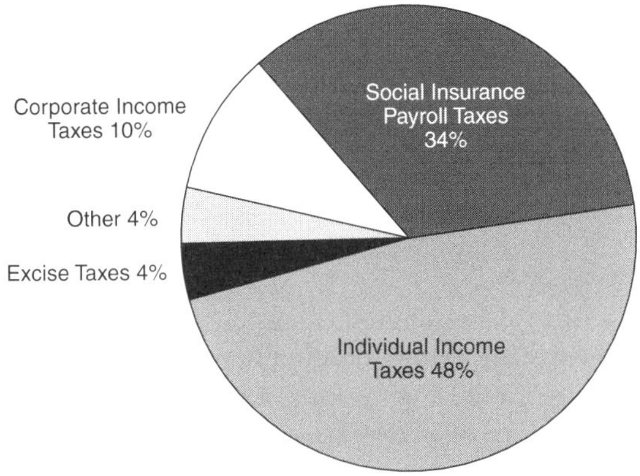

Corporate Income Taxes 10%

Other 4%

Excise Taxes 4%

Social Insurance Payroll Taxes 34%

Individual Income Taxes 48%

Source: Executive Office of the President, Office of Manpower and Budget, *A Citizen's Guide to the Federal Budget, Fiscal Year 2000* (Washington, D.C.: OMB, 1999), p. 7.

The difference between federal government revenues and expenditures is made up by borrowing, which is the responsibility of the U.S. Treasury. It can borrow by issuing three types of debt obligations, ranging from the sale of short-term Treasury bills to long-term Treasury bonds. Borrowing is an easy way out for politicians and the public. Politicians can spend more money, and the public can "have their cake and eat it too," in that they can postpone payment until a later date. But living beyond one's means can create problems for governments as well as individuals. It has increased interest payments, which is a fixed cost in the federal budget. Borrowing also has affected the foreign trade deficit, and has made the United States the world's leading debtor nation.

Expenditures   Federal government expenditures for the fiscal year 2000 are an estimated $1.8 trillion, which is around 20 percent of the U.S. Gross Domestic Product (GDP).[9] Expenditures can be divided into two major categories—discretionary and mandatory. Discretionary expenditures cover a wide variety of government functions and activities. About half of all discretionary expenditures go for national defense—a much smaller share than in the past. The remaining expenditures are for housing, agriculture, education, environmental protection, law enforcement, space exploration, research and development, international aid, and government operations. Conversely, mandatory expenditures consist mainly of large entitlement programs, such as Social Security, Medicare and Medicaid, and of interest payments on the federal debt. For most mandatory spending programs, the federal government is obligated to spending levels that depend on factors that are beyond its direct control.

Table 1-3 (on page 6) and Figure 1-2 (on page 7) present a breakdown of estimated federal government expenditures for the fiscal year 2000. Discretionary expenditures made up approximately one-third of the total net interest on the public debt, which is a fixed cost that has to be met, and accounted for $215 billion. Mandatory entitlement expenditures, which have risen rapidly over the last twenty-five years, can be expected to continue to increase. Beginning about the year 2010, the first wave of the baby-boom generation will reach retirement age, bringing unprecedented pressure on federal financing for Social Security, Medicare, and Medicaid programs. At about the same time, the number of people working and paying taxes to support these and other programs will rise more slowly.

STATE AND LOCAL GOVERNMENTS

The political structure of the United States is that of federalism, with sovereignty legally and constitutionally divided between the federal and state governments. Despite the increasing importance that the federal government has assumed since the start of World War II, any consideration of public finance would be incomplete without the inclusion of state and local government financial systems. One major item of federal government spending is national defense, a function that clearly belongs under its control. Related items such as foreign aid, aid to veterans, and interest on the national debt are also clearly the responsibility of the federal government. Social Security, which dates back to the Depression of the 1930s, is another responsibility of the federal government in order to assure uniformity in taxes, benefits, and standards.

The essential division of responsibility in a federal political system is that drawn between the powers of the federal government and those of the state governments. Within each state there is also a second division of responsibility between the powers of the state and those of local government units—counties,

TABLE 1-3   FEDERAL GOVERNMENT EXPENDITURES
FOR THE YEAR 2000[1] (BILLIONS OF DOLLARS)

SOURCES	AMOUNT
Discretionary	
Defense	262
Non-defense	330
Total discretionary	**592**
Mandatory	
Social Security	405
Medicare and Medicaid	328
Means-tested entitlements (except Medicaid)	112
Deposit insurance	−2
Other	116
Total mandatory	959
Net interest	215
Total mandatory	**1,766**

[1]Estimate

Source: Executive Office of the President, Office of Manpower and Budget, *Budget of the United States Government, Fiscal Year 2000* (Washington, D.C.: OMB, 1999), p. 12.

FIGURE 1-2   THE FEDERAL GOVERNMENT DOLLAR—WHERE IT GOES

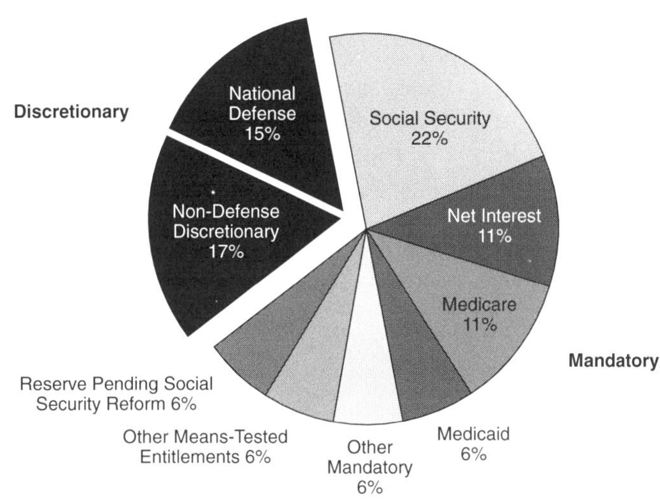

Source: Executive Office of the President, Office of Management and Budget, *A Citizen's Guide to the Federal Budget, Fiscal Year 2000* (Washington, D.C.: OMB, 1999), p. 10.

cities, school districts, and so forth. This division of responsibility is more administrative and legislative than constitutional. All local units of government are creations of the states, which hold the residual power to destroy them. The division of financial authority between the states and their subordinate local government units varies from state to state, and the administrative devices for coordinating their expenditure and tax systems are diverse. Broadly speaking, the more divisible and concentrated the benefits are from the service provided, the more advantageous it is to have the service provided by the local unit of government.

State and Local Government Revenues   For state governments, the sales tax is the single most important revenue source. Normally, the tax is imposed as a percentage of the retail selling price of goods and services. Income taxation is a second source of revenue for state governments. However, states tend to be limited in their usage of income taxation by the fact that the national economy is an integrated market. The freedom of migration for both humans and other resources across state boundaries tends to insure that state government will set relatively low tax rates on income. Local governments may also impose income taxes. Transfers from the federal government to state and local governments, which take the form of grants-in-aid, are a third important source of revenue. Property taxes are the primary revenue source for local governments. Property is not subject to federal government taxation, and state governments have generally left this revenue source to the localities. Table 1-4 (on page 8) presents the major revenue sources for state and local governments for 1997.

TABLE 1-4   MAJOR REVENUE SOURCES FOR STATE
AND LOCAL GOVERNMENTS (BILLIONS OF DOLLARS)

Revenues by Source	1,513.6
From Federal Government	234.8
From State and Local Sources	1,278.7
Taxes	689.0
Property	209.4
Sales	249.0
Personal income	146.8
Corporate income	32.0
Other	51.7
Charges and Miscellaneous	298.9
Education	49.7
Interest earnings	57.6
Sewerage	21.1
Hospitals	50.5
Interest earnings	57.6
Utility and Liquor Store Revenues	75.3
Insurance Trust Revenues	215.5

Source: U.S. Department of Commerce, Bureau of the Census, *Statistical Abstract of the United States, 1999* (Washington, D.C., 1999), p. 312.

State and Local Government Expenditures   State and local government expenditures for 1997 amounted to $1.4 billion.[10] Education, as Table 1-5 indicates, is the single most important component of expenditures, accounting for one-third of the total. One of the most striking of the post-World War II phenomena was the rapid increase in population, which continues to grow. Education expenditures increased almost six-fold during the period between 1946 and 1962. Moreover, as the United States has shifted from mass production industries to knowledge-based industries, demand for an educated labor force has increased. More students are finishing high school and more are going to college. New physical facilities are constantly in the process of construction. Expenditures on highways, hospitals, and other public facilities have also shown a marked increase in recent years. Affluence and the aging of the population are contributing factors.

A COMPARISON OF GOVERNMENT EXPENDITURES BY COUNTRIES

Government expenditures represent a transfer of resources from the private sector of an economy to the public sector, and they also represent the contribution of the government sector to the total Gross Domestic Product (GDP)[11] As Figure 1-3 shows, total government spending amounted to 29 percent of U.S. GDP in 1998, while private spending contributed 71 percent. The federal government spent about 20 percent of GDP, and state and local governments contributed 12 percent.

**TABLE 1-5   MAJOR EXPENDITURES OF STATE
AND LOCAL GOVERNMENTS (BILLIONS OF DOLLARS)**

Expenditures	1,397.6
Direct	1,393.7
General	1,189.4
Education	398.9
Hospitals	70.6
Health	40.2
Highways	79.1
Public welfare	40.6
Fire protection	17.7
Police protection	44.7
Corrections	37.5
Government administration	55.0
Interest on general debt	58.9
Utilities	92.5
Insurance trust expenditures	108.7

Source: U.S. Department of Commerce, Bureau of the Census, *Statistical Abstract of the United States, 1999* (Washington, D.C. 1999), p. 312.

FIGURE 1-3   GOVERNMENT SPENDING AS A SHARE OF GDP, 1998

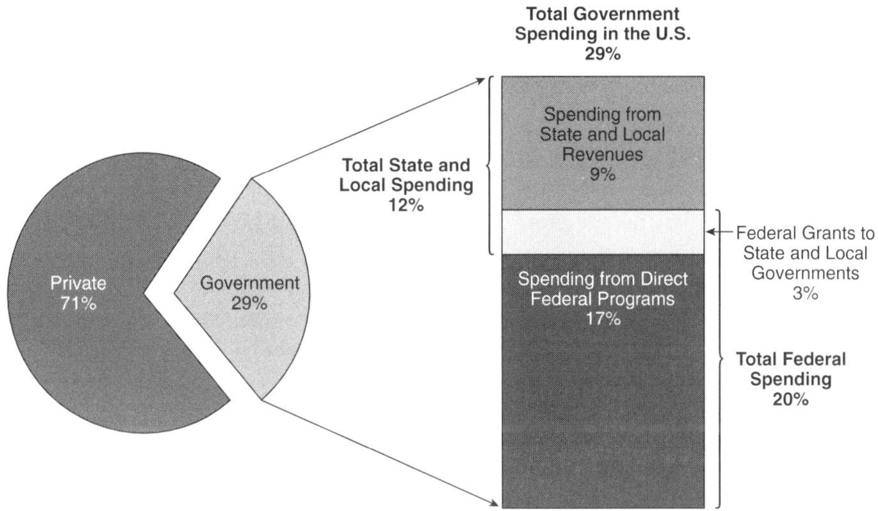

Note: Numbers do not add due to rounding.

Source: Executive Office of the President, Office of Management and Budget, *A Citizen's Guide to the Federal Budget, Fiscal Year 2000* (Washington, D.C.: OMB, 1999), p. 2.

However, as Table 1-6 (on page 10) shows, in comparison with other countries, total government expenditures expressed as a percentage of GDP is much smaller in the United States than in other major industrial countries, with the

TABLE 1-6   GOVERNMENT SPENDING AS A PERCENTAGE OF GDP FOR SELECTED COUNTRIES, 1996

COUNTRY	PERCENT
Canada	44.7
France	54.5
Germany	49.0
Japan	36.2
Italy	52.9
Sweden	64.7
United Kingdom	41.9
United States	33.3

Source: "A Survey of the World Economy: The Future of the State," *The Economist* (London, England; September 20, 1997), p. 8.

exception of Japan. This can be attributed to the fact that income transfer payments in these countries are much higher than they are in the United States. They would include family allowances, free medical care, paid maternity leave, old-age pensions, unemployment compensation, free college education, and accident benefits. However, there is also a reverse side to these expenditures; somebody has to pay for them. Thus, the level of taxation in these countries is going to be much higher than it is in the United States. In such countries as France and Sweden, it is going to be over half of their GDP.

ECONOMIC STABILIZATION POLICIES

It is generally accepted that the economic and political objectives of U.S. society are a high level of employment, price stability, economic growth, and a balance-of-payments equilibrium. Each goal does not necessarily lend itself to precise definition, and the attainment of one may not help achieve the others. Considerable government intervention is necessary. This intervention takes the form of macroeconomic stabilization of fiscal and monetary policies that are implemented by the federal government's use of taxation, payments, and transfer payments, and by the Federal Reserve's control over the money supply and interest rates.

Fiscal Policy   The term *fiscal policy* refers to the tax and expenditure policies of the federal government.[12] Its objective is either to increase or decrease the level of aggregate demand through changes in the level of government expenditures and taxation. For example, an expansionary fiscal policy is supposed to stimulate economic growth and employment through an increase in government spending, a decrease in taxation, or both. Conversely, fiscal policy can be used to contract the level of aggregate demand. Taxes can be raised, expenditures can be reduced, or a combination of these approaches can be used. The federal budget, because of its sheer size, exercises a considerable influence on the American economy.

Monetary Policy   Monetary policy is used by the Federal Reserve to control the level of national output and the price level through variations in the money supply.[13] An increase in the money supply will lower interest rates and stimulate private and public spending; a decrease in the money supply will raise interest rates and reduce public and private spending. The Federal Reserve cannot fix the amount of credit and its cost independently. If it wants to restrain the rate of growth in the money supply, it must allow interest rates to rise as high as possible. If it wants to keep interest rates low, it has to accept the consequences of an increase in the money supply. Monetary policy is independent from fiscal policy in that control over it is not in the hands of the federal government.

GOVERNMENT REGULATION

The legal basis for federal government regulation of certain economic activities is based on the Constitution of the United States. Its single most important provision is found in Article 1, Section 8, the commerce clause that states that Congress shall have the power to regulate commerce among the states and with foreign nations. Eventually, federal regulation of commerce became restricted to interstate commerce, as opposed to intrastate commerce that came under state jurisdiction. In addition, Article 1, Section 8, gave Congress the power to levy and collect taxes, to pay debts and provide for the general welfare of the people, and to coin money and regulate its value. Regulations to promote the general welfare of the people are usually of a negative character. For example, the producers of food may not ship their products in interstate commerce unless they meet certain purity standards prescribed by law.

RATIONALE FOR GOVERNMENT REGULATION

There are several reasons for government regulation. One is competition, which is considered one of the basic institutions of a capitalist free-market economy. It is based on the notion that it contributes to social welfare. It is a regulator of economic activity, and is thought to maximize productivity, prevent excessive concentration of economic power, and protect consumer interests. But both business and government have intervened in different ways to circumvent competition, which is a hard taskmaster, for there are losers as well as winners. Business firms have formed various combinations, such as cartels and trusts, to eliminate competition. They have also engaged in collusive practices, such as price-fixing and tying agreements, to eliminate competition. Government subsidies and restraint on foreign competition also protect businesses, farmers, and other groups against competition.

Economic Regulation   Antitrust laws provide an example of economic regulation. They are based on two premises. The first is the English common law as it evolved through court decisions over a period of time. In general, these decisions held that restraints on trade or commerce are not in the public interest. In interpreting the common law, courts in England and the United States ruled that contracts or agreements to restrain or attempt to restrain trade were illegal. Another example of economic regulation involves control over certain industries that directly affect the public interest. An example would be regulation of a natural monopoly, which refers to a market in which a single seller is required for efficient production. Public utilities can be natural monopolies, but the services they provide are regulated; otherwise, they would charge monopoly prices.

Social Regulation   Other defects in the market system are the inability of consumers to express negative wants in the marketplace through the price mechanism, and externalities, such as pollution, which are an external cost of production. Many people would be happier if they could prevent the production and sale of cigarettes or the emission of noxious fumes from a chemical plant. But there is no way in which the marketprice mechanism can take these preferences into account, except through government control over the output and use of goods deemed deleterious to the public interest. Pollution is an example of an externality because producers can impose a cost on consumers without having to pay compensation. Consumer spending cannot mandate a clean environment, but government regulation can. Thus, a series of laws were passed by the federal government that require the cleaning up of various forms of pollution.

STATE AND LOCAL GOVERNMENT REGULATION

State and local governments were involved in regulation long before the federal government became involved. For example, a number of midwestern state governments enacted a series of laws designed to regulate railroad abuses in the period immediately following the Civil War. In 1871 Illinois created a railroad commission, authorizing it to fix maximum rates for intrastate freight and passenger service. Federal regulation of the railroads did not occur until 1887. State and local governments were the first to pass laws to protect consumers. Sanitary regulations, inspection of weights and measures, and the like were established local government functions at the beginning of the nation's history. State laws to protect consumers against the adulteration of goods and drugs were first passed in Virginia in 1848 and Ohio in 1853. The federal government passed the Pure Food and Drug Act in 1906.

GOVERNMENT AS AN EMPLOYER

One measure of the public sector's size and importance to the American economy is the number of people employed by various government units. In 1997, 5.3 million people, including military personnel, were employed by the federal government, while state and local governments employed 16.1 million people.[14] The total number of government employees—federal, state, and local—amounted to 21.4 million, which was approximately 16 percent of a total American labor force of 131 million workers. Of this total, 12 million, or approximately 55 percent, worked for local governments and 4.7 million, or approximately 22 percent, worked for state governments.[15] State and local government employment are expected to increase in the future since the demand for social services will increase, particularly as the population continues to grow older.

Two sets of administrative hierarchies, one public and the other private, have grown at different times for different reasons to carry out different functions. The public hierarchy developed much later than the private hierarchy. In 1929 the federal government's labor force in Washington was a great deal smaller than that of U.S. Steel or General Motors; today, it is much larger than both companies combined. Numerous federal agencies have been created, and a new administrative culture has developed. The work, attitudes, and perspectives of the private sector administrator and the government administrator have become and will remain almost as distinct and separate as those of the scientist and humanist. The attitudes of these two hierarchies define relations between the private and public sectors of the American economy.

GOVERNMENT AS A LENDER AND INSURER

The federal government is the nation's single largest source of credit and underwriting of risk. It has a number of programs that offer financial assistance to its citizens. These programs give assistance to students, business firms, farmers, home buyers, banks, and exporters. Some of them are an important source of credit for various sectors of the American economy. For example, the housing industry relies on the various federal mortgage credit programs. The Direct Student Loan Program provides several types of loans for students, which carry interest rates lower than the going market rate. Rural electrification and telecommunications loans are for the construction and operation of generating plants, electric transmission, and distribution lines or systems. Exporters can obtain financial assistance form the Export-Import Bank (Eximbank).

DIRECT LOANS

Direct loans have several characteristics. First, they are designed to promote socially useful activities rather than to remove imperfections in the credit market. Second, they contain a subsidy element, in that interest rates charged are lower than prevailing market rates. Third, they are financed directly out of federal budget revenues. Fourth, foreign loans are the largest single component of direct loans. In quantity, the most important types of foreign loans are development loans and loans made by the Export-Import Bank (Eximbank). Both loans create a foreign demand for U.S. goods and services. Table 1-7 (on page 14) presents the total value of federal government direct loans as of September 30, 1997.

**TABLE 1-7   FEDERAL GOVERNMENT DIRECT LOANS
AS OF SEPTEMBER 30, 1997 (BILLIONS OF DOLLARS)**

Student loan programs	42.0
Rural electrification and telecommunications	28.3
Economic assistance loans	20.9
Agricultural credit insurance funds	10.7
Other loans outstanding	102.2
	216.6

Source: U.S. General Accounting Office, *Consolidated Financial Statement of the United States, Fiscal year 1997*, p. 46.

LOAN GUARANTEES

From the standpoint of the amount of money involved, insured loans are by far the most important segment of federal government credit. In 1997 insured loans by the federal government amounted to $876.8 billion. The government may either insure or guarantee loans made by private lenders. The difference between loan insurance and loan guarantees is that a fee is generally charged for insurance. The best example of loan insurance is the Federal Housing Administration (FHA) mortgage program, which is designed to encourage lenders to make credit available to expand home ownership. It predominantly serves borrowers that the conventional credit market does not adequately serve: first-time home buyers, minorities, lower-income families, and residents of underserved areas. The Federal Family Education Loan program is an example of a loan guarantee program. Table 1-8 presents the amount of loan guarantees outstanding as of September 30, 1997.

GOVERNMENT-SPONSORED FINANCIAL INSTITUTIONS

A third way in which the federal government allocates credit, although indirectly, is through privately owned government-sponsored financial enterprises. These enterprises have been created by the government to perform special credit functions. Three of them, the Federal National Mortgage Association

**TABLE 1-8   FEDERAL GOVERNMENT LOAN GUARANTEES
AS OF SEPTEMBER 30, 1997 (BILLIONS OF DOLLARS)**

Federal Housing Administration	454.5
Federal Family Education	99.0
Veterans housing benefits	198.0
All other loan guarantees	125.3
	876.8

Source: U.S. General Accounting Office, *Consolidated Financial Statement of the United States, Fiscal Year 1997*, p. 47.

(Fannie Mae), the Federal Home Loan Mortgage Bank (Freddie Mac), and the Federal Home Loan Banks, serve the housing market. The Farm Credit System finances agriculture, and the Student Loan Market Association (Sallie Mae) makes a secondary market in federally guaranteed student loans. Each issues securities and uses the proceeds to finance its lending activities, and their earnings are exempt from state and local income taxes. They can borrow at interest rates significantly lower than even the best-rate private borrowers, and can make loans at interest below prevailing market rates.

GOVERNMENT AND THE WORLD ECONOMY

The world has changed more rapidly since 1990 than at any time since the end of World War II in 1945. Probably the seminal event of this century has been the collapse of communism in 1989. The Soviet Union is now a thing of the past, and its former republics have become independent countries that are proceeding unevenly toward democracy and free market capitalism. Poland, the Czech Republic, Hungary, and other Eastern and Central European countries that were once a part of the Soviet bloc are, for the most part, well on their way to becoming democratic market economies. Most state-owned enterprises are now privately owned. Throughout most of the world, from Germany to Argentina, a trend toward privatization of state-owned enterprises has occurred.

A new type of economic and social revolution is also underway. The factor that is transforming the world environment and the relationship of the United States within it is technological change, which is moving more rapidly than at any time in history. Advances in computers and telecommunications have shrunk distances, eroded national boundaries, and enlarged the domain of the global economy. This is the most significant force that will shape the first half of this century. Money is immediately transferable; on a given day, some $1 trillion will cross country borders throughout the world. Many services have become internationally tradable and easier to ship from one country to another than goods are. The power of international market forces to allocate resources certainly will have an impact on the role of government in the future.

So, does this mean the end of national governments? It is argued by some that the Internet will make avoiding taxes so easy and riskless that sovereignty will shift to individuals, leaving governments to die of fiscal starvation. Another argument is that the volume of world money is so large that its movements in and out of a currency have an enormous impact on world financial markets. It has total mobility, serves no economic function and finances nothing, and is easily panicked by a rumor or unexpected event.[16] Currency instability is created by forces over which governments have little or no control. A third argument is that large corporations have become transnational. In a transnational company, there is only one economic unit, the world, and national boundaries have largely become irrelevant. This means that there will have to be the development of supranational organizations to make and enforce rules in a global economy.

Nevertheless, governments will continue to play an important role in their respective countries. In many countries, entitlements have become accepted as a right by their citizens. In fact, not only are entitlement expenditures the single largest component of the U.S. federal budget, they are also the single largest component of the budgets of other industrialized nations. As Table 1-6 indicated, the trend toward bigger governments in most of the industrialized nations has been universal. Spending on public consumption, such as education, health, and pensions, has risen substantially. The most important cause of the increase in government expenditures has been the development of the modern welfare state and the growth in income transfers and subsidies. In the United States, for example, transfers and subsidies accounted for 6 percent of GDP in 1968; by 1999, they accounted for 13 percent.[17]

SUMMARY

A considerable amount of government intervention is an indispensable requisite for the establishment of even the freest type of economy. The very atmosphere for the conduct of economic activity is created by the ability of government to establish and maintain private property, freedom of enterprise, money and credit, and a system of civil laws for adjusting the private disputes of individuals. Government regulation exists for several reasons. It is used to intervene between sellers and buyers in order to protect either or both from certain harmful practices that may arise. For example, it is unlawful to market certain drugs unless they have been approved by the Food and Drug Administration. Antitrust policies are designed to deal with industry conduct, such as price-fixing, that discriminates against consumers. A third area of regulation involves the misuse of public resources, such as air and water, that causes pollution.

QUESTIONS FOR DISCUSSION

1. What is the role of government in a market economy such as the United States?
2. What is the difference between discretionary and mandatory government expenditures?
3. It is said that technology will reduce the importance of national governments in the world economy. Do you agree?
4. What are the differences between direct loans and loan guarantees?
5. Discuss the differences between economic and social regulation.
6. What are entitlements? Why are they the fastest growing component of the federal budget?

NOTES

1. The naval victory of Athens over Persia at Salamis in 480 B.C. made Athens the leading sea power of the Eastern Mediterranean for some 100 years; hence its dominance in trade.
2. The Roman legal system became the foundation for civil, or code, law which is used in Europe, Latin America, Japan, and the state of Louisiana.
3. Venetian traders traveled as far as China. Venice developed a banking system and used letters of credit in foreign trade.
4. Mercantilist policies have been used to promote foreign trade in Japan and other East Asian countries.
5. Laissez-faire was developed by Adam Smith as a rule of practical economic conduct. According to Smith, the individual, if permitted to pursue his or her own self-interest, will promote the well-being of all.
6. Even without the war, the monarchical system of government was on its way out.
7. This can be called *Keynesian economics*.
8. In the case of taxes on tobacco, revenues are used to treat tobacco users who become ill from smoking.
9. This is much lower than it is in such countries as Sweden, where government expenditures are more than 50 percent of GDP.
10. Executive Office of the President, Office of Management and Budget, *A Citizen's Guide to the Federal Budget, Fiscal Year 2000* (Washington, D.C.: U.S. Government Printing Office, October 1999), p. 12.
11. Gross Domestic Product (GDP) measures the value of all goods and services that are produced each year in a country.
12. Fiscal policy is associated with what is called Keynesian economics, which is a school of economic thought based on the work of John Maynard Keynes, particularly The General Theory of Employment, Interest, and Money. Keynesian economics holds that government purchases of goods and services and tax collections are key instruments of government economic policy.
13. The money supply is the total quantity of money existing in an economy at a particular time.
14. U.S. Department of Commerce, Bureau of the Census, *Statistical Abstract of the United States 1999* (Washington, D.C.: U.S. Government Printing Office, 1999), pp. 338–339.
15. *Ibid.*, p. 39.
16. A very good example was the collapse of East Asian stock markets in October and November 1997.
17. *A Citizen's Guide to the Federal Budget, Fiscal Year 2000*, p. 11.

RECOMMENDED READING

Brooks, Clive. "The Future of the State." *The Economist*, London, England, September 20, 1997. World Survey: 1–24.

Evans, Harold. *An American Century*. New York: Knopf, 1998.

Executive Office of the President, Office of Manpower and Budget, *A Citizen's Guide to the Federal Budget, Fiscal Year 2000* (Washington, D.C.: Superintendent of Documents, U.S. Government Printing Office, 1999).

Landes, David S. *The Wealth and Poverty of Nations*. New York: W. W. Norton, 1998.

"Redefining the Role of Government in a Market Economy," *Economic Report of the President, 1997.* (Washington, D.C.: U.S. Government Printing Office, 1997), pp. 189–198.

CHAPTER 2

GOVERNMENT INVOLVEMENT IN THE AMERICAN ECONOMY

Some government intervention is necessary for the establishment of even the freest type of economic system. The very atmosphere for the conduct of business is created by the ability of government to establish and maintain private property, freedom of enterprise, money and credit, and a system of civil laws for adjudicating the private disputes of individuals. Such institutions make possible an elaborate system of private planning in which individuals, rather than government, organize and direct the production of goods and services in response to the desires of consumers.

Government involvement in the American economy can be divided into four time periods: In the first period, from 1787 to 1860, the government and business relationship mainly took the form of government support of developing U.S. industries through the imposition of protective tariffs. In the early part of the nineteenth century, government financed the development of canals, roads, and turnpikes. In the second period, from around 1865 to 1914, intervention was in the form of laws to regulate railroads and curb monopolies. The first laws to protect consumers were also passed during this period. The third period covers the Depression of the 1930s, probably the most active period ever in business-government relations, during which legislation was passed to regulate the activities of business. The fourth time period, from 1964 to the present, focuses on the attainment of social goals: environmental protection, consumer product safety, employment of women and minorities, job safety, and so forth.

THE BEGINNING OF INVOLVEMENT, 1789–1860

There never has been a purely free market economy in the United States. From its beginnings in 1787, the federal government became involved in the promotion of manufacturing, relying on the use of protective tariffs to protect American business interests from foreign competition. Federal government involvement increased in the early part of the last century, when financial aid was provided for the construction of canals, roads, and turnpikes. One example of financial support was the construction of the Cumberland Road that connected the Atlantic Seacoast to the Ohio Valley. It cost the federal government $6,821,000, but it became a convenient highway for westward migration and it greatly reduced the time and cost of transportation. The road was of great benefit to Philadelphia and Baltimore, and it brought prosperity to the areas through which it ran.

The Erie Canal, which was built by the state of New York at a cost of $7 million, ran from near Albany on the Hudson River to Buffalo on Lake Erie.[1] The economic consequences of its construction were considerable. The cost of transportation between Buffalo and New York were reduced by more than 74 percent, and the time consumed was cut by almost two-thirds. New York City replaced Philadelphia as the outlet for the products of the Great Lakes region and the Northwest. Western New York grew and expanded rapidly after the Canal was opened; agricultural products increased greatly in value; and Great Lakes ports thrived on the increased business.

Railroads also benefited from government support. The beginning of American steam railroads occurred in the late 1820s, and they almost immediately became the most important form of transportation in the United States. Great difficulty was encountered in obtaining capital; financial insecurity in an unsettled country made private investors wary, so much of the aid for railroad building came from state and local governments. Georgia actually built and operated a line between Atlanta and Chattanooga and operated it until after the end of the Civil War. Federal government aid to railroad construction before 1850 was limited to such indirect aids as mail contracts and cuts in the import duties on iron rails. However, in 1850 an era of federal land grants to railroads began and continued to 1871.[2]

A final area of government support of business was through the use of the tariff. In the earlier stages of economic development of the American economy, one industry after another was guaranteed a domestic market free from foreign competition. Between 1789 and 1815, the framework of American protectionist policy emerged. In 1789 Congress passed the first tariff act. Although it was mainly a revenue measure, it afforded some protection to American producers. The tariff was subsequently raised in 1790, 1792, and 1794. During the period 1816–1832, tariffs were constantly revised upward to protect American industries. The main reason was European resentment against the British after the end of the Napoleonic Wars in 1815. British goods flooded American markets and threatened to put domestic firms out of business. However, high tariffs encountered increasingly strong agrarian opposition and American farmers who had to buy manufactured goods from abroad had to pay higher tariffs.

THE DEVELOPMENT OF GOVERNMENT
REGULATION OF BUSINESS, 1870–1914

After the end of the Civil War in 1865, the United States began its transformation from an agrarian economy to an industrial economy. Industry became increasingly complex, and mass production techniques enabled producers to expand their output. The industrial development of the American economy was stimulated by several factors, not the least of which was an abundance of natural resources. The opening of the West was another factor that contributed to industrial development. The construction of transcontinental railroads facilitated the westward movement of settlers and the marketing of produce and raw materials. A third factor was foreign investment in the United States. Without large amounts of foreign capital, railroads and steel mills could not have been built.[3] Finally, industrial development was impossible without an adequate supply of labor. The necessary labor supply became available, for millions of immigrants came to the United States from all over Europe in the hope of finding a better life.

Government intervention increased during this time period. It took the form of laws to regulate railroads and to curb the power of monopolies. Only when the competitive, self-adjusting market mechanism broke down did the government undertake to correct its most serious failings. Various business abuses occurred that contributed to the decline of competition. One example was the creation of trusts that enabled their owners to gain control over supply and charge monopoly prices. The first laws to protect the interest of consumers were passed during this time period. Those laws regulating the railroads and monopolies usually were initiated by state governments and only later by the federal government. Laws were also passed to improve the lot of laborers, particularly with respect to working conditions, and to tax income and wealth.

RAILROAD REGULATION

Few inventions have had a greater impact on American life than the railroads. To the farmers, the railroads brought many blessings. They enabled the farmers to get their produce to market, supplied them with agricultural implements, catalogues, and other accoutrements of the outside world, and ended isolation as passenger trains connected the farms to the cities. The railroads contributed to the development of mass transportation and distribution and to large-scale corporations in their modern form. They also helped urbanize the American economy by carrying laborers and supplies to newly built factories in the cities. Many railroad innovations and inventions improved the economy—for example, the Pullman car and the creation of a standard gauge that enabled the integration of the nation's railroad system. Methods of financing and promoting railroad expansion also influenced the American economy. Railroad securities were one of the largest outlets for personal savings. State and local governments also extended financial aid to the railroads in the form of loans, grants, and property tax exemptions.

A characteristic of the railroads was the high ratio of fixed costs to variable, or operating, costs. Almost all railroads relied on bonds for financial expansion; however, the heavy fixed-interest charges they incurred often led to financial disaster. In addition, the purchase of expensive rolling stock such as locomotives and freight and passenger cars also increased fixed costs that had to be covered out of operating revenue. Increasing costs led to keen competition and a resulting tendency toward monopoly. Rate wars were common,[4] and in response, railroad owners began to consolidate their holdings through acquisitions of other railroads. Railroad pools were also created. Their purpose was to apportion business among members, fix rates, and thus avoid ruinous competition. For example, the five or six railroads that controlled coal shipment in northeastern Pennsylvania allocated to themselves a certain percentage of the total shipment of coal.

Reasons for Railroad Regulation　A number of abuses developed in which railroads disregarded the interest of consumers and shippers. Rate discrimination was one abuse that entailed setting different rates for different places, for different commodities, or for different firms. Railroads charged more for short hauls than for long hauls, and rates were higher between local, noncompetitive points.[5] Deviations from published tariffs were a common means of rate discrimination, and rebates were given to favorite shippers and localities. These various forms of price discrimination adversely affected farmers, small merchants, and consumers. Farmers were particularly hard hit because they were absolutely dependent on the railroads for survival. Their discontent coalesced in the Grange movement, which became an important political force at the state level.

State Regulation of Railroads　In 1871, Illinois created a railroad and warehouse commission authorized to fix maximum rates for intrastate freight and passenger service on the railroads, as well as rates for storing grain in public warehouses and grain elevators. The Commission was empowered to prosecute when a railroad charged a higher rate for a short haul than for a long haul over the same direction. Also, in 1871 the Minnesota legislature prescribed maximum rates for passengers and freight and appointed a railroad commission to enforce the railroad laws. The Iowa Railroad Act of 1874 followed the Minnesota model of setting maximum rates with provisions for a railroad commission that was empowered to reduce rates below the maximum when that could be done without injury to the railroad.

Federal Regulation of Railroads　State regulation of railroads proved to be inadequate. Some states had railroad regulations, while others did not. Bribing of state legislatures was common. The railroads continued to combine and strengthen, and the farmers continued to be exploited, suffering from high rail rates and rate discrimination. The high rates often attracted the attention of speculators and led to the building of more railroads. Thus, railroads were caught up in speculation and overbuilding, and they resorted to the issuance of common stock to provide investment funds. Various promoters were able to gain control over railroad systems by acquiring a majority interest in their common stock.[6] Railroads became monopolies, while the interest of shippers was neglected. The end result was the passage of laws by the federal government to regulate railroads.

1. The Interstate Commerce Act of 1887 created the Interstate Commerce Commission, the first major federal government regulatory agency. The act outlawed certain discriminatory acts used by railroads against shippers. For example, it made it unlawful for railroads to charge more for short hauls than for long hauls on shipments in the same direction. Schedules of freight rates and passenger rates alike had to be made public to prevent rate discrimination against shippers.
2. The Hepburn Act of 1906 broadened the jurisdiction of the Interstate Commerce Commission to cover other forms of transportation, such as pipelines and express companies.
3. The Mann-Elkins Act of 1910 extended this jurisdiction further to cover telephone, telegraph, and cable and wireless companies engaged in interstate commerce.

GOVERNMENT REGULATION OF MONOPOLIES—THE TRUST

An enormous growth in the size of business units, often with consequent damage to competition, took place in the period following the end of the Civil War and continued unabated to the end of the century. To circumvent competition, various forms of business combinations were formed—the pool, the trust, and the holding company. These combinations engaged in various forms of business abuses against consumers and other businesses. Consumers were at their mercy for through control over markets, they were able to set prices on basic necessities. Small business firms were put out of business through price-cutting, meaning combinations could sell at a loss and support the loss through profits made elsewhere. Once a competitor was ruined, a combination would raise prices.

The trust was the most visible form of business combination. Under a trust arrangement, owners of a controlling interest in all or almost all of an industry's firms would agree to entrust their ownership shares to the control of one or a few people called trustees, and to receive trust certificates in return. The trustees would direct all firms in the trust as though they were one firm. With monolithic power, they confronted the competition. An example was the Standard Oil Trust, which controlled not only the refining of oil but also its retail sales. It was organized to eliminate competition at these two levels of operation and it was quite successful at doing both. It was also able to control the transportation of petroleum by compelling railroads to charge it lower rates than they charged competitors.

State Antitrust Laws   The first antitrust laws were enacted by the states rather than by the federal government because popular discontent over trust abuses were first felt at the state level. In 1881 the State of Kansas passed a law outlawing trusts, which were defined as combinations formed to restrict trade, fix prices, or prevent competition. In the same year, laws were passed in Michigan, Tennessee, and Texas. By 1895 seventeen states had passed various types of antitrust laws. These laws varied in content, but almost all forbade monopolies and combinations in restraint of trade, and provided criminal penalties. In addition, they prohibited particular forms of agreements and specific practices that were thought likely to bring about control of the market. The state antitrust laws, however, were limited because in the U.S. system of government the states can only regulate intrastate commerce.

Federal Antitrust Laws   The movement toward industrial concentration in the hands of fewer firms was viewed with concern by many people, and this concern crystallized into populist reform programs.[7] In 1884 both major political parties referred in their presidential platforms to the dangers inherent in trusts, and in 1890 the Sherman Antitrust Act was passed. It is the most important of the federal government antimonopoly measures ever passed by Congress. It marked a major milestone in business-government relations, for with the passage of the act there was no turning back to a time period of unregulated capitalism. In 1914 the Clayton Act and the Federal Trade Commission Act were passed concurrently. Both acts increased the role of the federal government in the area of antitrust policy.

INCOME TAXATION

The growing concentration of economic power in the latter part of the last century also created another problem—extremes of poverty and wealth. The new aristocracy of the country was made up of wealthy entrepreneurs and business leaders. The prototypes of these leaders were John D. Rockefeller and Andrew Carnegie. They epitomized the Protestant work ethic, success in a competitive race in which victory went to the swift and resourceful. They and many other entrepreneurs of that time period were not particularly scrupulous, taking advantage of loopholes, corrupting government officials, and bribing rivals' employees in a no-holds-barred effort to ruin competitors.[8] But they were supported by a philosophy that helped explain and justify their preeminent position—social Darwinism. Put simply, it was the "survival of the fittest" principle applied to the business world.[9]

However, there were also hardworking people at the opposite end of the income and wealth spectrum. In 1890, Marshall Field, the department store magnate, made an income calculated to be $600 an hour. His shopgirls, earning salaries of $3 to $5 a week, had to work more than three years to earn that amount. Working conditions for most people were deplorable, and working twelve hours a day, seven days a week, was not uncommon. Wages were low, and there was no government intervention in the form of laws designed to provide unemployment benefits, workers' compensation, or any form of social security taken for granted in the industrial societies of today. Social and economic inequalities divided the United States, and by 1900, 1 percent of the population owned as much of the nation's wealth as the remaining 99 percent did.

Corporate and Individual Income Taxes   The corporate income tax was enacted in 1909, four years before the introduction of the personal income tax. To avoid a constitutional issue, Congress levied the tax as an excise on the privilege of doing business as a corporation. The law was challenged, but the Supreme Court upheld the authority of the federal government to impose such a tax and ruled that the privilege of doing corporate business could be measured by the corporation's profit. For most of the period beginning in 1913 when the individual income tax was introduced, the corporate income tax was the single most important source of revenue to the federal government; after the end of World War II, it began to decline in importance as a source of federal government revenue.[10]

The individual income tax was adopted in 1913, after the U.S. Constitution was amended to permit the direct taxation of income by the federal government.[11] For almost thirty years after its adoption, the tax applied mainly to a small number of high-income people. Exemptions were high, and few incomes were large enough to be subject to tax at the lowest rate, much less at the highest rate. The individual income tax became of increased importance as a source of government revenue during World War II. Although all advanced Western countries levy taxes on individual incomes, nowhere is this tax more important as a revenue source than in the United States.[12]

BANKING

The most important banking development during the period of 1865–1914 was the enactment by Congress of the Federal Reserve Act of 1913, which created the Federal Reserve System. The United States was divided into twelve economic districts, and a Federal Reserve Bank was established in the chief financial center in each district. National banks were required to join the system by subscribing 6 percent of their capital stock and surplus to their district Federal Reserve Bank. A Federal Reserve Board, consisting of eight members, was established to govern the system.[13] The Federal Reserve Banks serve as fiscal agents of the government. Among their more important functions are rediscounting member banks' commercial paper, buying and selling U.S. Treasury debt obligations in the open market, and control over legal reserve requirements commercial banks have to maintain against demand deposits.

Extension of Government Control: The New Deal

The Depression of the 1930s was an economic and social catastrophe with no previous parallel in U.S. history. Before the 1930s there had been periods of unemployment and falling prices, but they were rarely of long duration, and they were generally followed by a reasonably prompt recovery. But all this changed with the Depression, which began with the collapse of the stock market in the fall of 1929 and continued until 1941, when preparation for war eventually created full employment in the American economy. Prolonged mass unemployment became the norm for the decade. At its worst, 25 percent of the labor force was out of work. But the Depression meant more than unemployment; it also meant idle production capacity, loss of profits, business bankruptcies, a fall in living standards, the closing of banks, and considerable social unrest.

Table 2-1 presents the impact of the Depression on the American economy as measured by changes in gross national product, gross private domestic investment, and unemployment, for the period 1929–1941. It is necessary to point out that for most of that time period, there was no unemployment compensation or other benefits to provide a safety net for the unemployed. World War II actually ended the Depression. By 1941 the United States was providing armaments for Great Britain.

In the early stages of the Depression, President Herbert Hoover followed a traditional policy of laissez-faire and waited for the self-correcting forces of the

Table 2-1   Gross National Product, Gross Private Domestic Investment, and Unemployment, 1929–1941

Year	Gross National Product (billions of dollars)	Gross Private Domestic Investment (billions of dollars)	Unemployment (percent)
1929	104.4	16.2	3.2
1930	91.1	10.3	8.7
1931	76.3	5.5	15.9
1932	58.5	.9	23.6
1933	56.0	1.4	24.9
1934	65.0	2.9	21.7
1935	72.5	6.3	20.1
1936	82.7	8.4	16.9
1937	90.8	11.7	14.3
1938	85.2	6.7	19.0
1939	91.1	9.3	17.2
1940	100.6	13.2	14.6
1941	125.8	18.1	9.9

Source: *Economic Report of the President 1962* (Washington, D.C.: U.S. Government Printing Office, 1962), pp. 207, 220, 231.

market to work. Gradually, however, he began to use governmental powers and influence to relieve economic distress. The Reconstruction Finance Corporation was organized to assist banks, railroads, insurance companies, and other enterprises threatened with insolvency. The federal government contributed $500 million in capital, and the corporation was empowered to borrow an additional $1.5 billion through the sale of debenture bonds.[14] The creation of the corporation put the federal government in the business of making loans to private firms and set a precedent for a later time when the government would decide to make loans to firms faced with bankruptcy.

When Franklin D. Roosevelt became president in March, 1933, the nation was near economic collapse. Industry was operating at less than half its full capacity, prices were at their lowest point during the whole Depression, and the banking system was on the verge of disintegration. A number of economic measures were enacted, some of which were temporary and cosmetic but others of which permanently restructured the American economy. New Deal measures directly related to business can be divided into several broad categories: increased regulation and control of industry, reforms of the banking system, closer government control of the securities market, regulation of public utilities, and consumer protection. Other New Deal measures also had an impact on business. Minimum wage legislation was enacted and provisions were made for the retirement of older workers through the passage of the Social Security Act in 1935.

THE NATIONAL INDUSTRIAL RECOVERY ACT, 1933

The purpose of the National Industrial Recovery Act (NIRA) was to relax antitrust policies designed to promote competition and instead to permit business firms to modify or even to eliminate competition. The devices used included restricting an industry's total production and assigning quotas to individual producers. Although deliberate attempts to reduce competition and restrict output were socially undesirable, it was felt that once the industrial system was stabilized, an economy of abundance would be created. But the NIRA did not work as well in practice as it did in theory. One effect it had was to create a price structure unfair to the interest of consumers. It was also felt that the codes of fair competition were breeding monopolies. Moreover, the degree of government control necessary to prevent abuses of the code was immense. In 1935, NIRA was declared unconstitutional by the Supreme Court.[15]

REGULATION OF THE SECURITIES MARKET

The stock market crash of 1929 eventually brought to light many corporate abuses that had occurred during the 1920s. One abuse was that corporations, to capitalize on the demand for securities, would issue stock until it was worthless in terms of book value.[16] Another abuse was the use of various accounting methods to overstate the value of assets or to understate the extent of liabilities. Many business firms issued stock far beyond their need for financing and used the proceeds to invest in the stock market through loans to brokers. The public lacked adequate information to make rational buying decisions, for firms often did not reveal relevant data or, when they did, usually misrepresented the facts.

There were other abuses. Insiders on the stock exchanges who learned about corporate earnings in advance were able to make financial gains by manipulating the stock market. They would run up the price of stocks to induce buying by the general public and then sell out, causing stock prices to decline. They would also depress the price of stocks by selling "short," thus prompting the public to sell. Then, of course, they would repurchase the stocks at a lower price. Brokers were usually unlicensed and unregulated, and their records were not subject to government inspection.

Reforms of the Securities Market A series of laws were passed in order to achieve stock market reforms. The Securities Act of 1933 prohibited the public sale of securities in interstate commerce or through the mails unless detailed information concerning the securities had been filed with the Federal Trade Commission. Its objective was to protect the unwary investor from the sale of fraudulent securities through the mail and by door-to-door salesmen who peddled "get rich quick" schemes in such things as Florida real estate ventures and Nevada silver mine stock.[17]

A more important act was the Securities Exchange Act of 1934, which created the Securities and Exchange Commission. As mentioned above, widespread and flagrant abuses existed in the securities market during the 1920s. Through such abuses, prices of securities were either pushed up or forced down for the benefit of those in control. Uncontrolled margin requirements, in which a buyer puts up only a small percentage of the cost of securities, caused much speculation and accentuated the instability of the stock market.[18] The act outlawed the manipulation of stock prices in any manner. Under the act, corporate directors, officers, and insiders are not permitted to sell their company's stock short, and they must make public any intent to exercise stock options. The act also required that all securities listed on the national stock exchanges be registered with the SEC by the issuer.

The third act was the Public Utility Holding Company Act of 1935, which required public utility holding companies to register with the Securities and Exchange Commission. During the 1920s billions of dollars were lost in the collapse of public utility holding companies. Moreover, the electric and gas industries were controlled by holding companies.[19] Under the act, a holding company must register with the SEC; otherwise it is unlawful for it to sell, transport, or distribute gas or electricity across state lines. The act also has an antipyramiding provision, in that it requires the dissolution of holding companies above the second degree.[20]

REGULATION OF THE BANKING SYSTEM

The collapse of the American banking system was one of the cataclysmic results of the Depression. In 1929 the banking system was inherently weak, in part because of the large number of speculative loans made by bankers during the 1920s, and in part because of the large number of independent banks free from any form of government control. When the economy collapsed, these loans went into default as the market value of the borrowers' goods or the value of their collateral declined. When debtors defaulted on their loans, banks were unable to satisfy the demands of depositors who came to claim their deposits. Thus, one bank failure would lead to other bank failures, and these spread domino-like throughout the country. As income, employment, and property values fell, bank failures quickly became epidemic, and the collapse of the entire banking system became a distinct possibility.

The Glass-Steagall Act, 1933   The Glass-Steagall Act was designed to place the banking system under more centralized government control. It was designed to strengthen the commercial banks, weaken the link between speculation and banking, and give added power to the Federal Reserve system. It created the Federal Deposit Insurance Corporation (FDIC) to guarantee bank deposits.[21] The purpose of this guarantee was to prevent runs on banks by depositors who were fearful of losing their money. It required commercial banks to give up their securities affiliates and to abstain from investment banking. To prevent a recurrence of speculative transactions in corporate securities, real estate, and commodities financed by commercial banks, Federal Reserve Banks were required to supervise the use of credit made by them.

The Banking Act of 1935   The Banking Act of 1935 marked a further extension of government control over banking. With the passage of this act, the banking structure became inseparably connected with federal government monetary and fiscal policy, and the Federal Reserve and the U.S. Treasury operated in tandem. The act is also important because it provided for certain forms of centralized credit and monetary controls. It made the president's power to appoint and remove members of the Federal Reserve Board practically unlimited. The old Federal Reserve Board was dissolved and replaced by a board of governors composed of seven members appointed by the president. The board was given broader rediscounting power and mandatory power over legal reserve requirements against consumer demand and time deposits.

REGULATION OF PUBLIC UTILITIES AND TRANSPORTATION

Regulation of the electric power and transportation industries began at the state level. As electric power industry abuses against consumers developed, particularly in the form of high rates, states began to pass laws. Starting in 1907, regulatory commissions were established in New York and Wisconsin and spread rapidly to other jurisdictions. With the growing importance of interstate transmission of electric power, federal intervention became inevitable. In 1920 the Federal Power Commission (FPC) was established, with the authority to issue permits or licenses for private and public power projects involved in interstate commerce.

Regulation of transportation also began with state regulation of the railroads in the 1870s. The regulation of transportation was extended to cover motor carriers. State regulation of trucks and buses, introduced in the 1920s, was first concerned with safety, physical characteristics of vehicles, licensing of drivers, and the number of hours a driver might work. Soon, however, the states began to regulate the rates and services of common carriers. To prevent the evasion of such regulation, these controls were extended to contract carriers. But the impossibility of the states regulating interstate motor carriers led to federal regulation of motor carriers.

The Communications Act of 1934   The Communications Act of 1934 created the Federal Communications Commission (FCC) to regulate interstate and foreign commerce in telephone, telegraph, and radio communications.[22] The FCC was given power over rates, services, accounting, interconnections, facilities, and finances. Telephone and telegraph companies had to file their rates with the FCC and make them available for public inspection. Notice had to be given of rate changes. The FCC was given the authority to grant licenses to radio stations, assign them frequencies, fix their hours of operations, and prevent interference among stations.

The Motor Carrier Act, 1935   The Motor Carrier Act extended the jurisdiction of the Interstate Commerce Commission (ICC) to motor carriers engaged in interstate commerce. It established different degrees of regulation for common carriers, contract carriers, private carriers, and transportation brokers. A common carrier could only operate under a certificate from the ICC, after a finding that it was able to perform the proposed service. Rates and fares had to be published and could not be discriminatory. The ICC was also charged with enforcing safety standards. Minimum rates had to be made public and filed with the ICC.

The Civil Aeronautics Act of 1938   After 1918, the federal government had indirect control over air routes and types of planes allowed through its granting of conditional airmail contracts. The airmail acts of 1934 and 1935 gave the postmaster general the power to regulate schedules, frequencies, departure times, speed, stops, and load capacity. Regulation of air transportation, however, culminated in the passage of the Civil Aeronautics Act, which created the Civil Aeronautics Board (CAB) and gave it regulatory authority over entry, routes, rates, airmail payments, and subsidies of common carriers. Rates had to be approved by the board. The Civil Aeronautics Act was modified by an executive order in 1940 that created within the Department of Commerce a Civil Aeronautics Authority that maintains the national airway system and enforces safety, licensing, and traffic control regulations.[23]

ANTITRUST POLICIES

The Depression created demands for government assistance to small firms. The growth of the large chain stores, like A & P and People's Drugs, placed great competitive pressure on small business firms. The large chains were accused of engaging in practices that discriminated against small stores. One type of discrimination took the form of "loss leaders." The chains would often sell nationally advertised products at a price below cost to entice buyers away from the small independent stores.[24] Another form of price discrimination was called "whipsawing." When a chain operated in several geographic markets, prices were cut in one market and maintained in other markets. This device was used to eliminate local sellers that could not draw upon financial resources in other markets.

Two laws designed to help small business firms were passed. The first was the Robinson-Patman Act of 1936, commonly known as the Chain Store Act. Its objective was to limit certain unfair business practices, such as "whipsawing" and granting discounts to one group of buyers while not making the same discount available to other buyers.[25] The second law, the Miller-Tydings Act of 1937, legalized resale price maintenance agreements covering branded goods. It permitted the manufacturer or distributor of a branded product to set the minimum retail price at which the product would be sold. The purpose was to protect independent retail stores against the chains.[26]

LABOR UNIONS

The role of labor unions became increasingly important during the Depression as the New Deal programs of the Roosevelt administration improved the status of labor. In general, the climate before the 1930s was antiunion. Major impetus to the development of unions occurred during the industrial development after the Civil War. The Knights of Labor was formed as an industrial union in 1869. It was followed by the American Federation of Labor, which was formed as a craft union in 1881. A number of strikes occurred in the 1880s and 1890s, especially in the steel and railroad industries. The importance of unions began to decline during the 1920s. Business firms formed company unions to keep out the unions. The attitude of the federal government was unsympathetic to labor; government opposition helped to break strikes in the coal and steel industries.

The two most important New Deal acts pertaining to unions were the National Labor Relations Act of 1935 and the Fair Labor Standards Act of 1938. Under the provisions of the National Labor Relations Act, employers were forbidden to interfere with labor's right to bargain collectively, to refuse to bargain with unions, and to discriminate against union members. The Fair Labor

Standards Act enacted minimum wages and maximum hours for labor engaged in interstate commerce or in the production of goods involved in interstate commerce. Maximum working hours per week were set at forty-four, to be reduced to forty after two years. Minimum wages were set at twenty-five cents an hour. The act also required the payment of time and one-half for overtime work.

UNEMPLOYMENT RELIEF AND SOCIAL SECURITY

Mass unemployment will be forever associated with the Depression of the 1930s. Unlike the European countries, there was no safety net to protect those who were unemployed or were too old to work. It was the responsibility of the worker to look out for himself or herself. Moreover, it was felt that unemployment was a temporary phenomenon. Until the 1930s, the American economy had not experienced prolonged unemployment. This supported the view of classical economic theory that full employment of labor and other resources could be accepted as the norm.[27] The catalyst in classical economic theory was Say's Law of Markets, which states in effect that supply creates its own demand. Whatever is produced creates the demand for another product. Additional supply creates additional demand and any general overproduction is impossible. In an exchange economy, Say's Law meant that there would always be a sufficient rate of spending to maintain full employment.

However, unemployment continued to increase during the Depression,[28] and a number of short-term public works programs were introduced to provide jobs. The Civilian Conservation Corps (CCC) was created in 1933 to provide work on public works projects for young men. Some 300,000 men were employed in the first year of its operations.[29] The Public Works Administration (PWA) was also created in 1933 to create jobs on construction projects such as road building. It was followed in 1935 by the Works Progress Administration (WPA). It lasted until 1942, during which time it employed about 8.5 million people. Its accomplishments included the construction of public buildings, roads, airports, bridges, parks, and reservoirs. Through the Federal Arts Project and the National Youth Administration, WPA gave employment to artists, writers, white-collar workers, and college students.[30]

The Social Security Act of 1935   Until the mid-thirties, American legislation to provide social security for old age lagged behind that of most industrial nations, despite a steady growth in the number of older people. Before old-age insurance, the great majority were dependent for their support on family or on public or private social agencies. The Social Security Act of 1935 created a national system of old-age insurance. Through a contributory scheme that related benefits to contributions, protection was made available as a matter of right, without the use of a means test. It was financed by an income tax on employees and a payroll tax on employers. The program began in 1937, and the tax was 1 percent on an annual earnings base up to $3,000. The maximum tax was $30.00.[31] The original monthly pension ranged from $10.00 to $85.00.

The Social Security Act also provided for unemployment compensation. A federal tax was levied on the payrolls of all covered employers with eight or more employees. The tax was levied at a rate of 1 percent in 1936, 2 percent in 1937, and 3 percent thereafter. A credit of up to 90 percent of the tax was allowed to employers who paid taxes into state unemployment funds under state laws that met the standards prescribed in the Social Security Act. The state funds were to be deposited in the Unemployment Trust Fund in the U.S. Treasury where they were to be invested in government bonds. The states were given the authority to compute benefits, set maximum and minimum benefit standards, and set eligibility requirements.

RESULTS OF THE NEW DEAL

The New Deal did not end the Depression; World War II did that. However, it did represent the first broad effort in American history to promote economic recovery by means of government action. The federal government assumed an unparalleled burden of new welfare responsibilities. Expenditures on work relief and public works increased, and steps were taken to build a permanent social security system around unemployment compensation and old-age insurance. Government regulation of business markedly increased. A number of changes were made in the banking system, including the creation of the Federal Deposit Insurance Corporation to insure individual deposits against loss in the event of a bank failure. The position of the individual investor was improved by federal regulation designed to regulate the securities market. Direct government regulation was extended over electric power, telecommunications, and motor transportation.

The increased importance of the role of the federal government in the American economy during the period 1929–1941 can be seen in Table 2-2. The federal debt, which was $16.4 billion in 1929, increased to $64.3 billion in 1941.[32] Federal government expenditures in 1929 were $2.6 billion, compared to $7.7 billion for state and local governments.

WORLD WAR II AND ITS AFTERMATH

Two world events contributed to the end of the Depression. World War II began on September 1, 1939. The United States pursued a policy of neutrality.[33] However, in the spring of 1940, the German army defeated the French and British armies and occupied France. When it appeared that the Germans would invade England, the Roosevelt administration became involved in supplying arms and ships to England through Lend-Lease.[34] Defense expenditures increased at home, putting people to work. On June 22, 1941, the Germans invaded Russia, and it became more likely that the United States would eventually become involved. This involvement was precipitated on December 7, 1941, when the Japanese bombed Pearl Harbor. The Depression was over, and the unemployment rate, which was 10.1 percent in December 1941, dropped to 4.7 in 1942, 1.9 in 1943, 1.2 in 1944, and 1.9 percent in 1945.[35]

Table 2-3 presents the effect of World War II on the American economy. Government expenditures on goods and services, which amounted to $9.1 billion in 1940, increased to $98.3 billion in 1945, and the government debt increased from $43.0 billion in 1940 to $258.7 billion in 1945. The unemployment rate, which was 14.6 percent of the labor force in 1940, decreased to 1.9 percent in 1943 and 1.2 percent in 1944, as most of the unemployed workers were absorbed either into the armed forces or into the defense plants. Millions of women were also employed in the defense plants.

TABLE 2-2   THE INCREASED IMPORTANCE OF THE FEDERAL GOVERNMENT IN THE AMERICAN ECONOMY, 1929–1941 (BILLIONS OF DOLLARS)

	FEDERAL GOVERNMENT EXPENDITURES	STATE GOVERNMENT EXPENDITURES	LOCAL GOVERNMENT EXPENDITURES
1929	2.6	7.7	16.4
1930	2.8	8.4	16.0
1931	4.2	8.4	17.8
1932	3.2	7.6	20.8
1933	4.0	7.2	24.0
1934	6.4	8.1	31.5
1935	6.5	8.5	35.1
1936	8.5	8.1	39.1
1937	7.3	8.4	41.9
1938	8.5	8.9	44.4
1939	9.0	9.6	47.6
1940	10.1	9.2	50.9
1941	20.5	9.0	64.3

Source: *Economic Report of the President 1962* (Washington, D.C., U.S. Government Printing Office, 1962), pp. 269, 275.

TABLE 2-3   UNEMPLOYMENT, FEDERAL GOVERNMENT EXPENDITURES, AND DEBT, 1940–1945

	UNEMPLOYMENT (PERCENT)	EXPENDITURES (BILLIONS OF DOLLARS)	DEBT (BILLIONS OF DOLLARS)
1940	14.6	9.1	43.0
1941	9.9	13.3	49.0
1942	4.7	34.0	72.4
1943	1.9	79.4	136.7
1944	1.2	95.0	201.0
1945	1.9	98.3	258.7

Source: *Economic Report of the President 1962* (Washington, D.C.: U.S. Government Printing Office, 1962), pp. 230, 272.

The Employment Act of 1946   The Employment Act was a landmark act in that it gave legislative sanction to the view that the federal government had a direct responsibility for the level of employment and income prevailing in the economy. The rationale for its passage was based on the fact that the war, not government economic policies, had ended the Depression. The war was over and the problem was what to do with the demobilized veterans.[36] The significance of the act lies in the general direction it gives to economic policy and the machinery it established to enable both the executive and legislative branches of the federal government to assume responsibility for the overall functioning of the American economy. It had three public policies—maximum employment, price stability, and maximum production.[37]

Keynesian Economics   The aftermath of World War II[38] also marked the acceptance of Keynesian economic theory, first in Europe, and later in the United States. This theory offered an explanation for the mass unemployment that occurred during the Depression and a solution. Unemployment, according to the theory, was caused by a lack of aggregate demand. The policy implications were clear: The private sector could not generate enough demand to create jobs; it was the responsibility of government to do so. This was to be done through government monetary and fiscal policies that would stimulate consumption and investment expenditures. Income redistribution would be effected through progressive taxation and various social welfare measures designed to increase consumption. Thus, prosperity could be achieved by stimulating the purchasing power of consumers.

The American economy enjoyed a period of unprecedented prosperity for a twenty-year period following the end of World War II. The real income of most Americans more than doubled during the period. The rate of unemployment, which was 3.8 percent in 1946, fluctuated from a low of 2.9 percent in 1953 to a high of 6.8 percent in 1958, and averaged 4.5 percent during the period. The GNP increased from $212.0 billion in 1945 to $675.6 in 1965.[39] Federal government expenditures decreased from $98.3 billion in 1945 to a low of $32.9 billion in 1948. There was a gradual increase in government expenditures in the 1950s, primarily as a result of increased defense expenditures. It was not until 1963 that government expenditures were as high as they were in 1945. The national debt remained fairly constant during the twenty-year postwar period, increasing by an average of about $2 billion a year.[40]

SOCIAL REGULATION OF BUSINESS, 1964–PRESENT

The first three periods of government involvement in business were economic in nature. Tariffs were used to protect American industry against foreign competition and government subsidies were given to business to promote canal and railroad construction. The antitrust legislation of the last century and the first part of this century was also economic in nature. The laws dealt with specific economic issues: monopoly power, pricing, concentration of industry, and corporate economic power and its uses and abuses. Economic regulation often applied to specific industries. For example, the Interstate Commerce Commission was first created to regulate rates and services provided by the railroads, and its authority was extended over other forms of transportation. The Fair Labor Standards Act enacted minimum wages and maximum hours for labor employed in interstate commerce.

Social regulation is much more broad-based in its objective and enforcement. It focuses on the attainment of certain social goals: environmental protection, consumerism, employment of women and minorities, job safety, and so forth. These goals are associated with a change in societal values that is characterized by such terms as "rising entitlements" and "quality of life." Examples of legislation include the Civil Rights Act of 1964, the Age Discrimination in Employment Act of 1967, and the Consumer Product Safety Act of 1972. This kind of legislation also created a new type of regulatory agency that has a broader-based control over business activities and is more oriented toward accomplishing social objectives than the older regulatory agencies were.

REASONS FOR SOCIAL REGULATION

Social regulation reflects concern with the public welfare. One reason for social regulation is to provide better working conditions and safer products for people. For example, the Food and Drug Administration (FDA) attempts to protect the public against the use of impure and unsafe drugs, food, cosmetics, and other potentially hazardous products. A second reason is that the market mechanism does not prevent various forms of discrimination; humans do that. Laws became necessary to prevent discrimination, and it is the responsibility of the Equal Employment Opportunity Commission (EEOC) to provide equal opportunity access to jobs for workers who had been discriminated against in employment opportunities in the past. It also enforces fair access to better-paying jobs for women and minorities in the labor force.[41]

A third reason for social regulation was the externalities created by technological advances and shifts that were taking place in the American economy after World War II. Millions of Americans left the farms and small towns to move to the cities for employment. Rising living standards increased the demand for more cars, which increased air pollution, particularly in the cities. Pollution becomes an externality because one person can impose a cost on another without having to pay compensation.[42] This other person then demands government protection in the form of regulation prohibiting or limiting the action of the first person. As American society became more technologically advanced, one group's meat became another group's poison. Airports became more and more necessary to facilitate rapid transportation, but airplane noise damaged the environment to those who lived near them.

The last cycle of government regulation of business, which began in the 1960s, was marked by four types of social goals in business legislation: eliminating discrimination in employment, ensuring better and safer products for consumers, reducing environmental pollution, and creating safer working conditions. These goals resulted in the creation of a number of new federal agencies with regulatory functions—the Equal Employment Opportunity Commission (EEOC), the Environmental Protection Agency (EPA), the Consumer Product Safety Commission (CPSA), the Occupational Safety and Health Administration (OSHA), and a myriad of others. Their jurisdiction extends throughout most of the private sector and at times into the public sector.

EQUAL EMPLOYMENT OPPORTUNITY

Equality of opportunity is a *sine qua non* for a democratic society. It was and is the key factor that has attracted millions of immigrants to America. However, equality of opportunity has worked better in theory than in practice. The problem is that a number of impediments have hindered achieving true equality of opportunity. And equality of opportunity is only part of the picture, for opportunity is linked to income distribution. In part, income inequality is based on differences in people's abilities; often, however, it is based on sex, race, age, and disabilities, which may have little relation to ability. In 1964, the Civil Rights Act was enacted to eliminate job discrimination based on such factors as sex, race, and national origin, and it created the Equal Employment Opportunity Commission (EEOC) to investigate charges of job discrimination. In 1967, the Age Discrimination in Employment Act (ADEA) was passed, followed by the Americans with Disabilities Act of 1990.

CONSUMER PROTECTION

A number of consumer protection laws were enacted during the period 1964–1975. Many of them dealt with consumer product safety. An example would be the Consumer Product Safety Act of 1972 that set safety standards for consumer products and established the Consumer Product Safety Commission (CPSC). Another example is the Consumer Credit Protection Act of 1968 that requires full disclosure of terms and conditions of finance charges in credit transactions. These and other consumer laws were the result of a consumer movement that has fluctuated in intensity since the beginning of the twentieth century but that has never coalesced into an organized pressure group.[43] Occasional waves of popular indignation and, more frequently, identity of common interests between consumers and organized groups, have produced several kinds of special government protection of consumers.

ENVIRONMENTAL PROTECTION

Concern about the quality of the environment is probably the most important area affecting government and business relations. Although laws to protect the environment against industrial pollution have been on the books dating back to the last century, it was not until the 1970s that any major legislation was passed. Protection of the environment is partly a reflection of changing societal values, with more emphasis on the quality of life as opposed to mindless material consumption. The probability that pollution causes health hazards, some of which may endanger life itself, and the possibility that pollution may in time upset the balance of nature, have led to demands for stringent regulation of pollution. In 1970 the Environmental Protection Agency (EPA) was created to enforce the environmental protection laws.

OCCUPATIONAL SAFETY AND HEALTH

The development of high-risk industries such as agriculture, coal mining, railroading, shipbuilding, and automobile and steel production caused thousands of work-related accidents, many fatal, over the years. However, work-related deaths have declined in recent years. This can be attributed to a shift away from the manufacturing industries to the service industries. Nevertheless, an average of seventeen workers are killed in accidents each day in the United States, most of which are machine-related. Although laws designed to protect workers from job-related accidents date back to the last century, the most important is the Occupational Safety and Health Act of 1970. It created the Occupational Safety and Health Administration (OSHA). It was given the authority to inspect the workplace, develop safety standards, and inspect and approve plans to provide employee safety.

ENTITLEMENTS

The very nature of a market system provides for a certain amount of economic insecurity. A free enterprise system means the freedom to fail as well as the freedom to gain. Competition carries with it an element of social Darwinism—the efficient survive and the inefficient do not. The concept of individualism carried with it self-responsibility. A person was responsible for his or her own actions. The Protestant work ethic stressed thrift and hard work. Life's vicissitudes, such as unemployment and old age, were the responsibility of the individual, not the state, and savings were to be set aside to cover them. Life was for the venturesome—people who enjoyed the excitement of not knowing what the future holds for them and who welcome the challenge of adjustment.

However, in a very short period of time—just a little more than 100 years—changes have taken place in Western societies that have mandated some form of institutional protection for the individual who, in many cases, can no longer afford adequate self-protection. Consumer preferences may shift away from some product or production may be moved to other countries, causing a loss of jobs and a shutdown of plant facilities. Technological change is rapid, posing a constant threat that workers may lose their old jobs and need to undergo expensive and psychologically distressing retraining and education. In addition, improved health care means that more people are living longer and many are not able to accumulate the resources needed to support themselves during retirement.

The concept of entitlement is a product of the social upheaval of the 1960s. It has come to be expressed as a social right for specific groups of people. In terms of government expenditures, entitlement would include such categories as Medicare, Medicaid, and Social Security. For example, Medicare expenditures at its inception in 1966 were $100 million; by 1970, expenditures had increased to $6.2 billion; and by 1980, to $32.1 billion. Medicare expenditures continued to rise in the 1980s, and by 1990 amounted to $98.1 billion. In 1998 they amounted to $198 billion. Expenditures for Social Security have also increased dramatically. In 1965, Social Security expenditures amounted to $17.5 billion; in 1998 they were $381.5 billion. Table 2-4 presents the increase in various types of entitlements and in national defense expenditures for the period 1965–1997. Military expenditures, stabilized at around $80 billion during the period 1970–1975, began to increase, particularly during the Reagan presidency of the 1980s. In 1980, defense expenditures amounted to $134 billion; by 1990, they had increased to $289.8 billion.[44] The main reason for the increase in defense expenditures was the arms rivalry between the United States and the Soviet Union. The United States was better able to sustain these increases than the Soviet Union, and eventually the Soviet Union collapsed.[45]

SUMMARY

Government has played an important role in the American economy from its beginning. At first its functions were narrowly circumscribed. It was responsible for the conduct of national defense, foreign affairs, and tax collection. State

TABLE 2-4   FEDERAL GOVERNMENT RECEIPTS AND EXPENDITURES, FISCAL YEARS 1965–1997 (BILLIONS OF DOLLARS)

YEAR	RECEIPTS	EXPENDITURES			
		NATIONAL DEFENSE	*MEDICARE*	*INCOME SECURITY*	*SOCIAL SECURITY*
1965	116.8	50.6	—	9.5	17.5
1970	192.8	81.7	6.2	15.6	30.3
1975	279.1	86.5	12.9	50.2	64.7
1980	517.1	134.0	32.1	86.5	118.5
1985	734.1	245.2	65.8	128.2	188.6
1990	1,031.3	289.8	98.1	147.0	248.6
1991	1,054.3	262.4	104.5	170.3	269.0
1992	1,090.5	286.9	119.0	196.9	287.7
1993	1,153.5	278.6	130.6	207.3	304.6
1994	1,257.7	268.6	144.7	214.0	319.6
1995	1,350.6	259.6	159.9	220.2	335.8
1998	1,657.9	251.4	198.1	239.3	381.5

Source: *Economic Report of the President, 1996* (Washington, D.C.: U.S. Government Printing Office, 1998), pp. 369, 375.

governments played a major role in promoting economic development from after the American Revolution to the Civil War. After the Civil War, the role of the federal government expanded enormously. American life was reshaped by the rise of the industrial corporation. A vast increase in the size of business units occurred, in part as a result of the formation of trusts. Federal antitrust laws were passed to protect consumers and small business firms against various business abuses such as price-fixing. Federal regulatory agencies such as the Interstate Commerce Commission were created.

The Depression of the 1930s and World War II expanded the role of government. Under the New Deal the federal government assumed responsibility on a scale and range without precedent in American history. The majority of its reforms became permanent and accepted aspects of an altered role for government in the American economy. Social Security is an example. World War II also increased the involvement of the federal government in the world economy. Government expenditures increased as did the federal debt. National defense expenditures continued to be important during the Cold War. During the 1960s and 1970s, the role of the federal government increased in the areas of social regulation and entitlements. New government regulatory agencies were created to regulate the environment, employment, and occupational safety. Expenditures increased for social welfare programs such as Medicare.

QUESTIONS FOR DISCUSSION

1. Discuss the factors that led to the decline of competition in the last century.
2. What role did the federal government play in the economy of the United States from 1790 to 1860?
3. Why was it necessary to regulate railroads during the latter part of the last century?
4. What is a trust? Why did it become necessary to regulate trusts?
5. In what ways did the New Deal change the economy of the United States?
6. What impact did World War II have on the role of the federal government in the American economy?
7. What was the importance of the Employment Act of 1946?
8. Discuss the reasons for the development of social regulation in the 1960s.

NOTES

1. The Erie Canal was 363 miles long, 30 feet wide, 4 feet deep, and could accommodate 30-ton barges.
2. Railroad scandals and the feeling that public land should be open to settlers caused Congress to change.
3. Foreign capital invested in the United States increased from $600 million in 1860 to $4 billion by 1890.

4. Traffic attracted by charging rates that brought in anything at all over operating costs was better than no traffic at all; at least it brought in something to help defray fixed costs. It might be added that the same reason applies to airfare wars today. Airlines have to cover fixed costs of expensive equipment and interest on their debts.

5. For example, the rail freight charge for steel was based from Pittsburgh to the point of delivery. If steel was shipped fro Gary, Indiana, to Chicago, the freight charge was Pittsburgh to Chicago. This system was called Pittsburgh plus.

6. For example, the New York Central and the Pennsylvania Railroad established community of interest between themselves. The Pennsylvania Railroad controlled the Baltimore and Ohio and the Norfolk and Western, and the New York Central owned the Lake Erie and Western Railroad.

7. Populism was a political movement that developed during the latter part of the nineteenth century. It expressed the anger of the farmer, the factory worker, and the small business person against the trusts, railroads, and big banks. The trusts, they felt, overcharged them for what they had to buy; the railroads overcharged them for what they had to transport; and the banks charged them usurious rates when they had to borrow.

8. Matthew Josephson, *The Robber Barons* (New York: Harcourt, Brace, and World, 1934).

9. Social Darwinism was conceived by the British philosopher Herbert Spencer. According to Spencer, Carnegie, Rockefeller, and other tycoons earned their positions through a process of competitive selection.

10. In 1956, corporate income taxes accounted for 28 percent of U.S. government revenues, down to 11 percent in 1997.

11. This was the Sixteenth Amendment. The federal government imposed an income tax to raise revenue during the Civil War. It continued to use the tax after the war, but in the *Pollock* case of 1895, the Supreme Court declared its use unconstitutional.

12. The European countries rely more on consumer-based taxes such as the value-added tax.

13. The National Bank Act of 1864 created the National Bank system, which provided the United States with a nation-wide banking system and bank note structure. There were also state banks that joined the system. It proved incapable of handling financial panics.

14. Herbert Stein, *The Fiscal Revolution in America* (Chicago, IL: University of Chicago Press, 1969), pp. 6–26.

15. *Schechter Poultry Corporation v. U.S.*, 295 U.S. 495 (1935).

16. This was called "watered-down" stock.

17. Various states also enacted legislation called "blue-sky" laws to regulate the sale of securities. The laws varied widely in their scope and character, and were limited in their effectiveness.

18. A margin requirement is similar to a down payment on a car or house. During the 1920s, margin requirements were around 10 percent of the price of a security. A person could speculate by borrowing the remaining 90 percent from a broker by using the stock as collateral.

19. In 1932, thirteen holding companies controlled three-fourths of all privately owned utilities.

20. Pyramiding meant holding companies were built on other holding companies on the basis of stock ownership. Holding company A would be owned by holding company B, which would be owned by holding company C, and so forth.

21. The original guaranteed amount was $2,500. The amount today is $100,000.

22. The Federal Communications Commission replaced the Federal Radio Commission, which had responsibility for radio broadcasting. The radio industry developed in the 1920s.

23. The Civil Aeronautics Board is no longer in existence, and the Civil Aeronautics Authority is now the Federal Aviation Administration (FAA).
24. There is a parallel today in Wal-Mart, which stands accused of ruining many small business firms.
25. There was no widespread evidence of chain store abuses during the 1930s.
26. It was alleged that chain stores, because of their size, could compel their suppliers to give special discounts.
27. The term "classical economics" was used by Karl Marx to refer to the writings of Adam Smith and David Ricardo.
28. In early 1933, 12 million workers (one-fourth of the labor force) were unemployed.
29. The CCC lasted until 1942. It built the Blue Ridge Parkway, the Intercoastal Canal, and numerous state parks.
30. The Federal Arts Project sponsored a wide variety of programs ranging from musical concerts to painting of murals. It sponsored the writing of the history of the Appalachian region.
31. The maximum amount in 1998 is $5,130 on a maximum tax base of $68,400.
32. In 1997 the federal deficit amounted to $5.1 trillion. The U.S. GNP in 1941 was $125.8 billion; in 1997, it was $7.5 trillion.
33. Most Americans did not want to get involved in a European war that really did not concern them. Many felt that they had been pushed by British propaganda into World War I.
34. Lend Lease was a method of getting around public opposition to the war. Roosevelt could say that we were just loaning or leasing war supplies to England and Russia.
35. *Economic Report of the President 1962* (Washington, D.C.: U.S. Government Printing Office, 1962), p. 30.
36. Mass unemployment did not occur. The GI Bill of Rights sent many veterans to college. The Cold War began in 1947 and increased defense spending.
37. The act created the Council of Economic Advisers and the Joint Economic Committee of the U.S. Congress, charged with recommending national economic policy.
38. John Maynard Keynes, *General Theory of Employment, Interest, and Money* (New York: Harcourt, Brace, and Companies, 1936).
39. *Economic Report of the President 1966* (Washington, D.C.: U.S. Government Printing Office, 1966), p. 273.
40. The national debt began to accelerate during the Vietnam War. In 1964, the debt was $315.1 billion; by 1971 it had increased to $408.2 billion.
41. Abraham Maslow developed a theory of human needs as an explanation for motivation. The first, or lowest level, need is physiological and includes the need for water, food, and sex. Once these needs are satisfied, people proceed to the security need, which is the need for safety, order, and freedom from fear. The third need is belonging—the need for love and human contact. The next need is esteem, which involves achievement and respect from others. The fifth and highest level need is the need to grow and to feel fulfilled.
42. Lester C. Thurow, *The Zero-Sum Society* (New York: Basic Books, 1980), p. 124.
43. Probably the most effective special interest groups are the American Association of Retired Persons (AARP), the National Education Association (NEA), and the National Rifle Association (NRA).
44. *Economic Report of the President 1998* (Washington, D.C.: U.S. Government Printing Office, 1981), p. 373.
45. There were a number of factors contributing to the collapse of the Soviet Union. Its economy became isolated from the world economy and become obsolete.

Recommended Reading

Mitchell, Broadus. *American Economic History*. Boston, MA: Houghton Mifflin, 1947.

Tarbell, Ida M. *The History of the Standard Oil Company*. Gloucester, MA: Peter Smith, 1963.

Galbraith, John Kenneth. *The Great Crash*. Boston, MA: Houghton Mifflin, 1972.

U.S. Department of Labor. *Good for Business: Making Full Use of the Nation's Working Capital*. Washington, D.C.: U.S. Government Printing Office, 1995.

Allen, Frederick Lewis. *The Big Change: America Transforms Itself, 1900–1959*. New York: Harper & Row, 1952.

Mucciani, Gary. *Reversals of Fortune: Public Policy and Private Interests*. Washington, D.C.: The Brookings Institution, 1995.

Bourne, C. J. *Race and Sex Discrimination*. London: Sweet and Maxwell, 1997.

CHAPTER 3

GOVERNMENT REGULATION

The United States of today has changed considerably from the United States of the past. A laissez-faire economy existed through much of its history, predicated on the belief that government which governed the least, governed the best. Business owners ran their businesses pretty much as they pleased without government intervention. Consumers had little protection, with *caveat emptor* ("let the buyer beware") being the rule of the land. In terms of employment, the concept of employment at will prevailed. The employer owned property, set wages, and dictated working conditions. Workers could take it or leave it. If they did not like their jobs, they could quit; if they did not go to work, they were fired; and if they joined a union, they were also fired.

But all this changed drastically during the twentieth century. Government heavily regulates business. Local regulations tell a company where it may do business. State regulations cover the selling of securities, loan rates, and highway weight limits. Federal regulations are all-encompassing. Antitrust laws are designed to promote competition and to prevent various unfair business practices such as price-fixing. Consumers are protected by a variety of laws covering the sale of food and drugs, lending, warranties, and product safety. Federal and state regulations address pollution and the safety of employees in the workplace. There is also extensive federal and state regulation of labor, ranging from minimum wages to collective bargaining. In addition, there are federal and state laws designed to provide equal employment opportunity for persons who were historically foreclosed from the workplace.

THE POLITICAL SYSTEM OF THE UNITED STATES

The United States possesses what can be called a "marble cake" government. With the exception of Germany, the United States is unique in that it has a federal form of government that is divided into three parts—federal, state, and local. However, of the three levels, the federal government is clearly dominant in terms of its impact on business, consumers, taxpayers, and other groups. The Constitution of the United States provides for a distribution of power among the legislative, executive, and judicial branches of government. This provision was made to prevent an undue concentration of power within the federal government. An additional restriction on the exercise of political power was subsequently developed in the practice of judicial review. Soon after the federal courts began to function, they faced the question of whether or not certain acts of Congress were in harmony with the Constitution.[1]

LEGISLATIVE BRANCH

Congress is the most important legislative body in the land. It passes the laws that affect all of us. Sources of ideas for legislation are unlimited, and proposed drafts of bills can originate from many diverse sources, but only Congress can pass a bill. The United States today is composed of many special interest groups, each with its own constituency. The goals of these interest groups are often directly opposite—for example, pro-life versus abortion on demand. There is a trend toward a divided society and a multiplicity of special interest groups, and money is not likely to be lacking for any group with a good-sized bloc of voters. Congress is where the action begins, and the exercise of political power requires communication.

Committees   The committee system is the crux of the legislative process and is the basis for most legislative action. Ninety percent of all federal and state legislation is passed in the form reported by a particular committee. Some committees are of particular importance. At the federal level, the House Ways and Means Committee has the power to tax; all revenue-raising bills emanate from this committee. No one thing has more impact upon any individual or group than the power to tax. The House and Senate Appropriations Committees are also of prime importance for they determine how the money will be spent. The House Rules Committee is important because it has control over the order in which bills will be introduced in the House. The Senate Finance Committee and the Senate and House Judiciary Committees are also important.

Subcommittees   In addition to the committees, there are various subcommittees. The framework and parameters of most bills are settled in committees and subcommittees. Many subcommittees and their chairpersons and senior members have assumed considerable influence over the generally smaller slice of legislation they command. These subcommittees also have staff members, and chairpersons and higher ranking members also employ staff experts in the subject matter covered by these units. Staff members may play a major role in shaping legislation because their expertise is often greater than that of the typical legislator who has to be concerned with a myriad of other issues, constituent matters, and other problems. Thus, the power of Congress is dispersed, with legislative influence over policy decisions scattered over a large number of members who serve on many subcommittees.

EXECUTIVE BRANCH

The executive branch is the second branch of government. At the federal level of government, the executive branch consists of the president of the United States, his cabinet, and the bureaucracy. The framers of the Constitution created a presidency of limited powers. They wanted a presidential office that would stay clear of parties and factions, enforce the laws passed by Congress, deal with foreign governments, and help the states put down disorders. However, American presidents have been extending the limits of executive power, aided and abetted by Congress and the courts. In times of national emergency, Congress has increased the rule-making discretion of the executive branch. The growth in the role of the federal government has also enlarged the responsibility of the president. The presidency has increased in power, and White House aides are able to claim that it is the only place in government where it is possible to set national priorities.

The president of the United States has several responsibilities. First, the president is responsible for priority setting and policy formulation. Particularly since the New Deal, presidents have been expected to assume more responsibility in directing economic policy—fighting inflation and promoting economic growth. Second, the president is responsible for handling national emergencies. The military role of the president has increased in importance, as witnessed by U.S. involvement in the Persian Gulf region. Finally, the president is supposed to be the strongest mobilizer of public influence in the American system of power. This is facilitated by ready access to all communications media, which provides immediate contact with the people.

Departments and Agencies   However, the executive branch is by no means limited to the president. There is a host of departments and agencies that come under the jurisdiction of the executive branch. There is the Executive Office of the President, which consists of the Office of Management and Budget, the Council on Environmental Quality, the National Security Council, and other staff units. These units are supposed to coordinate administration policies before the Congress, help the president plan and set priorities, and monitor and evaluate progress toward achieving national objectives. Then there are the various departments of government, the heads of which are appointed by the president and form his cabinet. Then comes the government bureaucracy, which is the administrative arm of the government. Bureaucracy cannot be dismissed as simply part of the executive branch of government. Its power has increased and it has become an important force in the government system.

Bureaucracy   For practical purposes, the federal bureaucracy and Congress have the greatest impact upon the American public. Congress makes the laws and the bureaucracies of the many federal agencies enforce them. Only a small part of the bureaucracy works in Washington. The vast majority are employed in regional, field, and local offices scattered throughout the country. When one speaks of "big government," one is speaking about the bureaucracy. It provides an inviting target for politicians and the general public, because many have been hassled from time to time in dealing with such agencies as the Internal Revenue Service, which has been very much in the news, or the dozens of national regulatory agencies that have been created over the last thirty years.

JUDICIAL BRANCH

Courts, taken together, make up one of the three branches of government; therefore, as is also true of the legislative and executive branches, they are generally provided for in the federal and state constitutions. For example, Article III of the U.S. Constitution vests the judicial power of the United States "in one Supreme Court and in such inferior courts as the Congress may from time to time ordain and establish." The judicial branch of government has the power that allows the courts to make the ultimate decision as to where and how the other two branches of government may properly exercise their powers. There are two types of courts based on jurisdiction—federal court and state courts. Federal jurisdiction is derived from Article III of the Constitution. It would include all regulations of federal administrative agencies. For example, if a person is denied a job because of race, that would raise a federal question. State courts have the power to hear all matters with respect to state laws.

Federal Courts   The Supreme Court sits at the apex of the American judicial system. It is the only court created by the Constitution. It has nine judges, called justices, who are nominated by the president and confirmed by the Senate, and they serve for life. It has affected every stage in the transformation of government's role in the economic life of the United States, from its modest functions in 1789 to its all-pervasive role in the economy of today. However, its power is negative, one of veto rather than origination. Thus future economic and social policies are diverted into permitted channels confined within the orbit of judicial approval. For example, in recent years the Supreme Court has expanded the legal concept of class action to facilitate a much broader use of litigation as a form of interest-group social policy. It has also struck at various forms of discrimination.

In addition to the Supreme Court, the federal judicial system includes other types of courts. Congress has created federal district courts in each state. Each state has at least one; some states have many. The courts contained in each district constitute the general trial courts of the federal system. The district courts are grouped into circuits. There are thirteen circuits. Each circuit has a court of appeals in which appeals from the trial courts are heard. They do not retry the case; rather, they review the record to determine whether the trial court made errors of law. The decisions of these circuit courts of appeal are often final. In a few cases, further appeal may be made to the Supreme Court. Finally, there are specialized courts. An example would be the U.S. Claims Court.

In order for a lawsuit to be filed in a federal district court, it must come within the classes of cases to which the Constitution extends the federal judicial power: cases between citizens of different states and cases involving questions under federal laws or under the U.S. Constitution. Decisions of the district court are appealable, as a matter of right, to the appropriate U.S. court of appeals, and in a few cases directly to the Supreme Court of the United States. Most of the cases that reach the Supreme Court from the courts of appeals come by way of certiorari. In such cases, the party who lost the case is not given the right to appeal to the Supreme Court, but must persuade the Court that it should exercise its discretion and take the case for review because of some special importance it has.

State Courts   State courts include inferior trial courts, which include municipal courts, juvenile courts, domestic relations courts, and traffic courts. Then there are courts of general jurisdiction, meaning they have the power to hear all matters with respect to state law. In some jurisdictions, two courts may exist at this level: one to resolve all questions of law, and the other to resolve all matters of equity. Each state also has at least one court of appeals. It is usually, but not always, called the supreme court. Sometimes intermediate courts of appeals also exist, as in the federal system. These courts review the trial court record to determine whether or not there are any errors of law.

THE ADMINISTRATIVE AGENCIES

Almost every type of business activity falls within at least the indirect influence of a number of administrative agencies. It is important to study these agencies and their functions, though some general points should be made. Administrative agencies, regardless of responsibility, acquire their authority to act from the legislative branch of government. Because they do most of the day-to-day work of government, they make many significant policy decisions. Administrative agencies can be divided into two categories: independent regulatory commissions and agencies that are part of the executive branch of government.[2] In many areas of domestic policy formulation, independent agencies exercise more control, although different economic and political needs have produced administrative agencies exercising vast legislative and adjudicative powers that cannot be classified as independent regulatory agencies. Many executive agencies perform regulatory functions as part of their broader responsibility.

Most regulatory agencies that function within the executive department possess both quasi-legislative and quasi-judicial powers, just as the independent regulatory commissions do. The power to make rules and regulations has been delegated to these agencies by legislative fiat. The only important difference between an agency rule and a law enacted by a legislative body is that the rule may be only slightly more susceptible to attack because it was not made by elected officials. Administrative agencies can also implement policy or legislation through a process of initiating and settling specific cases. They also engage in administrative adjudication, which includes procedures used in deciding cases. For many types of cases, the procedures are carefully outlined: hearings are frequently prescribed, records are required, and so on. Furthermore, if the agencies overstep the boundaries of their authority, redress can always be secured in the courts.

Administrative agencies, as agents of Congress, reflect group demands for positive action. They are not supposed to be arbiters like the courts; rather, they should be activists who initiate policy in accordance with their policy. For example, when the Federal Trade Commission (FTC) ferrets out deceptive business practices, either through its own investigation or through information gained from outside sources, it initiates action in the name of the FTC against the party involved. It then adjudicates the very case it initiates. If the case reaches a formal hearing and goes to a hearing examiner for an initial decision, it is not, at that point, subject to commission control. But after the examiner renders a decision, the Commission may reverse it. The result is that the FTC can control the decisions rendered in almost all the cases it initiates.

SANCTIONS

Government intervention carries with it the threat and the actual application of sanctions to achieve desired economic and social outcomes. Sanctions may often be positive, taking the form of subsidies and tax incentives to promote a desired activity such as the construction of low-rent housing. When the target is an undesirable economic or social activity, negative sanctions are often used to enforce compliance with the law. They can designate noncompliance either as a criminal offense requiring the imposition of fines, imprisonment, or both, or as a civil offense involving the loss of the right or privilege to engage in economic transactions through the loss of licenses, permits, and franchises. For example, the Clean Air Act of 1970 subjects willful polluters to fines and jail sentences. Plants can be shut down and permits to operate canceled if pollution continues.

In applying negative sanctions, the intent is to use the coercive power of the state to enforce compliance. This is done by announcing to society or its components that various actions are not to be carried out and to ensure that fewer of them are. There is no choice other than to comply with a mandatory standard if the regulatory agency has sufficient enforcement tools. In addition, the regulatory agencies are expected to amass facts, to apply the law to these facts, and to impose the appropriate sanctions when noncompliance is found. Thus, the intent and process of regulation is more like adjudication than other types of political action. It can be said that violators of economic and social regulation differ from violators of criminal law only in the degree of responsibility for societal harm that is attributed to them by regulators and the community as a whole.

MAJOR REGULATORY AGENCIES

Some regulatory agencies are economic in their objectives, while other regulatory agencies have social goals, such as a clean environment. There are also some regulatory agencies that may have both economic and social goals. Economic regulation pertains to a specific industry. The Interstate Commerce Commission (ICC) was created in 1887 and was phased out in 1996. During its existence, it had control over rates and services that railroads, trucks, and buses could charge and provide in interstate commerce. Social regulation reflects concern for public welfare across all industries. Its aim is a better quality of life for all through the provision of a clean environment, better working conditions, and safe consumer products. For example, the Food and Drug Administration (FDA) protects consumers against the consumption of unsafe food, drugs, cosmetics, and other potentially hazardous products.

THE FEDERAL TRADE COMMISSION (FTC)

The Federal Trade Commission (FTC) is an example of a federal government agency that is engaged in both economic and social regulation. It was created by the Federal Trade Commission Act of 1914 to enforce compliance with the provisions of the Clayton Act that was also passed in 1914. Subsequent antitrust laws—such as the Robinson-Patman Act of 1936 and the Hart-Scott-Rodino Act of 1976—are also enforced by the FTC. The goals of these laws are economic. They are designed to promote competition. The Federal Trade Commission Act specifically prohibits unfair methods of competition, including price discrimination, and gives the FTC enforcement powers to seek civil and criminal remedies against violators of the act. The FTC, along with the antitrust division of the Justice Department, has jurisdiction over mergers.

However, the FTC is also involved in social regulation. It protects the public by preventing the dissemination of false or misleading food and drug advertising. It also has jurisdiction over various labeling laws, such as the Wool Products Labeling Act, that are designed to protect consumers from the misrepresentation of the product. Then there are various credit laws, such as the Truth-in-Lending Act of 1968, that require that borrowers be made aware of basic information about the terms and cost of credit. Finally, the Consumer Product Warranty Act of 1975 provides minimum disclosure standards for written consumer product warranties and defines federal content standards for these warranties.

THE SECURITIES AND EXCHANGE COMMISSION (SEC)

The Securities and Exchange Commission (SEC) was created by the Securities and Exchange Act of 1934 to prevent the widespread and flagrant abuses in the securities markets during the 1920s. The SEC consists of five members appointed by the president with the consent of the Senate, with each holding office for a period of five years. The act condemned a number of manipulative practices and gave the SEC the authority to check their use. Manipulation of stock prices in any manner is outlawed. Under the act, as seen in Chapter 2, corporate directors, officers, and insiders are not permitted to sell their company's stock short, and they must make public any intent to exercise stock options. Willful violations of an unfair practice are punishable by fines or imprisonment, or both. The act also requires all securities listed on national exchanges be registered with the SEC by the issuer, and that financial reports be in a form prescribed by the SEC.

THE FOOD AND DRUG ADMINISTRATION (FDA)

The Food and Drug Administration (FDA) is one of the most important social regulatory agencies in Washington. It monitors most laws involving food and drugs, and some laws dealing with disclosure. An example would be the Flammable Fabrics Act of 1953, which requires the labeling of highly flammable clothing. Also coming under FDA's jurisdiction are laws pertaining to the consumption of tobacco products. Cautionary notices have to be put on cigarette and small cigar packages as well as on containers of smokeless tobacco. An example is the Smokeless Tobacco Act of 1986 that requires producers, packagers, and importers of smokeless tobacco to label their products with such warnings as: "This product may cause mouth cancer," or, "This product may cause tooth disease and gum loss." The FDA also requires the testing of drugs before they can be sold to the public.

THE ENVIRONMENTAL PROTECTION AGENCY (EPA)

In July 1970, President Richard Nixon submitted to Congress a reorganizational plan to create an independent environmental protection agency. The organization was approved and the EPA was created in the executive branch of government. Functions that formerly belonged to the Department of the Interior relating to studies on the effects of insecticides and pesticides were transferred to this agency. Also transferred were functions belonging to the Department of Health, Education, and Welfare, including the creation of tolerance norms for pesticide chemicals under the Food, Drugs, and Cosmetics Act of 1938. The EPA was given supervision over air pollution standards as set forth in the Clean Air Act of 1970 and its subsequent amendments. The EPA was also given control over water pollution control programs, particularly those set forth later in the Water Pollution Control Act of 1972, including the setting of water quality standards. The jurisdiction of the EPA was also later extended to the Noise Control Act of 1972, and it became responsible for setting noise emission standards for products identified as major sources of noise. Subsequent environmental laws are also under the jurisdiction of the EPA.

THE OCCUPATIONAL SAFETY AND HEALTH ADMINISTRATION (OSHA)

OSHA was created as an agency of the Department of Labor to administer the Occupational Safety and Health Act of 1970. The purpose of the act is to assure safe and healthful working conditions. It requires employers to comply with safety and health standards promulgated by OSHA. In addition, every employer is required to furnish for his or her employees work free from recognizable hazards that cause or are likely to cause death or serious injury. Recognized hazards are defined as those that can be detected by the common human senses, unaided by testing devices, and that are generally known in the industry as hazardous. Further, a firm can be penalized under the general duty clause if the unsafe conditions have been cited by an inspector and the employer has refused to correct it in the specified time.

THE FEDERAL COMMUNICATIONS COMMISSION (FCC)

The Federal Communications Commission is an example of an economic regulatory agency in that it is concerned with the way business is done in a specific industry—telecommunications. It was created by the Communications Act of 1934. Prior to the passage of the act, Congress had given the Interstate Commerce Commission (ICC) jurisdiction over the operations in interstate commerce of telephone, telegraph, and radio companies. The FCC has control over maximum and minimum rates (except broadcasting charges), controls entry of new companies, and controls services companies can offer. It was eventually given control over the television industry; for example, the right to operate a local television station. The Telecommunications Act of 1996 will have some impact on the authority of the FCC, particularly with a long-distance entry approval procedure involving the regional Bell operating companies (RBOCs).

THE CONSUMER PRODUCT SAFETY COMMISSION (CPSC)

The Consumer Product Safety Commission was created in 1972 by the Consumer Product Safety Act, and functions as an independent regulatory commission. It has jurisdiction over most consumer products and has the power to inspect facilities where consumer products are made, stored, or transported. It can also require all manufacturers, private labelers, and distributors to establish and maintain books and records and to make available additional information if deemed necessary. It can require the use of specific labels that set forth the results of product testing. The greatest impact this requirement has is in the production process, in which the design of numerous products must conform to federal standards. Since safety standards are often formulated at various government and independent testing stations, a company may find that a finished product may no longer meet federal standards, and modification is necessary.

THE EQUAL EMPLOYMENT OPPORTUNITY COMMISSION (EEOC)

The EEOC was created by the Civil Rights Act of 1964 as an independent commission, and its enforcement authority was greatly increased by the Equal Employment Opportunity Act of 1972. It has the power to investigate and act on a charge of a pattern or practice of discrimination, whether filed by or on behalf of the person or group claiming to be aggrieved. It has the right to initiate civil suits against employers, labor unions, and any other group accused of practicing employment discrimination. Moreover, private individuals and groups have the right to sue under Title VII of the Civil Rights Act of 1964. The EEOC can also investigate company records to see whether a pattern of discrimination exists and can subpoena company records if necessary. Any organization subject to the Civil Rights Act of 1964 and subsequent executive orders must keep records that can determine whether unlawful practices have been committed.

STATE AND LOCAL GOVERNMENT REGULATORY AGENCIES

It is important to realize that state and local governments have their counterparts of the federal regulatory agencies. For example, federal laws pertaining to employment practices are not the only laws that affect business and other organizations; state and local government laws also exist. The degree of state and local government laws varies—some provide agencies to enforce laws, whereas others have voluntary enforcement. State and local governments also have environmental laws. The first consumer protection laws were passed by state and local governments long before consumer protection laws were introduced by the federal government. Regulations governing occupational safety and health and the sale of food and drug products are also among state and local laws.

INTERNATIONAL REGULATION

The globalization of national economies began with the communications revolution and continues unabated. Problems that were once the province of a particular country have become global. One problem is pollution of the environment that transcends national borders. Examples are pollution of the ocean and global warming. A second problem pertains to trade among nations. To prevent the use of deterrents to trade, such as protective tariffs and import quotas, most of the leading trading nations are signatories to the General Agreement on Tariffs and Trade (GATT) and its successor, the World Trade Organization (WTO). In 1994, Canada, Mexico, and the United States signed the North American Free Trade Agreement (NAFTA), creating a free-trade zone. Finally, in 1997, member nations of the Organization for Economic Cooperation and Development (OECD) agreed to create new laws to make bribery of a foreign public official illegal.

EXTRATERRITORIAL JURISDICTION

A question of jurisdiction is that of the power of a nation to regulate activities occurring beyond its borders. As markets become more global, the problems of regulating various types of unfair business conduct become more complex. In the United States, courts and regulators have struggled with the issue of the reach of their power. Some cases are relatively simple, involving conduct of foreign-owned businesses within the United States. In those instances, the jurisdictional principle of presence affords a basis for American courts or regulatory agencies to act. A more difficult question of authority arises when the alleged illegal conduct occurs in a foreign country but has an effect on the commerce of the United States. However, through legal precedence, U.S. laws, particularly in the areas of antitrust, employment, and corrupt practices, have been extended to actions of U.S. companies outside the United States.

Antitrust Laws   Although a number of countries have antitrust laws, they are not as far-reaching as those of the United States. As a consequence, actions taken by American corporations operating in a foreign country may be legal under its laws, but illegal in the United States. The American view that a freely competitive economic system is the most efficient, most desirable form of society, is not necessarily the view held by other major industrial countries. To compete more successfully in international commerce, the western European countries and Japan have permitted the use of such anticompetitive devices as cartels and other forms of business combinations that would be illegal in the United States.[3] One result is that the extent of industry and banking concentration is greater in those countries than in the United States.[4]

The application of American antitrust laws has been applied extraterritorially to American firms engaged in international commerce, thus subjecting their worldwide activities to national control. The first major international application of U.S. antitrust law came in the landmark American Tobacco case of 1911.[5] The American Tobacco Company and the Imperial Tobacco Company of Great Britain had agreed to divide world markets, with Imperial agreeing not to sell its tobacco products in the United States, except through American Tobacco. The two companies then formed a third corporation, the British-American Tobacco Company, which took over the foreign businesses of both companies. The U.S. Supreme Court ruled that this allocation of markets illegally restrained trade under the provisions of the Sherman Act.

Employment Laws   The U.S. government, particularly the Equal Employment Opportunity Commission (EEOC), has made an effort to apply U.S. employment laws to American firms operating overseas. These laws are the Civil Rights Act of 1964, particularly Title VII, the Age Discrimination in Employment Act (ADEA) of 1967, the Americans with Disabilities Act (ADA) of 1990, and the Civil Rights Act of 1991. The last act made clear that Americans employed abroad by U.S.-owned or U.S.-controlled firms can avail themselves of the protection of the Title VII, the ADEA, and the ADA unless compliance with these laws will constitute a violation of the laws of the country in which the American firm operates. American employment laws also apply to American workers employed by foreign firms operating in the United States, unless there is a need for these firms to employ their own citizens.

Bribery is an accepted way of life in many countries, a way to get things done. The moral implications of bribery are irrelevant in these countries, if indeed moral considerations are ever considered. Foreign firms, then, are often faced with a dilemma—do they play by the rules of the game, give a bribe and get what they want done, or do they stand on principle and refuse to play by the rules of the game. In an effort to address this problem, Congress passed the Foreign Corrupt Practices Act in 1977, which is an amendment to the Securities Exchange Act of 1934. The act prohibits the giving of money or anything else "of value" to foreign officials with the intent to corrupt. Enforcement comes under the jurisdiction of the Securities and Exchange Commission.

THE IMPACT OF REGULATION ON SOCIETY

There is more to regulation than the creation of a number of new government agencies. The laws creating these agencies also defined ambitious health, safety, and equity goals and in some cases established strict deadlines for attaining them nationally. Frequently, the laws have restricted agency discretion to moderate regulatory standards in view of economic or other considerations. They empower citizens' complainants and advocacy groups to sue business firms for damages and government officials for failure to promulgate strict rules of enforcement. Business firms are required to undertake extensive reporting of their compliance efforts. Local governments and school districts that fail to meet federally prescribed regulatory requirements have been threatened with debarment from federal grants-in-aid and contracts.

COSTS OF REGULATION

There are two types of regulatory costs—direct and indirect. Direct costs are of two types—paperwork and compliance. Paperwork costs involve the keeping of records and the filling out of required forms.[6] Compliance costs involve the installment of machinery and equipment. A university has to comply with the provisions of the Americans with Disabilities Act of 1990 by providing ramps, elevators, special parking facilities, and other devices necessary for use by the handicapped. The Clean Air Act of 1970 required the purchase of equipment, such as the catalytic converter and scrubbers, by companies to reduce the emission of pollutants into the atmosphere. Regulation also requires the creation of government regulatory agencies that employ people who are a part of the government payroll.

The indirect costs of regulation usually show up in higher prices for goods and services. For example, an automobile costs more because of government regulation. Federal safety standards promulgated in the 1960s and early 1970s involved accident avoidance, crash protection, and postcrash survivability. Accident avoidance standards were set for braking systems, tires, windshields, lamps, and transmission controls. Occupant protection standards included requirements for safety belts, head restraints, and highly penetration-resistant safety glass. Exterior penetration standards included the absorption capacity of front and rear bumpers. These and other standards that are presented in Table 3-1 added $671 to the price of the average automobile.

Opportunity Costs Opportunity costs are a type of indirect cost. Since resources are scarce, the decision to use them means that something else must be given up. When resources are used in a certain way, there is a simultaneous choice not to use them another way. The opportunity cost then can be defined as the value of the benefit lost as a result of choosing one alternative over another. It is an important concept because the real cost of any activity is measured by its opportunity cost, not by its outlay cost. Thus, if resources are used to control pollution or build safer automobiles, society gives up all the other goods and services that might have been obtained from the use of these resources. For example, resources devoted to the production of pollution control equipment might have been used to produce houses instead.

COST–BENEFIT ANALYSIS

The motive for incorporating cost-benefit analysis into the regulatory decision-making process is to achieve a more efficient allocation of resources. In making an investment decision, for example, it is necessary to compare the costs to be incurred to the expected benefits, namely, revenues. Very likely the investment will be pursued only if the expected costs are less than the expected revenues. If an investment will yield $20 and the cost is $10, the benefit obtained will be $10. Cost-benefit analysis can be applied to opportunity costs. For example, suppose that an individual has $10 that he or she wishes to spend on some benefits. His or her rational response would be to examine a number of possible uses of the money and ask which of them would yield the greatest benefit.

TABLE 3-1 SAFETY STANDARDS FOR PASSENGER CARS

STANDARD	DATE
Occupant protection in interior impact	1968
Head restraints	1969
Impact protection for driver from steering control	1968
Door locks	1968
Safety belt assemblies	1968
Windshield-wiping system	1968
Child protection system	1971
Side door strength	1973
Roof crash resistance	1973
Flammability of interior material	1972

Source: Robert W. Crandall, Howard K. Gruenspecht, Theodore F. Keeler, and Lester B. Lave, *Regulating the Automobile* (Washington, D.C.: The Brookings Institution, 1986), p. 48.

Table 3-2 provides an example of cost-benefit analysis applied to automobile safety regulation. The costs of safety standards are the original cost of meeting them as well as the costs of complying with them after the companies have had sufficient time to redesign the vehicles to accommodate the standards at the lowest cost. The benefits include a reduction in premature deaths, a large portion of which occurs among teenagers and adults. There has been a reduction in the number of highway deaths per 100 million vehicle miles driven. In 1965 the highway deaths were 5.52 per 100 million vehicle miles driven; in 1985 there were 2.21 highway deaths per 100 million vehicle miles driven; and in 1994 there were 1.53 highway deaths per 100 million vehicle miles driven.[7] These reductions can be attributed in part to improved safety standards for automobiles, but also in part to other factors such as drivers education and the 55 mile-per-hour speed limit then in effect.

Regulatory Impact Analysis (RIA) In 1981 President Reagan issued Executive Order No. 11291, which required that expensive new regulations should be implemented only if their benefits to society outweighed costs. Major regulations with an impact of $100 million or more required a regulatory impact analysis (RIA) from the sponsoring agency before going into effect. RIAs are used in environmental regulation where calculation of costs includes costs to industries for the installation of abatement measures, plant closures, lost jobs, medical costs, and the value of lives lost. In recent years the EPA has valued lives at between $400,000 and $7 million each.[8] The benefits of any environmental improvement can be the sum of the monetary values assigned to the effects of that improvement by those persons directly or indirectly affected by the action. Health benefits would be an example. Health can be improved by a reduction in pollution.

TABLE 3-2   ESTIMATES OF THE BENEFITS AND COSTS OF AUTOMOBILE SAFETY REGULATION

BENEFITS	
Reductions in premature deaths	23,400
Reductions in all deaths	35,100
Value at $1 million per fatality avoided (billions of dollars)	35.1
Value at $300,000 per fatality avoided (billions of dollars)	10.5
COSTS	
Cost per car (1981 dollars)	671
Annual cost (billions of dollars)	7.0
Annual cost without bumper standards (billions of dollars)	4.9
Benefits less costs – first estimate = 35.1 less 7.0 =	28.1
Benefits less costs – second estimate = 10.5 less 7.0 =	3.5

Source: Robert W. Crandall, Howard K. Gruenspecht, Theodore E. Keeler, and Lester B. Lave, *Regulating the Automobile* (Washington, D.C.: The Brookings Institution, 1986), p. 77.

DEREGULATION

A number of industries, including airlines, banking, railroads, trucking, natural gas, electricity, and telecommunications have been deregulated in recent years. The regulation was economic in nature, with regulatory agencies, such as the Civil Aeronautics Board (CAB), regulating specific industries. Most of these industries were natural monopolies. This can happen when economies of scale are so extensive in relation to the size of the market that only one firm can operate efficiently within that market. Thus, it is given a monopoly over a specific area. In return for its control over a given service area, a natural monopoly is subject to direct control of rates, services, and other functions by federal and state agencies to ensure the protection of the public interest.

In both electricity and telephones the most important natural monopoly was the local distribution network. It was considered wasteful to lay a set of parallel electric cables or telephone lines through cities and towns to enable different sellers to compete for customers. Accordingly, electricity and telephone service used to be provided by companies that managed virtually every aspect of the industry from top to bottom. Telephone services were largely the domain of the American Telephone and Telegraph Company (AT&T) which provided most local networks, long-distance services, and telephone equipment. Electric power companies generated power and transmitted it over high-voltage lines to their local distribution networks, which in turn delivered it to homes, offices, and factories. Both industries were subject to both federal and state regulation.

Deregulation has occurred for several reasons. The first is that technological change has eroded the natural monopoly characteristics of regulated industries. The telephone industry has seen the development of wireless technologies, along with the reductions in the cost of fiber-optic transmission lines that may someday route telephone calls over alternative pathways such as cable television systems. Second, it is felt that deregulation produces economic benefits when it leads to competition. If markets are competitive and function smoothly, they will lead to prices at which the amount sellers want to supply equals the amount sellers will demand. The benefits that accrue are a reduction in the cost of services and technological and operating innovation. Third, markets have information-processing skills and the preservation of individual incentives superior to those of the government when it comes to running an economy.

Table 3-3 (on page 58) lists the various deregulatory initiatives that have occurred since 1978 when the airline industry was deregulated.

REDEFINING THE ROLE OF GOVERNMENT IN THE U.S. MARKET ECONOMY

Attitudes toward the role of government in the U.S. market economy are in the process of change. For most of the twentieth century, government has expanded its role as regulator of economic activity in industries ranging from

TABLE 3-3 MAJOR DEREGULATORY INITIATIVES, 1978–1996

YEAR	INITIATIVE	PURPOSE
1978	Airline Deregulation Act	Deregulate interstate air transportation
1978	Natural Gas Policy Act	Deregulate interstate natural gas prices
1980	Motor Carrier Reform Act	Reduce federal control over entry and pricing of interstate trucking
1980	Depository Institutions Deregulation & Monetary Control Act	Reduce limitations on interest payable on bank depository accounts
1980	Staggers Railroad Act	Give railroads flexibility in setting rates
1982	Bus Regulatory Reform Act	Deregulate interstate bus transportation
1984	Cable Communications Policy Act	Deregulate 90 percent of cable TV rates by the end of 1986
1984	Breakup of AT&T	Promote more competition in the telephone industry
1996	Telecommunications Act	Deregulate the telecommunications industry
1996	Federal Energy Regulatory Commission, Orders No. 888 & 889	Set rules for opening up interstate transmission networks to all generators and resellers of electricity

banking to public utilities. The traditional relationship was between government-mandated regulation and reliance on market forces. But certain developments in the 1990s have forced a reappraisal of the proper role of government in the United States and throughout the world. The collapse of the centrally planned economies of the Soviet Union and Eastern and Central Europe demonstrated that state ownership and control of resources led to inefficiency, waste, and corruption. In Germany and other Western European countries, it has been demonstrated that excessive regulation has inhibited individual initiative and created high unemployment rates.[9]

A major problem confronting the United States and, for that matter, Canada, Western Europe, Japan, and the rich countries of the world is what to do about social security. In the United States, social security was introduced at a time when the average recipient, who was a male, lived only three years after the retirement age of sixty-five. But times have changed in the United States, and recipients are living an average of fourteen years after retirement. Thus, one of the most topical issues of the day is how to fix the social security systems so that benefits will be available for those who retire in the future. One proposal is to allow citizens to use the money they would invest in the social security system to invest in stocks, bonds, and mutual funds.[10]

It is also argued that the links between government and those citizens who reap the benefits and who bear the costs are very weak. In his book, *The Rise and Decline of Nations*, Mancur Olson combined economics and politics to explain why nations rose and declined.[11] The main reason was the rise in political importance of special interest groups. As they form, each gains and then fiercely defends some benefit for its members, usually with the help of government. Subsidies and other transfer payments flow to these groups, and a specialized class of lawyers, bureaucrats, and lobbyists who know how to work the system are created. Redistributive struggles displace productive ones when it comes to allocating resources. As a special interest group increases in numbers, its political clout increases, and it becomes more difficult to initiate reforms.[12]

THE PROPER ROLE OF MARKETS AND GOVERNMENT

The United States has a modified market economy where there is a primary reliance on the market mechanism to allocate resources, but also a considerable amount of government intervention in the form of regulation. The relationship between the market and government has been that one should be a substitute for the other and vice-versa. Those who advocate complete reliance on the market mechanism claim that it is much more efficient than government when it comes to resource allocation. Those who support an active role for government compare market failures with an idealized vision of a government possessing unlimited information and purely beneficial objectives. It can also be argued, based on the recent deregulation of telecommunications and electric power, that the relationship between the market and the government should be one of complementariness rather than substitution.[13]

The Proper Role of the Market   The price mechanism is the linchpin of a market system. Its function is to provide a coordinating mechanism for millions of decentralized production and distribution units. Because market prices measure the marginal benefits of goods and services, firms that maximize their profits also maximize the difference between benefits and costs. As tastes, technology, and resource availability change, market prices will also change to direct resources to the newly created ends. The interaction between prices and profits are supposed to keep economic mistakes down to a reasonable level. Profit, which depends on the selling price of goods and the cost of making them, indicates to businesses what people are buying.[14] In a market economy, profit is necessary for survival; it is the payment to owners of capital.

Given the institution of private property, which is indispensable for a market economy to function, the attempt of individuals and companies to further their economic self-interest results in competition. Competition is a requisite part of a market system. It is, therefore, not surprising that by statute and common law, the U.S. legal system has been actively concerned with the promotion of competition in the marketplace.[15] Certain benefits to society are thought to be derived from competition. The first benefit is that it expands consumer choice by providing a wide variety of goods and services. A second benefit is that it encourages product innovation. Finally, it promotes efficiency in that efficient firms are profitable and inefficient firms go bankrupt.

The Proper Role of Government   Government is necessary because it sets the formal rules—laws and regulation—that are a basic part of a country's institutional environment. These rules, along with the informal rules of the broader society, are the institutions that mediate human behavior. Without a government legal system to guarantee property rights and to enforce contracts, market exchange would virtually be impossible. Without regulation, firms can hinder competition through such devices as an agreement among themselves to maintain high prices or through the division of markets. The government also provides public goods, such as roads and education, that can have a spillover effect in the market sector. An example would be scientific research.[16] Finally, market efficiency is not the only way to judge an economy. Markets can be consistent with inequalities of opportunities and income resulting from various forms of discrimination.[17]

The Complementary Role of Markets and Government   Markets and government can complement each other. There are certain things that the market does best and there are certain things that government does best. Public policies can make the markets perform better, and market incentives can improve the performance of government. An example of the former is government deregulation of local telephone services and electricity generation to bring about competition and cost reduction to consumers. Conversely, markets can help the government to do its job more efficiently. An example is the use of tradable permit programs, in which the government issues rights to emit some pollutants and then allows firms to allocate those rights across their plants and to buy and sell them among themselves.

SUMMARY

Regulatory growth in the late 1960s and early 1970s created a number of new and important agencies that were social in nature. They included the Consumer Product Safety Commission, the Equal Employment Opportunity Commission, and the Environmental Protection Agency. These agencies were given the right to regulate certain business activities, including employment practices and the production of consumer goods. In the later 1970s and early 1980s, other industries were deregulated, and federal regulatory agencies that were economic in nature were eliminated. The Airline Deregulation Act of 1978 ended regulation of the fares, rates, schedules, and routes of passenger airlines in interstate commerce, eased entry into the airline industry, and phased out the Civil Aeronautics Board. The telecommunications and electric utilities industries were deregulated in the 1990s.

QUESTIONS FOR DISCUSSION

1. Discuss some of the reasons for the rapid expansion of the role of government in the American economy during the twentieth century.
2. What is the legal basis of government regulation of the American economy?
3. Discuss the differences between economic regulation and social regulation. Give examples of each type of regulation.
4. Discuss the division of responsibilities in the political system of the United States.
5. What is the role of profit in a market economy?

NOTES

1. *Marbury v. Madison*, 1 Cranch 137, 2 L.ED. 60 (1803).
2. An example of an independent regulatory agency is the Federal Trade Commission; an example of an agency that is a part of the executive branch of government is the Equal Employment Opportunity Commission.
3. This would represent a direct violation of Section 2 of the Sherman Act of 1890.
4. In Germany three major banks—the Dresdner Bank, the Commerz Bank, and the Deutsche Bank—dominate the credit market of the country.
5. *U.S. v. American Tobacco Co.*, 221 U.S. 10 C, 31 Sup. Ct. 632 (1911).
6. It is estimated that paperwork costs amount to around $30 billion a year to business firms and public institutions.
7. U.S. Department of Commerce, Bureau of the Census, *Statistical Abstract of the United States 1997* (Washington, D.C.: U.S. Government Printing Office, 1997), p. 636.
8. EPA evaluations of life are based on earnings surveys of dangerous occupations that try to measure the wage premium paid to attract people to risky work.
9. If anything, Russia has performed even worse during the 1990s. Corruption is widespread, income inequality has increased, crime is endemic, many workers do not get paid on time, and living standards for many people have declined.
10. This approach is predicated on the assumption that the stock market will continue to rise in the future. The performance of the stock market in the spring of 2000 shows that stocks can also fall and people can lose money.
11. Mancur Olsen, *The Rise and Fall of Nations* (New Haven, CT: Yale University Press, 1983).
12. The United States provides a number of good examples beginning with the AARP.
13. See Chapter 6, "Redefining the Role of Government in the U.S. Market Economy," in *Economic Report of the President 1997* (Washington, D.C.: U.S. Government Printing Office, 1997), pp. 189–234.
14. The reverse of profit is loss, and in a competitive market economy there are also losers.
15. It involves the Darwinist concept of "survival of the fittest."
16. Numerous recent initiatives, such as the Department of Transportation's programs to provide financing for public highways and private toll rolls, can generate benefits by promoting regional economic development.
17. There are a number of factors that inhibit true equality of opportunity. They would vary from country to country. In England, it would probably be social class and schools attended. It helps in life to have attended Eton or Harrow.

Recommended Reading

Buchanan, James M. "Why Does Government Grow?" In *Budgets and Bureaucrats: The Sources of Government Growth*, ed. Thomas Borcherding. Durham, NC: Duke University Press, 1977.

Executive Office of the President, Office of Manpower and Budget. *A Citizen's Guide to the Federal Budget, Fiscal Year 2000*. Washington, D.C.: U.S. Government Printing Office, October 1999.

Helm, Dieter, ed. *The Economic Borders of the State*. Oxford, England: Oxford University Press.

Israel, Arturo. "The Changing Role of the State: Institutional Dimension." PRE Working Paper 495. Washington, D.C.: Country Economics Department. The World Bank. 1990.

Lawrence, Robert Z., Albert Bress, and Takatoshi Ito. *A Vision for the World Economy*. Washington, D.C.: The Brookings Institution, 1996.

Rodrik, Dani. "Why Do More Open Economies Have Larger Governments?" Cambridge, MA: John F. Kennedy School of Government, Harvard University, 1996.

"A Survey of the World Economy: The Future of the State." *The Economist*. London, England (September 20, 1997): 1–48.

The World Bank, *World Development Report 1997: The State in a Changing World*. New York: Oxford University Press, 1997.

CHAPTER 4

SPECIAL INTEREST GROUPS AND THE PUBLIC INTEREST

The National Rifle Association (NRA) is one of the better-known special interest groups in the United States. Its purpose is to protect the rights of individuals to own guns as guaranteed by the Constitution of the United States.[1] Its spokesperson is the well-known actor Charlton Heston who, among his acting accomplishments, parted the Red Sea and won a chariot race.[2] In Europe, Japan, and other parts of the world, the right to own guns is circumscribed by law. They must be registered before a permit is issued. But the American psyche is different from the rest of the world. It is individualistic, and the individual is pretty much free to do what he or she pleases, including owning guns. American males, in particular, seem to be attached to owning guns.

School violence involving the use of guns has increased public interest in laws regulating gun ownership, which the NRA has adamantly opposed. However, the massacre of students at Columbine High School in Littleton, Colorado, in April 1999, galvanized public support in favor of laws regulating the use of guns, particularly by minors. In May 1999, as part of a bill aimed at curbing juvenile violence, the U.S. Senate passed measures mandating child safety locks on handguns and requiring background checks to be made on anyone who buys a weapon at a gun show. The House of Representatives began watering down the mandatory background checks. Both Democrats and Republicans participated in emasculating the measure, and gun control did not pass. The NRA was roundly blamed for its defeat.

However, the NRA is just one of a number of special groups that are involved in the making of public policy. As the United States has become a more pluralistic society, special interest groups have increased. One of the better-known and most powerful interest groups is the American Association of Retired Persons (AARP), which represents that segment of the population that depends on Social Security for retirement. The National Association of Women

(NOW) represents women on such issues as choice and affirmative action. The National Association of Manufacturers (NAM) represents the interest of business. Veterans are a special interest group and so are unions. Special interest groups are active at all levels of government. In Virginia, the Virginia Education Association (VEA) represents the interests of teachers. Special interest groups have learned the tools of political influence. They have become insiders in the high stakes game of public policymaking.

THE HISTORY OF SPECIAL INTEREST GROUPS

There is nothing new about special interest groups. Efforts to influence public policy through appropriate organizations have been a cardinal feature of the American economy since its inception in 1789. The three most important special interest groups over time have been those representing agriculture, business, and labor. In the period from 1789 to the beginning of the Civil War, canal builders and road builders looked to Washington and to state governments for financial help. Railroads and shipping companies also got support from Washington and the states to build railroads and steamboats. Small manufacturers petitioned Washington to raise tariffs on manufactured goods from Europe, arguing that they needed protection from more advanced European industries. Agrarian interests pressed for lower tariffs because they wanted to buy cheaper manufactured goods from Europe.

AGRICULTURE

Agriculture discontent after the Civil War asserted itself through the Grange movement. The discontent began for several reasons. The first was the decline of agricultural prices during the 1870s, and the others were high railroad rates, price gouging by middlemen, difficulty of getting credit, and a growing conflict between agrarian interests and commercial interests. The National Grange was created in 1867 and moved like a prairie fire across the Midwest. During the depression of 1873 it turned to politics, calling for regulation of warehouses and railroads, control of monopolies, creation of a Department of Agriculture, and broader government services for agriculture. In a short time it built up a membership of one million, captured control of several midwestern state governments, and passed laws regulating railroads and warehouses. But the Grange movement, like many political movements in America, was short-lived.

Populism   With the return of agricultural distress in the late 1880s, another movement called Populism developed. Two separate Farmers' Alliances, one in the Midwest and the other in the South, were created. They supported antimonopoly regulation, railroad regulation, and currency reforms. Their electoral successes stimulated agitation for the creation of a national party, and in 1892 the Populist Party was born. It wanted nationalization of the railroads, inflation based on a silver standard, regulation of banks, and rate regulation. Its peak was reached in 1892 when it polled twenty-two electoral votes and over one million votes. Like all third parties, it was absorbed into one of the major political parties.

VETERANS

Veterans are one of the strongest special interest groups in the United States. After the Civil War, thousands of Union soldiers were disbanded and became the backbone of the Republican Party. Support of veterans came mainly from the states, which provided pensions, land grants, and special poverty relief for disabled veterans. Many more Americans served in World War I than in the Civil War. Veterans formed a political group called the American Legion. It lobbied for veterans' hospitals and pensions for veterans and their dependents. One of the largest and most important special interest groups ever created in the United States was the veterans of World War II, some nineteen million of them. The Veterans' Administration helped them buy homes by providing them with loan guarantees; the federal government passed the GI bill of rights that provided them with free education; and various veterans' hospitals around the country provided them with free medical services. They were given preferential treatment when it came to getting jobs.

LABOR

Unions have become an important force in American politics. Much of their power developed during the 1930s, although they had been around a full century prior to this decade. Unions were generally split up into two types—those who recruited only skilled workers and those who recruited semiskilled and unskilled workers. The first were called craft unions, and the second were called industrial unions. Craft unions concentrated on "bread and butter" issues. They concentrated on the improvement of their own wages, hours, and working conditions, and showed little interest in wider reform or in politics in general. The first union to become actively involved in the political process was the Industrial Workers of the World (IWW), which supported a program of militant unions and the creation of a socialist economy. Its espousal of radical politics cost it any support it might have received from the craft unions, and it was outlawed during World War I with the passage of the Espionage Act.

Labor became a major special interest group during the Depression of the 1930s. The balance of power was strongly in favor of employers, who used every measure possible to keep unions from unionizing their workers. The typical device was the company union. As the Depression deepened, unions as represented by the American Federation of Labor increased their demands for government assistance.

Unions made enormous gains during the 1930s. Collective bargaining over wages, hours, and working conditions was recognized as legitimate and treated as legally enforceable. Gains in membership were made in the steel, tire, automobile, electric manufacturing, and other industries. Social legislation of interest to unions was passed, including retirement benefits, minimum wages, and overtime pay. The unions became one of the most powerful special interest groups as their membership increased. Most of the unions have traditionally supported the Democratic Party, particularly on social issues. They have supported protection against foreign imports when the issue is losing jobs. They were opposed to the North American Free Trade Agreement (NAFTA), because they visualized many American jobs being exported to Mexico if the agreement were passed.

CONSUMERS

Consumers are a special interest group, although they are not as well organized as other groups. They share a common interest in the most efficient conversion of their income into goods and services. They want accurate information about products they use—their variety, quantity, quality, price, and safety. They want a defense against product misrepresentation and injury. Consumers, who are all of us, are too many to organize into one organization, but they can coalesce around a single issue to demand product safety legislation. The sale of unsafe food and drugs led to consumer protest and the creation of the Food and Drug Administration in 1906. Automobile safety became an issue in the 1960s, leading to laws requiring the installation of seat belts and shatterproof glass. Various groups, such as the Consumers Union and Consumer Research, provide information and ratings of products that are available to consumers.

BUSINESS

Business is one of the most important special interest groups in the United States. Its concern with government dates back to the beginning of the country. It is the most visible element in American society. Attitudes toward business have fluctuated from good to bad during the two hundred years of our country's existence. During the latter part of the nineteenth century, such persons as John D. Rockefeller and Andrew Carnegie were referred to as "robber barons" and "malefactors of great wealth." Business had a bad name during the Depression of the 1930s and in the 1980s when corporate takeovers became common. In the 1990s, given the prosperity of the American economy, the image of business has improved as the number of billionaires and millionaires has increased.

Traditionally, business input into the political process has been done through the organization of industry trade associations and of regional and local business groups. In addition to crystallizing and registering the interests of the particular industry or area, these groups are important media for arousing and focusing general business reactions to broader policy issues.

They attempt to speak for the business community as a whole. The two most important business groups are the National Association of Manufacturers (NAM) and the Chamber of Commerce. NAM concentrates on representing manufacturing firms and is opposed to any form of government encroachment on the business decision-making process. The Chamber of Commerce represents a broader constituency. It is effective in presenting business views to legislative and administrative agencies and informing the business community of its stake in public policy issues.

ENVIRONMENTALISTS

Pollution of the environment is by no means a recent phenomenon. In one form or another it has existed since antiquity. In the United States, pollution as we know it today is a by-product of industrialization, urbanization, and population growth. In the nineteenth century, industrial cities such as Chicago and Pittsburgh were cited by foreign visitors as being particularly foul.[3] The largest assembly of stockyards in the world added a mephitic odor to Chicago's air, as if a poisonous or foul-smelling gas were being emitted from the earth. Natural drainage was nonexistent, flooding was habitual, and the surface of the Chicago River was so thick with grease that it looked like a liquid rainbow.[4] In New York, refuse including the carcasses of dead animals was thrown into the rivers or the Atlantic Ocean.

There is nothing new about environmentalism. Interest in preserving the environment dates back to John Audubon, who developed bird sanctuaries, and to the administration of Theodore Roosevelt, whose friend was the naturalist John Muir. Roosevelt set aside thousands of acres of forest land and designated them public property. But the one person who had the greatest impact on the environmental movement was Rachel Carson, who wrote the book *Silent Spring* in 1962.[5] She warned of the dangers of pesticides, in particular DDT. The use of DDT in the southern states against fire ants caused widespread damage to living creatures so that it had to be canceled. But pollution involved more than the use of pesticides. Rivers and lakes were polluted by runoffs of waste materials by chemical plants, paper mills, and oil refineries. The air in the cities was polluted by emissions from cars. Protection of the environment became very important to a large segment of the public, and another special interest group developed.

There are a number of environmentalist groups today and they are politically powerful. A number of these groups have more than half a million members and annual budgets in the tens of millions of dollars. They have large staffs who are able to churn out information and policy papers, and information still equates power with Congress and the news media. Some of the environmentalist groups, such as the Audubon Society, have been around for many years, which gives them credence in terms of their staying power. Table 4-1 (on page 68) presents the number of members in various environmental groups.

TABLE 4-1   MEMBERSHIP IN ENVIRONMENTALIST GROUPS, 1998

GROUP	MEMBERSHIP
Defenders of Wildlife	250,000
Environmental Action	16,000
Environmental Defense Fund	300,000
Friends of the Earth	50,000
Sierra Club	588,000
National Audubon Society	550,000
National Wildlife Federation	4,000,000
Nature Conservancy	900,000
Wilderness Society	200,000

Source: Jeffrey M. Berry, "Liberalism's Transformation," *Washington Post*, Sunday, July 11, 1999, p. B3.

SENIOR CITIZENS

People are living longer in the United States and many have reached that stage in life at which they have the title of senior citizen bestowed on them. It entitles them to many dispensations, including discounts at restaurants and stores, and fawning attention from the politicians.[6] It was not always that way. In 1900 the average American did not reach the age of fifty. There were many things that carried people off—poor dietary habits and a plethora of diseases ranging from typhoid fever and influenza to minor infections. Even when Social Security was created in the 1930s, the average American male lived only three years after he reached the age of sixty-five. But all this has changed dramatically, as healthier diets and the eradication of fatal diseases have increased the longevity of Americans and thereby increased the costs of pensions, medical care, and social services for retirees.

Older people, as represented by the American Association of Retired Persons (AARP), represent the strongest special interest group in the United States. No politician worth his or her salt would dare cross this group, because they vote more consistently than voters in any other special interest group. Their lobbyists are active at all levels of government for larger pensions, lower taxes, increased medical coverage, nursing home regulation, and other benefits of interest to the group. The entitlements for this special interest group comprise the largest expenditure in the federal budget, which will increase as more Americans grow older. The end result will be a continued increase in Social Security levied on workers to pay the cost of retirement benefits.

OTHER SPECIAL INTEREST GROUPS

There are many other special interest groups in the United States. They represent nonprofit organizations as well as profit organizations. They do not have to be American; they can represent the interests of other countries. China is an example. They can represent a large number of people or a small number of people. Although the number of farmers is declining nationally, in some states they are large enough to have a political impact. In Virginia, Kentucky, and North Carolina tobacco is an important product and tobacco farmers are a group that has an impact on how politicians from their states vote on tobacco legislation. Sugar beet farmers, although limited in number, have been successful in having restrictions placed on the import of cane sugar from other countries, even though it is cheaper than the beet sugar produced in the United States. Maritime unions have protected the jobs of their members by having requirements imposed on shipping goods on U.S. ships.

PROMOTION OF AN AGENDA

The public sector has grown rapidly because there has been a proliferation of economic and social responsibilities that various interest groups have asked government to perform. As a result, the federal government has extended its involvement in the market system. State and local governments have also become involved. More and more government effort is being directed toward cushioning individual risks and regulating personal and institutional conduct. The cumulative impact of its actions impinge upon all of us but in different ways, so we coalesce into special interest groups. There are a number of ways in which support or opposition to a particular measure that affects us can be expressed, the first of which is through lobbying.

LOBBYING

When Bill Clinton was running for president back in 1992, one of the things he promised to do if elected was to rid Washington of "lobbyists wearing Gucci shoes."[7] That promise, once he was elected, was promptly forgotten, probably because of his financial support from various lobbyists.[8] As the number of special interest groups has increased, so has the number of lobbyists. Washington has many of them, most of whom are lawyers who have had government experience in one form or another. Congresspersons who were defeated for reelection are likely to remain in Washington and become lobbyists for interest groups. The same holds true for government officials. Their knowledge of the ways of the political process is a strong selling point.

Although lobbyists are normally associated with the activities of the federal government, this is hardly the usual case. As state and local governments have increased in importance, so have the number of lobbyists. In Virginia the political action is in Richmond, and that is where the lobbyists are. There are 807 registered lobbyists in Richmond, and few of them wear Gucci shoes. They span a very diverse group of interests, ranging from Philip Morris, the Norfolk and Southern Railroad, and the Newport News Shipyards to volunteer environmental groups, home schoolers, and firefighters. The two major universities in the state—Virginia Tech and Virginia—also have lobbyists to represent them in Richmond before the state legislature.[9] The lobbyists have to be aware of shifting public sentiment and its impact on state education.[10]

FEDERAL LOBBYISTS

One may wonder what politicians do when they are not reelected to Congress. Do they go back to the districts from which they were elected and socialize with the people who elected them? Not hardly! Did Bob Dole go back to Russell, Kansas, his boyhood home, which he extolled when he was running for president in 1996? Not hardly! So what do they do with themselves? Do they emulate former president Jimmy Carter by working for Habitat for Humanity? Not hardly! They become lobbyists. But one does not have to be a former politician to become a lobbyist. One can be a former member of a congressional staff, or be involved one way or another with government, or have contacts with important people who usually do not live in Russell, Kansas. Vernon Jordan comes to mind.

As of 1998, there were 17,500 lobbyists in Washington.[11] The fifty best-known and most successful lobbyists took in $125 million in 1997. Add the revenues from subsidiary operations that do not require public disclosure, such as strategic advice and public relations services, and total income probably doubles. They are part of the power elite in Washington, and shape the decision-making process. They know what buttons need to be pushed in order to get things done. The backgrounds and clients of some of the most successful lobbyists in Washington are presented in the following paragraphs.

Gerald Cassidy of Cassidy and Associates was a former general counsel to Senator George McGovern's Committee on Hunger. Presumably this motivated him to build his company into Washington's most powerful lobbying firm. He earned a $4.5 million fee for getting the White House to allow an entry visa for Lee Teng-hiu, the president of Taiwan, so he could attend his Cornell University class reunion, as well as promoting Taiwan's entry into the World Trade Organization. To get the entry visa, Cassidy had influential Cornell graduates write their representatives and senators, and the president got his visa. Taiwan continues to pay Cassidy a retainer fee, and Cornell got a $2.5 million gift from its Taiwan alumni.

Vernon Jordan is well-known. He plays golf with Bill Clinton and supposedly tried to help Monica Lewinsky get a job. He is associated with the law firm of Akin, Gump, Straus, Hauer, and Feld. He is not a registered lobbyist as is required under the Lobbying Disclosure Act of 1995, but he has the contacts and he brings in hundreds of thousands of dollars in retainers to his firm. Beyond that, he sits on more corporate boards of directors than any other attorney in the United States. He is on the board of directors of J. C. Penney, Union Carbide, Sara Lee, Ryder Systems, and recently and rather appropriately joined the board of directors of Calloway Golf.

Robert Packwood, former senator from Oregon, achieved national notoriety for kissing almost every woman he could lay his hands on, and resigned his Senate seat. Rather than return to Oregon, he became a lobbyist. He is an expert on the tax code of the United States. A coalition of lumber mills and small business firms hired him to secure cuts in estate taxes to make it easier for heirs to keep businesses they inherit. He was successful in having the tax code changed. He also represents Northwest Airlines, which wanted to maintain its dominance in the Japanese market, by opposing the open-sky treaty that would let other airline companies in.

But men have no monopoly on becoming top lobbyists. Women are also lobbyists and an example is Deborah Steelman, who once worked for Senator John Danforth and then worked for the Bush administration in developing Social Security and Medicare policies and is now an adviser to presidential candidate George W. Bush of Texas. She is a lobbyist on health-care issues and represents such companies as Aetna, Johnson and Johnson, and Pfizer. She lobbied to defeat the Clintons' proposed health-care overhaul. Ann Wexler, a former aid to President Clinton, also has expertise on health care and is adept at building coalitions in support of such clients as Johnson and Johnson to increase Medicare funding for nonprescription drugs.

Lobbying is justified on the grounds that it gives more people access to the political decision-making process, but that is hardly the case. Special interest groups can afford to hire lobbyists; most people cannot. There is a redistribution of income in favor of groups that can pay to hire the best lobbyists. A state university that has a paid lobbyist is more likely to get funding for a new building than a state university without a lobbyist. Consumers are often the losers. When union and automobile company lobbyists lobbied Congress to use import quotas to reduce the number of Japanese cars that could be sold in the United States, the intent was to protect workers against loss of jobs and the automobile industry against possible bankruptcy. The end result was that consumers had to pay $3,000 more for both American and Japanese cars. The automobile companies made money, their executives got richer, and the jobs that were saved were eventually lost to automation.

POLITICAL ACTION COMMITTEES (PACS)

American politics is very expensive. Candidates for office at every level of government, from local government officials to the president of the United States, are forced to spend money to get elected. Costs range from a few thousand dollars in local elections to tens of millions of dollars for U.S. senate and presidential elections. Thus, long before the presidential election of 2000, the candidates were beating the bushes for donations. By July 1999 George W. Bush, the governor of Texas, had already raised more than $30 million, and he eventually got the Republican nomination for president. Vice-President Al

Gore raised more money than his opponent Bill Bradley, close to $20 million by July 1999, and he eventually got the Democratic nomination for president. Both men are wealthy and have friends who are wealthy.

An important way in which candidates raise money to run for political office is through financial support from Political Action Committees (PACs). PACs are independently incorporated organizations that can solicit contributions from employees, union members, or shareholders, and then channel the funds to those seeking political office. Companies that have organized PACs are not permitted to donate corporate funds to the PAC or to any political candidate; all donations to company-organized PACs must come from individuals. Labor unions also have PACs, as do trade and health organizations. One of the more important trade organizations is the National Association of Realtors. Table 4-2 presents the number of PACs by committee type. Corporate PACs are the most numerous. Table 4-3 presents the money outlays made by PACs. Labor and trade and health PACs spent the most money.

The Federal Election Commission has established rules to regulate PACs. For example, PACs are not allowed to give more than $5,000 to a single candidate for a single election. These limits were imposed on all PACs to reduce the role of concentrated wealth in determining the result of elections to public office. Candidates and donors get around these limits by using loopholes. One popular method has been the payment of "soft money." This loophole refers to funds directly donated to political parties to support party activities such as televised commercials that do not support a specific candidate, get-out-the-vote drives, and other activities in conjunction with presidential and congressional races.

THE 1996 ELECTIONS

In 1996, spending on election campaigns reached a record high. The majority of the funds involved came through what is called soft money loopholes. Soft money can be defined as funds that are contributed to a political party instead of a political candidate. By law, it should be spent on party-building activities

TABLE 4-2   NUMBER OF POLITICAL ACTION COMMITTEES BY COMMITTEE TYPES, 1996

Corporate	1,642
Labor	332
Trade, health	838
Nonconnected	1,103
Cooperatives	41
Other	123
Total	**4,079**

Source: U.S. Department of Commerce, Economics and Statistics Administration, Bureau of the Census, *Statistical Abstract of the United States 1998* (Springfield, VA: National Technical Information Services, 1998), p. 301.

TABLE 4-3 FINANCIAL ACTIVITY OF POLITICAL ACTION COMMITTEES, 1996
(MILLIONS OF DOLLARS)

COMMITTEE	DISBURSEMENTS
Corporate	130.6
Labor	99.8
Trade and Health	105.4
Nonconnected	81.3
Cooperatives	4.2
Other	8.7
Total	**430.0**

Source: U.S. Department of Commerce, Economics and Statistical Administration, Bureau of the Census, *Statistical Abstract of the United States 1998* (Springfield, VA: National Technical Information Services, 1998), p. 301.

and not on campaigns. However, that is not what happens. Much of it is used to finance campaigns and to gain access to powerful politicians who can grant favors. This type of contribution helped to finance the campaigns of 1996 because no limits are placed on the amount of soft money that can be given.

Table 4-4 presents the top ten contributors to the political campaigns in 1996. Some gave more money to Republicans, while others gave money to Democrats. None of them gave money out of the goodness of their hearts or because they had a conversion experience on the road to Damascus; all of them wanted something in return. The tobacco companies gave money to Republicans because they would be less likely to impose restrictions on the tobacco industry. The Association of Trial Lawyers gave money to the Democrats because they would be less likely to impose caps on punitive damage awards

TABLE 4-4 TOP 10 CONTRIBUTIONS TO CAMPAIGNS IN 1996[1]

CONTRIBUTOR	DEMOCRATS	REPUBLICANS
Philip Morris	$608,704	$2,131,955
AT&T	858,462	1,270,583
Association of Trial Lawyers of America	1,747,725	353,600
Teamsters Union	2,005,250	87,160
Laborers Union	1,778,750	153,500
International Brotherhood of Electrical Workers	1,785,260	31,950
RJR Nabisco	341,406	1,423,900
National Education Association	1,618,110	38,850
American Medical Association	321,114	1,309,166
American Federation of State/County/ Municipal Workers	1,578,700	32,425

[1]Includes soft money to the national parties, PAC money to candidates, PAC and individual contributions to the Clinton and Dole campaigns, and individual campaign contributions to all federal candidates.

and lessen lawyers' fees.[12] The top overall contributor was Wall Street, which gave $60 billion, mostly to Republicans who are usually more likely to buy *The Wall Street Journal* than are Democrats.[13]

CAMPAIGN REFORMS

The great majority of Americans give $200 or less to political campaigns, and that is not likely to buy them a cabinet seat or an ambassadorship to the Court of St. James.[14] The political process is subverted by the use of money, but there is nothing new about it. Politicians since time immemorial have rewarded their faithful followers based on services performed. What is new are the flagrant violations that are involved in campaign financing. One of the most egregious violations of campaign financing is the selling of a night at the White House. Apparently, spending a night at the White House is a prestige symbol for which some people are willing to pay a lot of money. To sleep in the Lincoln bedroom can cost a contributor $250,000, not including breakfast. To schmooze with a government official of the contributor's choice can cost an additional $50,000, but as a happy businessman said: "If I had known all the contacts I was going to make, I would have given $600,000."

Times have changed from the old days when all a politician had to do to get reelected was to attend fish fries, march in the Fourth of July parade wearing his VFW hat to proclaim he was a veteran, and send congratulatory notes to graduating high school seniors even though most of them had never heard of him. He usually maintained one office in his district; his office staff in Washington plus the office staff at home numbered around five or six people.[15] But times have changed drastically from the old days. As the country has become more complex and the number of special interest groups has multiplied like dandelions, political campaigns have become expensive and costs have skyrocketed for virtually every local, state, and elected official. The high cost of running for political office in the United States has had a deleterious effect on the American political process. Politicians must now engage in continuous fund-raising; there was a time when fund-raising was done just before an election, but this is no longer true.

One factor that has driven up the cost of elections is the need for media exposure, which has become very expensive. In the old days, advertising in the local newspapers was a good way to get exposure or, as Harry Truman did in the 1948 presidential election, "whistle-stopping" throughout the country by railroad. Television has become the most important medium to reach the most people. Ads can cost thousands of dollars. A candidate also has to hire a pollster to tell him or her what issues to stress. Then there are campaign managers and their assistants, so a politician has to employ a retinue of experts to turnout policy papers. Advertising firms are also hired to turn out clever commercials that voters remember when they go to the polls to vote.

The McCain-Feingold bill, sponsored by Senators John McCain of Arizona and Russell Feingold of Wisconsin, represents a bipartisan attempt to reform campaign financing. The bill would limit personal and corporate spending, restrict out-of-state contributions, eliminate soft money contributions to parties after existing limits on contributions to individual candidates had been reached, and ban corporate and labor union contributions to political parties. In addition, the bill would bar contributions by noncitizens. Testimony at Senate investigatory hearings showed that China, Indonesia, and other countries employed a variety of agents and intermediaries to funnel money to the Clinton campaign.

MADD V. NATIONAL BEER WHOLESALERS ASSOCIATION

MADD (Mothers Against Drunk Driving) is an organization that wants stiffer penalties imposed on drunk drivers who kill or maim children. It also sees alcohol as a gateway to the use of more serious drugs. It and its supporters wanted to include antidrinking messages as a part of a $1 billion, five-year advertising campaign by the Office of National Drug Control Policy against the use of illegal drugs. However, it was necessary for MADD to make its case for the inclusion of the antidrinking message before the House and Senate Appropriations Committee.

The inclusion of the message was opposed by the beer industry, as represented by the National Beer Wholesalers Association, on the grounds that it conveyed the idea that sipping a beer was tantamount to injecting oneself with a needle. Beer and wine interests maintain active lobbies on Capitol Hill. The political action committees gave $2.3 million to congressional candidates of both parties during the 1998 elections. The top lobbyist for the National Beer Wholesalers Association, David Rehr, lobbied representatives and senators of the Appropriation Committees. He and other lobbyists for the alcohol industry sent fax messages to committee senators and representatives. The MADD lobbyists also worked to present their views, including a statement by the president of MADD who said: "We will learn whether the House Appropriations Committee will see Mr. Rehr's face or the faces of thousands of young people who die each year from alcohol abuse."

In the end, the beer industry carried the day; the full House Appropriations Committee voted 32 to 23 to kill the underage drinking language. One who voted to kill the bill was Representative Anne Northup of Kentucky, a recipient of beer contributions, who thought that the proposal to include underage drinking could undermine the effectiveness of the federal government's battle against illegal drugs. "Alcohol and drugs," she said, "are two very different substances." Drugs are illegal. They are bad for you at any time. The beer wholesalers also enlisted the support of two senators who would support their views. One of the senators lost his sister to alcohol-related abuse, and the other's mother was killed by a drunken driver.

SUMMARY

Campaign spending has reached record highs in the United States, which purports to be democratic country but in reality is not. Wealth counts because the wealthy can buy influence through campaign donations. Then there are a congeries of special interest groups that combine their resources and form PACs to lobby for their chosen objectives. Politicians have come to depend on much of their support from these groups, whose objectives are often mutually exclusive. It is obvious what the NEA wanted when they gave 99 percent of their campaign contributions to Democrats during the 1996 election campaign, and it is equally obvious what Philip Morris and RJR Nabisco wanted when they gave most of their campaign contributions to the Republicans during the 1996 election campaigns. Most voters have a negative image of PACs, and cynicism, as reflected by a decline in voters' participation in national elections, is an end result.

QUESTIONS FOR DISCUSSION

1. Do lobbyists perform a useful service for society? Discuss.
2. What are special interest groups? Why have they increased in recent years?
3. What impact do special interest groups have on the redistribution of income in the American economy?
4. What are PACs? Do they serve a useful purpose?

NOTES

1. The Second Amendment of the Constitution is as follows: "A well Regulated Militia, being necessary to the security of a free State, the Right of the people to bear Arms, shall not be infringed." At the time of the writing of the Constitution, the idea was to create a citizens' militia to provide for the defense of the new nation. The possibility of incursion by Indians or foreign powers was real. Also, hunting was necessary for most people to put provisions on their tables. There is little relevance to today's world.
2. The movies were *The Ten Commandments* and *Ben Hur*, the latter for which Heston won the Academy Award for best actor.
3. Rudyard Kipling, *Actions and Reactions* (New York: Doubleday and Page, 1909).
4. Louis Mumford, *The City in History* (New York: Harcourt, Brace, and World), p. 461.
5. Rachel Carson, *Silent Spring* (Boston, MA: Houghton-Mifflin, 1962).
6. The author of this chapter had a politician friend who wanted to change Social Security for the elderly, and he is no longer in office.
7. There is an element of populism here because most Americans do not know what Gucci shoes are, but the name sounds foreign.
8. The China lobby that was involved in Clinton's election campaign comes to mind.
9. The lobbyist for Virginia Tech has the campus title of Director of Government Relations.

10. A former governor of Virginia once said: "Shrubs are shrubs and we don't need to pay a bunch of farm extension agents to tell people how to grow them." Virginia Tech did not fare well during his administration.
11. Kim I. Eisler, "Show Me The Money," *The Washingtonian* (January 1998): 81. Subsequent data on the top lobbyists can be found in pp. 81 and 170–177.
12. On July 9, 1999, a California jury awarded plaintiffs in an automobile damage suit $107 million in compensatory damages and $4.8 billion in punitive damages. The lawyers for the plaintiffs hailed the award as a victory for consumers, but did not mention the fact that the award was also a victory for them. If the award stands, they will collect probably a third of it. In Alabama a jury awarded plaintiffs, in a suit involving overcharging for the purchase of a television disc, $529 million.
13. *The Wall Street Journal* advertises itself as the publication that is read by those people who are on their way up in the world, which excludes most college professors. A recent commercial showed a young man who gets into an elevator. He is standing between two men who are reading *The Wall Street Journal*. The implication is clear. If he wants to make anything of himself, he had better start reading *The Wall Street Journal*.
14. To put things in perspective, 99.97 percent of Americans do not give more than $200 in political contributions, which means that .03 percent of the population has the strongest political influence.
15. In the 1960s the congressman from the author's district had a total of seven staff members, two of whom worked in his office in the district, and the rest were in his office in Washington. Today, the congressman from the same district has around forty people on his staff.

RECOMMENDED READING

Birnbaum, Jeffrey H. *The Money Men*. New York: Times Books, 2000.
Drew, Elizabeth. *The Corruption of American Politics*. New York: Overlook, 2000.
Johnson, Haynes, and David S. Broder. *The System: The American Way of Politics at the Breaking Point*. Boston, MA: Little, Brown and Company, 1996.
Phillips, Kevin. *Arrogant Capital: Washington, Wall Street, and the Frustration of American Politics*. Boston, MA: Little, Brown and Company, 1994.

CHAPTER 5

THE SUPREME COURT AND THE SHERMAN ACT

On July 2, 1890, the Congress of the United States passed "An Act to Protect Trade and Commerce against Unlawful Restraints and Monopolies," more commonly known as the Sherman Antitrust Act. The Justice Department is charged with enforcing it, and in 1903 created a special antitrust division for that purpose. Section 1 of the law states that "Every contract, combination in the form of trust or otherwise, or conspiracy, in restraint of trade or commerce among the several States, or with foreign nations, is declared to be illegal." These offenses, known as *per se* violations, include some price-fixing; divisions of customers, markets, and volume of production; boycotts or concerted refusals to sell; and tie-in sales.

Section 2 of the law states that "Every person or persons, who shall monopolize, or attempt to monopolize, or combine or conspire with any other person to monopolize any part of the trade or commerce among the several States, or with foreign nations, shall be deemed guilty of a misdemeanor." Section 4 of the law allows for civil suits to be brought by the Attorney General, with such remedies as dissolution, divestiture, or divorcement, as well as the remedy of an injunction. Section 7 of the law allows for private parties to sue for three times the amount of damages sustained.

Important provisions of the Sherman Antitrust Act are listed below:

<u>Important Provisions of the Sherman Antitrust Act</u>

Section 1:	prohibits price-fixing; divisions of customers, markets, and volume of production; boycotts or concerted refusals to sell; tie-in sales
Section 2:	prohibits monopolies or attempts at monopolies
Section 4:	allows civil suits for divestiture and injunctions
Section 7:	allows private parties to sue for triple damages

Should the government decide to use criminal penalties, violations of Sections 1 and 2 are subject to fines, not to exceed $100,000 for each violation, or by imprisonment, not to exceed three years, or both. The government often brings suits alleging violations of both Sections 1 and 2, and there are sometimes cases in which the government brings a criminal action to which the defendant will plead *nolo contendere*. If accepted by the Court, this means the defendant, without making a contention of guilt or innocence, agrees to accept whatever penalties the Court imposes. In addition, there are instances in which a private party will bring a suit under another law, such as the Clayton Antitrust Act, and a court in arriving at a decision might rely upon the Sherman Act for guidance.

Sherman Act cases are heard in U.S. District Courts, with appeals, if any, to the U.S. Courts of Appeals. A case of relative importance might well end up in the Supreme Court of the United States. The Court has, indeed, rendered decisions in many Sherman Act cases over the years, and that has resulted in the development of case law in this area that is constantly evolving and changing.

SHERMAN ACT CASE LAW DEVELOPMENT

THE EARLY YEARS

The first time the Court looked at the Sherman Act, it gave such a narrow interpretation of it that the law might have been doomed from the start except for subsequent cases. That case, in 1895, was *United States v. E.C. Knight Co.*[1] The government was attempting to make the American Sugar Refining Company, chartered in New Jersey, divest itself of the stock it had acquired of four Philadelphia refineries who refined 33 percent of the sugar in the United States and who were competitors with American. The acquisition gave American 98 percent control of the sugar refining in the United States, and, once refined, the sugar went into commerce among the several states. However, an 8–1 Court, speaking through Chief Justice Fuller, held that the Sherman Act was inapplicable because it is based on the government's commerce power, and the refineries in question were involved with the manufacture of the product. Commerce succeeds to manufacture and is not part of it, according to Fuller. He did not find any intention to put a restraint upon trade or commerce, and the fact that trade or commerce might be indirectly affected was not enough. Only Justice Harlan dissented.

Fortunately for the government, the Court in 1897 was going to find a Sherman Act violation, although by only a 5–4 vote. The case was *United States v. Trans-Missouri Freight Association*,[2] and the defendant was a grouping of eighteen railroads formed for the purpose of balancing the freight rates between the states. Any rate change was to be made at a monthly meeting. If one of the railroads felt compelled to cut a rate between meetings and that rate was in violation of the agreement, the offending railroad was fined $100 by the group.

Justice Peckham held that the Sherman Act applies to all contracts in restraint of trade or commerce, not just those that are unreasonable, and therefore Section 1 was violated. The government does not have to prove the purpose as long as restraint is the necessary effect, as in this case. The dissenters felt that railroads came under the Interstate Commerce Act and not the Sherman Act.

Once the government was able to dissolve the Association, it was able to do it again the next year in a case in which thirty-one railroads operating between Chicago and the Atlantic coast had joined together on rates.[3] However, later that year the Court ruled against the government in two cases involving Live Stock Exchanges,[4] finding only an indirect and incidental effect upon interstate commerce. The government did gain a major victory in the 1899 case of *Addyston Pipe and Steel Co. v. United States.*[5] Once again Peckham authored the opinion, this time unanimous, in dissolving an association of six companies who were practically the only manufacturers of cast iron in the United States. They agreed not to compete with each other in the sale of pipe and they allotted territories. If a sale took place in a territory not assigned to a member, the association decided which one would get the bid, and the others would then submit higher bids to insure the one they selected would get the sale. Peckham said the direct effect of the association was to regulate interstate commerce and therefore there was a Section 1 violation.

Significant government antitrust victories in the Supreme Court are listed below:

Government Antitrust Victories in the Supreme Court, 1895–1939

1. *United States v. Trans-Missouri Freight Association,* 1897.
2. *United States v. Joint Traffic Association,* 1898.
3. *Addyston Pipe and Steel Company v. United States,* 1899.
4. *Northern Securities Co. v. United States,* 1904.
5. *Swift & Company v. United States,* 1905.
6. *Standard Oil Co. v. United States,* 1911.
7. *United States v. American Tobacco Co.,* 1911.
8. *United States v. Union Pacific Railroad Co.,* 1912.
9. *Eastern States Retail Lumber Dealers' Association v. United States,* 1914.
10. *American Column and Lumber Co. v. United States,* 1921.
11. *United States v. American Linseed Oil Co.,* 1923.
12. *United States v. Trenton Potteries Co.,* 1927.
13. *Sugar Institute v. United States,* 1936.
14. *Interstate Circuit, Inc. v. United States,* 1939.

INTO THE TWENTIETH CENTURY

The year 1904 found the Court sharply divided in a case of national importance. It was *Northern Securities Co. v. United States,*[6] and involved a holding company organized in New Jersey that held the stock of two railroad giant competitors: the Great Northern and Northern Pacific, along with the stock of the Chicago, Burlington, and Quincy. President Theodore Roosevelt was advocating the breakup of the holding company, and Justice Harlan, for a 5–4 Court, agreed with him. Harlan felt that every corporation created by a state is subject to the supreme law of the land and therefore cannot circumvent the Sherman Act. The railroads whose stock was held had substantially parallel lines and Congress, in regulating interstate commerce, cannot be subordinate to the will of the states. If the Sherman Act cannot cover this, said Harlan, then the plain intention of Congress would be defeated. Although happy at the result, Roosevelt was disturbed that Justice Holmes, his first appointment to the Court two years earlier, had dissented, saying that the holding company was not in and of itself an interstate commerce company.

Holmes redeemed himself in Roosevelt's eyes one year later, in 1905, in the case of *Swift & Company v. United States*.[7] The issue was a combination of the dominant dealers in fresh meat throughout the United States to regulate prices. Holmes wrote the unanimous decision dissolving the combination, as he said it embraced and was directed at commerce among the states and therefore had a direct effect upon it. He found intent, not merely to restrict competition among the parties, but to aid in an attempt to monopolize commerce. He found a current of commerce, meaning that even though the combining companies were located in the same place, the fact that the meat originated in other states and would eventually end up in other states made for interstate commerce and the application of the Sherman Act. The next year the Court held that a city is a person and can bring a Sherman Act Section 7 triple damage suit.[8]

Although the Sherman Act was directed against business it did not explicitly say that, and thus the Court was able to uphold its use against a labor union in the 1908 case of *Loewe v. Lawlor*.[9] A combination of labor organizations had tried to compel a manufacturer whose goods were sold almost entirely in other states (he made hats in Danbury, Ct.) to unionize. The union, United Hatters of North America, which was part of the American Federation of Labor, was sued by the manufacturer for triple damages because of the boycott, and Chief Justice Fuller for a unanimous Court agreed with him and awarded him $240,000. Fuller held that the Sherman Act includes restraints of trade aimed at compelling third parties and strangers involuntarily not to engage in the course of interstate trade except on conditions that the combination imposes. The persons in the combination do not themselves have to be engaged in interstate trade, and organizations of farmers and laborers were not exempted from the Sherman Act.

The year of 1911 saw the Court render three Sherman Act decisions. In one of them, it ruled that a system of contracts between manufacturers and wholesale and retail merchants to control prices fell under the Sherman Act.[10] Then came two attempts by the government to break up giant corporations: *Standard Oil Co. v. United States*[11] and *United States v. American Tobacco Co.*[12] In the former, John D. Rockefeller had chartered the company in New Jersey and it had control over thirty-seven subsidiary corporations. When Theodore Roosevelt was president he called Standard Oil a bad trust and had the Justice Department try to dissolve it. Chief Justice White, for a unanimous Court, agreed with the president and, in so doing, formulated the rule of reason. He thought Standard Oil was guilty of violating both Sections 1 and 2 of the Sherman Act, but Section 2 only because the monopoly was unreasonable (i.e., it was achieved by unnecessarily abusive business practices). He found a *prima facie* presumption of intent and purpose to maintain dominancy over the oil business. The end result was that Standard Oil was divested into thirty-four smaller companies, each dominant in their region and run by the same persons who had run the parent company. Nevertheless it was a big victory for the government, and was followed by a similar victory in the second case.

In that case, American Tobacco and sixty-four other American companies along with two English companies were tied together by their stock and controlled 86 percent of the cigarettes produced in the United States. They also had big monopolies in other aspects of the tobacco industry. White, again unanimously and again using the rule of reason, agreed that Sections 1 and 2 had been violated. As in the previous case, the subsidiaries became new companies, and because American Tobacco was not totally unreasonable, only two other full-line companies were created to give it competition: Liggett and Myers, and P. Lorillard.

THE INTERIM PERIOD

Once the Court formulated the rule of reason, it began to swing back and forth in its Sherman Act decisions. For example, in the following year (1912) it did not find a violation when the holder of a patent for making stencil-duplicating machines would license the machines with a restriction that his unpatented articles, such as the stencil paper, ink, and other supplies, must be the only ones used by the licensee.[13] However, it did find Sections 1 and 2 violated when one railroad bought 46 percent of the stock of a competitor.[14] Similarly, two years later the Court held that Section 1 was violated by a report circulated among a retail lumber dealers' association listing wholesale dealers who sold directly to customers, which tended to prevent members of the association from dealing with those consumers.[15] Yet four years after that it found no violation when the Chicago Board of Trade prohibited its members from purchasing, or offering to purchase, anything other than what the closing bid had been at the time the Board closed in the afternoon until it opened the next morning.[16] It also found no violation later that year when the government charged a company who had, through patents and acquisitions, ownership or control of all concerns engaged in the manufacturing of all kinds of shoe machinery.[17] Again, a year later it upheld the resale price arrangements made by a manufacturer with its dealers.[18]

Significant government antitrust losses in the Supreme Court are listed at the top of page 83:

<u>Government Antitrust Losses in the Supreme Court, 1895–1939</u>

1. *United States v. E.C. Knight Co.*, 1895.
2. *Hopkins v. United States*, 1898.
3. *Anderson v. United States*, 1898.
4. *Board of Trade of the City of Chicago v. United States*, 1918.
5. *United States v. United Shoe Machinery Co.*, 1918.
6. *United States v. Colgate*, 1919.
7. *United States v. U.S. Steel Corporation*, 1920.
8. *Maple Flooring Manufacturers' Association v. United States*, 1925.
9. *Cement Manufacturers' Protective Association v. United States*, 1925.
10. *United States v. General Electric Co.*, 1926.
11. *United States v. International Harvester Co.*, 1927.
12. *Appalachian Coals, Inc. v. United States*, 1933.

THE CONSERVATIVE 1920S

The Court's increasing reluctance to interfere with big business was never more evident than in the 1920 case of *United States v. U.S. Steel Corporation*.[19] The government was attempting to break it up due to its being a monopoly, but Justice McKenna, for a unanimous Court, refused to do so. While conceding that the company had more power than any one competitor, he said that it was not greater than that possessed by all the competitors, so there was no monopoly. Mere size is not illegal. Even though the corporation actually was a holding company for twelve manufacturers, he felt there was no public interest served by dissolving it or by separating it from some of its subsidiaries. Instead, such action would actually pose a risk of injury to the public interest and would hurt this country in foreign trade.

The next year, in 1921, the Court decided *Duplex Printing Press Co. v. Deering*.[20] It was a mixture of Sherman and Clayton Acts, since, under the latter, peaceful picketing by labor was not supposed to be enjoined by federal courts, and labor was not commerce and thus should not be prevented from doing legitimate activities. In this case, a union was trying to get a manufacturer of printing presses to unionize its factory in Michigan. Since the union of machinists was in New York, they engaged in a boycott of the company's products in New York City and vicinity. The Court, in a 6–3 decision given by Justice Pitney (Holmes, Brandeis, and Clarke dissenting), allowed the injunction against the boycott, saying that the Sherman Act, as amended by the Clayton, permitted it because the boycott was a secondary one, which is illegal, and under Clayton, labor organizations and its members cannot do illegal conspiracies. Therefore, the section forbidding injunctions was not applicable.

The government did win a case later that year when the Court found Section 1 violated by manufacturers of one-third of the hardwood output in the United States. They had instituted a plan by which they exchanged full and minute disclosures of their business to a central office, which then distributed back to them analytical digests of the information, plus suggestions for future production and prices by an expert agent, supplemented by frequent meetings and discussions.[21] Similarly, two years later (1923) the government won again when twelve corporations entered into agreements to suppress competition in trade between the states. Each company had to reveal to all the others the intimate details of its business affairs.[22] However, two years later, in 1925, the government lost companion cases. In the first one, twenty-two corporations controlling 74.2 percent of the total production of maple flooring gathered information and disseminated it, and in the second one several companies gathered and disseminated pertinent information with respect to the sale and distribution of cement.[23] Again the following year, in 1926, the government lost when it tried to prevent a company who owned patents for electric lamps with tungsten filaments from licensing them out but fixing the prices while doing so.[24] One year later the government did manage to win a victory involving an agreement by twenty-three corporations controlling over 82 percent of the business of manufacturing and distributing sanitary pottery in the United States to fix prices.[25]

In that year of 1927, the Court heard another case similar to *Duplex* in that it concerned labor, combined the Sherman and Clayton Acts, and also went against labor. It was *Bedford Cut Stone Co. v. Journeymen Stone Cutters' Association of North America*.[26] At issue was a conspiracy by a union of stone-cutters to restrain the interstate commerce of certain building-stone producers by declaring their stone, cut by nonunion workers, "unfair" and forbidding members of the union to work on it in building construction in other states. Justice Sutherland, in a 7–2 opinion (Brandeis and Holmes dissenting), found the union to be in violation of the Sherman Act because it directly and substantially curtailed, or threatened to curtail, the natural flow of interstate commerce of a very large proportion of the building limestone of the entire country. It was a strike against the product in order to coerce or induce the local employers to refrain from purchasing such a product. Due to the illegal activity, an injunction under Clayton was appropriate.

Fittingly for the 1920s, in that same year the Court refused to divide a company, a combination of five separate firms controlling 85 percent of the harvesting machinery business, into separate and distinct corporations in order to restore the competitive conditions that had existed some sixteen years previously. The company had already agreed to limit its sales agencies and dispose of some of its lines to independent manufacturers, and the Court felt that was sufficient for competitive conditions to exist.[27]

Significant private antitrust suits in the Supreme Court are listed below:

<u>Private Antitrust Suits in the Supreme Court, 1895–1939</u>

Victories for Plaintiffs

   1. *Chattanooga Foundry and Pipe Works v. City of Atlanta*, 1906.

   2. *Loewe v. Lawlor*, 1908.

3. *Dr. Miles Medical Co. v. John D. Park & Sons Co.*, 1911.

4. *Duplex Printing Press Co. v. Deering*, 1921.

5. *Bedford Cut Stone Co. v. Journeymen Stone Cutters' Association of North America*, 1927.

6. *Story Parchment Company v. Paterson Parchment Paper Company*, 1931.

Loss by Plaintiff

1. *Henry v. A.B. Dick Co.*, 1912.

THE DEPRESSION AND WAR YEARS

As would be expected, Sherman Act cases were few in number during the Depression years. In 1931 the Court did allow a company to collect triple damages based on a Section 2 allegation that three companies were monopolizing interstate trade and commerce in vegetable parchment with the resultant price-cutting against the company. What made the case interesting was the holding that the damages can be based on estimated prices.[28] Two years later, in 1933, the Court refused to break up a corporation formed by some 137 producers of bituminous coal to act as their selling agent with authority to set the prices. The group had 73 percent control in the immediate region, but the great bulk of their coal was marketed in another and highly competitive region. The fact that the industry was one in grave distress helped the Court arrive at its decision.[29] However, three years later, in 1936, the Court did break up a trade association formed by fifteen companies that controlled 70–80 percent of the refined sugar in the United States. Its purpose was to do away with unfair merchandising practices, especially the granting of secret concessions and rebates. The association made each member publicly announce in advance its prices, terms, and conditions of sale, and also imposed numerous supporting restrictions. The Court concluded that the end did not justify the illegal means.[30] Three years after that, the Court upheld the use of Section 1 to stop distributors of 75 percent of interstate motion picture films from making agreements with the owners of theaters in certain cities that showed first-run exhibitions of movies. The agreements said that when the distributors licensed other theater owners in the same cities for subsequent runs of the films, the licenses would mandate a minimum price of admission, and the theaters would not show another picture with it. This would maintain the higher prices of the first-run theaters and protect them from competition.[31]

Once the country started to get out of the Depression, the government began to initiate Sherman Act cases with renewed determination. In 1940 the Court held that Section 1 was violated by a company that was making agreements in the midwestern area to fix prices in interstate commerce. Even though the company contended that there were competitive abuses or evils that it was trying to stop, the Court held that price-fixing is illegal *per se*.[32] The following year, labor unions finally received a big boost from the Court in the antitrust area. In *United States v. Hutcheson*[33] the government charged a union with violating Section 1, but Justice Frankfurter, in a 6–2 opinion, held that the Clayton Act and the 1932 Norris-LaGuardia Act immunized trade union activities from being a violation of any U.S. law, including the Sherman Act. He did say, however, that this immunization would be lost if labor combined with nonlabor groups to restrain trade. In that same year the Court held that the United States was not a person under the Sherman Act and therefore could not bring a civil action for triple damages.[34] However, the following year it did consider a state a person for damage awards.[35]

Also in 1942, the Court held that Sections 1 and 2 were violated by ten companies who either made or sold building materials. Each was tied to the dominant company by an agreement that expressly recognized the validity of that company's patents during the life of the agreement and that required the distribution of the patented products at fixed prices. Again, the price-fixing made for the illegality.[36] The next year, on the other hand, the Court made states immune from the Sherman Act, since that law makes no mention of states and there is no suggestion of a purpose to restrain state action in its legislative history.[37]

Significant government antitrust victories and losses in the Supreme Court are listed below:

Government Antitrust Victories in the Supreme Court, 1940–Present

1. *United States v. Socony-Vacuum Oil Company*, 1940.
2. *United States v. Masonite Corporation*, 1942.
3. *American Tobacco Company v. United States*, 1946.
4. *United States v. Yellow Cab Company*, 1947.
5. *United States v. National Lead Company*, 1947.
6. *International Salt Company v. United States*, 1947.
7. *United States v. United States Gypsum Company*, 1948.
8. *United States v. Griffith*, 1948.
9. *Schine Chain Theatres v. United States*, 1948.
10. *United States v. Paramount Pictures*, 1948.
11. *Timken Roller Bearing Company v. United States*, 1951.
12. *Northern Pacific Railway Company v. United States*, 1958.
13. *United States v. Parke, Davis and Company*, 1960.
14. *United States v. Loew's Incorporated*, 1962.
15. *United States v. First National Bank and Trust Company of Lexington*, 1964.
16. *United States v. General Motors Corporation*, 1966.
17. *United States v. Arnold, Schwinn & Company*, 1967.
18. *United States v. Container Corporation of America*, 1969.
19. *United States v. Topco Associates, Inc.*, 1972.
20. *Otter Tail Power Company v. United States*, 1973.
21. *National Society of Professional Engineers v. United States*, 1978.

Government Antitrust Losses in the Supreme Court, 1940–Present

1. *United States v. Hutcheson*, 1941.
2. *United States v. Cooper Corporation*, 1941.

3. *United States v. Columbia Steel Company,* 1948.
4. *Times-Picayune Publishing Company v. United States,* 1953.

THE POSTWAR YEARS AND THE FIFTIES

In a 1946 case that was a preview of what was going to occur in the 1990s, the Court ruled that three tobacco companies had a monopoly of over two-thirds of the domestic cigarette market and over 80 percent of comparable cigarettes, with the resultant fixing and controlling of prices.[38] The next year, the Court found that there was a combination and conspiracy to restrain and monopolize interstate trade and commerce in the sale of motor vehicles for use as taxicabs to the principal cab companies in certain cities. The companies bought their cabs exclusively from one manufacturer and an appreciable amount of interstate commerce was affected. In addition, two of the defendants in the case would not compete with a third one for contracts with railroads or railroad terminal associations to transport passengers and their luggage, and that involved a stream of interstate commerce.[39]

In 1947 the government continued with its string of victories. It won a case against an international cartel that was retraining trade and commerce in the titanium products industry among the several states and with foreign nations by pooling patents and allocating markets.[40] Another case was won against a firm owning patents on machines utilizing salt that leased them subject to the condition that the salt be purchased from them.[41] The next year the Court found Sections 1 and 2 violated by six corporations that conspired to restrain and monopolize trade in gypsum products through patent licensing. The dominant firm granted the patents and the others accepted. The Sherman Act bans patent exploitations such as this, and the efforts to monopolize the patents were unreasonable.[42]

Also in 1948, the Court in companion cases held Sections 1 and 2 violated. In one case, four affiliated corporations operated motion picture theaters in three states, and used their monopoly power to prevent their competitors from obtaining first- or second-run films. In the other case, a company and five subsidiaries owned or had a financial interest in a large chain of motion picture theaters in six states. In negotiating for films, they combined theaters in towns in which they had a monopoly with those in towns in which they had competition.[43] In yet another case that year, Sections 1 and 2 were again used against eight corporations in the motion picture industry for price-fixing and monopoly.[44] Finally, in that year, the government lost when the Court refused to dissolve a merger in which a major steel company got the assets of the largest steel company on the West Coast. The Court found a normal business purpose, namely the expansion of facilities to meet the needs of new markets of a community. Vertical integration was not illegal *per se*.[45]

In 1951 the Court upheld both a triple damage suit due to an agreement among competitors in interstate commerce to fix the maximum resale prices of their products,[46] and a Section 1 case against a company that made antifriction bearings but that combined with a British corporation and a French corporation to allocate territories and fix prices. The latter case, even though it involved foreign trade, still fell under our antitrust laws.[47] In 1953 the Court refused to use Sections 1 and 2 against a publishing company that put out a morning and evening newspaper (there was only one other evening paper in the city) and that adopted a unit rate for advertising space (i.e., one who buys advertising space in the morning paper must also buy it in the evening paper). The Court found no intent to put an unreasonable restraint on interstate commerce nor had it had that effect, and there was no intent to monopolize.[48] Similarly, in 1954 the Court refused to allow triple damages or an injunction in the case brought by a suburban theater owner who claimed that a film distributor conspired to restrict first-run pictures to downtown theaters. It held that proof of parallel business behavior does not conclusively establish agreement, nor does such behavior itself violate the law.[49]

The government did win a Section 1 case in 1957 against a railroad for preferential routing agreements made in deeds or leases to several million acres of land in several northwestern states. Under these agreements, all commodities produced or manufactured on the land would have to be shipped over the railroad's lines. The Court said that a tying arrangement *per se* is unlawful whenever the seller has sufficient economic power and a substantial amount of interstate commerce is affected.[50] One year later the Court upheld a triple damage award because a chain of department stores had violated Sections 1 and 2 by conspiring with ten national manufacturers and their distributors either not to sell to a particular company, or to do so only at discriminatory prices and highly unfavorable terms. The law forbids all contracts and combinations that tend to create a monopoly, even if done one company at a time rather than in large groups.[51]

THE FIRST SEVENTY YEARS IN RETROSPECT

The Supreme Court gave varying interpretations of the Sherman Act during its first seven decades of cases involving the law. It broke up monopolies and refused to break up others. It found restraints of trade in some combinations but not in others. It developed the rule of reason and the current of commerce. It even applied it to labor, despite Congress's attempt in the Clayton Act to prevent that. It is true that seldom do two cases have identical facts, so the Court can make differentiations between them. Nevertheless, the Court consists of nine persons who bring to it their own political, social, and economic values, and those values also play a role in decision making. Therefore, there is an explanation to the Court's decisions, and whether one agrees with a decision or not the fact remains that the Court does have the ultimate say as to what the Sherman Act means. In those first seventy years, both supporters and opponents of vigorous Sherman Act enforcement could find a mixed bag of Court opinions.

THE 1960S

The last decade for sheer volume of Sherman Act cases before the Court was that of the 1960s. It began with a 1960 case. The government won an injunction due to a Section 1 violation in which a company had combined and conspired to maintain resale prices of its more than six hundred pharmaceutical products in areas that did not allow that practice. The company refused to deal with retailers who failed to observe suggested minimum prices or who advertised discount prices; five other wholesalers were persuaded to do the same. The company also told a number of retailers that if each would adhere, so would one of their principal competitors. Once a retailer agreed to stop the price-cutting, it could resume purchasing the products. The Court held that the law had been broken even though the plan was not based on any contract.[52] The next year, 1961, the Court did not find Sections 1 and 2 violated and thus refused to issue an injunction or award triple damages to a group of trucking companies and their trade association. The truckers brought the case against a group of railroads, a railroad association, and a public relations firm that had conducted a publicity campaign against the truckers. The campaign's goal was to get laws and law enforcement practices hostile to truckers and to create an atmosphere of distaste for truckers among the general public, thus impairing relationships between the truckers and their customers. The Court felt that people have the right to get together to get laws passed or enforced.[53]

In 1962 the government won a Section 1 suit against six major distributors of pre-1948 copyrighted motion picture feature films for television exhibition. These distributors engaged in blockbooking—selling one or more films on condition the station buy a block of less popular or inferior films.[54] Two years later, in 1964, the government again won, this time a Sections 1 and 2 case stopping the consolidation of the largest and fourth largest of the six commercial banks in a county, even though there was no predatory purpose.[55] In 1966 the Court ruled against a conspiracy wherein a company restrained trade by eliminating sales of its new automobiles through discount houses and referral services. The company got promises from every dealer in the area not to deal with any discounters. The result was a substantial restraint upon competition, a goal unlawful *per se* when sought to be effected by a combination or conspiracy.[56]

One year later, in 1967, the Court found Section 1 violated by a manufacturer and its distributors who established exclusive territories, meaning the distributors could only sell within their territory and could only sell that product, not those of competitors. The manufacturer also sold to franchised retailers who could sell competitors' products as long as its product was given equal prominence and they did not sell to discounters. Anyone breaking the agreement would be terminated. The Court felt that one should be able to dispose of products purchased from a manufacturer without restrictions. Only those who received a product on consignment could have restrictions imposed, as the manufacturer still retains ownership and has not parted with the title.[57] The next year the Court upheld a triple damage suit brought by an independent newspaper carrier who sold the papers at a price higher than that set by the publisher and was terminated. The problem of fixing maximum prices was revisited by the Court in the 1990s.[58]

Nineteen sixty-nine found the Court upholding a Section 1 suit against companies who controlled about 90 percent of the shipment of corrugated containers from plants in the southeastern United States. Each of the companies would, upon the request of a competitor, furnish information as to the most recent price charged or quoted to individual customers, with the expectation of reciprocity and the understanding that it represented the price currently being bid. The Court felt the exchange was concerted action to establish a combination or conspiracy, and the price stabilization had an anticompetitive effect in the industry, thus hurting price competition.[59] That same year, the Court upheld an injunction and triple damages against a company and its wholly owned subsidiary due to violations of Sections 1 and 2. In order to obtain credit at advantageous terms, a housing developer would have to purchase at artificially high prices prefabricated houses made by the manufacturer. The Court held it to be an illegal tie-in sale because there was a substantial volume of commerce foreclosed due to the total volume of sales.[60]

Significant private antitrust suits in the Supreme Court are listed below:

Private Antitrust Suits in the Supreme Court, 1940–Present

Victories for Plaintiffs

1. *Georgia* v. *Evans*, 1942.
2. *Kiefer-Stewart Company* v. *Seagram & Sons, Inc.*, 1951.
3. *Klor's Inc.* v. *Broadway-Hale Stores, Inc.*, 1959.
4. *Albrecht* v. *Herald Company*, 1968.
5. *Fortner Enterprises, Inc.* v. *United States Steel Corporation*, 1969.
6. *Goldfarb* v. *Virginia State Bar*, 1995.
7. *Cantor* v. *Detroit Edison Company*, 1976.
8. *Continental T.V., Inc.* v. *GTE Sylvania, Inc.*, 1977.
9. *Catalano, Inc.* v. *Target Sales, Inc.*, 1980.
10. *Arizona* v. *Maricopa County Medical Society*, 1982.
11. *Monsanto Company* v. *Spray-Rite Service Corporation*, 1984.
12. *National Collegiate Athletic Association* v. *Board of Regents of the University of Oklahoma*, 1984.
13. *Aspen Skiing Company* v. *Aspen Highlands Skiing Corporation*, 1985.

Losses by Plaintiffs

1. *Parker* v. *Brown*, 1943.
2. *Theatre Enterprises, Inc.* v. *Paramount Film Distributing Corporation*, 1954.
3. *Eastern Railroad Presidents Conference* v. *Noerr Motor Freight, Inc.*, 1961.
4. *Broadcast Music, Inc.* v. *Columbia Broadcasting System, Inc.*, 1979.

5. *Jefferson Parish Hospital District No. 2* v. *Hyde*, 1984.
6. *Business Electronics Corporation* v. *Sharp Electronics Corporation*, 1988.
7. *State Oil Company* v. *Khan*, 1997.

THE 1970S AND 1980S

In 1972 the Court upheld a Section 1 suit against a cooperative association of twenty-five supermarket chains in thirty-three states. They had a company that was their purchasing agent with more than one thousand items, most of which bore its name. The sales of the members were exceeded only by three national grocery chains. No member was allowed to sell the agent's brand products outside the territory in which it was licensed to sell unless the member whose territory was being invaded agreed. Also, no member could sell any product supplied by the association at wholesale without permission that was subject to conditions. The Court found it a horizontal restraint, a *per se* violation that minimized competition at both the retail and wholesale levels.[61] One year later the government again won, this time a Section 2 case against a supplier of electric power to many municipalities in the Midwest. When its franchises expired and the towns wanted to establish their own power systems, the supplier refused to sell wholesale power to them. The company also refused to transfer power over its facilities from other sources, litigated in order to delay things, and invoked transmission contract provisions to forestall other companies from supplying power. The Court found that the company used its monopoly power to foreclose competition or gain a competitive advantage, or to destroy a competitor, all in violation of the antitrust laws.[62]

In 1975 the Court found a Section 1 violation by a state bar association for enforcing fees set by a county bar association. The decision found that the practice established a fixed, rigid price floor that affected interstate commerce.[63] One year later the Court held illegal as a tie-in arrangement a practice of the sole supplier of electricity in a part of a state of furnishing its customers, without charge, almost 50 percent of the most frequently used standard size light bulbs.[64] The next year, in 1977, the Court again found a Section 1 violation, when a manufacturer of television sets limited the number of retail franchises granted for any given area and required each franchisee to sell the product only from where it was franchised. The Court felt the company acted unreasonably and that location restriction is *per se* illegal because it limits the retailer's freedom to dispose of the purchased products and reduced intrabrand competition. The Court did not differentiate between sale and nonsale transactions, such as in consignments: All were illegal if they included location restrictions.[65]

The year 1978 saw the government win a Section 1 case in which the canon of ethics of engineers prohibited members of their national society from submitting competitive bids for engineering services. This was a suppression of competition.[66] One year later, the Court refused to find a Section 1 violation by two organizations in the music industry that awarded blanket licenses to copyrighted musical compositions at fees negotiated by them. Blanket licenses are included in the 1976 Copyright Act. They guard against unauthorized copyright use, which would be difficult and expensive protection if left to individual users and copyright owners. Therefore, the blanket licenses were reasonable.[67]

In a 1980 case the Court ruled that Section 1 had been violated by some wholesalers who made an agreement to eliminate the short-term credit formerly granted to retailers, requiring them instead to make payment in cash. It was anticompetitive in that it eliminated discounts, since discounts had been given by the wholesalers when they competed with each other on credit terms.[68] Two years later the Court again found Section 1 violated, this time by a county medical society that established maximum fees that doctors could claim. It was illegal, horizontal price-fixing that did not enhance competition.[69] In 1984 the Court found vertical price-fixing, and held illegal the refusal of a manufacturer to renew an agreement to sell to a wholesale distributor because the latter was selling at discount prices. Other distributors either refused to sell their products to the discounter or sold them too late to be of use (the product was herbicides). The Court said the standard for finding a conspiracy in these cases must be evidence that reasonably tends to prove that the manufacturer and others had a conscious commitment to a common scheme designed to achieve an unlawful objective. That standard was reached in this case.[70] However, in that same year the Court did not find Section 1 violated by a tying arrangement in the form of a contract between a hospital and a firm of four anesthesiologists requiring all anesthesiology services for hospital patients to be performed by that firm. There was no evidence that price, quality, or supply and demand had been adversely affected and no showing that the market as a whole had been affected at all by the contract.[71]

Also in 1984, the Court did find Section 1 violated by the National Collegiate Athletic Association when it made contracts to televise football games but limited both the total of games telecast and the number of times any one college could appear. It further said that no school could act independently. When the major football schools formed their own association and made their own television contract the NCAA threatened sanctions. In its ruling the Court could find no legitimate procompetitive purpose, saying that the NCAA had restricted rather than enhanced the place of intercollegiate athletics in the nation's life by these actions.[72] The following year, in 1985, the Court found Section 2 violated and awarded triple damages to a skiing company when a rival company made changes in the pattern of distributing tickets under a joint marketing program that had been in effect for several years. When the changes became economically detrimental to the smaller company it refused to go along, and the larger company then refused to deal with it. The Court found no valid reasons for that; rather, the only reason was to harm a smaller competitor and there was no efficiency justification for its pattern of conduct.[73] Three years later in 1988, the Court did not find Section 1 violated by a company who terminated another company because the latter sold the former's product at low prices. The Court said a vertical restraint is not illegal unless it includes some arrangement on price or price levels, which did not happen here.[74]

THE 1990S

The Court in 1997 rendered a decision that was of major significance. The case was *State Oil Company v. Khan*,[75] and the issue was whether a manufacturer or supplier necessarily violate Section 1 by placing a ceiling on the retail price a dealer can charge for its products. Even though an earlier case had held that all limits on retail markups were a violation, Justice O'Connor, for a unanimous Court, said that the legality of markup limits will now be determined case by case with reasonableness being the standard. In this particular case, the oil company had tried to tell a gasoline dealer that he had to rebate to it any excess over the allowed markup of 3.25 cents a gallon. The Court felt there was insufficient economic justification to prohibit the practice, and that an inability to limit markups could actually harm consumers by leading to monopoly behavior by dealers who serve exclusive territories, as well as causing higher prices. The Court noted, however, that it is still illegal for a manufacturer to impose minimum prices on dealers.

In 1998, the Justice Department initiated an antitrust suit against Microsoft. This was a long trial, and the case is significant in several respects. First of all, it is the first antitrust suit of major proportions brought by the government in many years. Microsoft is the number one company in the computer field (Explorer Browser, 64 percent control; Windows, 85 percent), and the fact that the Justice Department decided to take it on, alleging predatory practices in order to hurt its competitors, is a major step forward in antitrust law enforcement. The last major case brought by the government that ended at the Supreme Court level was in 1978. This case might not get to the Supreme Court, as shown by the case against AT&T, which will be discussed in a later chapter.

The Microsoft case is also significant in that the field of communications, which includes the computer area, has been the scene of many megamergers in recent years. Is this case a portent of things to come, or is it an isolated case based solely on a dominant company's particular practices? The case's outcome might provide the answer, as a government loss might end any future attempts to rein in this field whose technology is growing so rapidly. Of course, even should the government lose, it might try to derail some of the announced mergers, since the Microsoft case is not about mergers. The same could be said, naturally, with a government victory, in that the government might say this was not about mergers and it will not try to stop any of them.

Yet another significant point in the Microsoft case is the effect it will have on this country's ability to engage competitively in international trade. U.S. companies already think our laws and regulations hurt them in this field, and a decision against one of the American giants might indeed make it even more difficult for our companies to compete. In any event, the stakes are high and the final outcome should be of utmost importance.

The trial judge for the Microsoft case felt that Microsoft plotted to control the browser markets and bullied rivals into altering their products, and he did rule that Microsoft is a monopoly. In April 2000, the judge found Microsoft guilty of violating the Sherman Act due to its using anticompetitive means to maintain a monopoly for its PC operating system software, its attempt to monopolize the Web-browser software market, and its tying its Internet Explorer browser to the Windows operating system. The only point in which the judge ruled for Microsoft was his holding that its marketing contracts with other companies did not deprive Netscape of the ability to distribute its Web browser.

In June 2000, the judge issued his remedy, and the most important part of it called for splitting Microsoft into two companies. One company would make the Windows operating system, and the other would make the applications that are run by the operating system, and would also include Microsoft's Internet and computer hardware businesses. The two entities would have separate employees, assets, and intellectual properties, and there would be separate stock. The judge also issued a long list of restrictions on Microsoft's conduct that would last three years if the breakup order withstands appeal, and ten years if it does not. Microsoft announced that it would appeal the breakup plan and would also ask that the conduct restrictions be stayed while the appeal proceeds, and the judge did stay them.

What Does It All Mean?

Sometimes it is difficult for people to understand the significance of the Sherman Act and the Supreme Court decisions interpreting it. One reason for that is the recent decline in these cases. Why has the government not been as active in this area as formerly, especially in view of the fact that it has been remarkably successful in winning its suits? Is it because business has, to a large extent, stopped its Sherman Act violations? The answer to the latter depends on the viewpoint of the person being asked, because there is so much subjectivity in the law. For example, as can be seen from the cases, it used to be that only monopolies were subject to the rule of reason, meaning that only bad monopolies violated the law, and what was bad depended upon various players, such as the president, the Justice Department, and the Court. Now even placing ceilings on retail prices, which used to be illegal *per se* no matter how reasonable the price, can be reasonable. This, coupled with the fact that recent administrations have tended to be more business-friendly, has led to the decrease in cases brought by the government.

Still another reason for the decline of cases has been the perception that the federal courts, including the Supreme Court, are also more business-friendly than before and thus would be more likely to rule against the government. This is due to the influx of judges appointed by more conservative presidents, such judges usually taking the side of business against the government. The reality is that this perception is probably right, but just the perception itself is enough to make the government decide not to bring a suit even if it were inclined to do so.

A further reason for the decline of cases is that there has also been a decline in Sherman Act cases brought by businesses and individuals, although not as noticeable a decline as government cases. That is due in part to the above-mentioned perception that the federal courts are more conservative and therefore less likely to find illegality in business activities. It is also due in part to the tendency of businesses, especially big ones, to cooperate more with each other than to fight each other, with the resultant increase in practices such as mergers. A healthy economy is also conducive to more friendly relations among businesses.

Will this trend continue? On the surface it would appear so, but history tends to be cyclical, and thus one cannot rule out a renewed interest in Sherman Act prosecutions. For example, besides the Microsoft suit, the government in 1998 initiated a suit against the credit card companies MasterCard and VISA. It is too early to discern if these are isolated incidents or a trend. A Republican victory, for example, in the 2000 presidential election, would probably end any possible trend since Republican administrations tend to be more business-friendly than do Democratic administrations.

One other important point is that the Sherman Act is not the government's only antitrust law. There are others that can be used, as we will see in the next chapter.

SUMMARY

The Sherman Act was the government's first major law to try to curb the abuses of big business (except for the railroads, as will be shown in a later chapter, which were regulated three years earlier). As with any important law, its significance depends upon its enforcement by the executive branch, and its interpretation by the judicial branch, especially the Supreme Court. This chapter has attempted to show the Court's interpretation by pointing out the most significant cases brought both by the government and by private persons, including corporations, in a chronological manner so as to see the Court's growth in this area. As was shown, the growth has been steady, albeit uneven at times, but no study of the role of government and business in the American economy can be complete without this inclusion. With the relative dearth of cases in recent years, there is a tendency to downplay the significance of antitrust history. As mentioned previously, that may or may not change, but whether it does or not is insignificant due to the role it has played. It is sometimes hard to find where antitrust history fits, but indeed it does, as this and the next chapter should make abundantly clear.

Questions for Discussion

1. What does a *per se* violation of the Sherman Act mean?
2. What does the "rule of reason" mean with regard to the Sherman Act?
3. What is the importance of allowing private parties to sue for triple damages?
4. What is meant by the "current of commerce" doctrine?
5. Was the Sherman Act meant to be applied to labor?
6. Was the Supreme Court consistent or inconsistent in its interpretation of the Sherman Act?
7. Why has the government not pursued antitrust suits despite their high winning percentage?
8. Do private antitrust suits stand a better chance of victory in the courts than do government suits?
9. Do you agree that the rule of reason should apply to maximum resale prices?
10. Why has the government renewed its antitrust activity?
11. Are antitrust suits helpful or detrimental to the economy?
12. Is the Sherman Act still an important law?

Notes

1. 156 U.S. 1 (1895).
2. 166 U.S. 290 (1897).
3. *United States v. Joint Traffic Association,* 171 U.S. 505 (1898).
4. *Hopkins v. United States,* 171 U.S. 578 (1898); *Anderson v. United States,* 171 U.S. 604 (1898).
5. 175 U.S. 611 (1899).
6. 193 U.S. 197 (1904).
7. 196 U.S. 375 (1905).
8. *Chattanooga Foundry and Pipe Works v. City of Atlanta,* 203 U.S. 390 (1906).
9. 208 U.S. 274 (1908).
10. *Dr. Miles Medical Company v. John D. Park & Sons Co.,* 220 U.S. 373 (1911).
11. 221 U.S. 1 (1911).
12. 221 U.S. 106 (1911).
13. *Henry v. A.B. Dick Co.,* 224 U.S. 1 (1912).
14. *United States v. Union Pacific Railroad Co.,* 226 U.S. 61 (1912).
15. *Eastern States Retail Lumber Dealers' Association v. United States,* 234 U.S. 600 (1914).
16. *Board of Trade of the City of Chicago v. United States,* 246 U.S. 231 (1918).
17. *United States v. United Shoe Machinery Co.,* 247 U.S. 32 (1918).
18. *United States v. Colgate,* 250 U.S. 300 (1919).

19. 251 U.S. 417 (1920).
20. 254 U.S. 443 (1921).
21. *American Column and Lumber Co. v. United States*, 257 U.S. 377 (1921).
22. *United States v. American Linseed Oil Co.*, 262 U.S. 371 (1923).
23. *Maple Flooring Manufacturers' Association v. United States*, 268 U.S. 563 (1925); *Cement Manufacturers' Protective Association v. United States*, 268 U.S. 588 (1925).
24. *United States v. General Electric Co.*, 272 U.S. 476 (1926).
25. *United States v. Trenton Potteries Co.*, 273 U.S. 392 (1927).
26. 274 U.S. 37 (1927).
27. *United States v. International Harvester Co.*, 274 U.S. 37 (1927).
28. *Story Parchment Co. v. Paterson Parchment Paper Co.*, 282 U.S. 555 (1931).
29. *Appalachian Coals, Inc. v. United States*, 288 U.S. 344 (1933).
30. *Sugar Institute v. United States*, 297 U.S. 553 (1936).
31. *Interstate Circuit, Inc. v. United States*, 306 U.S. 208 (1939).
32. *United States v. Socony-Vacuum Oil Co.*, 310 U.S. 150 (1940).
33. 312 U.S. 219 (1941).
34. *United States v. Cooper Corporation*, 312 U.S. 600 (1941).
35. *Georgia v. Evans*, 316 U.S. 159 (1942).
36. *United States v. Masonite Corporation*, 316 U.S. 265 (1942).
37. *Parker v. Brown*, 317 U.S. 341 (1943).
38. *American Tobacco Co. v. United States*, 328 U.S. 781 (1946).
39. *United States v. Yellow Cab Co.*, 332 U.S. 218 (1947).
40. *United States v. National Lead Co.*, 332 U.S. 319 (1947).
41. *International Salt Co. v. United States*, 332 U.S. 392 (1947).
42. *United States v. United States Gypsum Co.*, 333 U.S. 364 (1948).
43. *United States v. Griffith*, 334 U.S. 100 (1948); *Schine Chain Theatres v. United States*, 334 U.S. 110 (1948).
44. *United States v. Paramount Pictures*, 334 U.S. 131 (1948).
45. *United States v. Columbia Steel Co.*, 334 U.S. 495 (1948).
46. *Kiefer-Stewart Co. v. Seagram & Sons, Inc.*, 340 U.S. 211 (1951).
47. *Timken Roller Bearing Co. v. United States*, 341 U.S. 593 (1951).
48. *Times-Picayune Publishing Co. v. United States*, 345 U.S. 594 (1953).
49. *Theatre Enterprises, Inc. v. Paramount Film Distributing Corporation*, 346 U.S. 537 (1954).
50. *Northern Pacific Railway Co. v. United States*, 356 U.S. 1 (1958).
51. *Klor's Inc. v. Broadway-Hale Stores, Inc.*, 359 U.S. 207 (1959).
52. *United States v. Parke, Davis and Co.*, 362 U.S. 29 (1960).
53. *Eastern Railroad Presidents Conference v. Noerr Motor Freight, Inc.*, 365 U.S. 127 (1961).
54. *United States v. Loew's Inc.*, 371 U.S. 38 (1962).
55. *United States v. First National Bank and Trust Co. of Lexington*, 376 U.S. 665 (1964).
56. *United States v. General Motors Corporation*, 384 U.S. 127 (1966).
57. *United States v. Arnold, Schwinn & Co.*, 388 U.S. 365 (1967).
58. *Albrecht v. Herald Co.*, 390 U.S. 145 (1968).
59. *United States v. Container Corporation of America*, 393 U.S. 333 (1969).
60. *Fortner Enterprises, Inc. v. United States Steel Corporation*, 394 U.S. 495 (1969).
61. *United States v. Topco Associates, Inc.*, 405 U.S. 596 (1972).
62. *Otter Tail Power Co. v. United States*, 410 U.S. 366 (1973).
63. *Goldfarb v. Virginia State Bar*, 421 U.S. 773 (1975).
64. *Cantor v. Detroit Edison Co.*, 428 U.S. 579 (1976).
65. *Continental T.V., Inc. v. GTE Sylvania Inc.*, 433 U.S. 36 (1977).
66. *National Society of Professional Engineers v. United States*, 435 U.S. 679 (1978).
67. *Broadcast Music, Inc. v. Columbia Broadcasting System, Inc.*, 441 U.S. 1 (1979).
68. *Catalano, Inc. v. Target Sales, Inc.*, 446 U.S. 643 (1980).
69. *Arizona v. Maricopa County Medical Society*, 457 U.S. 332 (1982).

70. *Monsanto Co. v. Spray-Rite Service Corporation,* 465 U.S. 752 (1984).
71. *Jefferson Parish Hospital District No. 2 v. Hyde,* 466 U.S. 2 (1984).
72. *National Collegiate Athletic Association v. Board of Regents of the University of Oklahoma,* 468 U.S. 85 (1984).
73. *Aspen Skiing Co. v. Aspen Highlands Skiing Corporation,* 472 U.S. 585 (1985).
74. *Business Electronics Corporation v. Sharp Electronics Corporation,* 485 U.S. 717 (1988).
75. 118 S. Ct. 275 (1997).

Recommended Reading

Kaserman, David, and John Mayo. *Government and Business.* Fort Worth, TX: The Dryden Press, 1995.
Langran, Robert W. *The United States Supreme Court.* 4th ed. Needham Heights, MA: Pearson Custom Publishing. 1999. Chapters 4–15.
Schnitzer, Martin. *Contemporary Government and Business Relations.* 4th ed. Boston, MA: Houghton Mifflin Co., 1990. Chapters 6, 7, and 9.

CHAPTER 6

The Supreme Court and the Federal Trade Commission and Clayton Acts

When Woodrow Wilson became president in 1913, he perceived that the Sherman Act needed augmenting. As a result, Congress in 1914 passed two more laws to try to keep our market system competitive and to curb abuses. The first one, the Federal Trade Commission Act, was passed on September 26. It created an independent regulatory commission, the Federal Trade Commission, composed of five members appointed by the president with Senate approval, with each member holding office for seven years. Section 5 of the act gives the FTC the power to prevent unfair methods of competition and unfair or deceptive acts or practices in or affecting commerce. The second part, concerning unfair or deceptive acts or practices, was actually added in 1938 when Congress amended Section 5 with the Wheeler-Lea Amendment due to a Supreme Court decision, to be examined later, that did not think unfair methods of competition prevention included efforts to protect consumers. The amendment also specifically forbids false or misleading advertisements for food, drugs, cosmetics, and therapeutic devices sold in interstate commerce. However, the Commission cannot award monetary damages to victimized consumers under the amendment, thereby weakening the consumer's incentive to lodge complaints and weakening the seller's incentive to comply. A fraudulent seller, if successfully prosecuted, will not be allowed to continue or repeat the violation, but may keep any of the profits obtained during the period of the violation. The respondent has sixty days to appeal the Commission's cease and desist order to a court of appeals, but once the order is finalized, any subsequent violation subjects the respondent to contempt proceedings and a civil penalty of up to $5,000 for each day of continuing violation or for each separate offense.

The second law, the Clayton Antitrust Act, was passed on October 15, 1914. Probably its most important provision is Section 2, which deals with primary-line price discrimination (i.e., a geographic line where goods are sold at a higher price in one area and a lower price in another, to the injury of a local seller). It may also occur within the same geographic area. One cannot engage in price discrimination in the sale of goods of like grade or quality when the effect is to injure or prevent competition. In 1936, Congress amended the Clayton Act, especially Section 2, when it passed the Robinson-Patman Act, commonly known as the Chain Store Act. It prohibits secondary-line price discrimination, which is the sale of the same goods to different buyers in the same geographic area at different prices when there is no cost difference. One cannot practice price discrimination when the end result is to lessen competition, when it tends to create a monopoly in any line of commerce, or when it injures, destroys, or prevents competition with any person who either grants or knowingly receives the benefits of such discrimination. The law does permit a seller to show that lower prices to some buyers are based on cost differences related to different methods or quantities involved in the sale or delivery of the product. Other actions prohibited are the payment of brokerage fees when no independent broker was involved (some chains had been demanding the regular brokerage fees at a discount when they purchased directly from the manufacturers), and advertising allowances, unless they were made on equal terms to all competing purchasers.

Section 3 of the Clayton Act prohibits tying contracts, which are the lease or sale of a particular product conditional on the lessee's or purchaser's use of associated products sold by the same manufacturer, and exclusive dealing arrangements, in which one firm induces another not to deal with the former's competitors. These have generally been condemned by the courts only when the seller enjoys substantial market power and they result in a lessening of competition.

Section 4 allows a person to sue for triple damages, and the important Section 7 prohibits any corporation engaged in commerce from acquiring the stock of another corporation when the effect may be to reduce competition substantially or to create a monopoly in any line of business and in any section of the country. It applies to both interstate and foreign commerce. In 1950, Congress passed the Celler-Kefauver Act to plug a loophole in Section 7. It is now illegal for one corporation to acquire the stock or assets of another corporation when the end result might be to lessen competition substantially or to tend to create a monopoly. It makes a merger illegal if there was a trend toward concentration in an industry. Small firms that merge to improve their competitive position are generally not challenged, but mergers that would ordinarily be allowed in concentrated industries may well be challenged if a large firm acquires a small competitor.

Section 8 applies to interlocking directorates, saying that no person shall be a director in two or more corporations if they are competitors and if they have capital, surplus, and undivided profits in excess of one million dollars.

The government does not have to prove that competition has been reduced. The fact of the interlock itself makes for illegality.

Section 14 provides that individual directors or officers of a corporation can be fined as much as $5,000, or sentenced to prison for up to one year, or both, and the Federal Trade Commission was given joint responsibility with the Justice Department to enforce the act, the violations of which are considered civil offenses. Section 15 gives the U.S. district courts jurisdiction over these cases, and Section 16 permits any person or firm to sue for and have injunctive relief against potential loss or damage by violations.

Below is a listing of important provisions of the Federal Trade Commission and Clayton Acts:

Important Provisions of the Federal Trade Commission Act and the Clayton Act

FTC Act

Section 5:   prohibits unfair methods of competition and unfair or deceptive acts or practices

Clayton Act

Section 2:   prohibits price discrimination
Section 3:   prohibits tying contracts and exclusive dealing arrangements
Section 4:   allows a person to sue for triple damages
Section 7:   prohibits anticompetitive acquiring of stocks or assets
Section 8:   prohibits anticompetitive interlocking directorates
Section 14:   provides for fines and jail sentences
Section 15:   gives jurisdiction to U.S. district courts
Section 16:   provides injunctive relief

Before looking at the major Court cases, there is one other law of note with regard to antitrust law. It is the 1976 Hart-Scott-Rodino Act, and it made a number of procedural changes. The Justice Department now has the authority to issue civil investigative demands to third parties, such as competitors of those companies under investigation, and to compel oral testimony and answers to written questions. It also requires notice to the antitrust division of the Justice Department and to the Federal Trade Commission, thirty days in advance, of mergers involving companies with stock or assets of $100 million or more that plan to merge with companies worth $10 million or more when the transaction involves acquisitions of more than $15 million in stock or assets. This gives them time in which to challenge the merger, because the firms must provide the government with extensive information pertaining to the merger. The government might decide to approve the merger subject to certain conditions. This provision benefits the government because once a merger takes place it is often difficult to stop it since the length of time needed to arrive at decisions allows firms time to consolidate their assets; it also benefits the firms because they will know of the challenge before the merger is finalized rather than after it has been finalized. Finally, the law authorizes state attorneys general to bring triple damage suits on behalf of state citizens injured by violations of the Sherman Act. This has increased the amount of antitrust enforcement by state governments, and the courts will exclude from the amount of monetary relief any amount duplicating an award for the same injury.

An important point to remember about antitrust enforcement is that the majority of cases initiated by the federal government are settled by a consent decree approved by the judge, a violation of which would result in contempt of court. Although saving the time and expense of a trial, its drawback is that if the government had won the suit, that would have constituted *prima facie* evidence of the violation and would be used by a private plaintiff in a triple damage suit.

Federal Trade Commission and Clayton Act Case Law Development

THE EARLY YEARS

The Federal Trade Commission tried using its own law in the 1920 case of *FTC v. Gratz*[1] by bringing unfair competition charges against a company for refusing to sell steel ties unless prospective purchasers bought bagging to be used with them. However, Justice McReynolds, for a 7–2 Court, ruled against the FTC, saying it was up to the courts to decide what is unfair competition. Since Gratz sold at fair prices to those willing to take those terms, the public did not suffer injury and therefore the law was not broken.

Two years later, in 1922, the Federal Trade Commission again brought a case to the Court involving its own law, but this time fared better. The Court ruled against a company who refused to sell to those who did not observe the resale price set by it, even though there was no contract to fix the price, and it refused to sell to those who sold to other dealers who failed to sell at the set price. The Court felt it was a suppression of competition after the company had sold the products, which was unfair competition.[2] That same year the Court voided a contract under Section 3 of the Clayton Act. Under it a manufacturer who controlled 40 percent of the industry bound a retailer to sell only the manufacturer's products. However, the retailer stopped selling those products and began selling those of a rival company. The Court held that the law condemns sales of agreements where the effect may be to substantially lessen competition or tend to create a monopoly.[3] Again that year, the Federal Trade Commission won another case enforcing its law, this time against a manufacturer selling products with misleading labels as to what fabric was in the products. The Court found unfair competition even though competitors and eventually retailers knew what the company was doing.[4]

In 1923 the Court ruled against an attempt by the Federal Trade Commission to use its own law as well as Section 3 of the Clayton Act. The case was *FTC v. Curtis Publishing Co.*,[5] and it involved a contract made between the publisher and a distributor to consign publications until they are sold at specified prices and to have the distributor act as an exclusive agent, meaning it would not carry any other publisher's materials. Justice McReynolds in a 7–2 opinion held that the contract was not a violation of the Clayton Act, and the exclusive agency did not violate the FTC Act if done in an orderly development of business and without an unlawful motive, as was the case here. He also said that the courts are the ultimate determiners of unfair competition and that they can look at the record of a case to see if there were any material facts not reported by the FTC. The Court ruled the same way later that year in a case against four companies who leased equipment to retailers, who in turn had to use the product it produced when they used that equipment. The Court felt that those who give time, skill, and capital should have large freedom of action in the conduct of their affairs.[6]

In 1927 the Court upheld a Section 4 triple damage suit against a manufacturer who refused to sell to a company at dealers' discounts, which violated Section 2 of the Sherman Act as it was an attempt to monopolize. An interesting holding of the case was that one does not have to prove the actual cost of doing business in order to calculate damages.[7] Four years later, in 1931, came the aforementioned decision that led to the passage of the Wheeler-Lea Amendment. The Court ruled against an FTC attempt to stop a company that made a product from advertising it as a cure for obesity. The Court said that the company did not represent the product as being scientific, and no competition was injured.[8] The FTC was able to win two cases in 1934. One involved a trade name that was misleading and that caused both confusion and prejudice to retailers, architects, builders, and consumers (the product was a type of lumber),[9] and the other involved a manufacturer who made a product (candy) that contained material attractive to children in each package. The problem was that the package explained that either the price or the amount of candy was affected by chance. It was also inferior in size and quality to their other candy. The Court found it unfair competition even if there was no fraud or deception.[10] Two years later the Court found no violation of Section 3 of the Clayton Act when automobile manufacturers made dealers agree not to sell, offer for sale, or use in repairs second-hand or used parts not manufactured or authorized by the manufacturer. It felt the arrangement did not substantially lessen competition nor create a monopoly.[11]

Significant government victories and losses in the Supreme Court are listed below:

<u>**Government Federal Trade Commission and Clayton Act Cases in the Supreme Court, 1920–1959**</u>

Government Victories

   1. *FTC v. Beech-Nut Packing Company*, 1922.

2. *FTC v. Winsted Company*, 1922.
3. *FTC v. Algoma Lumber Company*, 1934.
4. *FTC v. R. F. Keppel & Brothers, Inc.*, 1934.
5. *Corn Products Refining Company v. FTC*, 1945.
6. *FTC v. A. E. Staley Manufacturing Company*, 1945.
7. *FTC v. Cement Institute*, 1948.
8. *FTC v. Morton Salt Company*, 1948.
9. *Standard Oil of California v. United States*, 1949.
10. *FTC v. Motion Picture Advertising Service Company*, 1953.
11. *United States v. duPont and Company*, 1956.
12. *FTC v. Simplicity Pattern Company, Inc.*, 1959.

Government Losses

1. *FTC v. Gratz*, 1920.
2. *FTC v. Curtis Publishing Company*, 1923.
3. *FTC v. Sinclair Refining Company*, 1923.
4. *FTC v. Raladam Company*, 1931.
5. *Standard Oil Company v. FTC*, 1951.
6. *Automatic Canteen Company of America v. FTC*, 1953.

THE 1940S AND 1950S

In 1945 the FTC was successful in breaking up two basing-point schemes. Basing-point is a system in which the companies involved will only sell at delivered prices, which avoids giving firms located near a consuming center an advantage in obtaining business. The delivered prices were the sum of the base price added to the cost of transportation to the destination, regardless of the origin of the shipment or the actual freight cost. The steel industry was one of the first to utilize the practice, although these two cases involved the glucose industry. In the first case, the Court found Section 2 of the Clayton Act plus the Robinson-Patman Act violated because the allowance of discounts to purchasers of by-products was a substantial threat to competition, as were the advertising discounts that were given because they were not on terms proportionally accorded other purchasers.[12] In the second case, the Court said there was no good-faith effort to meet competition, the FTC can decide that fact, and the fact that competitors are also doing it does not justify price discrimination.[13]

The following year, 1946, the Court awarded triple damages under both Section 4 of the Clayton Act and Section 7 of the Sherman Act, and allowed an injunction to be issued under Section 16 of the Clayton Act against film distributors plus those who owned or controlled theaters in a city. They had conspired to prevent an owner of motion picture theaters from showing pictures until after the preferred theaters had shown them, a violation of Sections 1 and 2 of the Sherman Act. An interesting facet to this case was that the plaintiff could not prove what his earnings would have been over a five-year period under fully competitive conditions, and the Court said that the wrongdoer should bear the risk of the uncertainty in computing the damages he has created.[14] Two years later, in 1948, the FTC won two cases. In one, the Court decided that Section 5 of the FTC Act and Section 2 of the Clayton Act and the Robinson-Patman Act were violated by seventy-four corporations who were acting in concert through a multiple basing-point system, resulting in price discrimination that was not made in good faith to meet the equally low price of a competitor.[15] In the other, a company was selling with quantity discounts that were not justified by cost savings. The Court found there was a reasonable possibility that the discrimination harmed competition because certain merchants had to pay more since they could not qualify for any discounts because they could not purchase the amount necessary.[16] The next year, 1949, the government won a Clayton Act Section 3 suit against a company that made contracts under which independent dealers had to purchase exclusively from the company all requirements of one or more of the products they marketed. Since these agreements accounted for 6.7 percent of the company's total sales in a seven-state area, the Court felt that competition was foreclosed in a substantial share of the line of commerce affected.[17]

In 1951 the Court did not find Section 2 of the Clayton Act plus the Robinson-Patman Act violated by a company that sold to four large customers in a city more cheaply than it sold to small customers. The Court accepted the defense that it was doing so in order to retain each of the four as a customer, and was, in good faith, meeting the lawful price of a competitor, even if it resulted in competition being injured, destroyed, or prevented.[18] Two years later, in 1953, the FTC was more fortunate and won a case against a company under the FTC Act. The company had made exclusive contracts with 40 percent of its customers in an area, and, together with three other companies, had 75 percent control nationally. The Court found unfair competition, but did not end the contracts totally. Instead, the Court said the contracts could be for only one year (the majority of them had been from one to two years).[19] That same year the FTC lost a case, with the Court finding no violation of Section 2 of the Robinson-Patman Act by a large buyer of products who received as much as one-third lower price than others. The Court felt that the burden of proof in these cases is on the government to show that there was no cost justification for the practice or any other defense, or that the buyer knew that those defenses were not present in this case.[20]

In an interesting 1956 case, the government was successful in using Sections 7 and 15 of the Clayton Act to make a company divest itself of stock it had purchased between 1917 and 1919. The problem was that the company made automotive finishes and fabrics, among other things, and the stock was in an automobile company. The Court held that there was a reasonable possibility of restricting commerce or tending to create a monopoly in that line of commerce.[21] Three years later, in 1959, the FTC was able to win a Section 2

Clayton and Robinson-Patman Act case against a company that discriminated in favor of larger customers by furnishing them services and facilities not given smaller customers on proportionally equal terms. The Court said that since these customers were competitors, neither the absence of competitive injury nor the presence of cost justification can be a defense.[22]

THE FIRST FORTY YEARS IN RETROSPECT

It is possible to see something of a pattern in the first four decades of Supreme Court decisions interpreting the Federal Trade Commission, Clayton, and Robinson-Patman Acts. Each act attempted to do something about business activity intended to subvert the forces of competition. The Federal Trade Commission brought almost all the government's cases, leaving the Justice Department to concentrate on the Sherman Act. It won two-thirds of them, despite the Supreme Court justices who were, at least until the mid-1950s, inclined to prevent too much government interference in the economy. This shows both the strength of many of the government's cases, along with the accompanying attempts by business to circumvent the market. One other pattern deserving of mention is the reluctance of businesses to take advantage of the Clayton Act and bring suits themselves. The fact that they won the few suits they brought should have indicated that it was a viable way to proceed. However, they were on the whole enjoying prosperity in the 1920s, fighting a depression in the 1930s, fighting a war in the 1940s, and again enjoying prosperity in the 1950s. As the adage goes, why knock a good thing? Whether that would continue will be the focus of the look at the next four decades of the enforcement of these three statutes.

Significant private suits in the Supreme Court are listed below:

<u>Private Federal Trade Commission and Clayton Act Cases
in the Supreme Court, 1920–1959</u>

Victories for Plaintiffs

1. *Standard Fashion Company v. Magrane-Houston Company*, 1922.
2. *Eastman Kodak Company v. Southern Photo Company*, 1927.
3. *Bigelow v. RKO Radio Pictures, Inc.*, 1946.

Loss by Plaintiff

1. *Pick Manufacturing Company v. General Motors Corporation*, 1936.

THE TURBULENT 1960S

The Federal Trade Commission and Clayton Acts, along with the latter's Robinson-Patman and Celler-Kefauver Acts, found their way to the Supreme Court in a great many cases during the 1960s. In theory it was an ideal time to bring these cases, because the Court was often dominated by its liberal wing, which is usually more agreeable to government intervention in the economy and to the attempt to try to curb the abuses of big business. That fact, together with the Democratic administrations through most of the decade, meant that suits would be initiated and that business would be in for a severe fight if, indeed, those cases ever found their way to the Court. It would also seem the appropriate time for businesses to use the laws against each other in suits for triple damages as well as for injunctive relief.

The decade started with the FTC victorious in two 1960 cases. In one, the Court agreed that Section 2 of the Clayton and Robinson-Patman Acts was violated by a company whose broker reduced his commission from 5 percent to 3 percent in order to meet the bid of a favored buyer. The company, accordingly, reduced its price only for that buyer in that and subsequent sales. The Court held that one cannot make any allowance in lieu of brokerage to the other party in a transaction. The fact that the buyer was unaware was immaterial, and it did not matter whether it was done from the broker to the buyer directly or, as in this case, indirectly through the seller.[23] In the other case the Court again found a violation of Section 2 of the Clayton and Robinson-Patman Acts by a company that reduced its prices in one area of the country (around a city). That is primary line discrimination, even though all competitive purchasers paid the same price. One does not have to show prices either below cost or unreasonably low in order to prove that a firm was trying to eliminate competition and get a monopoly. The price difference broke the law.[24] One year later, in 1961, the Court found no violation of Section 3 of the Clayton Act in a contract made between an electric company and a coal company in which the former agreed to buy all its coal from the latter for the next twenty years. However, when the price of coal rose, the coal company repudiated the contract, claiming it broke Section 3. The Court disagreed and made the company honor the contract, saying that the coal company was responsible for only 1 percent of the coal produced and supplied by seven hundred coal suppliers in that area. Therefore, the contract did not foreclose a substantial volume of competition.[25]

The following year, in 1962, the government won two cases. In the first, Section 7 of the Clayton Act and the Celler-Kefauver Act was used to stop a merger between two shoe companies, one of which was the nation's third largest retailer and fourth largest manufacturer, with the other the eighth largest retailer and twelfth largest manufacturer. It was an industry in which the top four manufacturers produced 23 percent of the nation's shoes. The result would be a lessening of competition in retail sales, particularly in cities of over 10,000 population.[26] In the second, Section 2 of the Clayton Act was used to stop the price discrimination being practiced by a company selling milk in a metropolitan area. It sold more cheaply to two chains than it did to 1,322 independent grocery stores, but could not show actual cost savings.[27] The next year, 1963, the government won three more cases. In the first the Court found Section 2 of the Clayton and Robinson-Patman Acts violated by a company giving only one of its independently owned retailers in a particular region a lower price than it gave any others, so that retailer could meet the price reductions of a competitor. The Court said that the good-faith meeting of competition in order to practice price discrimination must be done with your own competitor, not someone else's.[28] In the second, the Court found Section 3 of the Robinson-Patman Act violated by a company selling goods in a metropolitan area at unreasonably low prices for the purpose of destroying competition or eliminating a competitor. The Court found no legitimate commercial activity by the company's practice.[29] In the third case, Section 7 of the Clayton Act and the Celler-Kefauver Act were used to block a merger between the second and third largest commercial banks in a metropolitan area. At least 30 percent of the relevant market would be in the hands of the bank after the merger, and it would increase concentration in the banking industry in the area by one-third, resulting in a substantial lessening of competition.[30]

In 1964 the government continued its streak with four more victories. First, Section 7 of the Clayton Act was used to stop the acquisition by a natural gas company of one of the two major interstate pipelines serving that part of the country, due to the probability of substantially lessening competition there.[31] Then Section 7 of the Clayton Act was again used, this time to stop a company that was the largest in its field from acquiring the ninth largest one, which was also the fourth largest independent. The merger would have a probable anticompetitive effect in a oligopolistic industry (that produced aluminum conductors), where the prevention of increased competition was important. The merger resulted in a substantial lessening of competition.[32] Then a joint venture was broken up because it might well have eliminated any prospective competition between the two companies. The Court felt that the presence of a potential competitor having the capability of entering an oligopolistic market may be a substantial incentive to competition.[33] Finally, Section 7 of the Clayton Act was again used to stop the acquisition of the third largest producer of glass containers by the second largest producer of metal containers. In the combined container field, six companies dominated, with the acquiring company being number two and the acquired company number six; the two combined held 25 percent of the market. The Court felt that when there was a trend toward concentration, any further concentration should be stopped, and in a highly concentrated industry, even slight increases should be prevented.[34]

In 1965 the government won two more cases. In one, the FTC used Section 5 of the FTC Act to stop a deceptive television commercial. The Court felt that great weight must be given to what the FTC says constitutes a deceptive practice, especially deceptive advertising. The misrepresentation of any fact, so long as it materially induces a purchaser's decision to buy, is a deception prohibited by the law.[35] In the other, Section 7 of the Clayton Act was used to make a company give up another company it had acquired, because the acquiring company tried to induce reciprocal buying of the acquired company's products by the former's suppliers. Since this was an oligopolistic industry, the Court said there was a probability of substantially lessening competition.[36] Similarly, one year later the government won twice again. In one case, Section 7 of the Clayton Act and the Celler-Kefauver Act were used to stop a merger of two grocery stores in a metropolitan area. The problem was that they were two of the largest and most successful in a market characterized by a steady decline in the number of small grocery companies, and by a significant absorption of small firms by larger ones. The Court said that this was a market exhibiting a marked trend toward concentration, and the merger would probably destroy competition in the future.[37] In the other, Section 7 of the Clayton Act was used to stop a merger of the tenth largest beer brewer in the country with the eighteenth, which resulted in the former becoming number five with 4.49 percent of the market. The Court felt this was an industry that was rapidly becoming more concentrated and thus the merger would injure competition.[38]

In 1967 the Court used Section 7 of the Clayton Act and the Celler-Kefauver Act to make a company divest itself of the assets of a company it had obtained ten years earlier. The acquiring company, dominant in several areas, decided to extend its product line by merging with the other company, which was number one in its area. The acquired company's area was an oligopolistic industry, and the substitution of a powerful acquiring firm for the smaller dominant firm might reduce the competitive structure of the industry by dissuading the smaller firms from competing aggressively, resulting in a more rigid oligopoly with the acquiring firm as the price leader. The Court also felt the merger tended to raise the barriers to new entrants because of the acquiring firm's large advertising budget, thus, the merger eliminated that firm's likely entrance into that market as a potential competitor.[39] That same year the Court upheld Section 2 of the Clayton and Robinson-Patman Acts as well as Sections 1 and 2 of the Sherman Act being used against three companies engaged in predatory pricing to get rid of a local competitor in a city. The Court said that the law can be used against price discrimination that erodes competition as well as that which does it immediately. In this case there was a drastically declining price structure.[40]

The impressive string of government victories came to a halt in a 1968 case in which the FTC tried to use Section 2 of the Clayton and Robinson-Patman Acts against a chain of supermarkets, charging the company with unlawfully inducing suppliers to engage in discriminatory pricing and sales promotion activities while not giving these benefits to wholesalers who would sell to its retail competitors. The Court felt the government could only act against discrimination between customers competing for resales at the same functional level. The responsibility should, in cases such as this, be on the supplier to make promotional allowances available to the reseller. It was not up to the defendant company to do that.[41] That same year the Court upheld a Clayton Act Section 4 triple damage suit, as well as a Section 5 charge. That section states that a final judgment or decree in a government antitrust suit is *prima facie* evidence in a private suit. The suit charged that a company's practice of leasing and refusing to sell its major machines was illegal monopolization, and that it overcharged when it did lease. The defense was that the company leasing the machines simply passed the illegal charges on to its customers in the form of higher prices, but the Court disagreed, saying that the possibility of recoupment that way is not relevant. It is not a valid defense, and the company was guilty of breaking the law.[42] The very busy 1960s concluded the next year with a case in which the Court upheld Section 2 of the Clayton and Robinson-Patman Acts against a company charging higher prices to an independent wholesale and retail distributor than it did its branded dealers. The suit had an interesting twist, in that a wholesaler had sold to a subsidiary that had sold to its subsidiary, and it was the latter that was a competitor of the plaintiff.[43]

Significant government victories and losses in the Supreme Court are listed below:

<u>Government Federal Trade Commission and Clayton Act Cases in the Supreme Court, 1960–Present</u>

Government Victories

1. *FTC v. Henry Brock and Company*, 1960.
2. *FTC v. Anheuser-Busch, Inc.*, 1960.
3. *Brown Shoe Company v. United States*, 1962.
4. *United States v. Borden Company*, 1962.
5. *FTC v. Sun Oil Company*, 1963.
6. *United States v. National Dairy Products Corporation*, 1963.
7. *United States v. Philadelphia National Bank*, 1963.
8. *United States v. El Paso Natural Gas Company*, 1964.
9. *United States v. Aluminum Company of America*, 1964.
10. *United States v. Penn-Olin Chemical Company*, 1964.
11. *United States v. Continental Can Company*, 1964.
12. *FTC v. Colgate-Palmolive Company*, 1965.
13. *FTC v. Consolidated Foods*, 1965.
14. *United States v. Von's Grocery Company*, 1966.
15. *United States v. Pabst Brewing Company*, 1966.
16. *FTC v. Procter & Gamble Company*, 1967.
17. *Ford Motor Company v. United States*, 1972.
18. *United States v. Falstaff Brewing Corporation*, 1973.
19. *California Dental Association v. FTC*, 1999.

Government Losses

1. *FTC v. Fred Meyer, Inc.*, 1968.
2. *United States v. General Dynamics Corporation*, 1974.
3. *Great Atlantic & Pacific Tea Company, Inc. v. FTC*, 1979.

THE 1970S TO THE PRESENT

Since the 1960s were unusually busy with these cases, a slowdown seemed likely, and it began in the 1970s and continues through the present. The government did win a case in 1972 when the Court upheld a Section 7 Celler-Kefauver Act suit against the nation's number two automobile manufacturer who had bought the assets of an independent manufacturer of spark plugs. Prior to the acquisition, the automobile company was the number one purchaser of plugs from independents. The Court held that the acquisition of the assets and the trade name might substantially lessen competition.[44] The government won again the next year when Section 7 of the Clayton Act was used to make the country's fourth largest beer producer divest itself of the largest seller of beer in a regional market. The Court said the acquiring company was a potential competitor to the acquired one, even though it would not have been a new entrant to the market. Its position on the edge of a market exerted a beneficial influence on the market's competitive condition.[45] One year later, in 1974, the government lost a Clayton Act Section 7 case it brought against a deep-mining coal company that had acquired a strip-mining company. The Court said there was not a substantial lessening of competition, as the acquired company did not have sufficient reserves to make it a significant competitive force. It could not compete effectively for long-term contracts.[46]

In 1977 the Court dismissed a Clayton Act Sections 4 and 7 suit brought against one of the country's two largest bowling equipment manufacturers who was also the largest operator of bowling centers. It had acquired some bowling centers that had defaulted in their payments for bowling equipment, but a regional operator of bowling centers claimed injury due to the acquisitions. The Court, however, said the regional company would have suffered the same loss had the acquired centers secured refinancing or had they been bought by someone else, and that the company was trying to get damages for profits it would have received had the acquired centers been closed.[47] That same year the Court denied a Clayton Act Section 4 suit, as well as a Sherman Act Section 1 suit, against manufacturers who had sold to specialized contractors, who in turn sold to general contractors who then sold to state and local governments. The latter alleged price-fixing and wanted triple damages. However, the Court refused to use the pass-on theory by an indirect purchaser. It would create a serious risk of multiple liability for the defendants. There would be massive multiparty litigation involving many distribution levels and including large classes of ultimate consumers remote from the defendant. Therefore, only direct purchasers have standing to bring triple damage suits.[48] One year later, in 1978, the Court did allow a foreign nation to bring triple damage suits.[49] The following year the Court ruled against the government's attempt to use Section 2 of the Clayton and Robinson-Patman Acts against a large supermarket chain that made a deal with a dairy company to supply it with private label milk in a metropolitan area, then solicited other dairy companies to do the same. It then went back to the first company and told them to make a better offer, which they did. The Court said that since the dairy company was just meeting competition, the supermarket company was not liable.[50]

There were three suits of note in the 1980s. A 1983 case found Section 2 of the Clayton and Robinson-Patman Acts violated by the selling of a product to a wholesaler in one state at a higher price than to one in a neighboring state, without proof that competition was being met.[51] In 1986 the Court dismissed a Section 2 Robinson-Patman Act and Sections 1 and 2 Sherman Act case against twenty-one Japanese corporations or Japanese-controlled American corporations by a United States manufacturer of color television sets. The claim was that, over a twenty-year period, the companies had conspired to drive American firms from the market by predatory pricing. The Court held that these types of conspiracies are speculative in that they must sustain substantiated losses in order to recover uncertain gains. In this case the alleged conspiracy was implausible because it had not succeeded. The firms had not, despite the period of years, been able to dominate the market here, at least to the extent of being able to reap monopoly prices.[52] In that same year, the Court turned down a Clayton Act Section 16 request for an injunction by the fifth largest beef packer in the country to stop a proposed merger of the second and third largest companies. The Court felt the merger did not constitute a threat of antitrust injury.[53]

Four more cases appeared in the 1990s, two of which came in 1990. In one, the Court ruled against a Clayton Act Section 4 triple damage suit that was accompanied by a Sherman Act Section 1 claim. One company sued another because the latter encouraged its dealers to match the prices of independents, causing the sales of the company bringing the suit to drop. However, the Court found no antitrust injury. The losses did not flow from the harmful effects on dealers and consumers. Cutting prices to increase business is often the essence of competition, and the prices were above predatory levels.[54] In the other case, a Section 2 Robinson-Patman Act suit was upheld. It was brought against a company that sold gasoline to independent retailers in a metropolitan area but also sold to two distributors and that gave the latter substantial discounts. Both distributors eventually sold the gas at retail and their sales volumes increased while the other stations declined. The Court felt that the discount was illegal because it was not tied to the supplier's savings or the wholesalers' costs.[55]

In 1993 a case concerned a fight within the tobacco industry itself. It was a Section 2 Clayton and Robinson-Patman Act suit brought by one company against another, and they were two of the six firms that dominate the concentrated industry. It involved an allegation of predatory pricing. The Court dismissed the suit, holding that the laws are applicable only if price discrimination threatens to injure competition, and that predatory pricing schemes, in general, are implausible, and are even more improbable when they require coordinated action among several firms.[56]

In 1999 the Court rendered a decision favorable to the Federal Trade Commission. The case was *California Dental Association v. Federal Trade Commission,*[57] and the issue was whether the FTC had jurisdiction over the advertising guidelines the group issued to its members. The agency said those guidelines violated Section 5 in that they restricted two types of truthful, nondeceptive advertising: price advertising, particularly discounted fees, and advertising relating to the quality of dental services. A unanimous Court speaking through Justice Souter held that the FTC Act did give the agency jurisdiction over an association that provides substantial economic benefit to its for-profit members, even though the association itself was a nonprofit one.

Significant private suits in the Supreme Court are listed below:

<u>Private Federal Trade Commission and Clayton Act Cases
in the Supreme Court, 1960–Present</u>

Victories for Plaintiffs

1. *Utah Pie Company v. Continental Baking Company,* 1967.
2. *Hanover Shoe v. United Shoe Machinery Corporation,* 1968.
3. *Perkins v. Standard Oil Company of California,* 1969.
4. *Pfizer, Inc. v. Government of India,* 1978.
5. *Falls City Industries, Inc. v. Vanco Beverage, Inc.,* 1983.
6. *Texaco, Inc. v. Hasbrouck,* 1990.

Losses by Plaintiffs

1. *Tampa Electric Company v. Nashville Coal Company,* 1961.
2. *Brunswick Corporation v. Pueblo Bowl-O-Mat, Inc.,* 1977.
3. *Illinois Brick Company v. Illinois,* 1977.
4. *Matushita Electric Industrial Corporation v. Zenith Radio Corporation,* 1986.
5. *Cargill, Inc. v. Montfort of Colorado, Inc.,* 1986.
6. *Atlantic Richfield Company v. USA Petroleum Company,* 1990.
7. *Brooke Group, Ltd. v. Brown and Williamson Tobacco Corporation,* 1993.

WHAT DOES IT ALL MEAN?

As with the Sherman Act, it is sometimes difficult to understand the significance of the Federal Trade Commission, Clayton, Robinson-Patman, and Celler-Kefauver Acts, as well as the Supreme Court decisions interpreting them. Again, an obvious reason for that has been the steady decline of cases since the end of the 1960s. As mentioned with regard to the Sherman Act, courts in general and the Supreme Court in particular have become conservative in nature due to appointments by conservative presidents, resulting in a reluctance to interfere in business activities. Government staff in charge of antitrust prosecutions, such as the Justice Department and the Federal Trade Commission, take their lead from the president, and therefore do not bring many cases. Another pattern follows: The government has had just one major suit (1999) under these statutes reach the Supreme Court since the end of the 1970s. The other suits that have reached the Court since are private ones, and those bringing them lose about two-thirds of the time, making the filing of these suits even less likely. Ironically, private suits were seldom brought in the 1960s, when the chances of winning were better, but that might have been because the government was taking care of the situation. Both the Justice Department and the Federal Trade Commission were bringing cases and were winning almost every one they brought. Presidents and their administrations were vigorous in bringing cases, and the Supreme Court, with its liberal bent, was highly receptive to the government's position. Since history tends to be cyclical, the days of the big antitrust suits might return, but it will take changes in executive and judicial thinking for that to happen. As mentioned previously, perhaps the Microsoft case is an inkling of what might be ahead, for in May, 1999, the Justice Department did file an antitrust suit against American Airlines.

SUMMARY

The Federal Trade Commission Act as well as the Clayton Act and its amendments were passed to try to eliminate the gaps in the Sherman Act. To a large extent they succeeded, mainly due to administrations that were eager to use the laws, and the Supreme Court's willingness to interpret them the government's way. This chapter has attempted to trace the evolution of the Court's interpretation of these laws in a chronological fashion in order to better understand the evolutionary role of laws and to show the development of patterns in their interpretation. As has been apparent, the Supreme Court justices do not mechanically apply the law to the case, due to an element of subjectivity. The justices have their political, social, and economic values, and these, by their nature, play a role in decision making, as does the time frame in which the decisions are given (i.e., conservative times, more liberal times, a healthy economy, an economy marred by high inflation or a recession, or even national emergencies). Thus, decisions of the Court must be looked at in their various settings, and the chronological approach is helpful. One other fact that should be apparent is that laws are seldom 100 percent precise. That is because most major laws are a result of compromise, which means that differing ideas are included in them. The lack of precision, in turn, gives the justices more room to interpret the laws as they think most proper. The fact that many laws are imprecise is good, because the resultant flexibility renders the law adaptable to changing situations without the necessity of amending or rewriting the law. In any event, antitrust history is important in any examination of the role of government in our economy. If there is an impetus for a revival of antitrust activity, it might come from the enormity of the mergers taking place recently. As will be seen in later chapters, these megamergers, both within industries and cutting across industries, might just force the government, however reluctantly, to bring some suits. Whether the courts will respond favorably to these suits is another matter. Certainly the current Supreme Court is not receptive to the government taking an active role in the economy.

Questions for Discussion

1. Why was the Wheeler-Lea Amendment needed?
2. Why was the Robinson-Patman Act needed?
3. Why was the Celler-Kefauver Act needed?
4. What procedural changes did the Hart-Scott-Rodino Act enact?
5. Is it important that the FTC brought most of the pre-1960 Clayton Act cases instead of the Justice Department?
6. Why did private parties not bring many cases under the FTC and Clayton Acts (pre–1960)?
7. With the government winning almost every case since the start of the sixties, why has it stopped bringing FTC and Clayton Act cases?
8. Why have private FTC and Clayton Act suits not fared well before the Supreme Court in recent years?
9. Is the Federal Trade Commission still an important agency?
10. Is the Clayton Act still an important law?
11. Are megamergers something to be concerned about?
12. Do you foresee a renewal of antitrust activity?

Notes

1. 253 U.S. 421, 1920.
2. *FTC v. Beech-Nut Packing Co.*, 257 U.S. 346 (1922).
3. *Standard Fashion Co. v. Magrane-Houston Co.*, 258 U.S. 346 (1922).
4. *FTC v. Winsted Co.*, 258 U.S. 483 (1922).
5. 260 U.S. 568 (1923).
6. *FTC v. Sinclair Refining Co.*, 261 U.S. 463 (1923).
7. *Eastman Kodak Co. v. Southern Photo Co.*, 273 U.S. 359 (1927).
8. *FTC v. Raladam Co.*, 283 U.S. 643 (1931).
9. *FTC v. Algoma Lumber Co.*, 291 U.S. 67 (1934).
10. *FTC v. R. F. Keppel & Brothers, Inc.*, 291 U.S. 304 (1934).
11. *Pick Manufacturing Co. v. General Motors Corporation*, 299 U.S. 3 (1936).
12. *Corn Products Refining Co. v. FTC*, 324 U.S. 726 (1945).
13. *FTC v. A. E. Staley Manufacturing Co.*, 324 U.S. 746 (1945).
14. *Bigelow v. RKO Radio Pictures, Inc.*, 327 U.S. 251 (1946).
15. *FTC v. Cement Institute*, 333 U.S. 683 (1948).
16. *FTC v. Morton Salt Co.*, 334 U.S. 586 (1948).
17. *Standard Oil of California v. United States*, 337 U.S. 293 (1949).

18. *Standard Oil Co. v. FTC*, 340 U.S. 231 (1951).
19. *FTC v. Motion Picture Advertising Service Co.*, 344 U.S. 392 (1953).
20. *Automatic Canteen Company of America v. FTC*, 346 U.S. 61 (1953).
21. *United States v. duPont and Co.*, 353 U.S. 586 (1956).
22. *FTC v. Simplicity Pattern Co., Inc.*, 360 U.S. 55 (1959).
23. *FTC v. Henry Brock and Co.*, 363 U.S. 166 (1960).
24. *FTC v. Anheuser-Busch, Inc.*, 363 U.S. 536 (1960).
25. *Tampa Electric Co. v. Nashville Coal Co.*, 365 U.S. 320 (1961).
26. *Brown Shoe Co. v. United States*, 370 U.S. 294 (1962).
27. *United States v. Borden Co.*, 370 U.S. 460 (1962).
28. *FTC v. Sun Oil Co.*, 371 U.S. 505 (1963).
29. *United States v. National Dairy Products Corporation*, 372 U.S. 29 (1963).
30. *United States v. Philadelphia National Bank*, 374 U.S. 321 (1963).
31. *United States v. El Paso Natural Gas Co.*, 376 U.S. 651 (1964).
32. *United States v. Aluminum Company of America*, 377 U.S. 271 (1964).
33. *United States v. Penn-Olin Chemical Co.*, 378 U.S. 158 (1964).
34. *United States v. Continental Can Co.*, 378 U.S. 441 (1964).
35. *FTC v. Colgate-Palmolive Co.*, 380 U.S. 375 (1965).
36. *FTC v. Consolidated Foods*, 380 U.S. 592 (1965).
37. *United States v. Von's Grocery Co.*, 384 U.S. 270 (1966).
38. *United States v. Pabst Brewing Co.*, 384 U.S. 546 (1966).
39. *FTC v. Procter & Gamble Co.*, 386 U.S. 568 (1967).
40. *Utah Pie Co. v. Continental Baking Co.*, 386 U.S. 685 (1967).
41. *FTC v. Fred Meyer, Inc.*, 390 U.S. 341 (1968).
42. *Hanover Shoe v. United Shoe Machinery Corporation*, 392 U.S. 481 (1968).
43. *Perkins v. Standard Oil Company of California*, 395 U.S. 642 (1969).
44. *Ford Motor Co. v. United States*, 405 U.S. 562 (1972).
45. *United States v. Falstaff Brewing Corporation*, 410 U.S. 526 (1973).
46. *United States v. General Dynamics Corporation*, 415 U.S. 486 (1974).
47. *Brunswick Corporation v. Pueblo Bowl-O-Mat, Inc.*, 429 U.S. 477 (1977).
48. *Illinois Brick Co. v. Illinois*, 431 U.S. 720 (1977).
49. *Pfizer, Inc. v. Government of India*, 434 U.S. 308 (1978).
50. *Great Atlantic & Pacific Tea Co., Inc. v. FTC*, 440 U.S. 69 (1979).
51. *Falls City Industries, Inc. v. Vanco*, 460 U.S. 428 (1983).
52. *Matsushita Electric Industrial Corporation v. Zenith Radio Corporation*, 475 U.S. 574 (1986).
53. *Cargill, Inc., v. Montfort of Colorado, Inc.*, 479 U.S. 104 (1986).
54. *Atlantic Richfield Co. v. USA Petroleum Co.*, 495 U.S. 328 (1990).
55. *Texaco, Inc. v. Hasbrouck*, 496 U.S. 543 (1990).
56. *Brooke Group, Ltd. v. Brown and Williamson Tobacco Corporation*, 509 U.S. 209 (1993).
57. *California Dental Association v. FTC*, 119 S.Ct. 1604 (1999).

RECOMMENDED READING

Kaserman, David, and John Mayo. *Government and Business*. Fort Worth, TX: The Dryden Press, 1995.

Langran, Robert W. *The United States Supreme Court*. 4th ed. Needham Heights, MA: Pearson Custom Publishing. 1999. Chapters 5–15.

Schnitzer, Martin. *Contemporary Government and Business Relations*. 4th ed. Boston, MA: Houghton Mifflin Co., 1990. Chapters 6 and 8.

GOVERNMENT AND THE CONSUMER

In a market economy, consumer sovereignty is an important institution because consumption is supposed to be the basic rationale for economic activity. As Adam Smith said, "Consumption is the sole end and purpose of all production; and the interest of the producer ought to be attended to only as far as it is necessary for promoting that of the consumer."[1] Production is the means; consumption is the end. On the one hand, those producers that effectively satisfy the wants of consumers are rewarded by large monetary returns, which in turn enable them to purchase the goods and services they require in their operations. On the other hand, those producers that do not respond to the wants of consumers will not remain in business long.

Freedom of choice is linked to consumer sovereignty. In fact, a basic rationale that is offered for the existence of a market economy is the freedom of choice it offers to consumers.[2] They are free to accept or reject whatever is produced in the marketplace; thus they are paramount to the operation of a market economy, since production has to be oriented toward fulfilling their desires. It is assumed that consumers are capable of making rational decisions, and in an economy dominated by the existence of a large number of buyers and sellers, this assumption has some merit.[3] But parity between consumers and producers does not exist in the complex world of today. Consumers are confronted with many products and not enough information to make rational choices.

CONSUMER PROTECTION

For many years the relationship between buyer and seller was governed by the common-law concept of *caveat emptor*, "Let the buyer beware." Thus, in an argument between the buyer and seller over the purchase of a horse that turned out to be lame, the burden of proof was on the buyer to convince a judge or jury that the seller deliberately misrepresented the condition of the horse before it was purchased. There had to be a legal precedent before the buyer could prove his case. Otherwise, it was assumed that both buyer and seller were equally knowledgeable when it came to horse trading. If one was not, that was his misfortune.

Two things happened that eventually led to consumer protection laws. The first was the Industrial Revolution, which provided a wide variety of manufactured products ranging from cars to refrigerators. The average person—in fact, even the most intelligent—did not have the ability nor the time to be an expert on the intricacies of the many products that industry produced. Second, the advantage passed to the producers because they were able to take the initiative in changing the techniques of production that increased the volume and variety of consumer goods. They were also able to develop skilled marketing techniques, including advertising, that influenced the consumer's choice of goods. It can be argued that the purpose of advertising is to entice consumers into buying products they do not need.

THE CONSUMER MOVEMENT

Consumer movements have not been as strong or exercised as much influence in the United States as other movements, such as the civil rights and environmental movements of the 1960s. Consumers are much more numerous and harder to organize than environmentalists, nor do they have the fervor. Generally, consumers coalesce around a particular issue, such as automobile safety. Then when laws are passed, the issues tend to disappear. The occasional identification of consumer interests, however, does not eliminate their frequent conflicts with producers over a wide variety of areas, ranging from false or misleading advertising to product safety. There has been an increase in the number of consumer groups in the United States in recent years. Examples are the National Consumer's League and Consumers Union.[4] They have expanded the policy area of consumerism.

Consumer movements have been much stronger in Europe than in the United States. The oldest type of consumer organization is the cooperative, which originated in Rochdale, England, in 1844. European cooperatives handle a significant volume of retail trade. They obtain their capital from members on the basis of a fixed return. American cooperative experience has been far more limited. The efficiency and low profit margins of American grocery chains and supermarkets have provided stiff competition to cooperatives and have weakened their appeal to consumers. While they have had some success, it is limited to certain areas of the country.

The laws protecting consumers are of an infinite variety, but it is possible to divide them into three main categories. The first category includes laws designed to protect consumers from the adulteration, misbranding, or mislabeling of food, drugs, and cosmetics.[5] The second category includes laws designed to protect consumers from unfair competition, such as false or misleading advertising or various forms of product misrepresentation. These laws generally involve some form of disclosure. An example is the Consumer Credit Protection Act of 1968, which requires banks to provide information on the true rate of interest charged to borrowers. The third category of consumer protection laws involves product safety. Their purpose is to protect consumers from the harmful use of products. Implicit in product safety legislation is that the concept of consumer sovereignty is inadequate if there are external costs in a product's consumption.

CONSUMER PROTECTION AND THE LAW

PURE FOOD, DRUGS, AND COSMETICS LEGISLATION

State and local government provisions against product adulteration or fraud have a long history. Sanitary regulation, inspection of weights and measures, and the like were established functions when the country was created. With relatively local self-sufficiency, particularly in food, local regulation protected the public reasonably well. However, development of mass transportation and the improvement of food processing techniques made the problem of consumer protection more complex. State legislation against the adulteration of food and drugs began in Virginia in 1848 and Ohio in 1853. It spread to most of the other states during the remainder of the century. But interstate competition prevented any state from raising its standards far out of line with other states and made federal regulation necessary.[6]

The Pure Food and Drug Act of 1906   The Pure Food and Drug Act of 1906 was adopted only after several decades of public concern about food adulteration and patent medicine fraud. Pure food bills were first introduced in Congress as early as 1890, but were opposed by business interests. However, public sentiment for protection increased, which eventually led to the passage of the act. There were several factors that were responsible for the increase in public interest, not the least of which was the publication of *The Jungle*, a book written by Upton Sinclair in 1906[7] that described business practices in the meat-packing industry in Chicago. Companies were alleged to have used chemical substances to hide the odor of spoiled meat that was sold to the public. The companies were also supposed to have used coloring substances to make the meat look fresh. The book was an immediate bestseller.

President Theodore Roosevelt, who read the book,[8] ordered an immediate investigation of the meat-packing industry, and a pure food bill that had been bottled up in committee took a new lease on life and was passed. The Pure Food and Drug Act of 1906 is considered to be the first significant piece of consumer protection legislation in the nation's history. Its main provisions are as follows:

1. The Federal Food and Drug Administration was formed to administer and enforce the provisions of the act.
2. The law prohibited the sale in interstate commerce of adulterated or misbranded food and drugs. Adulteration was defined as the hiding of damage or inferiority through the use of artificial covering or coating, the addition of poisonous or other deleterious ingredients injurious to health, and the inclusion of decomposed or diseased animals in vegetable substances.
3. Food and drugs were considered misbranded if their packages or labels bore statements that were false and misleading, or if one was sold under the label of another. Food was regarded as misbranded if its weight or measure was not plainly shown, as were drugs if their packages or labels bore false claims of their curative powers.[9]
4. Criminal sanctions were provided, with a fine of up to $200 for a first offense and $300 or one year in prison for subsequent offenses.
5. Forfeiture of adulterated or misbranded products upon their entry into interstate commerce was used as a remedy to prevent public injury.

The Food and Drug Act was, for the most part, largely ineffective. Its administration was hampered by inadequate congressional appropriations. Political pressure was placed on the Food and Drug Administration to weaken its enforcement of the law. It did have some successes, notably in barring the sale of dangerous products to the public, and in the area of product liability. Its remedies were weak. Fines were small, and juries were reluctant to convict local manufacturers.

The Food, Drug, and Cosmetics Act of 1938   The rationale for the passage of this act was a resurgence of public interest in consumer protection that developed during the Depression of the 1930s. A number of books were published that exposed various consumer abuses, including false or misleading advertising. The FDA itself exhibited products that it had seized. Filthy, decayed, and insect-infested food was displayed for the public to see. Pictures of women blinded, disfigured, or paralyzed from the use of patent medicine were shown. The catalyst for the passage of the Food, Drug, and Cosmetics Act occurred when almost one hundred persons were killed by consuming a product called Elixir Sulfanilamide that had been marketed without ever being tested for toxicity.

The Food, Drug, and Cosmetics Act expanded consumer protection in the following ways:

1. It enlarged the range of affected products to include cosmetics and therapeutic devices.
2. It broadened the definition of adulteration and misbranding. Food was defined as adulterated if it contained any poisonous or deleterious substances,

or if it was prepared under conditions that might result in contamination with filth or injury to health.

3. A food sold under another name had to be marked clearly as an imitation, and foods bearing proprietary names had to be labeled with the common or usual name of the product.

Drug Amendments of 1958 and 1962   The Food, Drug, and Cosmetics Act of 1938 was amended by the Delaney clause of 1958, which prohibits the addition to food of any substance known to produce cancer in any form, dosage, or under any set of circumstances.[10] The act was also amended in 1962 to extend the authority of the FDA, particularly in the area of drugs. The reason for this amendment came from hearings held in 1959 by the Senate Antitrust and Monopoly Subcommittee. It was argued that drug companies devoted inordinate time and research to the development of patented new drugs that represented only a minor modification of existing formulas. The companies would then exploit the patent protection through expensive promotion campaigns in which extravagant claims for these drugs were impressed on doctors and consumers.[11] Most drug innovations were characterized as socially wasteful.[12]

Thus, it was apparent that accurate information about new drugs would be provided only if the federal government regulated the manufacturers' claim of effectiveness. The primary feature of this amendment is that a manufacturer must prove to the satisfaction of the FDA that a drug must have the curative powers the manufacturer claims for it. No drug can be put on the market unless approved by the FDA, which can also remove a drug from the market if it has evidence that the drug carries a threat to health.

The Medical Device Amendment of 1976   Concern over medical devices, particularly the Dalkon Shield, led to this amendment to the Food, Drug, and Cosmetics Act of 1938. The Dalkon Shield was an Intra-Uterine Device (IUD) that was used for birth control.[13] It was a copper device shaped like a coil that was inserted into a woman's uterus. It caused a number of health problems among women, including infertility, scarring, and infection. This amendment gave the FDA the right to require premarket safety testing of medical devices. It exempted medical devices that had been on the market prior to its passage, including breast implants, which have created problems for some women. However, if the FDA believes an exempted product is dangerous, it can require manufacturers to prove its safety.

Other Food and Drug Laws   The Meat Inspection Act of 1907 was a companion to the Food and Drug Act of 1906. It prohibited the use of adulterants to hide meat decay or to color meat. It also provided that the Department of Agriculture must inspect the slaughtering, packing, and canning plants that ship meat in interstate commerce. The Wholesale Meat Inspection Act of 1967 amended the 1907 act. It is designed to force states to raise their inspection standards to those of the federal government. The Poultry Products Inspection Act of 1957 gave the Department of Agriculture the right to inspect poultry sold in interstate commerce. The Wholesale Poultry Act of 1968 offers federal government aid to the states so that they can establish their own inspection program. In drugs, the Public Health and Service Act of 1944 gave the FDA the authority to ensure the safety of vaccines, blood, serum, and other biological products. The Nutrition, Labeling, and Education Act of 1990 requires the agency to develop nutrition labeling for packaged food items, and the Generic Drug Enforcement Act of 1992 permits it to oversee the generic drug industry.

The Food and Drug Administration   The FDA is a regulatory agency that exists within the executive branch of government as a part of the Department of Health and Human Services. It possesses quasi-legislative and quasi-judicial powers, as all regulatory agencies do. The power to make rules and regulations has been delegated to these agencies by legislative fiat. The only important different between an agency rule and a law enacted by a legislative body is that the rule may be slightly more susceptible to attack because it was not made by elected officials. They can also implement policy or legislation through a process of initiating and settling cases. For many types of cases, the procedures are carefully outlined: Hearings are often prescribed, records are required, and so on. Furthermore, there are often elaborate provisions for judicial review.

All regulatory agencies, including the FDA, as agents of Congress, reflect group demands for positive action. They are not supposed to be judges like the courts; rather, they are supposed to be activists and initiate policy in accordance with their policy interests. For example, when the FDA ferrets out deceptive practices involving food, drugs, and cosmetics either through its own investigation or through information gained from an outside source, it initiates action in the name of the FDA against the party involved. It then adjudicates the very case it initiates. If the case reaches a formal hearing and goes to a hearing examiner for an initial decision, it is not at that point subject to FDA control. But after the examiner renders the decision, the FDA may reverse it. The result is that the FDA can control the decisions rendered in almost all the cases it initiates.

The FDA and Diet Pills   Many Americans resort to the use of diet pills as an easy way to lose weight, and numerous remedies are on the market. One such remedy is called Pondimin, the brand name for fenfluramine which was manufactured and sold by American Home Products and its subsidiary Wyeth-Ayers Laboratories. It also sold a companion drug called Redux. Fenfluramine had been sold since the 1970s but became widely used in the 1990s when doctors prescribed it in combination with phentermine. When taken alone, phentermine was never associated with health problems and it remains on the market.

However, in 1997 the FDA pushed for the withdrawal of Pondimin and Redux, citing a study that linked the drugs to potentially fatal health problems.

A 36-year-old woman named Debbie Lovett sued American Home Products and Wyeth-Ayers Laboratories over health problems she contended were caused by the drug she had taken for more than three months starting in October 1995. Her attorney argued before a jury that Lovett suffered from fatigue and shortness of breath and probably would need surgery to replace heart valves as her ailment progressed. Lawyers for American Home Products argued that Lovett was seeking compensation for a health condition she had before using the drug and said her weight was a bigger problem than the drug. A jury in Canton, Texas awarded her $23 million in damages, but a settlement was reached out of court.[14]

The Lovett lawsuit was only one of many brought against American Home Products, which agreed in January 2000 to pay up to $4.8 billion over 16 years to settle claims for more than three thousand consumers to took the weight-loss drug.[15] The agreement would establish a $1 billion fund for medical tests to check for heart damage for anybody who took the drug and to provide treatment if necessary. An addition $2.3 billion would be used to pay damages to those who now suffer or later develop moderate to severe heart-valve problems. Payment, based on age and severity of condition, would range from $500 to $1.4 million. Those with less severe problems could get more money later if their condition worsens. Lest we forget, up to $429 million would go to the plaintiffs' lawyers.

DISCLOSURE

A second area of government involvement in consumer protection is the various forms of disclosure such as advertising and product warranties. This area is rather broad, but generally the practices that come under its purview are covered by Section 5 of the Federal Trade Commission Act of 1914, which gives the FTC the right to prevent unfair competition practices, including those that affect consumers adversely. A rather common practice over the years has been false or misleading advertising. But advertising is only one area of the entire subject of disclosure. There are various product labeling requirements designed to protect consumers against misrepresentation and fraud. There are also laws designed to protect consumers against excessive credit charges. Finally, there are laws that cover the terms of consumer product warranties.

ADVERTISING

The rationale for advertising is that for markets to work effectively, buyers must have accurate information about the quality and the characteristics of products offered for sale. Otherwise, markets are unlikely to enable consumers to make purchases maximizing their welfare within the limits of their resources. As a result of the increases in the complexity and variety of products and the value of people's time, there has been a major shift from consumer to seller in the comparative advantages of supplying consumer product information. But this increased reliance on sellers for information about products does not mean the information provided will be truthful. A seller's general purpose is to provide information that, if believed, will induce consumers to buy this product in preference to other sellers' products.

The first demands for the control of advertising came at the turn of this century as a result of the false claims made by the many charlatans who populated the food and drug industries. Although the early postal laws were meant to deal with the wholesale distribution of false advertising by mail, it was not until 1914 when the Federal Trade Commission Act was passed that broad federal legal weapons against false or misleading advertising came into existence. As mentioned earlier, Section 5 of the act declared that unfair methods of competition in commerce were unlawful. Its intention went deep, for it authorized the FTC to proceed against various forms of antisocial business conduct over and above the unfair practices proscribed by the Sherman and Clayton Acts; for example, price-fixing and group buyouts.

The FTC did make up an attempt to prosecute consumer fraud, but the courts generally took the side of the advertiser. For example, in 1931, as mentioned in Chapter 6, the Supreme Court overturned an FTC ruling that Raladam, the manufacturer of Marmola, cease and desist from representing its product as a remedy for obesity. The Court found misrepresentation common among vendors of such nostrums and concluded that no damage had been done to Raladam's competitors.[16] The Court held that in the absence of proof to such an effect, the FTC could not act against consumer fraud. This decision led to proposals to amend the original Federal Trade Commission Act, which eventually led to the passage by Congress of the Wheeler-Lea Amendment of 1938.

The Wheeler-Lea Amendment   A Supreme Court justice once said about pornography that he couldn't define it, but he would know it if he saw it. The same can be said for deceptive advertising. The legal definitions of deceptive advertising are rather abstruse. The Federal Trade Commission Act contains a general prohibition of deceptive advertising and a definition of false advertising that makes clear that false representations are illegal and that failure to disclose material facts can be illegal. The FTC has used the following criteria in determining whether an advertisement is illegal.[17] An advertisement is illegal if:

1. it deceives a significant number of customers;
2. a false presentation or omission relates to facts important to consumers in their purchasing decisions, and
3. a false implication relates to facts that consumers use in their purchasing decisions.

Deceptive advertising can be harmful to the public interest for two reasons.[18] First, it harms consumers by causing them to have false beliefs about the nature of the products being advertised and thereby causes consumers to make different purchasing decisions from those they otherwise would have made. For example, a consumer may buy Product A because it promises to make him or her a better athlete, even though Product B is the better product. Second, it can be argued that, apart from its immediate bad consequences, deceptive advertising can lower the general level of trust essential to the proper functioning of a free market economy. Consequently, there is a strong feeling against deception even though it does no immediate harm.

Enforcement Procedure   The FTC has one standard procedure by which it can act to prevent deceptive practices such as false or misleading advertising. It can make a formal complaint against a company engaged in deceptive practices. The company, which is the respondent or accused party, is given an opportunity to enter into a consent settlement without formal litigation. If the respondent decides to contest the complaint, the matter is set for trial before an administrative law judge or hearing examiner, appointed by the FTC. The Commission and the respondent each are represented by their own attorneys. At the conclusion of the hearings, the judge issues his or her findings and an initial decision which, if it goes against the prosecution, can be appealed to the full commission. The respondent can also appeal if the decision is against him or her.

Sweepstakes Advertising   Getting rich is an integral part of the American dream, and since the founding of our country, there have been many ways in which Americans have tried to do it. One way was to trade whiskey to the Native Americans for valuable furs which could be sold in Europe. Another way was to prospect for gold, first in California and then in Alaska. This required very hard work, and few people struck it rich. But as America became prosperous, more civilized ways developed to make a person wealthy. One way was to speculate in the stock market, but the problem is that you have to put up your own money with the risk that the stock market can crash. One can also play the lottery for a dollar or two. Then there are sweepstakes, such as the ones sponsored by the American Family Publishers and Publishers Clearing House. These sweepstakes sponsors send out form letters insinuating that the recipients of the letters have won the grand prize; never mind that approximately 200 million such letters are sent out with each mailing.[19] Moreover, as Table 7-1 (on page 126) indicates, the chances of winning are very remote.

Sweepstakes, particularly the ones run by American Family Publishers and Publishers Clearing House, have come under fire, and rightfully so, because their mailings are very misleading. The fine print is hard to find, and many people assume they have won.[20] In fact, over a two-year period a Virginia man won $1 million, $3.5 million, $5 million, and $11.2 million from Publishers Clearing House. At least, that is what the letter said. The only problem was that

TABLE 7-1   WHAT ARE THE ODDS?

Winning the American Family Publishers $11 million sweepstakes	1 in 150,000,000
Winning powerball	1 in 80,089,128
Winning the Publishers Clearing House $10 million sweepstakes	1 in 50,000,000
Winning the Virginia "Lotto"	1 in 7,059,057
Winning the Maryland "Lotto"	1 in 7,000,000
Dying in a fireworks accident	1 in 1,733,250
Getting a royal flush in five-card poker	1 in 649,739
Dying from snake or spider bites	1 in 216,656
Dying in an airplane crash	1 in 4,073

the money never materialized. There is also the inference that your chances are enhanced if you buy the magazines the publishers push. Some thirty-two states and the District of Columbia have initiated class-action suits against American Family Publishers, and twenty-six states have initiated class-action suits against Publishers Clearing House. On March 2, 2000 a settlement was reached whereby American Family Publishers agreed to pay $1.23 million in damages.[21] In New York the company agreed to pay $60 each to 12,000 New Yorkers who bought the magazines believing that would enhance their chances of winning.

Criticisms of Advertising   Advertising has been criticized for several reasons. First, it relies on psychological needs that play on human emotion rather than reason. An example would be alcohol and cigarette advertising that play on a person's desire to feel grown-up or to fit in. However, both contain powerful addictive drugs, which are a source of pleasure but also can damage one's health. Other ads play on the desire to achieve economic and social status. Second, children are also influenced by advertising to consume certain products that can be harmful. They are often led to consume a product because some sports hero or movie star endorses it.[22] Sometimes it can be a fictitious character such as Joe Camel, who is supposedly as recognizable as Mickey Mouse to children under the age of ten. The ad, which was sponsored by R.J. Reynolds, portrayed a hip camel with a baseball cap on backwards and a cigarette hanging out of his mouth. The implication was that it is cool to smoke.

LABELING

Labeling of products is the second area of disclosure. It is designed to protect consumers from product misrepresentation. An example would be the claim by a clothing manufacturer that its men's suits are 100 percent wool when they are not. In 1939 Congress passed the Wool Products Labeling Act that requires that most products containing wool must show on the label the percentage of wool and other fibers used. The Fur Products Labeling Act of 1951 was passed to protect consumers against the mislabeling of furs, such as rabbit fur being called mink. Manufacturers are required to attach labels to a garment showing the true name of the animal that produced the fur and indicating whether the fur is bleached or dyed. The Textile Fiber Products Identification Act of 1958, which covers the labeling of textiles and fibers, protects consumers by requiring a disclosure on the label and in advertising of the exact fiber contents of all textile fibers other than wool marketed in interstate commerce.

Other Labeling Laws The Flammable Fabrics Act of 1954 was passed as a result of deaths that had occurred when clothes, such as evening gowns, caught on fire.[23] The act requires that clothing labels contain notice that the product is highly flammable. Then there is the Cigarette Labeling and Advertising Act of 1965, which requires that cigarettes sold in interstate commerce be packaged and labeled with the warning that cigarettes can be injurious to health. The Poison Prevention Act of 1970 is designed to keep unsafe products from being used by children. Some drugs may also be required to carry the notice that their use may be habit-forming. Still other drugs must state on their label that they are not to be taken by pregnant women without first consulting a physician.

CREDIT

In the old days, Americans were accustomed to putting aside sufficient savings in order to purchase homes, cars, appliances, clothes, and vacations. But all that began to change in the 1920s when charge accounts were introduced by companies such as Sears Roebuck and Montgomery Ward. Credit cards were introduced in the 1960s and 1970s, so Americans no longer had to postpone self-gratification. Just about anything could be purchased by using credit cards. Banks, to remain competitive, also made credit easier to obtain. However, consumer information as to the terms of credit was incomplete, so it was difficult to make a rational choice between various alternative forms of loans. Today, most consumers are constantly bombarded by advertisements from banks and other lending institutions for credit cards that supposedly offer a low interest rate.

For many years, state laws regulated consumer credit activities. But the lack of uniformity among such laws, coupled with the need to protect consumers against fraudulent or unfair practices, led to the enactment of a number of federal laws. One of the most significant of these laws is the Consumer Credit Protection Act, more commonly known as the Truth-in-Lending Act (TILA), which was passed in 1968.

Truth-in-Lending Act (TILA) of 1968   TILA is a disclosure law designed to force creditors to inform consumers of the actual cost of credit. It requires that lenders disclose to borrowers basic information about the cost and terms of credit by providing every borrower with a separate disclosure statement. It regulates transactions in which a borrower puts up his or her home as collateral. A purpose of credit disclosure is to encourage competition in financing by making borrowers more aware of specific charges and other relevant credit information, thus enabling them to shop for the most favorable terms of credit. TILA also prohibits the issuance of a credit card except in response to an oral or written agreement.

Fair Credit Reporting Act of 1970   The Fair Credit Reporting Act requires consumer reporting companies to provide consumers with information in his or her file to verify whether the credit is accurate or inaccurate. The purpose of the act is to protect the privacy of consumers against the issuance of credit reports that may contain erroneous information. It expressly obligates every consumer reporting agency to report only accurate and up-to-date information to creditors who would seek information about the creditworthiness of consumers. Anyone seeking this credit information must identify themselves and certify the purpose for which they are seeking this information.

Fair Debt Collection Practices Act of 1977   This act limits the ways in which a debt collector can deal with a debtor. Overt force or other forms of coercion were often used to force debtors to pay their debts. The act limits the ways in which the debt collector can communicate with a debtor. The collector cannot communicate with the debtor at the debtor's place of employment where such communication is prohibited by the employer. The debt collector can only communicate with the debtor during certain hours of the day.[24] The act permits the cessation of communications between the debt collector and debtor if the latter in writing notifies the collector that he or she refused to pay the debt.

The Credit Card Disclosure Act of 1988   This act requires banks, department stores, and other issuers of credit cards to disclose clearly their interest rates, fees, method of calculating interest charges, and the grace period before interest charges begin to accrue. The act specifically aims at bulk mail credit card solicitations to potential consumers that do not disclose application fees. The act makes it easier for consumers to shop around for lower interest rates.

WARRANTIES

A warranty under common law is a promise that affirms a fact or makes an affirmation related to the goods being sold. Since a warranty involves a promise, it becomes part of a contract.[25] Warranties are of two types—expressed and implied. An express warranty can be given only by the seller. For example, any affirmation of a fact or a promise that relates to the goods creates an express warranty that the goods will match the fact or the promise. An implied warranty is automatically present in the contract unless it is surrendered by the buyer or excluded by the seller. An example of an implied warranty is a warranty of title by the seller. This ensures the buyer that no one can assert a hidden claim to the goods that is superior to the claims of the buyer.

The Consumer Product Warranty Act of 1975   This act was passed because consumers had become increasingly dissatisfied with product warranties, and had to resort to the courts for redress. Generally, this dissatisfaction centered on such problems as the purchase of a product that turned out to be a "lemon," delays in making repairs, excessive labor charges, the failure of companies to honor guarantees, unscrupulous service operators, and consumers' total lack of power to enforce compliance. The act's major provisions may be divided into two categories, which are as follows:

1. The first category pertains to consumer warranty provisions. To increase the product information available to consumers, prevent deception, and promote competition in the marketplace, any warrantor offering a written warranty must disclose the terms of the warranty in easily understood language.
2. The second category extended the Federal Trade Commissions' consumer protection powers to prescribe rules and regulations for deceptive practices. It was given the authority to move against local consumer abuses when state or local protection agencies were ineffectual. With respect to defective warranties, the FTC was given the power to seek injunctions against offenders and to represent itself in litigation. In addition, the FTC can initiate civil suits against offenders that knowingly engage in an act or practice determined to be unfair or deceptive.

THE FEDERAL TRADE COMMISSION

The Federal Trade Commission Act of 1914, as mentioned in Chapter 6, created the Federal Trade Commission, an independent regulatory agency consisting of five members, each holding office for seven years. Section 5 of the act empowers the FTC to prevent unfair methods of competition and unfair or deceptive acts or practices in or affecting commerce. Originally, Section 5 was used to stop practices before they developed into violations of the antitrust laws. However, it has been interpreted to go further than the antitrust laws do to reach unfair business practices, whether or not they have an impact on competition. The current aim of the FTC's enforcement activities under Section 5 is both to protect fair competition and to assure that the consumer is not subjected to unfair or deceptive practices, without regard to their effect on competition. The responsibilities of the FTC can be broken down into two main categories—antitrust and unfair and deceptive business practices. The FTC is responsible for enforcing the following antitrust laws:

<u>Antitrust Laws</u>

1. The Clayton Act of 1914, specifically Section 2, which pertains to price discrimination; Section 3, which prohibits the use of tying contracts and exclusive dealership arrangements when they lessen competition; Section 7, which pertains to mergers and acquisitions; and Section 8, which pertains to interlocking directorates.
2. The Robinson-Patman Act of 1936, which amended Section 2 of the Clayton Act.
3. The Celler-Kefauver Act of 1950, which amended Section 7 of the Clayton Act.
4. The Hart-Scott-Rodino Antitrust Improvements Act of 1976, which requires advance notice of proposed mergers.

The FTC is responsible for monitoring unfair and deceptive business practices in the following areas:

<u>Unfair and Deceptive Practices</u>

Advertising

1. The Wheeler-Lea Amendment to the Clayton Act, 1938

Labeling

1. The Wool Products Labeling Act of 1940
2. The Fur Products Labeling Act of 1951
3. The Textile Fibers and Product Identification Act of 1958
4. The Cigarette Labeling and Advertising Act of 1965
5. The Fair Packaging and Labeling Act of 1966

Credit

1. The Truth-in-Lending Act of 1968
2. The Fair Credit Reporting Act of 1970
3. The Fair Debt and Collection Practices Act of 1977
4. The Credit Card Disclosure Act of 1988

Warranties

1. The Consumer Product Warranty Act of 1975

PRODUCT SAFETY

Until the 1960s, national product safety legislation consisted of isolated statutes designed to remedy specific hazards existing in a narrow range of product categories. Moreover, enforcement authority was divided among a number of federal agencies. For example, the Flammable Fabrics Act of 1953 was passed after serious injuries and deaths had resulted from the ignition of clothes made from synthetic fibers. Enforcement measures by the FDA include cease-and-desist orders, seizures of offending goods, and criminal penalties of a year's imprisonment, or fines of up to $5,000 for willful violations. Tests of flammability are established by the Bureau of Standards.

Other examples of product safety laws and the agencies responsible for their enforcement are as follows:

1. The Federal Hazardous Substances Labeling Act of 1960 mandates warnings on the labels of potentially hazardous substances such as cleansing agents and paint removers. This act is administered by the Food and Drug Administration.
2. The Child Protection Act of 1966, also administered by the Food and Drug Administration, prevents the marketing of potentially harmful toys.
3. The National Traffic and Motor Vehicle Safety Act of 1966 concerns automobiles that include such features as an impact-absorbing steering wheel and column, safety latches and hinges, safety glass, and impact-resistant gasoline tanks and connections. This act comes under the jurisdiction of the National Highway Traffic Safety Administration. Tires must be labeled with the name of the manufacturer or retreader and with certain safety information, including the maximum permissible load for the tire.
4. The Public Health Smoking Act of 1970 extends warnings about the hazards of cigarette smoking, and the Poison Prevention Packaging Act of the same year authorized the standards for child-resistant packaging of hazardous substances.

THE CONSUMER PRODUCT SAFETY ACT OF 1972

One of the most important laws to be passed in a long time is the Consumer Product Safety Act. Fragmentation of legislation and generally ineffective controls over product hazards prompted the federal government to introduce new product safety legislation to protect the consumer. The act was a result of congressional findings that unsafe consumer products were widely distributed, and hence consumers were frequently unable to anticipate and guard against the risks entailed in their use. Findings before the Senate Committee on Commerce indicated that more than 20 million people were injured by consumer products annually.[26] Of that total, 110,000 people were permanently disabled, and 30,000 lost their lives. The annual cost to consumers was around $5.5 billion. It was estimated that 20 percent of those injuries could have been prevented if the manufacturers had produced safe, well-designed products.

The origins of the Consumer Products Safety Act are in the common law in that the manufacturer or seller is liable for injuries to a buyer or others caused by a defective or hazardous product. The common law imposes liability on a broad group of people involved in the marketing process, including suppliers, wholesalers, and retailers. Liability is assumed for injuries to the consumer when the results of such injury are reasonably foreseeable, regardless of whether the product itself is dangerous or harmful. A consumer need not prove that a manufacturer was guilty of negligence.

Provisions of the Consumer Product Safety Act   The Consumer Product Safety Act is broad in scope and affects those consumer products not already regulated by the federal government. When compared to earlier consumer-oriented legislation, the act not only possesses more effective legal and administrative sanctions, but also allows application of safety standards. Its basic provisions are as follows:

1. It created a five-member Consumer Product Safety Commission that functions as an independent regulatory agency. A major function of the Commission is the gathering and dissemination of information related to product injuries. In addition, the Commission was empowered to create an advisory council of fifteen members to provide information on product safety.
2. Section 14 of the act requires manufacturers to conduct a testing program to assure their products conform to established safety standards. After the products are tested, a manufacturer must provide distributors or retailers with a certificate stating that all applicable consumer product safety standards have been met. Section 14 also holds the manufacturer accountable for knowing all safety criteria applicable to the product and requires that safety standards be described in detail.
3. The Consumer Product Safety Commission also can require the use of specific labels that set forth the results of product testing. This requirement has a significant impact on the production process in which the design of new products must conform to federal safety standards that are formulated at various governmental and independent testing stations.
4. Section 15 requires a manufacturer to take corrective steps if he or she becomes aware that a product either fails to comply with an applicable consumer product safety rule or contains a defect that could create a substantial product hazard. The manufacturer has to inform the CPSC of the defect. If, after investigation, the Commission determines that a product hazard exists, the manufacturer—or distributor or retailer, for that matter—may be required to publicize the information to consumers.

In addition to the Consumer Product Safety Act, the Consumer Product Safety Commission is responsible for the administration of the following acts:

1. The Flammable Fabrics Labeling Act of 1954
2. The Refrigerator Safety Act of 1956
3. The Hazardous Substance Act of 1964
4. The Poison Prevention Packaging Act of 1970

AUTOMOBILE SAFETY REGULATION

Before the 1960s the automobile industry was largely unregulated. However, this changed dramatically during the 1960s when Ralph Nader wrote his book, *Unsafe at Any Speed,*[27] which dealt with what he called dangerous designs in American cars, particularly the Corvair produced by General Motors. Helped by General Motors' response, which was to hire investigators to find damaging evidence against him, Nader became the leader in a consumer movement that catalyzed around a demand for safer cars. Federal safety standards promulgated in the 1960s involved accident avoidance, crash protection, and postcrash survivability. Accident avoidance standards were set for braking systems, tires, windshields, lamps, and transmission controls. Occupant protection standards included requirements for seat belts, head restraints, and high-penetration resistant windshield glass. Exterior protection standards included the absorption capacity of front and rear bumpers. These and other standards are presented in Table 7-2.

THE NATIONAL HIGHWAY TRAFFIC SAFETY ADMINISTRATION

The National Highway Traffic Safety Administration (NHTSA) was created in 1966 to set safety standards for automobiles and other types of motor vehicles. It has the authority to establish minimum safety standards for automobiles, trucks, and their accessories. It also has the right to set standards for fuel economy and emissions, and it regulates the safety and performance of new and used automobiles and trucks. It has initiated such safety features as air bags, safety belts, collapsible steering columns, and penetration-resistant windshields, and it has the power to order the recall of defective products. It administers state and local community grant programs, and it conducts research and development of new automobile safety techniques.

Costs of Automobile Safety Standards   Using the automobile industry as an example, there are both costs and benefits of safety standards. The costs of safety standards are the original cost of meeting them as well as the costs of

TABLE 7-2   SAFETY STANDARDS FOR PASSENGER CARS

STANDARD	EFFECTIVE DATE
Occupant protection in interior impact	1968
Door locks	1968
Impact protection for driver from steering control	1968
Seat belt assemblies	1968
Windshield wiping system	1968
Head restraints	1969
Child seating system	1971
Flammability of interior materials	1972
Side door strength	1972
Roof crash resistance	1973

Source: Robert W. Crandall, Howard K. Gruenspecht, Theodore E. Keeler, and Lester B. Lave, *Regulating the Automobile* (Washington, D.C.: The Brookings Institution, 1986), p. 47.

complying with them after the companies have had sufficient time to redesign the vehicles to accommodate the standards at the lowest cost.[28] There
is the cost of variable inputs required to produce such safety devices as seat
belts, padded dashboards, and other interior protection devices. There is also
the cost of external production devices, including the installation of safer,
more durable bumpers. An important part of safety standards cost is the fuel
penalty that motorists have to pay as a result of the weight added to cars,
which is due in part to bumper standards.

The automobile industry had to meet additional safety standards by 1999.
Dual air bags were required. An anti-lock brake system that would keep cars
from skidding had been proposed. Beginning with 1997 models, all cars had
to have stronger side guards that required thicker padding. More roof padding
was required to provide head protection. Cleaner exhaust had been mandated. Already, government regulations had eliminated 95 percent of pollutants out of car exhaust. However, catalytic converters that clean exhaust do
not work until they get hot. Cold-start pollution had to be cut beginning with
1996 car models. This required the introduction of either a preheated catalyst or a converter.

Benefits of Automobile Safety Standards   Benefits accrue to persons and to
society as a whole as a result of safety standards. One obvious benefit is the
reduction in the number of injuries and fatalities caused by automobiles and
other forms of auto-related accidents. There has been a reduction in the number of highway fatalities even though the population of the United States
today is larger than it was when most of these safety standards were implemented. The reductions can be attributed in part to improved safety standards for automobiles, but also in part to other factors such as driver education
and the 55-mile-per-hour speed limits.[29]

Table 7-3 presents deaths and death rates from motor vehicle accidents
for selected time periods.

PRODUCT LIABILITY

The United States is a litigious society, which explains why it has more lawyers
than the rest of the world combined. One area of litigation is product liability, which is a part of tort law. This field of the law is concerned with com-
pensating one person for harm caused by the wrongful conduct of another.
Courts impose monetary liability on firms whose products have caused personal injury. Liability originally depended on showing that a firm had acted
negligently, which meant it had failed to exercise that degree of due care as
would be reasonably expected in similar circumstances. However, liability
has become stricter in that the fault or negligence of the manufacturer is irrelevant; it is now imposed if the product is defective and the defect is unexpected by the consumer and causes injury.

TABLE 7-3   DEATHS AND DEATH RATES FROM MOTOR VEHICLE ACCIDENTS, 1970–1996

YEAR	NUMBER OF DEATHS	RATE PER 100,000 POPULATION
1970	54,633	26.9
1980	53,172	23.5
1990	46,814	18.8
1991	43,536	17.3
1992	40,982	16.1
1994	42,524	16.3
1995	43,363	16.5
1996	43,649	16.5

Source: *Statistical Abstract of the United States 1999* (Washington, D.C.: U.S. Government Printing Office, 1999), p. 106.

MACPHERSON V. BUICK MOTOR COMPANY

Prior to this landmark case, privity of contract governed the relationships between buyer and seller. It meant that a plaintiff could sue only when he or she had a legally binding contract with the defendant. Thus, if a manufacturer caused the product defect, the consumer had no right to recovery because the consumer's contract was with the retailer, not the manufacturer. *MacPherson v. Buick* changed all this.[30] MacPherson, the owner of a Buick automobile, was injured when a defective spoke in a wheel broke when he was driving. He sued the company but it denied responsibility for two reasons. First, it had not produced the wheel, but had purchased it from a supplier; so if liability is attached to the defect in the wheel, the supplier should be the liable party. Second, Buick claimed lack of privity in that MacPherson had purchased the car from a dealer, not from Buick.

However, Buick's arguments were rejected by the Court. The decision ended the privity of contract requirement in product liability cases. Regardless of any contractual obligations, the Court held the manufacturer liable for injuries caused by its product. After this decision, product liability became a subset of tort law rather than contract law. The significance of the case is that plaintiffs in a suit can go directly to the manufacturer and bypass any intermediary, such as a retailer or wholesaler. They have to prove fault, which means that adequate warnings or reasonable safety features have not been provided.

Each year thousands of Americans sue manufacturers in a broad array of industries, alleging they were injured by unreasonably dangerous products including asbestos, drugs, medical devices, cars and trucks, toxic chemicals, and toys. Almost all plaintiffs settle out of court. Of the small proportion who go to trial, more than half win damage awards—multimillion dollar sums in a few cases. Nevertheless, the whole process can be expensive. In total, U.S. injury claims cost $152 billion in 1994. The U.S. tort system is the most expensive in the world. As a percentage of GDP, it takes up 2.2 percent, two and one-half times the average of industrial countries. Of every dollar awarded by the courts, less than half goes to victims.[31] It can prove to be very expensive to business firms. Insurance rates go up and bankruptcy can result.

TORT LAW

Product liability is a part of tort law, which is concerned with a body of private wrongs. Tort law has evolved over hundreds of years to support the protection of an individual's rights with respect to persons and property. In addition, tort law is based on common law and, consequently, the rules vary from state to state. There are three areas of tort law—intentional tort, negligence, and strict liability. An example of an intentional tort would be physical assault by one person against another person. Negligence would involve a careless act that injures a person. An example would be leaving a pair of roller skates on a sidewalk where someone might trip over them. Strict liability carries negligence one step further. An example would be someone undertaking a hazardous activity by which it is foreseeable that injury can result.

Negligence   Many product liability suits, including the aforementioned landmark case of *MacPherson v. Buick*, are based on negligence. Negligence can be said to exist when certain conditions are met, one of which is foreseeability, which addresses the likelihood that something will happen in the future. Second, there must be causation. When an injured person alleges negligence in a product liability damage suit, there must be a close causal relationship between the negligence and the injury. For example, in *MacPherson v. Buick*, a judge held the Buick Motor Company liable for the defective wooden spoke that caused the accident because it was negligent when it had not properly inspected the wheel before it was put on the car. However, if a plaintiff has not been harmed, the defendant is not liable.

Strict Liability   Strict liability is liability for an action simply because it occurred, not because it is the fault of the person who must pay. For example, a person builds a dam with the intent of creating a fish pond. The dam breaks and the water floods a neighbor's property, causing extensive damage. The person who built the dam is liable. Business firms can be held liable for defects even though they may have been unaware of their existence at the time their products were produced. This was the case in *MacPherson v. Buick*. They are also liable for failure to warn consumers of a known danger commonly faced when using a product. The application of strict liability varies from state to state and from court to court.

Compensatory and Punitive Damages   What is the basis for damage awards in a tort law suit? There are two types of damages—compensatory and punitive. The most common type of damage is compensatory damage, which is a sum of money that will place a person in the same economic position that he or she would have attained had the contract been performed. An injured person may recover only the damages that he or she could reasonably foresee. Punitive damage is damage that a court may award in order to deter the defendant from further wrongdoing. The following case involves the use of compensatory and punitive damages. As the case indicates, states differ in their application of tort law to damage awards. Some states place a cap on the amount of money that can be awarded in punitive damages, while other states do not.

BMW OF NORTH AMERICA INC. V. IRA GORE JR.[32]

In January 1990, Dr. Ira Gore Jr. purchased a black BMW sports sedan for $40,750.88 from a BMW dealer in Birmingham, Alabama. After driving the car for approximately nine months, and without noticing any flaws in its appearance, Dr. Gore took the car to "Slick Finish," an independent detailer, to make the car look "snazzier than it normally would appear." Mr. Slick, the proprietor, detected evidence that the car had been repainted. Convinced that he had been cheated, Dr. Gore brought suit against BMW of North America, the American distributor of BMW automobiles, the German manufacturer, and the Birmingham BMW dealership. He asked for $500,000 in compensatory damages.

At trial BMW acknowledged that it had adopted a nationwide policy in 1983 concerning cars that were damaged in the course of manufacturing or transportation. The top, hood, trunk, and quarter panels of Dr. Gore's car had been repainted at BMW's preparation center at Brunswick, Georgia. The damage to the car had been caused by exposure to acid rain during the transit from the manufacturing plant in Munich, Germany, to the preparation center in Brunswick, Georgia. BMW's policy was that if the cost of repairing the damaged exceeded 3 percent of the car's suggested retail price, the car was placed in company service for a period of time and then sold as used. If the repair cost did not exceed 3 percent of the suggested retail price, the car was sold as new without advising a dealer that any repairs had been made. The cost of repairing Dr. Gore's car was $601.37, or 1.5 percent of the purchase price.

A jury returned a verdict finding BMW and the Birmingham dealership liable for compensatory damages of $4,000 and assessed an additional $4 million in punitive damages.[33] BMW filed a posttrial motion to set aside the punitive damages award. It argued that its disclosure policy was consistent with the laws of thirty-five states defining the disclosure obligations of car manufacturers. It also argued that its disclosure policy had never been adjudged unlawful before this case was filed. The motion was denied, BMW then appealed to the Alabama Supreme Court, which reduced the punitive damage award to $2 million. It found that the amount of punitive damage had been improperly computed because similar sales in the other states involved different jurisdictions.[34]

The case was then appealed to the U.S. Supreme Court, which ruled that the two million punitive damage award was excessive. The court was concerned that BMW was being punished for an activity which was lawful in other states. It held that an award of punitive damages can be grossly excessive. It then set three guidelines by which reviewing courts could determine whether puni-tive damages were excessive. The first guideline is the degree of reprehensibil-ity of the defendant's conduct.[35] The second guideline is the ratio between the plaintiff's award of compensatory damages and the amount of the punitive damages. The third guideline is the difference between the punitive damage award and civil or criminal sanctions that could have been used. The court found that BMW's conduct was not sufficiently reprehensible to justify such a large award, and the punitive damage was five hundred times the amount of the compensatory damage. The case was remanded to the Alabama Supreme Court, and Gore was awarded $50,000.

THE TOBACCO INDUSTRY

The tobacco industry is the most maligned industry in the United States. It is held responsible for the deaths of some 400,000 Americans annually, mainly from lung cancer, emphysema, strokes, and heart disease. It is also held re-sponsible for targeting children through advertising designed to make smoking appear attractive and sophisticated. An example was the Joe Camel ads spon-sored by R.J. Reynolds. Tobacco company executives are accused of willfully lying to a Congressional subcommittee which was investigating the impact of smoking on children. They are accused of withholding documents and claim-ing that cigarette smoking is not addictive. Finally, various company documents placed on line have revealed incriminating evidence including that companies have boosted their sales by enhancing their cigarettes' nicotine levels. Other rev-elations are as follows:[36]

1. Cigarette marketers tracked the smoking habits of customers as young as 13. A Philip Morris memo in 1979 showed that Marlboro dominates the 17 and younger market.
2. The creator of R.J. Reynolds' Joe Camel campaign in 1988 termed it a drawback that the cartoon would attract children, but the campaign con-tinued.
3. In contrast to the public position of tobacco executives that there was no proof that smoking caused disease or that nicotine was addictive, industry scientists privately believed otherwise. In 1961, the research director of Philip Morris stated carcinogens are found in practically every class of com-pounds in smoke.
4. A strategy proposed at a 1981 industry-wide meeting of lawyers was the prevention of the government from learning about poisonous cigarette ad-ditives by keeping tests in company hands where could be easily destroyed.

CHARACTERISTICS OF THE TOBACCO INDUSTRY

The tobacco industry is an oligopolistic industry dominated by Philip Morris and R.J. Reynolds, which supply 72 percent of the cigarettes sold in the Unit-ed States. Both are multinational conglomerates. In 1999 Philip Morris was the ninth largest American company, with total sales of $61.7 billion and a profit of $7.7 billion.[37] Its Marlboro brand is the most popular cigarette in the world. Although tobacco is its most important product in terms of sales and profits, it produces a wide variety of products ranging from breakfast foods to candy. R.J. Reynolds is the second largest producer of cigarettes in the United States. It, too, is a multinational conglomerate. In 1999 RJR Nabisco's total sales consisted of $11.4 billion and its loss amounted to $2.3 billion.[38]

In 1997, there were 61 million smokers in the United States, of whom 4.5 million were between the ages of twelve and seventeen.[39] Although the percentage of Americans who smoke is declining, there are more than a billion cigarette smokers in the world, and the number is growing. Cigarette sales internationally are growing at the rate of 3 percent to 5 percent a year. China is the single largest market for cigarettes, and Marlboro is the most popular cigarette. Ninety percent of Chinese smokers are men. Cigarette consumption is also high in Japan and other East Asian countries. In the Russian Federation and countries that were also formerly a part of the Soviet Union, cigarette consumption was high under communism and remains high, with Marlboro remaining the most important cigarette.

Tobacco companies do not compete against each other in terms of price competition. Instead, they practice product differentiation through advertising. One seller, in an attempt to gain a competitive advantage over its rivals, will make claims about its product to differentiate it from other products. Philip Morris enjoyed enormous success through the use of its Marlboro Man advertisements, which introduced an element of machismo in smoking. The Joe Camel ads enabled Reynolds to double its market share of Camel cigarettes. By and large, only the largest firms in an oligopolistic industry can afford the high cost of advertising. In 1997 Philip Morris and Reynolds spent $5 billion on advertising and other forms of promotion.[40]

PRODUCT LIABILITY SUITS

The tobacco companies have had a good record of winning product liability suits. Very few plaintiffs won their cases. Lawyers for the tobacco companies have argued that smoking is a matter of choice, which is a basic consumer right in a market economy. As consumers, we are free to smoke or not to smoke. Second, they have argued that Congress preempted the entire field of cigarette information under the 1965 Cigarette Labeling and Advertising Act and the subsequent Public Health Smoking Act of 1970. A third defense is comparable fault in product liability. The comparable fault doctrine looks at the plaintiff's conduct in determining the extent to which he or she has caused his or her harm. It is expected that consumers are aware of risk when it comes to smoking.

TOBACCO SETTLEMENTS

Public sentiment has turned against the tobacco industry and has led individuals and states to initiate lawsuits against the industry. Some forty states filed lawsuits, with the intent of making the industry pay for medical expenses they have incurred in treating tobacco smokers. Tobacco settlements were reached with Florida, Minnesota, Mississippi, and Texas. Florida settled for $11.3 billion, which is supposed to compensate it for the cost of treating smokers in state-supported hospitals. In addition to the settlement, the tobacco industry also agreed to pull down all of its billboards within six months, starting with signs within 1000 feet of schools. Vending machines where children have access to cigarettes are to be removed, and also outdoor advertising in sports arenas and on mass transit conveyances.

On Friday, November 21, 1998, the tobacco industry agreed to a $206 billion settlement of all state lawsuits pending against it.[41] The settlement, agreed to by forty-six states and the District of Columbia, will not impose mandatory price increases on cigarettes, grant the Food and Drug Administration (FDA) broad regulatory authority over tobacco products,[42] and impose financial penalties if smoking by teenagers does not decline by a specific time period. The settlement would limit, but not abolish, the use of cartoons and human figures from cigarette ads, and it would also limit, but not abolish, sponsorship of sporting events such as NASCAR racing. It would not provide broad protection from individual and class-action lawsuits, including one that was underway in Florida, and it will be paid primarily by smokers who will have to pay more for tobacco products.

By no means are the problems of the tobacco industry over. If anything, they are getting worse. There are individual and class-action suits against the industry.[43] On July 7, 1999, a Florida jury ruled against the tobacco industry in the first class-action suit to be brought by sick smokers to come to trial. The jury concluded that cigarette makers addicted and defrauded customers by concealing the dangers of cigarette smoking and making a product that caused more than one dozen deadly diseases, ranging from heart disease to cancer. The defendants are the five largest tobacco companies—Philip Morris, R.J. Reynolds, Brown & Williamson, Lorillard Tobacco, and the Liggett Group.

On July 14, 2000, the Florida jury handed down the largest punitive damage award in the history of the United States, ordering the tobacco industry to pay $145 billion to approximately five hundred thousand Florida smokers who suffer from diseases related to cigarette smoking. (The largest previous award was $5 billion against Exxon in 1994 for the Exxon Valdez oil spill. That award is still under appeal.) To put things in perspective, the award, if it stands, is larger than the GNPs of Portugal or Greece. Philip Morris, which sells half of the twenty billion packs of cigarettes sold annually in the United States, was ordered to pay $73.9 billion of the award. The remainder of the award payment was distributed as follows: R.J. Reynolds $36.3 billion, Brown & Williamson $17.6 billion, Lorillard Tobacco $16.3 billion, and the Liggett Group $790 million. Lawyers will receive approximately one-third of the total award.

There are several important points to discuss: The first is the appeals process, which could take many years before a final settlement is reached. Second, punitive damage awards are generally reduced by the higher courts (see the *Gore* case on pages 137–138). Third, what implications will this settlement have on the $246 billion settlement already reached between the industry and the forty-some states involved (money that state legislatures have been eagerly spending on projects that usually have nothing to do with the prevention of teenage smoking)? Finally, there is the question of whether or not the award will bankrupt the tobacco industry as their lawyers claim. (The stock market generally reacted with indifference when the damage award was announced.) The companies have been diversifying, and much of their earnings come from abroad.

SUMMARY

One of the fundamental tenets supporting a market economy is consumer sovereignty, which is based on the idea that ultimate decisions as to what will be produced rest with the consumer. This presumes that consumers have the information necessary to make rational choices in the marketplace. If this is true, consumer expenditures guide resource allocation into chosen products. But in a complex modern society, it is difficult for consumers to have the expertise necessary to distinguish among many products. In addition, consumers are led by advertising to make product choices on the basis of subjective factors. Therefore, laws have been passed to protect consumers against those practices considered harmful to their interests. These laws cover a wide variety of areas ranging from pure food and drug laws to disclosures on credit and warranties on products sold to the public. Tort law also pertains to consumer protection.

QUESTIONS FOR DISCUSSION

1. What is meant by consumer sovereignty? Are consumers really sovereign?
2. What is considered false or deceptive advertising?
3. There are costs as well as benefits in consumer protection legislation. Discuss.
4. Are some beer, wine, liquor, or tobacco ads misleading? What specifically is misleading?
5. Should caps be placed on punitive damage awards?
6. The state of California has proposed a fifty cent tax increase per package of cigarettes sold. What impact do you think this will have on cigarette consumption?
7. Should companies producing alcoholic beverages be held liable for deaths resulting from alcohol consumption?
8. Should fast-food companies be held responsible for deaths that can be related to the consumption of high-calorie foods?
9. What is the difference between compensatory and punitive damages?
10. Why is *MacPherson v. Buick* considered a landmark case?

NOTES

1. Adam Smith, *The Wealth of Nations* (New York: The Modern Library, 1937), p. 38.
2. There was no freedom of choice in the former communist countries. Resources were allocated by central economic planning.
3. This is called pure competition, an ideal market situation that rarely exists.
4. The Consumer Federation of America is the most important consumer group.
5. The doctrine of breach of warranty affords remedies for misrepresentation that can be extended beyond the retailer as far back as the manufacturer.
6. Federal regulation in 1872 forbade the use of the mails to defraud.
7. Upton Sinclair, *The Jungle* (New York: Doubleday and Page, 1906).
8. Some 1.5 million copies of the book were sold during its printings.
9. There were all sorts of ads in the newspapers of that time period that claimed curative powers for their products.
10. In 1970 all cyclamate-sweetened soft drinks were banned from the market. This was based on tests made on rats showing that they developed bladder cancer when given strict doses of cyclamates.
11. Sam Peltzman, *Regulation of Pharmaceutical Innovation: The 1962 Amendment* (Washington, D.C.: American Enterprise Institute, 1974).
12. The waste was said to result from product differentiation in an imperfect market permeated by physicians and consumer ignorance.
13. The device was made by the A.H. Robins Co. of Richmond, VA.
14. *The Roanoke Times*, Friday, August 20, 1999, p. 2.
15. Julie Appleby, "Diet Drug Maker Settles for $4.8 billion," *USA Today* Thursday, February 24, 2000, p. 1.
16. FTC v. Raladam Co., 283 U.S. 643 (1931).
17. Lewis W. Stern and Thomas L. Fovaldi, *Legal Aspects of Marketing Strategy: Antitrust and Consumer Protection Issues* (Englewood Cliff, N.J.: Prentice-Hall, 1984), pp. 371–372.
18. Thomas L. Carson, Richard E. Wokutch, and James E. Brown Jr., "An Ethical Analysis of Deceptive Advertising." *Journal of Business Ethics* (Winter, 1985), pp. 99–101.
19. Two hundred million letters multiplied by the amount of money that could be won comes out to $200 trillion which is five times the GNP of the world.
20. An elderly man, thinking that he had won the grand prize, flew to Tampa to claim it. He was going to give the money to his children. Dreams often die hard.
21. *The Roanoke Times*, Monday, February 28, 2000, p. 2.
22. Wheaties cereal used to be called "the breakfast of champions." It was endorsed by professional athletes who implied that they owed their success to eating Wheaties.
23. In Selma, Alabama, several women were burned to death when a Christmas tree caught fire, setting their billowy gowns on fire.
24. He or she cannot call before 8:00 A.M. or after 9:00 P.M.
25. Both federal and state laws on warranties conform to the Uniform Commercial Code (UCC) which follows common law theory that a product, when sold, carries with it the promise that it is fit for common use.
26. U.S. Senate Committee on Commerce, *Hearing of National Commission on Product Safety*, 91st Cong., 2nd Sess., 1972, p. 37.
27. Ralph Nader, *Unsafe at Any Speed* (New York: Pocket Books, 1966).
28. Cadillac, to meet government rules, came out with a V-8-6-4 engine in 1981. To save gas, it shut down pairs of cylinders automatically as the car got to cruising speed. But it bucked, misfired, and lacked power, and was discontinued.

29. This is no longer in effect. The limit is now up to each state to determine.
30. MacPherson v. Buick Motor Co., 217 N.Y., 382, 111 N.E. 1050 (1916).
31. *USA Today*, Thursday: June 27, 1996, p. 13A.
32. Supreme Court of the United States, Syllabus, *BMW of North America, Inc. v. Gore*, No. 94-896. Decided May 20, 1996, pp. 1–27.
33. The amount was based on the evidence that between 1983 and 1990, BMW had sold 983 repainted cars in the United States as new, including 14 in Alabama. This number was multiplied by the $4 thousand in compensatory damage awarded to Dr. Gore to arrive at $4 million.
34. When the original $4 million verdict was returned, BMW instituted a nationwide policy of full disclosure of all repairs, no matter how minor.
35. The Supreme Court described reprehensible conduct as consisting of the following: Crimes marked by violence or threats of violence; trickery and deceit; intentional malice; repeated engagement in unlawful conduct; bad faith actions; and deliberate false statements or concealment of evidence of improper motives.
36. *USA Today*, Thursday, April 23, 1998, p. 7A.
37. "America's Largest Corporations," *Fortune*, April 17, 2000, pp. F1, F7. While Philip Morris's 1999 sales were $61.7 billion and profits were $7.7 billion, R.J. Reynolds's 1999 sales were $17 billion and profits were $2.3 billion.
38. Nabisco, which was formerly a part of RJR Nabisco, is now a separate company.
39. *Value Line*, "The Tobacco Industry," January 19, 1998, pp. 1574–1579.
40. *Ibid.*, p. 1574.
41. Florida, Mississippi, Texas, and Minnesota had already concluded settlements with the tobacco industry.
42. On March 21, 2000, the Supreme Court by a 5–4 decision rejected the government's attempt to have nicotine declared a drug and thus regulated by the Food and Drug Administration.
43. On March 27, 2000, a California jury ordered Philip Morris and R.J. Reynolds to pay $20 million in punitive damages and $1.7 million in compensatory damages to a dying ex-smoker who took up the habit after the surgeon-general's warning appeared on cigarette packs during the 1960s. The verdict was the first for a smoker who took up the habit after 1969, after the warning was on the packs. This smoker started smoking in 1972 when she was 13 until she was diagnosed as having lung cancer in 1998.

RECOMMENDED READING

No industry has received as much attention in recent years as the tobacco industry. Some forty states have lawsuits against the tobacco industry. The following readings on the subject are recommended:

Kluger, Richard. *Ashes to Ashes: America's Hundred-Year Cigarette War, the Public Health, and the Unabashed Triumph of Philip Morris*. New York: Alfred A. Knopf, 1997.

Mollenkamp, Carrick, et al., *The People v. Big Tobacco: How the People Took on the Cigarette Giant*. Princeton, N.J.: Bloomburg Press, 1998.

Pringle, Peter. *Cornered: Big Tobacco at the Court of Justice*. New York: H. Holt, 1998.

On jury awards, see:

"How a Jury Decided a Coffee Spill Is Worth $2.9 Million," *The Wall Street Journal*, September 1, 1994, pp. A1, A5.

For the increase in product liability lawsuits, see John Gilbeaut, "At the Crossroads," *American Bar Association Journal*, March 1998.

CHAPTER 8

EMPLOYMENT POLICY

The rationale for government intervention in employment and education is that equal employment opportunity is considered to be a basic right of the American democratic process—everyone should have the same opportunity to achieve material success. When opportunity is equal, competition and market forces determine one's worth in the marketplace. The idea behind equal employment opportunity is that if everyone is given the same or substantially the same starting position in a race, the winners will have to achieve their rewards through merit rather than through any favored position. Reward would be based on merit, and the result would be the creation of a meritocratic society.[1] Logically, if everyone is given the same opportunity and there is no discrimination based on sex, age, or other factors, the rewards should be distributed fairly uniformly.

However, the problem is that a number of impediments hinder achieving true equality of opportunity. Clearly, discrimination on the basis of sex, color, religion, or any criterion outside of professional qualifications prevent any genuine equality of opportunity. And equality of opportunity is only part of the future, for opportunity is linked to the distribution of income. In part, income inequality is based on differences in people's abilities; sometimes, however, it is based on sex, race, and age, which have little or no relationship to ability. Income inequality can also be based on the distribution of wealth, the great bulk of which is held by those who are in the upper 5 percent of income earners in the United States.[2]

INCOME DISTRIBUTION IN THE UNITED STATES

Income inequality is greater in the United States than in any other major industrial country, and it has increased in recent years. From 1980 to 1997, the top 20 percent of American families saw their incomes, measured in terms of purchasing power, increase while the bottom 60 percent of families saw a decrease. From 1950 to 1978, all income groups gained as the American economy grew. It was a time when unskilled assembly-line workers, with little if any education beyond a high school diploma, were able to achieve a middle-class standard of living. U.S. firms had very little competition from abroad and foreign wages were not a factor that affected U.S. wages. But all of this began to change during 1970 when foreign competition began to catch up with U.S. companies.

Faced with this competition, U.S. manufacturers turned to technology to increase productivity, substituting machines for people wherever possible. Companies began to eliminate thousands of workers from their payrolls, sometimes more than half the industrial labor force. As manufacturing employment decreased, employment in the service industries was growing faster than in any other sector, often providing jobs without benefits such as health insurance. Moreover, the competition for jobs increased in the 1980s, as those who were born during the post-World War II era began entering the labor force. Women, too, entered the labor force in large numbers. The technological revolution that hit the manufacturing sector then reached the service sector, replacing bank tellers with automatic teller machines and telephone operators with automatic switching equipment.

Table 8-1 presents the distribution of money income of U.S. families by quintiles and income at selected positions in constant U.S. dollars for 1980 and

TABLE 8-1   MONEY INCOME OF U.S. FAMILIES: PERCENTAGE DISTRIBUTION
OF AGGREGATE INCOME RECEIVED BY QUINTILE AND INCOME
AT SELECTED POSITIONS, 1980 AND 1997 (1997 DOLLARS)

	ALL FAMILIES IN 1980	ALL FAMILIES IN 1997
Number (1,000)	60,309	70,884
PERCENTAGE DISTRIBUTION		
Lowest fifth	5.3	4.2
Second fifth	11.6	9.9
Third fifth	17.6	15.7
Fourth fifth	24.4	23.0
Top fifth	41.1	47.2
Top 5 percent	14.6	20.7
UPPER INCOME AT SELECTED POSITIONS		
Lowest	$19,258	$20,586
Second	32,424	36,000
Third	45,929	53,616
Fourth	64,441	80,000
Top 5 percent	101,847	137,080

Source: U.S. Department of Commerce, Bureau of the Census, *Statistical Abstract of the United States, 1999* (Washington, D.C.: U.S. Government Printing Office, 1999), p. 479.

1997. As the table indicates, there was a decline in real income for the bottom 80 percent of the families and a gain for the top 20 percent.[3] The lowest one-fifth of families had their share of income reduced from 5.3 percent in 1980 to 4.2 percent in 1997. Conversely, the share of income received by the top 20 percent of families increased from 41.1 percent in 1980 to 47.2 percent in 1997, and the share of income received by the top 5 percent of families increased from 14.6 percent in 1980 to 20.7 percent in 1997. Income inequality was greater for black and Hispanic families in 1997 than it was for white families.

Table 8-2 presents the share of income of families by race for 1997. As the table indicates, more blacks and Hispanics are concentrated in the two lowest levels of income, while whites are concentrated in the two highest levels of income. Twenty-six percent of black families and 24 percent of Hispanic families made less than $15,000 a year, while 47 percent of white families made more than $50,000 a year.

DEMOGRAPHIC CHARACTERISTICS OF INCOME DISTRIBUTION

Political and economic conditions in the United States have focused on the rights of the individual—equality of opportunity, voting rights, and support for those people who in some sense have fallen below society's norm of acceptability. However, the United States has become a pluralistic society and group consciousness has developed, with each group wanting a larger share of the economic pie. Therefore, a more complete analysis of income distribution based on the demographic characteristics of sex, race, and age is necessary. Income distribution shows disparities related to each of these characteristics, and has created a demand for government policies, such as affirmative action, that force attention on reducing these disparities.

TABLE 8-2   MONEY INCOME OF FAMILIES: PERCENT DISTRIBUTION BY INCOME LEVEL, RACE, AND HISPANIC ORIGIN (CONSTANT 1997 DOLLARS)

	WHITE	BLACK	HISPANIC
Under 10,000	5.3	17.0	13.8
10,000–14,999	5.1	9.8	10.9
15,000–24,999	12.5	17.7	20.1
25,000–34,999	12.7	14.2	15.3
35,000–49,999	17.7	15.5	17.2
50,000–74,999	22.1	16.0	12.7
75,000 and over	24.5	9.9	10.0

Source: U.S. Department of Commerce, Bureau of the Census, *Statistical Abstract of the United States, 1999* (Washington, D.C.: U.S. Government Printing Office, 1999), p. 475.

Sex One of the defining movements of this century has been the struggle for gender equality, led mostly by women. It was not until this century that women were given the right to vote in the major industrial countries. Women in all countries earn less than men. Moreover, 70 percent of those who live in poverty throughout the world are women, and the rate of illiteracy is much higher among women.[4] In India, for example, two-thirds of the population that is illiterate are women. In many countries women have few legal rights regarding marital relations, the division of property, or land tenure. In some countries men can divorce their wives but not the other way around; also, it is difficult for the women to get any form of alimony.[5]

The percentage of American women who have entered the labor force has increased dramatically in recent years. In 1950, 31.4 percent of women worked; by 1970, it had increased to 42.6 percent; and by 1998, 59.8 percent of all women were employed. The most dramatic increase in employment involved married women with children. In 1960, 18.6 percent of women in the labor force were married women with children; in 1998 it was 71.1 percent.[6] In 1980, 61.5 million males were employed compared to 45.5 million females; in 1998, 74.0 million males were employed compared to 63.7 million females.[7] Many women today have more financial responsibility than in the past because more of them are single heads of families. In 1998, for example, one out of every five women who worked was a single mother with a family to raise.

Two things have happened as more women have entered the labor force. First, there has been a shift in employment by occupations as more women are entering occupations once considered the preserve of men. As Table 8-3 (on page 148) indicates, the percentage of women who have entered such high-paying professions as engineering, law, and medicine has shown a marked increase. Second, wages of women relative to men have also shown an increase. In 1950 the pay ratio of women to men was 48.6 percent. Between 1960 and 1980, there was little change in the ratio, which was 60.7 percent in 1960 and 60.2 percent in 1980. In 1990 the ratio was 71.6 percent and in 1997 it was 70.5 percent.[8] Table 8-4 (on page 149) presents a comparison of men's and women's pay by occupations for 1995. Women's pay in some of the higher-paying professions has shown little gain or has decreased.

There are several reasons that women have not made income gains relative to men's income. For one thing, women by the thousands have flocked to such lucrative professions as law and medicine, thus increasing the supply of workers. In fact, the medical profession is reputed to be overcrowded, and the AMA has asked medical schools to decrease admissions.[9] Another factor is discrimination. Women are often given the lower-paying jobs and are denied promotion. Home Depot, the home improvement chain, was accused in a class-action suit of putting women behind cash registers instead of putting them on the sales floor where they could earn commissions and get promoted.[10] Third, there is networking, or contacts, that have been built up by men over an extended period of time, and that works to their advantage in employment.

	1970	1995
Total workforce	38.0	46.1
CONSIDERABLE CHANGE		
Insurance adjusters	29.6	73.9
Typesetters	16.8	67.3
Educational administrators	27.8	58.7
Publicists	26.6	57.9
Bartenders	21.0	53.5
Government administrators	21.7	49.8
College faculty	29.1	45.2
Insurance agents	12.9	37.1
Pharmacists	12.1	36.2
Photographers	14.8	27.1
Lawyers	4.9	26.4
Physicians	9.7	24.4
Butchers and meat cutters	11.4	21.6
Architects	4.0	19.8
Telephone installers	2.8	16.0
Dentists	3.5	13.4
Police officers	3.7	12.9
Clergy	2.9	11.1
Engineers	1.7	8.4
Sheet-metal workers	1.9	7.5
MODEST CHANGE		
Hotel receptionists	51.4	75.2
Social workers	63.3	67.9
High school teachers	49.6	57.0
Journalists	41.6	53.2
Realtors	31.2	50.7
Computer programmers	24.2	29.5
ESSENTIALLY NO CHANGE		
Dental hygienists	94.0	99.4
Secretaries	97.8	98.5
Registered nurses	97.3	93.1
Elementary school teachers	83.9	84.1
Librarians	82.1	83.2
MEN REPLACING WOMEN		
Telephone operators	94.0	88.4
Data entry keyers	93.7	82.9
Waiters and waitresses	90.8	77.7
Cooks and chefs	67.2	44.5

Source: Andrew Hacker, *MONEY: Who Has How Much and Why?* (New York, NY: Scribner, 1997), p. 197.

TABLE 8-4   A COMPARISON OF MEN AND WOMEN'S PAY BY OCCUPATIONS, 1983–1995 (WOMEN'S EARNINGS PER $1,000 RECEIVED BY MEN)

OCCUPATION	1983	1995
MORE THAN 10 PERCENT IMPROVEMENT		
Chefs and cooks	$711	$885
Realtors	683	794
Production inspectors	563	649
Waiters and waitresses	721	822
Public administrators	701	786
Computer analysts	703	860
LESS THAN 10 PERCENT		
Journalists	782	855
Retail sales	636	693
Insurance adjusters	651	691
Financial managers	638	674
Engineers	828	862
Accountants	706	734
College faculty	773	781
DETERIORATION		
High school teachers	886	881
Health technicians	839	813
Lawyers	890	818
Physicians	816	649

Source: Andrew Hacker, *Money: Who Has How Much and Why* (New York, NY: Scribner, 1997), p. 191.

Race   In the case of blacks and other minorities, income differences can be explained in part by overt discrimination. Over an extended period of time, blacks have been systematically denied the same educational opportunities as whites, which is reflected in the occupations of blacks. A majority still work the low-pay, low-skill jobs. There has also been discrimination in hiring and promotion policies toward other minority groups. Hispanics are an example. Often the discrimination is indirect, as in testing that, although it can be a legitimate device to find out something about employee aptitudes and qualifications, may be culturally biased in favor of certain types of job applicants. Blacks and other minorities have often been unable to obtain jobs commensurate with their training.

Table 8-5 (on page 150) presents a comparison of white, black, and Hispanic household median income in constant 1995 dollars for the period 1970–1997. There has been some narrowing of the gap between black and white household median income during the period; conversely, the gap between white and Hispanic household median income has widened. In terms of purchasing power, the median income of Hispanics has shown a decline during the period, while the median income of black and white households increased by less than 10 percent.

CIVIL RIGHTS LAWS

Civil rights are extremely important in the litigious world of today and have their historical background in the first ten amendments of the U.S. Constitution. Persons are protected in the free exercise of their speech, are free to choose or not to choose a religion, can peacefully assemble, and may petition their government for a redress of grievances. They also have the right to keep and bear arms, the right to be free of unreasonable searches and seizures, and the right to a jury trial. These rights are bestowed by the government upon the people. Coupled with civil rights are natural rights to which a person is entitled because he or she is human and that cannot be taken away by government.[11]

HISTORY OF CIVIL RIGHTS LAWS

The first civil rights laws had their origin in the Civil War. After the battle of Antietam, which was fought in September 1862, President Lincoln issued the Emancipation Proclamation that freed the slaves. After the war was over, several constitutional amendments were passed that had a direct impact upon the treatment of blacks, The Thirteenth Amendment in 1865 abolished slavery; the Fourteenth Amendment in 1868 was designed to prevent southern states from passing discriminatory laws against blacks; and the Fifteenth Amendment

TABLE 8-5   MEDIAN INCOME OF U.S. HOUSEHOLDS
BY RACE AND HISPANIC ORIGIN (IN CONSTANT 1997 DOLLARS)

YEAR	ALL HOUSEHOLDS	WHITE	BLACK	HISPANIC
1970	33,942	35,353	21,518	(NA)
1980	34,536	36,437	20,992	26,622
1985	35,229	37,154	22,105	26,051
1990	36,770	38,352	22,934	27,421
1991	35,501	37,201	22,162	26,739
1992	35,047	36,846	21,455	25,850
1993	34,700	36,610	21,696	25,420
1994	34,942	36,852	22,772	25,365
1995	35,887	37,667	23,583	24,075
1996	36,306	38,014	24,021	25,477
1997	37,005	38,972	25,050	26,628

Source: U.S. Department of Commerce, Bureau of the Census, *Statistical Abstract of the United States, 1999* (Washington, D.C.: U.S. Government Printing Office, 1999), p. 475.

in 1870 was designed to prevent race discrimination in voting. The Civil Rights Act of 1866 was passed by Congress to protect blacks from employment discrimination and the Civil Rights Act of 1875 was designed to protect them against discrimination in housing and transportation. It provided for a fine of up to $1,000 or imprisonment of up to one year for violation.

The two laws had very little impact on improving the lot of blacks, particularly in the South. Resentment against the North increased during the period of reconstruction. Southern states passed Jim Crow laws designed to segregate blacks. The concept of separate but equal accommodations came out of the *Plessy v. Ferguson* case of 1896, which legitimized segregation.[12] This ruling provided the foundation for making segregation legal. There were separate schools for whites and blacks, separate accommodations, and separate facilities such as toilets and drinking fountains. *Plessy v. Ferguson* was eventually reversed by the *Brown v. Board of Education* case of 1954 in which the Supreme Court ruled that the separate but equal doctrine followed by the states had resulted in unequal education facilities for blacks.[13] But other forms of discrimination against blacks and other minorities continued to exist.

THE CIVIL RIGHTS ACT OF 1964

Title VII of the act specifically deals with discrimination in employment. It is designed to protect individuals from job discrimination on the basis of race, color, sex, religion, or national origin. It prohibits discrimination with respect to compensation, contract terms, and conditions or privileges of employment. The most common Title VII claims involve failure to hire, failure to promote, discipline, discharge, pay discrimination, and sexual harassment. It applies to employers who have fifteen or more employees for each working day in each of twenty or more calendar weeks per year. The act also created the Equal Employment Opportunity Commission (EEOC) to handle claims of employment discrimination. The responsibility of EEOC was subsequently extended to apply to the Age Discrimination in Employment Act (ADEA), the Americans with Disabilities Act (ADA), and the Equal Pay Act. Title IX prohibits discrimination on the basis of sex in educational programs receiving government financial assistance.

THE AGE DISCRIMINATION IN EMPLOYMENT ACT OF 1967

The poet Byron once wrote, "The days of our youth are the days of our glory." No society in the world believes that more firmly than Americans, who are firmly committed to the pursuit of youth. The notion that older people lose their mental faculties and are unable to perform as well as younger workers is not uncommon in the American workplace. Employers have often refused to hire and promote workers and have also fired them, all on the basis of age. The Age Discrimination in Employment Act (ADEA) is designed to prohibit discrimination based on age. It protects workers who have reached the age of forty and older. It applies to employers with at least twenty employees for each day of twenty or more calendar days.

THE AMERICANS WITH DISABILITIES ACT OF 1990

This act, which is an extension of the Rehabilitation Act of 1973, makes it unlawful to discriminate against a qualified individual with a disability. A person is said to have a disability if he or she has a physical or mental impairment that substantially limits or restricts a major life activity such as hearing, seeing, breathing, performing manual tasks, walking, or caring for oneself. The act mandates that employees make reasonable accommodations for the disabled. Reasonable accommodation is any change that is necessary to permit a worker to do the job. It may involve modifying equipment or making the workplace readily accessible to persons with disabilities. It also may mean part-time or modified work schedules. ADA applies to all employers, including state and local governments, with fifteen or more employees.

BONA FIDE OCCUPATION QUALIFICATION (BFOQ)

BFOQ exemptions to employment laws can be used in certain circumstances. In terms of safety, the courts have allowed an employer to limit its recruiting and hiring for certain types of individuals when either the safety of the public or the employees are involved. BFOQ exemptions are given when it can be shown that being a member of a particular group is necessary for serving in a given job, such as an acting job, that may require a person to be a male or female. An exemption may also be given for jobs that involve legitimate privacy concerns. An example would be the hiring of a female attendant for a women's locker room in a health club. Religion can sometimes be used as a BFOQ; an example would be teaching at a religious school where teaching involves the propagation of certain religious beliefs.[14]

OTHER LAWS FORBIDDING WORKPLACE DISCRIMINATION

There are several other antidiscrimination laws that should be noted. The Equal Pay Act of 1963 requires equal pay for men and women doing the same job. The Vocational Rehabilitation Act of 1973 requires federal contractors to take affirmative action in hiring the qualified handicapped. The Pregnancy Discrimination Act of 1978 forbids discrimination against women if they decide to have a child. The Civil Rights Act of 1991 broadens the scope of federal antidiscrimination law. It makes clear that Americans employed abroad by U.S.-owned or U.S.-controlled firms can avail themselves of the protection of Title VII of the Civil Rights Act of 1964 and ADEA, unless compliance with these laws violate the host country's laws. It broadened the categories of victims who can seek compensatory and punitive damages. The Family and Medical Leave Act of 1993 protects job rights of employees who can take up to twelve weeks leave for family reasons such as childbirth.

EMPLOYMENT DISCRIMINATION—DISPARATE TREATMENT AND DISPARATE IMPACT

Employment discrimination claims brought under Title VII of the Civil Rights Act of 1964 have been approached through the use of two legal theories—disparate treatment and disparate impact. Under the disparate treatment theory, an employer may be liable if he or she impermissibly differentiates among employers or applicants or treats some unfavorably based on their race, sex, religion, or national origin. This discrimination may often be invisible. For example, an employer may have used job requirements that appear merit-based, but in fact were not. An example would be educational requirements that have the effect of favoring whites over blacks or strength tests that would favor men over women.

Griggs v. Duke Power[15]   Griggs, a black worker, applied for a semiskilled job at the Duke Power Company. However, the requisite for the job was a high school diploma or, in lieu of that, he could take the Wonderlic and Bennett tests that measured intelligence and mechanical aptitude. If he scored at the same level as whites with a high school diploma, he could get the job. In North Carolina, fewer blacks than whites had received a high school education, so blacks were limited to the lowest paying jobs. Griggs and other blacks argued that the educational requirements screened them from getting the better-paying jobs that whites were getting. The Supreme Court ruled that there was no satisfactory relationship between the educational requirements and job performance.

While the disparate treatment approach aims at the elimination of discrimination that is usually intentional, disparate impact is designed to eliminate racially neutral employment policies that have a disproportionate impact on members of a protected class and that cannot be justified by legitimate business considerations. The employment practice may appear neutral, but it is not. The focus is on the effect of an employer's practices, not the intent of establishing these practices. To establish a *prima facie* claim of disparate impact discrimination, a plaintiff must prove that a particular practice adversely affects employment opportunities of one group of workers as compared to the effect the same practice has on the opportunities of other groups.

Watson v. Fort Worth Bank and Trust[16]   Clara Watson, a black employee at the Fort Worth Bank and Trust, tried without success to obtain several promotions. The bank relied on the subjective judgment of a supervisor as to who would receive promotions. Watson filed a lawsuit but a trial court dismissed the action after finding that Watson had failed to prove racial discrimination under the standards of disparate or unequal treatment. Under disparate treatment, an employer may be liable if he or she impermissibly differentiates among employees on the basis of their race, sex, color, religion, or national origin. Watson argued that disparate impact should have been applied in her case and eventually the case went to the Supreme Court, which ruled in her favor.

Disparate impact focuses on the effects of an employer's practice, not the intent in establishing those practices. To establish proof of disparate impact, statistical analysis can be used. Two types of statistical evidence—pass/fail comparisons and population/work force comparisons—have frequently been introduced as evidence in disparate impact cases. Thus an employee may support an individual claim of discrimination with statistical evidence showing that women or minorities are underrepresented in the workplace instead of having to prove intentional discrimination. In the case of Watson, all the jobs to which she aspired were filled by whites.

CLASS-ACTION EMPLOYMENT SUITS

A class-action suit is a lawsuit filed by a group of people who have a grievance against a particular company. It is less expensive to file than an individual lawsuit. An example of a class-action suit was one that was filed against Texaco by six black employees and a 1,500-member class of current and former employees, over the failure of the company to promote and compensate fairly. The suit involved several claims by the plaintiffs. The first was statistical underrepresentation of minorities in upper management. A second claim was disparate promotion rates. Other claims included a low minority representation at Texaco relative to the oil industry as a whole, and the existence of a secret high-potential promotion list with no minority representation. Texaco, as Table 8-6 indicates, settled the suit for $172 million.

AFFIRMATIVE ACTION

Affirmative action means active efforts by employers to correct any racial, sexual, or other minority imbalance that may exist in a labor force. The general principle behind affirmative action is the accordance of special treatment to groups that have suffered discrimination in the past. It is far more comprehensive than simple employment discrimination, which may involve only one person over some issue such as age or sex. It requires employers with federal contracts to evaluate their work forces, to analyze their employment needs, and to actively solicit minority employees. Affirmative action programs must meet certain minimum requirements in which the burden is on the employer. A program must contain certain basic information. For example, the work force must be analyzed to determine where minorities are being underused, why they are being underused, and how this situation can be corrected.

TABLE 8-6   EMPLOYMENT DISCRIMINATION CLASS-ACTION SETTLEMENTS, 1992–1997

DATE OF SETTLEMENT	COMPANY	AMOUNT	CLASS DESCRIPTION
9/97	Home Depot	$87.5 million	25,000 women claiming discrimination in promotion
3/97	Texaco	$172 million	1,500 past and current African-American employees
11/96	Chevron	$7.4 million	800 current and former female employees alleging sex discrimination in promotions and salaries
10/96	Southern California Edison	$18.2 million	2,500 African Americans alleging race discrimination
10/94	Albertson's, Inc.	$29.4 million	Women and Hispanics claiming race and sex discrimination
6/94	Denny's	$54 million	4,500 people alleging race discrimination
4/94	Lucky Stores	$107.2 million	14,000 women alleging sex discrimination
1/93	Shoney's	$133 million	African-American employees alleging race discrimination
10/92	State Farm	$250 million	Sex discrimination

Source: Jeffrey A. Norris, President, Equal Employment Council, Washington, D.C., May, 1997) unpublished data.

The principle of affirmative action goes back much further than the civil rights legislation of the 1960s and extends well beyond questions involving ethnic minorities or women. In 1935 the Wagner Act prescribed affirmative action as well as cease-and-desist remedies against employers whose antiunion activities had violated the law. Thus, in the landmark *Jones and Laughlin Steel* case, which established the constitutionality of the act, the National Labor Relations Board ordered the company not only to stop discriminating against employees who were union members, but also to post notices in conspicuous places announcing they would reinstate back pay to unlawfully discharged workers. Had the company been ordered merely to cease and desist from economic retaliation against union members, the effect of its past intimidation would have continued to hamper the free choice of election guaranteed by the Wagner Act.[17]

EXECUTIVE ORDERS

An executive order can be issued by the president of the United States requiring that a certain action be taken. There are limits within which it can be done. For example, it can be challenged by Congress as an usurpation of its powers.

Executive orders issued by Presidents Lyndon Johnson and Richard Nixon declared it a matter of public policy that affirmative action must be taken to rectify discrimination against minorities. President Johnson issued Executive Order 11246 in 1965, which stated that in all federal contracts or in any employment situation that uses federal funds, employers have to prove they have sought out qualified applicants from disadvantaged groups, and must hire preferentially from minority group members when their qualifications are roughly equal to those of other applicants.

Executive Order 11375, which was issued by President Johnson in 1967, banned discrimination in federal employment on the basis of race, sex, color, and national origin. Directors of federal agencies were required to draw up a positive program of equal employment opportunity for all employees, and to hire more women and minorities at all levels. Affirmative action was eventually extended to universities, and each school with federal contracts was asked to provide information on the number of women and minority members in each position, academic and nonacademic. They were also required to set specific goals for increasing the number of women and minorities in each position.

Executive Order 4, issued by President Nixon in 1971, is the basis for most affirmative action programs. Under this order, affirmative action is required from all employers who hold federal contracts. The type of affirmative action employers must take is determined by the nature of the federal contract they hold. A written affirmative action program, demanded by the Office of Federal Contract Compliance (OFCC) regulations, applies to all nonconstruction contractors and subcontractors of the federal government and to agencies of the federal government that employ fifty or more employees and have a contract in excess of $50,000 a year. All business firms or government agencies that meet these criteria must file a written affirmative action program that contains a statement of good faith efforts to achieve equal employment opportunity. Such efforts must include an analysis of deficiencies in the use of minorities, a timetable for correcting such deficiencies, and a plan for achieving these goals. Revised Order 14, issued by the Labor Department in July 1974, gave approval to the procedures that federal agencies must use in evaluating government contractors' affirmative action programs. Among other things, contractors must list each job title as it appears in their union agreements or payrolls, rather than listing only job groups as was formerly required. The job titles must be ranked from the lowest paid to the highest paid within each department. Further, if there are separate work units or lines of progression within a department, separate lists must be provided for each unit or line, including unit supervisors. For lines of progression, the order of jobs in the line through which an employer can move to the job must be indicated. For each job title, two breakdowns are required. Besides the total number of male and female jobholders, it is necessary to have the total number of male and female jobholders in each of the following groups: blacks, Hispanics, Native Americans, and Asians.

APPLICATION OF AFFIRMATIVE ACTION

Affirmative action is very controversial. It has come under criticism for several reasons. The first involves Title VII of the Civil Rights Act of 1964, which was supposed to create an employment-neutral playing field by prohibiting discrimination based on race, sex, religion, color, or national origin. The intent of Congress in passing the act was reasonably explicit. It did not force employers to achieve any kind of racial balance in their work force by giving any kind of preferential treatment to any individual or group.[18] Affirmative action, it is argued, goes far beyond this intent by requiring preferential treatment. The second criticism involves the problem of fairness when it comes to admission to colleges or to medical and law schools. The plaintiff in the so-called *Bakke* case argued that he was denied admission to medical school even though his grades were higher than those of minority students who were admitted.

United Steelworkers of America v. Weber[19]   The United Steelworkers Union and Kaiser Aluminum entered into an agreement covering an affirmative action plan designed to eliminate racial imbalance in the Kaiser plants throughout the country. Black hiring goals were set in each plant equal to the percentage of blacks in the respective labor forces. In the Gramercy, Louisiana, plant, 39 percent of the area work force was black but only 18 percent of the plant workers were black, and only 2 percent of black workers held craft positions. Kaiser established a goal for the plant whereby it was required that 50 percent of openings in craft-training positions be reserved for blacks. Brian Weber, who applied for a position, was turned down. Arguing that he had seniority, he charged reverse discrimination. The case went to the U.S. Supreme Court, which upheld the quota system for the training program.

A number of other affirmative action cases followed *Weber*. In 1984, the Supreme Court upheld the seniority system in the *Stotts* case.[20] In the New York Sheetmetal Union Case of 1986, the justices upheld by a five-to-four vote a federal court order for a local sheetmetal workers' union in New York to meet specific minority hiring requirements of 29.23 percent.[21] In the same year in the *Cleveland Firefighters* case, it upheld a decision by a lower court settlement between the City of Cleveland and minority firefighters that called for the promotion of one minority for one white, with the intent of increasing to a certain percentage the number of black officers in each rank.[22] These and other cases delineated several factors that are important in determining whether or not an affirmative action plan that involves preferential treatment complies with Title VII of the Civil Rights Act of 1964.

1. An affirmative action plan should be remedial in nature. If an employer's work force is imbalanced, an affirmative action plan can be justified.

2. A plan should not exclude all nonminorities. In the *Weber* case, the Supreme Court emphasized that a 50 percent minority admissions quota did not create a bar to nonminorities.
3. An affirmative action plan should be temporary. Once the goals have been met, the plan should be discontinued.

MINORITY SET-ASIDES

Minority set-asides are an area of affirmative action designed to provide preferential treatment for women- and minority-owned businesses. In addition to the federal government, state and local governments have similar programs of set-asides for preferred groups. The rationale for these programs is to encourage more women and minorities to become involved in business, and to prevent discrimination that is often based on factors that have little to do with efficiency. In some cases, these businesses may be awarded contracts by federal agencies without competitive bidding.

City of Richmond v. J.A. Croson Co.[23]   In 1989 the U.S. Supreme Court ruled against a minority set-aside program that had been established by the City of Richmond. It had set aside 30 percent of construction funds for minority contractors. A contractor, J. A. Croson Co., had bid on a city contract but was rejected on the grounds that it had not made sufficient efforts to find minority subcontractors. It argued that it had made a good faith effort but was unable to find qualified minority subcontractors. The Court, by a 6–3 decision, found the Richmond ordinance unconstitutional. Justice Sandra Day O'Connor, in writing the key opinion, argued that affirmative action programs could be justified only on the evidence of prior discrimination. She stressed that this discrimination must be specific and identifiable and this the city had failed to prove. She also held that the plan was not narrowly tailored to fit a specific disadvantaged group; it was too broad-based in its preference.[24]

Adarand Constructors, Inc. v. Pena[25]   This case involved a challenge to a federal program that granted special treatment to minority subcontractors. A large construction company received a contract to build highways in southern Colorado. It requested bids to build guardrails. Two subcontractors made bids, one white-owned and one minority-owned. Adarand, the white-owned company, made a bid that was $1,700 lower than the bid of the other company. The contract went to the other company because the main contract was with the federal government, which provided a 10 percent bonus to the contractor if it used a minority contractor. In this case, the Supreme Court decided in favor of Adarand, holding that all racial classifications, used by whatever level of government, must conform to strict scrutiny standards.[26] It ruled that only affirmative action plans that would respond to provable past discrimination would be legal.

AFFIRMATIVE ACTION AND EDUCATION

In no one area has affirmative action become more controversial than in college education. The main issue is over the use of race in college admissions and the use of different and lower selection criteria for minority applicants. Supporters of affirmative action argue that different admission policies are necessary to ensure that students of all backgrounds have access to a college education in order to create cultural diversity. However, proposals to roll back affirmative action have increased. Opponents of the use of racial preferences in admission won in California with Proposition 209. A major affirmative action case involved a white teacher who was laid off, rather than an equally qualified black teacher.[27] A lawsuit has been filed against the University of Michigan by white students who contend that racial preference denied them admission.[28]

Cheryl Hopwood v. Texas[29]   In 1992 hundreds of students were denied admission to the prestigious University of Texas School of Law. However, four of the applicants, including Cheryl Hopwood, sued, charging that the University of Texas had discriminated against them on the basis of their race in violation of the Fourteenth Amendment and Title VII of the Civil Rights Act of 1964. The plaintiffs challenged the admissions process used by the University of Texas in which Mexican Americans and African Americans were admitted pursuant to a different and lower standard for admittance than other students. Under the 1992 admissions system, a nonpreferred applicant could have a substantially higher Texas Index score and be denied admission while a preferred minority with a lower TI could be admitted. Preferred minority applicants were color-coded and reviewed by a separate minority subcommittee, while all other applicants were reviewed by the regular admissions committee.

A district court upheld the concept of UT's affirmative action program, based on the idea that obtaining educational benefits from a racially and ethnically diverse student body is a sufficiently compelling reason to support the use of racial classifications.[30] It held that the plaintiffs had to show that they would have been admitted to the law school if a constitutionally permissible admissions system had been in place. It found the plaintiffs had failed to show this, awarded them $1.00 each in nominal damages, and ordered that they be allowed to reapply to the law school without further costs. However, the Court, in justifying the rationale for affirmative action for admission to the law school, stated that the approach was flawed because UT failed to give comparative evaluation to all applicants.

The university appealed this part and the case went to the Fifth Circuit Court of Appeals, which ruled that any consideration of race or ethnicity by the law school for the purpose of achieving a diverse student body is not a compelling interest under the Fourteenth Amendment. The Fifth Circuit majority relied on two Supreme Court decisions, *City of Richmond v. J. A. Croson Co.* and *Adarand v. Pena*, for the contention that modern equal protection has only one compelling interest, namely, remedying the effect of past discrimination. It removed diversity as a compelling interest for the use of racial classification. It declared that only past discrimination could be remedied by the use of racial classifications.[31]

Sexual Harassment

Sexual harassment is a very important subject. It is a form of discrimination and falls within the statutory prohibitions against sex discrimination. It is covered by the Civil Rights Act of 1964. Title VII, which prohibits discrimination on the basis of ascriptive characteristics such as sex in any employment condition, also includes behavior that has an adverse effect on the work environment. This has come to include any verbal, nonverbal, or physical behavior that has an adverse effect on work conditions. It is divided into two categories, the first of which is quid pro quo harassment, and the second of which is a hostile work environment. Quid pro quo harassment involves the exchange of sexual favors for some type of employment benefit, such as a promotion or pay raise. A hostile work environment can be created by one's coworkers, supervisors, or clients who ask for dates, post suggestive pictures, or make lewd gestures or remarks.

QUID PRO QUO HARASSMENT

Williams v. Saxbe serves as an excellent example of quid pro quo sexual harassment.[32] The plaintiff in *Williams* was an employee of the Department of Justice. She brought an action under Title VII of the Civil Rights Act of 1967, claiming that her supervisor made sexual advances toward her. She accused her supervisor of retaliatory conduct in response to her refusal to submit to his sexual requests. Ultimately, she was fired. A court ruled that her supervisor was in a position to hire, fire, or promote her, or at least to influence others who had that influence over her. If she denied her supervisor's requests her position would have been jeopardized, as it was. The supervisor's retaliatory action of firing her represented a sanction only an employer can impose, and such employer behavior violated Title VII of the Civil Rights Act.

HOSTILE WORK ENVIRONMENT

The first major case that came under the category of hostile work environment was *Vinson v. Meritor Savings and Loan*.[33] The plaintiff, Michelle Vinson, was employed as a teller-trainee and was promoted. Eventually she took an excessive number of days of sick leave and was fired. She then brought action against the bank, claiming she had been sexually harassed by her supervisor. She claimed that she had complied with his demand for sex because she was afraid she would lose her job. She also contended that he fondled her in front of other employees, and exposed himself to her in the women's bathroom. Vinson asked for injunctive relief as well as compensatory and punitive damages against her supervisor and the bank, alleging unwelcome sexual advances created a hostile work environment in violation of Title VII.

There were countercharges by the supervisor and the bank. One was that Vinson dressed provocatively, and another was she had engaged in sexual fantasies. The bank stated that if her supervisor had sexually harassed her, it was unknown to the bank and was engaged in without its consent or approval. In addressing the issues, a district court labeled Vinson's relations with her supervisor as voluntary and said that it had nothing to do with her employment advancement. It also found that, even if the supervisor had harassed Vinson, Meritor was not liable for his action, and held that evidence of Vinson's dress and personal fantasies was admissible. The court ruled in favor of Meritor. Vinson then took the case to an appeals court, which ruled in her favor. The Supreme Court upheld the court of appeals, finding that Vinson's voluntary sexual relationship was not a defense to a sexual harassment case. The decision strengthened the hostile environment theory of sexual harassment.[34]

Application of Meritor v. Vinson   Catherine A. Broderick was employed as an enforcement attorney in the Washington office of the Securities and Exchange Commission. When first employed, her performance rating was high, but later she was criticized for a poor attitude. She complained that her emotional state was caused by sexual harassment on the job. She contended that the head of the SEC's regional office got drunk at a party and fondled her and tried to undress her. A supervisor had an affair with his secretary and arranged for her promotion. A third executive also had an affair with his secretary. This woman received a cash bonus, a superlative performance rating, and two in-grade promotions.

Her complaint resulted in a district court finding of sexual harassment. Even though her employment benefits were not directly affected, the court was clear.[35] It said that the record established that Broderick and other women were, for obvious reasons, reluctant to voice their displeasure, and when they did, management treated them in a hostile manner. While there was no direct tie between the sexually hostile environment and the employment of Broderick, the court ruled that she was a victim of sexual harassment.

Ellison v. Brady—The Reasonable Woman Standard[36]   In this case, Kerry Ellison worked for the IRS. Sterling Gray, who worked near her, kept pestering her for dates and wrote her love notes. She filed a complaint with her employer alleging sexual harassment. Gray was counseled, told to leave her alone, and was transferred to another location. Eventually, he was brought back without Ellison's knowledge. She requested a transfer, which she got, and then filed suit. An appellate court ruled that a hostile work environment must be judged from the perspective of the victim—in this case, the reasonable woman. This meant that the victim's feelings must play an important role in identifying a series of actions as sexual harassment. The mere presence of an employee who has harassed a coworker may constitute a hostile work environment.

Robinson v. Jacksonville Shipyards[37]   Lois Robinson was one of six women among 846 skilled craft workers employed by Jacksonville Shipyards. She and two other female workers accused their employer of ignoring pornographic pinups displayed by male workers on their lockers, including a picture of a nude female with USDA CHOICE written on it. She claimed that she and other women had to endure a barrage of sexual comments from their male peers on the way to their lockers. She complained about the pictures to her male supervisor, but was told that the men had a constitutional right to post them. She took her case to the federal district court in Jacksonville, Florida, which ruled that pictures of naked and scantily clad women qualified as sexual harassment under Title VII of the Civil Rights Act of 1964. A "boys' club" atmosphere, wrote the presiding judge, is no less destructive to workplace equality than a sign declaring "men only."

Harris v. Forklift Systems[38]   As the only female supervisor in her company, which sold and leased forklifts, Teresa Harris tried to get along with her male counterparts. She attended some of their beer-drinking parties at a bar after work, exchanged dirty jokes, and incorporated into her vocabulary some of the off-color language the men used. But in 1987, after two years on the job, she quit and filed a lawsuit accusing her boss of ignoring her requests to stop sexually harassing her. He used crude language and sexual innuendos toward her in front of other men. He also allegedly dropped things on the floor and made her pick them up; suggested to her that she should dress in a way that would expose her legs and breasts; and asked her if she had sex with clients in order to get their business.

She claimed that this sexual harassment caused her to drink excessively and to cry all the time. The lawyer for her boss claimed she put herself in this position by conducting herself as "just one of the boys." Her boss claimed he was just joking and she should not have taken him seriously. A district court found that his conduct did not constitute a hostile work environment; even though his comments were offensive and abrasive, they were not serious enough to affect Harris's well-being. A reasonable woman manager under like circumstances would have been offended, but his conduct would not have affected her performance. Moreover, the court ruled that Harris was not subjectively so offended that she suffered psychological damage. The decision went to an appellate court, which upheld the decision.

The case then went to the Supreme Court, which decided in her favor. The ruling may well affect every workplace in the nation and will define, once and for all, the point at which sexual comments and tasteless jokes on the job constitute sexual harassment. In the past, many federal courts have required women to demonstrate how they have been psychologically injured. They have had to prove that the conduct was so severe that it altered the victim's work conditions and produced a hostile work environment. The Supreme Court decision changes this.

Burlington Industries v. Ellerth[39]   Several major sexual harassment cases were resolved by the U.S. Supreme Court in 1998. One involved Kimberly Ellerth, a marketing assistant in the mattress-fabric division of Burlington Industries, whose boss asked her to wear short skirts, grabbed her knee, and said, "You know, Kim, I could make your job very hard or very easy here." Despite a constant barrage of sexual comments, innuendos, and sexual suggestions from her boss, she was promoted. She sued the company on the grounds of sexual harassment even though she rejected him and was promoted anyway. A circuit court allowed the case to advance to the Supreme Court, saying that a person could claim she was subjected to quid pro quo harassment and hold a company liable even when a supervisor's threat had no adverse effect on her job advancement. The Supreme Court ruled that harassment is defined by the ugly behavior of the manager, not by what happens to the worker consequently.

Faragher v. City of Boca Raton[40]   Beth Ann Faragher, now a lawyer, was formerly a lifeguard in Boca Raton, Florida. In her sexual harassment suit against the city, she contended that she and other female lifeguards were harassed by their supervisors who would request sexual favors, grab them by the breasts and buttocks, and try to break in on their showers. But Faragher never complained to recreation department officials about the misconduct of her supervisors, and the Eleventh U.S. Circuit Court of Appeals said the City of Boca Raton was not liable. It held that an agent (lifeguard) is not acting within the scope of his employment when he is going on a frolic of his own. The City of Boca Raton argued that it should not be held liable because it had a clear policy against sexual harassment. The Supreme Court ruled that it is not enough to have a policy; it must be disseminated and enforced effectively.

Oncale v. Sundowner Offshore Services[41]   Joseph Oncale was a roustabout who worked on an oil rig off the coast of Louisiana. He was constantly sexually harassed by his boss and coworkers. They called him vile names and propositioned him for sex. He filed a sexual harassment lawsuit against the company, Sundowner Offshore Services, but a lower court ruled that Title VII of the Civil Rights Act of 1964 only covered harassment of women by men, and harassment of men by women, but not same-sex harassment. In this particular case, the Supreme Court ruled that the Title VII provision applied even when the victim and the harasser were of the same sex. The case was remanded back to the Louisiana court that originally heard the case.

VIOLENCE AGAINST WOMEN ACT OF 1994

Violence in the workplace is of increasing concern in the United States. Much of the violence is directed against women. A remedy is the Violence Against Women Act (VAWA) that was passed in 1994 after nearly four years of hearings and extensive debate concerning the pervasive nature and widespread effects of violence against women. As a result of the hearings, Congress determined that a comprehensive federal approach was called for to stem the increase in gender-motivated violence and to address a perception that this type of violence was not as serious as other crimes. Gender-motivated violence was determined to be a hate crime; and guidelines for determining hate crimes included the following:

1. language used by the perpetrator;
2. the severity of the attack including mutilation;
3. the lack of provocation;
4. previous history of similar incidents;
5. the absence of any other apparent motive, such as robbery.

VAWA has two major provisions:

1. It authorized $1.6 billion in federal spending over a six-year period to aid state and local attempts to reduce violence against women, including money for education and prevention, battered women's shelters, and a national domestic violence hotline.
2. Title III of the act provides a civil rights remedy. It is statutorily limited to violent crimes committed because of gender or on the basis of gender, and due, at least in part, to hate based on the victim's gender. A crime of violence is defined as an act or series of acts that would constitute a felony if the conduct presents a serious risk of physical injury to another person. The person injured may sue for compensatory and punitive damages, and injunctive and declaratory relief.

STATE FAIR EMPLOYMENT LAWS

Federal laws pertaining to employment practices are not the only laws that affect employers; there also are state laws. In fact, federal laws are often designed to stimulate activity by the states under their existing laws. The Civil Rights Act of 1964 directed the EEOC to defer to the states for a reasonable time when there is a charge of discrimination. A number of local governments also have antidiscrimination laws. Almost all states provide for an administrative hearing and the judicial enforcement of orders of an administrative agency or officials, and carry penalties for violating the laws. State laws apply to all employers, unions, and employment agencies located within a state without being restricted to those engaged solely in intrastate operations. This application of state laws to interstate employees has been upheld by the Supreme Court.

State laws vary in their coverage but generally prohibit discrimination on the basis of race, sex, age, and national origin, unless a necessary occupational requirement. Apart from laws governing the practices of business firms, many states have separate laws requiring equal pay for equal work by male and female employees. These laws are limited to eliminating discrimination in wage differences and do not touch other forms of job discrimination. In addition to the equal pay laws, discrimination in compensation based on sex also is barred, either specifically or by implication, in states that include sex bias in their unemployment practice laws.

RECRUITMENT AND TESTING OF WORKERS

Employers are also affected by laws concerning the recruitment and testing of workers. In advertising for workers, it is unlawful for an employer to print or publish an advertisement related to employment that expresses a preference based on sex, except when sex is a necessary requisite for employment. Somewhat similar requirements have been applied to application forms with respect to race, though it quickly became apparent that if there were no records concerning race, there would be insufficient statistical evidence on which to prove discrimination or the lack of it. Thus, the EEOC had to grapple with the fact that the logical time and place to gather certain significant information about a person's qualifications is also the time when there is the greatest likelihood of discrimination in recruitment and hiring.

EMPLOYMENT INTERVIEWS

In hiring workers, employers can run afoul of Title VII of the Civil Rights Act of 1964 or other legislation regulating employment practices. One of the greatest areas of potential problems is in the employment interview, since virtually all employers use it. There are basically three types of questions that are illegal. First, it is illegal to ask questions about race, sex, or age in the employment interview unless they are relevant to the job. Second, questions asked of one group but not another are generally illegal. An example would be that asking a woman how many children she has without asking the same question of male applicants is usually illegal. Third, questions that would have an adverse effect on employment should not be asked unless they are job related. Table 8-7 (on page 166) provides examples of questions that can and cannot be asked.

TESTING

Certain personnel problems confronting businesses are quite subtle. The entire area of testing is an excellent example of how genuine efforts at compliance with civil rights laws can still be construed as noncompliance. Courts have held that

TABLE 8-7 PRE-EMPLOYMENT INTERVIEWS: WHAT IS LAWFUL AND WHAT IS UNLAWFUL

QUESTION	LAWFUL	UNLAWFUL
Name	First, middle, last—use of any name necessary for checking previous work experience	Requirement of prefix Mr., Ms., Mrs. or inquiries about names changed by marriage or divorce
Height and Weight		Questions are unlawful unless there is a BFOQ
Religion	Only questions based on BFOQ	Questions not based on BFOQ
Age	Questions as to whether or not applicants meet minimum/ maximum age standards	How old are you? Birth date
Marital Status	Whether person can meet specific work schedules, or has responsibility that would interfere with work	Whether person is single, married, divorced, or engaged; number and ages of dependent children; all questions related to pregnancy.
Photograph	May be required after employment	Requirement that applicant attach photo
Criminal Record	Have you ever been convicted of a crime?	Have you ever been arrested?
Credit Rating		All questions regarding credit ratings, charge accounts, or other indebtedness
Military History	Military experience of relevance to the job	Type of discharge, military discipline record
National Origin	Languages applicant speaks, reads, or writes	Birthplace of applicant; how foreign languages were learned

Source: Jeffrey A. Norris, President, Equal Employment Opportunity Council. (Washington, D.C., May 1997) unpublished data.

inquiries into a prospective employee's criminal record would be racially discriminatory unless the inquiry and the answer it was designed to elicit were somehow directly related to the total assessment of the employee. The same is true of all other types of preemptive testing and standards, such as aptitude tests, IQ tests, and educational achievement tests. That there was no intent to discriminate does not matter.

OTHER EMPLOYMENT LAWS

There are other important employment laws that are worthy of note. One is the Family and Medical Leave Act of 1993, which is designed to provide job security for workers who have to take leave to care for a child, spouse, or other relatives. Unlike similar laws in the European countries that provide paid leave, often for up to one year, American workers can only take unpaid leave. The second act is the Occupational Safety and Health Act of 1970, which is designed to reduce the number of injuries and fatalities incurred in the workplace.

THE FAMILY AND MEDICAL LEAVE ACT (FMLA)

FMLA, which is under the jurisdiction of the Department of Labor, covers public employers of any size and private employers with fifty or more employees during each of twenty or more calendar work weeks in the current or preceding calendar year. Employees eligible to take leave under the act must have worked for an employer for at least twelve months and for at least 1,250 hours immediately preceding the commencement of any leave taken under the act. An eligible employee can take a total of twelve work weeks unpaid leave during any twelve-month period for the birth of a child; adoption; the care of a child, spouse, or parent; and a serious health problem that would make him or her unable to perform the job. Eligible employees can use any accrued vacation or personal leave for FMLA purposes.[42]

THE OCCUPATIONAL SAFETY AND HEALTH ACT (OSHA)

OSHA covers most employers and employees, including agricultural workers, nonprofit organizations, and professionals. The purpose of the act is to assure safe and healthful working conditions for men and women. It requires employers to comply with safety and health standards promulgated by OSHA. In addition, every employer is required to furnish for each of his or her employees a job free from recognized hazards that cause or are likely to cause death or serious injury. Recognized hazards are defined as those that can be recognized by the common human senses, unaided by testing devices, and those that are generally known in the industry as hazardous. Further, a firm can be penalized only if the unsafe condition has been cited by an inspector and the employer has refused to correct it in the specified time.

MITSUBISHI MOTORS MANUFACTURING COMPANY OF AMERICA v. EEOC

In April 1996 the Chicago office of the Equal Employment Opportunity Commission (EEOC) filed a class-action suit against Mitsubishi Motors Manufacturing Company of America (MMMA), a subsidiary of Mitsubishi Motors Corporation of Japan, charging it with condoning sexual harassment of women workers at its plant in Normal, Illinois. EEOC alleged that as many as seven hundred women were harassed for years while plant managers did nothing. The suit claimed the breasts, buttocks, and genitals of female assembly line workers were groped and fondled, obscene remarks were made, and sexual graffiti covered the walls. Separately, a private lawsuit in the Peoria, Illinois, federal court was brought by twenty-nine women alleging sexual harassment at the MMMA plant. The suit contended that women were retaliated against by other workers, and that company officials tried to intimidate them.

The company retaliated against EEOC by staging a rally outside their Chicago office to protest the class-action suit. It shut down its production line for a day and offered all employees who wanted to participate a free lunch and a trip aboard one of the thirty-nine buses it rented for the occasion. An estimated 3,000 workers attended the rally. The purpose of the rally was to counter what the company said was a politically motivated lawsuit by the federal government. Wages at the Mitsubishi plant were quite high for that area of Illinois, averaging better than $30,000 a year. Lawyers representing the company alleged that one of the twenty-nine women had a pattern of promiscuous behavior.

Conversely, EEOC contended that MMMA made no effort to cooperate during the investigation that began in April 1994. Apparently the company refused to let EEOC representatives interview management-level personnel accused of harassment. Requests for interviews with witnesses of sexual harassment were also turned down. Companies under investigation usually make an effort to improve their practices so that they are in compliance with the law. However, MMMA did not. Moreover, the company was not interested in settling out of court. Eventually public pressure caused MMMA to try to settle the case. Although sexual harassment is common in Japan, it is not considered important. What was important to top management executives in Tokyo was the effect that a high-level lawsuit would have on the sales of Mitsubishi products in the United States.

MMMA AND THE MITSUBISHI KEIRETSU

MMMA is a subsidiary of Mitsubishi Motor Corporation of Japan, which in turn is part of a giant Japanese combine called a keiretsu bearing the same name. The original Mitsubishi company was formed in 1879 and developed into a combine called a zaibatsu. Included in the zaibatsu were industrial companies, insurance companies, banks, and trading companies. By the 1930s six zaibatsus accounted for 90 percent of the total industrial output of Japan. When World War II was over, the zaibatsus were broken up by the American occupational authorities. Later, they reemerged in the form of keiretsus. Today, some forty companies, most with the Mitsubishi name, belong to the Mitsubishi keiretsu, which is the largest industrial combine in the world with total assets of more than $1 trillion. Member firms of the keiretsu do business with each other, and the presidents of each firm meet regularly to discuss business strategy.

Of the seventy-one executives of the MMMA plant in Illinois, seventy were Japanese. Management culture is a reflection of their country's culture.

Japan is a male-dominated society, and the great majority of business executives are males. Group consensus is the name of the game in Japan. Male bonding is important and after hours, male executives go to karaoke bars to drink and to sing. This is an important part of the Japanese corporate culture. Women simply are not a part of it. One of the sexual harassment charges against the MMMA plant in Illinois was that photographs of male workers having sex with prostitutes at various parties were passed around on the job. It was alleged that managers attended some parties, knew that the pictures were being passed around, and did nothing to stop it. Some of the American workers claimed they saw the same thing happen when they visited the parent company in Japan.

JAPAN AND SEX DISCRIMINATION

Japan passed an Equal Opportunity Law in 1986 that specifies that companies make an effort to prevent discrimination against women, but provides no penalties for companies that violate this law. Consequently, blatant and pervasive incidents of sex discrimination and sexual harassment continue. Japanese companies skirt these laws by using a two-track hiring system in which 98 percent of women employees are placed on a career track to lower-paying positions with little chance of promotion. While the educational level of women has been increasing, most college-educated Japanese women who work are considered office ladies who answer phones and serve tea to their male colleagues. Employers often specify a gender preference when they advertise and ask personal questions of women, but not men, during interviews. Unwritten policies against hiring older women because they are less attractive are prevalent. Women are expected to handle lewd comments and gestures quietly, and are considered immature if they don't.

The Japanese culture places much emphasis on family and the roles of women as housewife and mother. This view has roots in religion as well as tradition. Since the eighth century, Confucian and Buddhist thought supported a patrilineal descent system that discriminated against women in the legal codes and ascribed to them an inferior social and religious status. Emphasis on women's roles as mother and caregiver has given Japanese women a sense of power and pride in the households that could not be achieved in other roles. The Japanese stress the importance of the group over the individual and respect for the elders. There are many multigenerational households where women are charged with the care of elderly family members as well as children.

However, as more and more Japanese women enter the workplace, change has occurred. A ruling by the Tokyo district court in November 1996 found the Shiba Shinyo credit union guilty of sex discrimination, ordering it to pay twelve female employees $900,000 in damages and to promote eleven of the women to management positions. This is the first case in a Japanese court that has held a company liable for denying promotions because of gender.

MITSUBISHI REFORMS

The Martin report has resulted in a number of reforms that have been initiated by Mitsubishi to curb sexual harassment at its plant. Workers must now attend eight hours of antiharassment classes, but supervisors have to spend ninety-nine hours learning how to curb misbehavior and resolve conflicts, among other skills. Managers' raises are now based in part on how well they handle sexual harassment issues. Requirements that supervisors rotate between day and night shifts have been changed, making it easier for women with children to advance. After many women complained that they thought promotions were handled through an "old boys' network," the company began to post job openings on bulletin boards. Sixteen men have been fired for sexual harassment, while other men have had their pay docked and their job grades reduced.

SUMMARY

In recent years, the focus of government regulation has been on the achievement of social goals. An example is the regulation pertaining to the employment of women and members of minority groups. In 1964 the Civil Rights Act was passed to prevent discrimination based on race, color, sex, religion, or national origin. Other acts were passed to prevent discrimination based on age and disability and to provide equal pay for equal work. Executive orders in 1965 and 1967 introduced the idea of affirmative action, which has come to be associated with the hiring and promotion of more women and minorities. Sexual harassment has also become an important workplace issue. It is a form of discrimination and falls within the statutory provisions against sex discrimination.

QUESTIONS FOR DISCUSSION

1. What is quid pro quo sexual harassment?
2. Affirmative action is a very controversial subject. Discuss the arguments for and against it.
3. Discuss the difference between disparate impact and disparate treatment in employment.
4. Explain why incomes of women lawyers and physicians are relatively no better off in comparison to the earnings of men in the same professions than they were twenty years ago.
5. What is the reasonable woman defense?
6. Why is the case of *Oncale v. Sundowner Offshore Services* significant?
7. Discuss some of the questions that can and cannot be used in employment interviews.

NOTES

1. Daniel Bell, "On Meritocracy and Equality," *The Public Interest*. Vol. 29 (Fall 1972): 18–21.
2. U.S. Bureau of the Census. *Statistical Abstract of the United States: 1999* (Washington, D.C.: October 1999), p. 488.
3. *Ibid.*, p. 479.
4. United Nations Development Program, *Human Development Report 1997* (New York: Oxford University Press, 1997), p. 170.
5. Jodi L. Jacobson, *Gender Bias: Roadblock to Sustainable Development.* (Washington, D.C.: World Watch, September 1992).
6. *Statistical Abstract of the United States 1999*, p. 416.
7. *Ibid.*, p. 417.
8. *Ibid.*, p. 414.
9. The mean income of all physicians in 1995 was $182,400, which was down from the two previous years.
10. Barbara F. Reskin and Heidi I. Hartmann, eds. *Women's Work, Men's Work: Sex Segregation on the Job* (Washington, D.C.: National Academy Press, 1996), pp. 27–41.
11. Daniel Bell, *The Cultural Contradictions of Capitalism* (New York: Basic Books, 1976), p. 275.
12. *Plessy v. Ferguson*, 163 U.S. 540 (1896).
13. *Brown v. Board of Education*, 347 U.S. 483 (1954).
14. *Abrams v. Baylor College*, 805 F. 2d 528 (5th Cir. 1980).
15. *Griggs v. Duke Power Co.*, 401 U.S. 424 (1971).
16. *Watson v. Fort Worth Bank and Trust*, No. 86-6139 S.C. (1988).
17. Harry A. Millis and Emily Clark Brown, *From the Wagner Act to Taft-Hartley.* (Chicago, IL: University of Chicago Press, 1950), p. 97.
18. U.S. Equal Employment Opportunity Commission, *Legislative History of Titles VII and XI of Civil Rights Act of 1964* (Washington, D.C.: U.S. Government Printing Office, 1969), p. 3005.
19. *U.S. Steelworkers v. Brian Weber*, 61 U.S. 480 (1979).
20. *Firefighters Local Union No. 1784 v. Stotts*, U.S. No. 82-206 (1984).
21. *Sheetmetal Workers of N.Y. Local 28 v. EEOC*, 54 USLW 3596 (1986).
22. *IAFF v. Cleveland*, 54 USLW 3573 (1986).
23. *City of Richmond v. J.A. Croson Co.*, 488 U.S. 469 (1989).
24. *City of Richmond v. J.A. Croson Co.*, 57 Law Week 9132 (January 23, 1989).
25. *Adarand Constructors, Inc. v. Pena*, 115 S. Ct. 2097 (1995).
26. Under this standard, only affirmative action plans that respond to specific, provable past discrimination and that are narrowly tailored to eliminate such bias would be legal.
27. White teacher Sharon Taxman claimed her school board violated her rights when it made a racially based decision to lay her off rather than an equally qualified black teacher. She eventually got her job back and was compensated through a settlement with the NAACP.
28. The University of Michigan suit, filed by Jennifer Gratz, a white student who was denied admission, is aimed at the Supreme Court's decision in the two-decade-old *Bakke* decision; it upheld the use of race as a plus factor in college admissions but barred the use of quotas and separate tracks for minorities and white students. Gratz, who had a 3.76 GPA in high school and scored a 25 on the ACT, was active in a number of extracurricular activities.
29. *Texas v. Hopwood*, 116 S. Ct. 2581 (1996).
30. *Hopwood v. Texas*, 861 F. Supp. 551, 557-63 (W. D. Texas 1994).
31. *Hopwood v. Texas*, 78 F. 3d 932, 937 (5th Cir. 1996).

32. *Williams v. Saxbe*, 413 F. Supp. 654 (D.C. Cir. 1976).
33. *Meritor Savings Bank FSB v. Vinson*, 106 S. Ct. 2399 (1986).
34. Maria Morlacri, "Sexual Harassment Law and the Impact of Vinson," *Employee Relations Law Journal*. Vol. 13 (Winter 1987/88): 501–513.
35. *Broderick v. Ruder, Chairman U.S. SEC*. 685 S. 1269 (May 13, 1988).
36. *Ellison v. Brady, Sec. of the Treasury*, 924 F. 2d 872 (1991).
37. *Robinson v. Jacksonville Shipyards*, 760 F. Supp. 1486 (M.D. Fla, 1991).
38. *Harris v. Forklift Systems, Inc.*, 114 S. Ct. 367 (1993).
39. *Burlington Industries, Inc. v. Kimberly B. Ellerth*, 118 S. Ct. 2257, June 26, 1998.
40. *Beth Ann Faragher v. City of Boca Raton*, 118 S. Ct. 2275, June 26, 1998.
41. *Oncale v. Sundowner Offshore Services*, 118 S. Ct. 75, 1998.
42. The act requires employers to post notices regarding the FMLA at the work site. An employer's failure to do so can result in fines up to $100 per offense.

RECOMMENDED READING

Bennett-Alexander, Dawn D. "Same-Gender Sexual Harassment: The Supreme Court Allows Coverage Under Title VII." *Labor Law Journal*, No. 4 (April 1998): 927–940.

Chay, Kenneth. "The Impact of Federal Civil Rights Policy on Black Economic Progress: Evidence from the Equal Employment Opportunity Act of 1972." *Industrial and Labor Relations Review*, Vol. 51, No. 4 (July 1998): 608–632.

Greenlaw, Paul S., and John P. Kohl. "Proving Age Discrimination in the Court's View." *Labor Law Journal*, No. 1 (January 1997): 50–56.

Lavelle, Marianne. "The New Rules of Sexual Harassment," *U.S. News and World Report* (July 6, 1998): 30–31.

Siegel, Matt, "Yes, They Can Fire You." *Fortune* (October 26, 1998): 301.

United Nations Development Program. *Human Development Report, 1995*. New York: Oxford University Press. 1995. The entire report deals with gender inequality throughout the world.

Zachary, Mary-Kathryn. "The Violence against Women Act—An Emerging Employment Remedy." *Labor Law Journal*, No. 3 (March 1998): 888–896.

CHAPTER 9

ENVIRONMENTAL PROTECTION

One of the major areas of social regulation of business is environmental protection. In fact, pollution control costs are by far the most important regulatory costs imposed on business. There are not only the incremental costs of such items as emission control devices and paperwork costs, but also the secondary effects such as opportunity costs, changes in productivity, and costs of regulation-imposed delays. An example of an opportunity cost would be money spent in cleaning up the environment that could have been spent in modernizing industrial plants to meet foreign competition. There is also the economic cost of lost jobs when a plant shuts down as a result of environmental compliance costs.

Why are these costs imposed upon business? The major reason is because of health benefits. Pollution, whether it be air, water, noise, or any other type, causes problems. Air pollution increases the mortality rate and respiratory ailments, particularly among older people. From 1990–1997, although the share of polluting fuels was reduced by more than 40 percent, each year nearly three million deaths were traced to air pollution. There is also a relationship between air pollution and the incidence of lung cancer. Outbreaks of infectious diseases have been traced to contaminants in municipal water supplies (nearly 1.3 million people do not have access to clean water), and certain chemicals in water supplies have been linked with increased rates of cancer. From 1990–1997, more than five million people died from diseases caused by water contamination.

Another reason to try to curb pollution is that it can have an adverse effect on economic activities. Agricultural production can be harmed by rising acidity in the soil. Lowered water control standards have had an adverse effect on commercial fishing production.

Finally, there are aesthetic benefits to curbing pollution. Air and water pollution can cause odors and tastes that affect people's ability to function well. Oil slicks on a beach or fish killed by a chemical spill are unpleasant, as is noise pollution. Pollutants that are visibly unpleasant can have an adverse effect on property values.

TYPES OF POLLUTION

Pollution of the environment is not a recent phenomenon, either in this country or around the world. In the United States it is a by-product of industrialization, which was stimulated by the Civil War. Examples of environmental problems are numerous. One that has received some attention in recent years is radon, an odorless, colorless radioactive gas produced by the decay of uranium in rocks and soils, and a major cause of lung cancer. Manufacturers have made radon detectors so that people can see if their homes have a problem.

The environmental problem that has received the most attention worldwide lately has been the so-called greenhouse effect, wherein the earth has been getting warmer by over one degree Fahrenheit in the last century.[1] A leading cause is carbon dioxide from the burning of fossil fuels such as oil, coal (half of the electricity in the United States comes from coal), and natural gas. The carbon from the fuel meets the oxygen from the air and the resultant carbon dioxide accumulates in the atmosphere. Another cause is from gases such as chlorofluorocarbons, although the United States banned most imports of them as of January 1, 1996. These and other gases come from a variety of sources, such as vehicle exhausts and industrial solvents.

The first large-scale increase in carbon dioxide levels came with the clearing of North American and European forests. Then, after a period of stability, the levels began to rise when coal was used for steam power in locomotives, factories, and ships, followed by oil, which surpassed coal as the world's leading primary energy source in the mid-1960s. One of the factors in the greenhouse effect is that since 1960 the number of automobiles worldwide has increased more than twice as fast as the population. Added to this is the burning of the Amazon rain forest, which began in earnest in the 1980s and continues today.

What happens when the gases such as carbon dioxide, methane, nitrous oxide (which collectively make up some 80 percent of the gases), sulfur hexafluoride, hydrofluorocarbons, and perfluorocarbons are released into the atmosphere? They act like the glass in a greenhouse, in that they let in the sunlight but trap the heat. About one-half of the sun's energy, solar radiation, is absorbed by the earth and converted into heat, which is then trapped, especially by carbon dioxide. The gases absorb rather than reflect the infrared radiation that produces heat. As the heat rises from the earth's surface, it strikes molecules of carbon dioxide and other gases, setting them vibrating. The gas molecules reflect some of the heat back to earth, which intensifies the warming or greenhouse effect. As more heat is trapped, the earth's overall temperature rises. If the troposphere (sea level to ten miles up) gets moisture (and water vapor is a greenhouse gas), the warming could accelerate. Water vapor, in fact, makes up 98 percent of the gases. Without the water vapor and the other gases such as carbon dioxide, the earth would be 61 degrees Fahrenheit colder. The warming is greater near the Arctic than near the equator (in the past thirty years temperatures in the Alaskan Arctic have risen twice as much as in the rest of the world), is greater at night than during the day, and is greater in winter than in summer. Unless some action is taken to curb these gases, predictions have been made that the average temperature will rise another three to seven degrees Fahrenheit in the future. Already, six of the warmest years on record have occurred in the 1990s. Most of the members of the United Nations have ratified protocols to cut down on greenhouse gases but, even if all comply, it would not be until around the years 2050 to 2070 that recovery would take place.

The next question is, why is it so important to curtail the use of these gases? First, the melting of the polar ice cap due to the warmth can produce more icebergs that can endanger shipping. Also, water expands when heated, and oceans have risen some four to ten inches this century. Countries that are already adversely affected by flooding will have more flooding. In addition, the warming produces hotter and drier summers, which hurts farming and could cause crop failures. Tropical diseases could follow the rising mercury. The increase in warmth could also affect the world's wildlife, such as birds, that have adapted to the climate in which they are located.

Who are the world's biggest emitters of heat-trapping gases? To nobody's surprise, the United States, despite a drop in the 1970s due to the energy crisis, is number one. The top five nations account for more than one-half the carbon dioxide emissions. The United States, despite having just 4.6 percent of the world's population, consumes 24.4 percent of the world's energy and emits 23.5 percent of the carbon dioxide. Next is China; with 21 percent of the world's population, it consumes 9.9 percent of the world's energy but emits 14.1 percent of its carbon dioxide. Then come the former parts of the USSR; with 5 percent of the world's population they consume 11.1 percent of the world's energy and emit 11.2 percent of its carbon dioxide. Japan follows; with 2.2 percent of the world's population, it consumes 5.9 percent of the world's energy, and emits 5.2 percent of its carbon dioxide. Rounding out the top five is Germany; with 1.4 percent of the world's population, it consumes 3.8 percent of the world's energy, and emits 4.1 percent of its carbon dioxide. India and Britain follow as the countries that also emit the most carbon dioxide. All countries combined emit some seven billion tons of carbon dioxide into the atmosphere each year; there is 30 percent more carbon dioxide in the air today than there was in 1860. A country such as Brazil also emits much carbon dioxide due to the previously mentioned burning of the rain forest.

In the United States alone, carbon dioxide emissions have risen 9 percent

Table 9-1 A Comparison of Per Capita Carbon Dioxide Emissions for Selected Countries, 1996* (Metric Tons)

Country	Per Capita Metric Tons
Australia	16.7
Belgium	10.4
Canada	13.7
China	2.8
France	6.2
Germany	10.5
India	1.1
Italy	7.0
Japan	9.3
Norway	15.3
Russian Federation**	10.7
Singapore	21.6
United Kingdom	9.5
United States	20.0

*Average for low-income countries including China and India, 1.4 per capita metric tons. Average for high-income countries, 12.5 metric tons.

**The Russian Federation is a lower-middle-income country. Little attention was given to pollution when the Soviet Union and Eastern Europe were communist.

Source: The World Bank, *1999 World Development Indicators* (Washington, D.C.: The World Bank, 1999), pp. 148–150.

since 1980, in part because car usage has more than doubled since 1970. In 1997, petroleum accounted for 38.19 percent of the emissions, natural gas 24.1 percent, coal 22.3 percent, renewable energy 7.9 percent, and nuclear energy 7.6 percent. Of the energy used that year, 37.8 percent was for industrial use (up from 32.5 percent the year before), 36.1 percent was for residential and commercial use (up from 35.3 percent the year before, of which residential was 19.6 percent and commercial 15.7 percent), and transportation was 26 percent (down from 32.2 percent the year before). Just since 1990, the emission of carbon dioxide in the United States has increased some 7.4 percent through 1996, and the forecast from the Clinton administration is that it will be 13 percent higher by the end of the decade than it was in 1990.

The greenhouse effect problem has been compounded by the fact that carbon dioxide stays in the atmosphere for a century, on average. There were 280 parts per million of carbon dioxide before the Industrial Revolution, and 360 parts per million today. One result of all this is that the nations of the world have decided to try to do something about the problem. In 1992, at an Earth Summit held in Rio de Janeiro, Brazil, attended by 166 nations, an agreement to limit harmful climate change was signed. The developed nations pledged to reduce emissions of greenhouse gases by the year 2000. However, some countries, such as the United States, are falling short of that target. Therefore another conference on climate change, sponsored by the United Nations, met in Kyoto, Japan in December 1997. Some 159 nations were represented by more than five thousand delegates. The goal now for the United States is to reduce greenhouse gas levels by 7 percent of 1990 levels by the year 2012. Other nations and regions of the world have their own goals and timetables. The problem, in addition to meeting goals and timetables, is that not everyone is committed to them. For example, some members of the U.S. Congress have declared themselves against this goal for various reasons. Thus, the future of the greenhouse effect is still uncertain. The United States did sign the Kyoto Pact at an international conference held in Buenos Aires, Argentina, in November, 1998, but it still must be approved by the Senate.

There are, of course, other types of environmental problems, not the least of which is the depletion of the earth's ozone layer. That layer protects living organisms by using up ultraviolet and other high-energy forms of radiation through a cycle of chemical reactions. When the layer is weakened, ultraviolet radiation interacts with genetic material. The result is an increased incidence of skin cancer. What causes the depletion of the ozone layer? The chief culprits are freons, which are gases commonly used as solvents, refrigerants, and aerosol propellants. Freon reacts with ozone by converting it to atmospheric oxygen, thereby reducing the amount available to interact with ultraviolet radiation. Besides skin cancer in both humans and animals, there is a possibility that the depletion of the ozone layer might lower crop yields. The ozone layer has been depleted by some 30–35 percent since 1957. In fact, it was depleted by 10 percent alone in the year 1995, with the last three months of that year being the fastest ever, up to that time. The hole over Antarctica caused by the depletion is 3.9 million square miles, which is the size of Europe. The use of ozone-depleting substances is down by 70 percent since 1987, but there have been ozone losses as high as 55 percent in the year 2000.

Another environmental problem is acid rain, caused by acid deposition in the atmosphere. What happens is that sulfuric acid and nitric acid are oxidized, the former primarily by coal-fueled electric utilities, the latter primarily by motor vehicles and electric utilities. Also, a variety of volatile organic compounds are released during petroleum refining, chemical manufacturing, and with the use of paints and solvents, and they too oxidize into acid rain. The problem, of course, is that when the acid rain falls to earth it affects metals, paint systems, stones, and other materials sensitive to it. It can affect the growth of forests, and it may affect agricultural growth. Also, aquatic organisms can be damaged when acid rain falls into lakes and streams. Sulfur emissions are down 40 percent in the United States, but will triple in Asia by 2010.

Pesticides are yet another environmental problem, as they are hazardous to some forms of life and their misuse can cause environmental contamination. They can be ingested by humans because some may get into food products. DDT, which is now banned in the United States, is the classic example; it got into streams and lakes, poisoning fish and the people who ate them. Any pesticide that is water soluble can get into food crops, which are then consumed by humans. One of the biggest problems with pesticides is their increased use by developing countries; misuse can not only affect those who live there but those from the industrialized countries, since the pesticides can be reimported as residues on food. The U.S. government was concerned enough about the pesticide problem to unanimously pass a law in 1996, the Food Quality Protection Act, tightening the regulation of pesticides and imposing tougher rules to curb the risks for children. The EPA must apply a margin of safety ten times larger than the limits it previously set on cumulative exposure to traces of the chemicals. In 1999, in the first regulations intended specifically to protect children, it banned most uses of a pesticide applied widely for years on fruits and vegetables, and tightened restrictions on another.

Hazardous waste, both solid and toxic, creates another environmental problem. Solid waste includes garbage, disposable cartons, and other items emitted by consumers. The problem is what to do with it in our increasingly consumptive society. Landfills are full, and incineration can cause pollution. People in the United States have endorsed the concept of recycling, but some recyclers have more material than they can handle. The United States recycled approximately one billion pounds of plastic in 1998. As for toxic waste, that is caused by various by-products of industrial production. For example, nitrous acid is released by the production of fertilizers, and usually disposed of in barrels that are buried in the earth. The barrels, unfortunately, can sometimes leak and cause pollution. Another example is wastewater from factories and sewage treatment plants, because it includes such toxic substances as heavy metals, including lead and mercury. They, in turn, have been responsible for the decimation of oysters, lobsters, and crabs in some places such as Chesapeake Bay.

A potential problem in the environmental area is the possibility of a nuclear accident with the accompanying radiation danger. The meltdown of the nuclear power plant in Chernobyl in the former Soviet Union has been the biggest accident thus far, with a number of fatalities among workers who were employed at the plant as well as radiation damage that extended to neighboring countries, with contaminated milk as one example.

Perhaps the most important of all environmental problems is deforestation, because trees provide oxygen and prevent soil erosion. The average annual deforestation rate, from 1990–1995, was 38,610 square miles. The major forests of the world are the tropical rain forests, and those of the Amazon River and equatorial Africa have been disappearing at an alarming rate. Half of the world's tropical rain forests have been destroyed in the past one hundred years. One side effect is that wildlife populations native to the regions are in danger of becoming extinct or, at the very least, endangered. (These wildlife populations are further endangered by illegal wildlife trade, which garners $2–3 billion per year.) Also, since the deforestation occurs in very poor areas of the world, the little food supply that exists is reduced by the leaching of the soil, the polluting of water supplies, and the land becoming less arable. Another item of

TABLE 9-2   AVERAGE ANNUAL DEFORESTATION RATES FOR POOR
AND LOWER-MIDDLE-INCOME COUNTRIES, 1990–1995 (SQUARE KILOMETERS)*

COUNTRY	SQUARE KILOMETERS**
Brazil	25,544
Indonesia	10,844
Malaysia	4,002
Mexico	5,080
Myanmar	3,874
Paraguay	3,266
Peru	2,168
Philippines	2,624
Sudan	3,526
Tanzania	3,226
Thailand	3,294
Venezuela	5,034

*One square kilometer = 0.386 square miles = 246 acres.

**Low-income countries = 6,227 square kilometers.

Lower-middle income countries = 12,884 square kilometers.

High-income countries = –11,564 square kilometers, which means that these countries are replacing forests more rapidly than they are destroying them.

Source: The World Bank, *1990 World Development Indicators* (Washington, D.C.: The World Bank, 1999), pp. 120, 121, 122.

worry associated with deforestation is the disappearance of the carbon sink, which is anything that absorbs and retains carbon dioxide. Oceans are one type of sink, but so are forests and soils. When deforestation occurs, the trees are not there to absorb the carbon dioxide and so it goes into the atmosphere, helping to cause the greenhouse effect.

As can be seen, pollution is a global problem that transcends national boundaries and from which no country is immune. A good example is the pollution of the seas. Persons who traverse waters, whether they be recreational boaters, people who fish, or even those who operate ocean-going ships, have dumped their garbage overboard. The resultant debris entangles many different marine species, and some species even ingest it. In addition, persons on land can dump pollutants into rivers that eventually make their way to the sea. Finally, a combination of marine pollution plus overfishing can cause a declining food supply.

Another point that should be apparent is that pollution comes from many sources. For one thing, the simple matter of population density means there will be more waste created in those areas. Just in the United States, more than half the people live in 1 percent of the total land area, and two-thirds live in 9 percent of the area. Along with the density, there is widespread affluence in Western industrial society. Two cars per family is common, which means that many cars are junked each year, along with other items such as bottles and cans. People want creature comforts. Even something such as air conditioning can lead to environmental pollution. The following is a summation of major environmental problems today:

1. Radon
2. Greenhouse effect
3. Acid rain
4. Pesticides
5. Hazardous waste—solid and toxic
6. Nuclear accidents
7. Deforestation
8. Water pollution

Industry does have its share of responsibility. Steel was one of the industries that polluted places, such as Lake Erie, with its wastes. Even something as innocuous as changing the way steel is made lessened the demand for scrap metal, which in turn lessened the incentive for junk dealers to salvage old cars, which in turn led to the problem many cities face of having to dispose of old automobiles. The governments of the world share some of the blame, as they have often been lax in disposing of sewage and solid wastes and have ended up polluting rivers and the air. Many cities operate their own public utilities and have polluted, as has the federal government with some of its facilities.

SOLUTIONS TO POLLUTION

What can be done by governments to help solve the many environmental problems? They can regulate by such methods as legislation and the requiring of licenses, permits, and registration, along with zoning. An advantage of regulation is that similar standards are established for all business firms. A disadvantage is that it could lead to rigidities and might be unwieldy and inefficient. Governments could also try levying emission charges, such as taxes or fees, against polluters. Subsidies to business firms to defray the cost of compliance with pollution control standards are another possibility. Examples of subsidies are tax credits to compensate for the cost of buying pollution abatement equipment, outright cash payments to reduce the level of pollution, accelerated depletion allowances to let business firms write off the cost of pollution control equipment in a shorter time than usual, and property tax exemptions on pollution control equipment by state and local governments. Although subsidies sound good, they do have disadvantages, such as less pressure on a firm to find alternate ways of dealing with pollution. Subsidies are also financed out of general tax revenues, which violates the principle of equity because not all taxpayers are involved with the making or consuming of those products. All these approaches can be used in combinations; they are not mutually exclusive.

How has the U.S. government responded to the problems affecting the environment? It has passed many laws over the years to try to handle the various issues. The following is a list of U.S. environmental laws:

1. 1899 Refuse Act
2. 1924 Oil Pollution Act
3. 1948, 1956, and 1972 Water Pollution Control Acts and Amendments
4. 1963 and 1970 Clean Air Acts and Amendments
5. 1965 and 1970 Water Quality Acts
6. 1967 Air Quality Act
7. 1972 Noise Control Act
8. 1973 Endangered Species Act
9. 1975 Energy Policy and Conservation Act Amendments
10. 1976 Toxic Substances Control Act
11. 1976 Resource Conservation and Recovery Act
12. 1980 Comprehensive Environmental Response, Compensation, and Liability Act
13. 1984 Hazardous and Solid Waste Amendments
14. 1986 Emergency Planning and Community Right-to-Know Act
15. 1992 Safe Water Drinking Act Amendments plus 1996 Safe Water Drinking Act Renewal
16. 1996 Magnuson Fishery Conservation and Management Act
17. 1996 Food Quality Protection Act

The 1899 Refuse Act prohibited the discharge of waste materials into navigable waters. The 1924 Oil Pollution Act forbade the discharge of oil into coastal waters, and the 1948 Water Pollution Control Act authorized the Public Health Service to coordinate research, provide technical information and, on request from the states involved, provide limited supervision of interstate waterways. Congress then turned its attention to air pollution in 1955 by authorizing technical assistance to states and localities and setting up a research program. In 1956 the Water Pollution Control Act, amended in 1961, 1965, 1966, and 1970, considerably extended federal involvement, both regulatory and financial, in water pollution.

Congress then returned to air pollution with the 1963 Clean Air Act, which gave states grants to improve pollution control programs and to provide for federal enforcement in interstate pollution cases. It also expanded federal research, particularly in connection with pollution from motor vehicles and from the burning of coal and fuel oil, and it emphasized the need for controlling pollution from facilities operated by the federal government. The act was amended in 1965 to authorize federal regulation of motor vehicles through standards that became effective in 1968. It was amended again in 1966 to broaden the federal aid program, making grants available for state and local control programs. Meanwhile, in 1965, Congress revisited water pollution by passing the Water Quality Act, which created the Water Pollution Control Administration that was almost immediately transferred to the Department of the Interior. Then Congress went right back to air pollution with the 1967 Air Quality Act that directed the Department of Health, Education, and Welfare (the agency handling air pollution problems) to delineate broad atmospheric areas for the entire country, as well as air quality control regions. It continued and strengthened most of the provisions of the earlier laws and provided for special studies of jet aircraft emissions, the need for national emission standards, and labor and training problems. It also established the Presidential Air Quality Advisory Board.

With all the previously discussed laws and with the problem of two agencies trying to coordinate their enforcement, President Nixon in 1970 sent a reorganization plan to Congress to create an independent agency to handle all environmental problems. Congress approved the plan and the Environmental Protection Agency was created in the executive branch. Besides air and water pollution problems, the EPA was given other environmental problems that had been in various agencies, such as studies on the effects of insecticides and pesticides, and the creation of tolerance norms for pesticide chemicals.

Now that the EPA was in place, Congress passed probably the most important of all federal laws governing pollution, the 1970 Clean Air Act. Among other points, the act required that new cars be virtually pollution free by 1975, and specified that emissions of hydrocarbons and carbon monoxide gases had to be 90 percent less than levels permissible in 1970. When automobile manufacturers had difficulty meeting the requirement due to costs, the date was pushed to 1981. The manufacturers also had to offer a 50,000-mile warranty on emission control devices, and the law established strict controls for fuel additives.

In addition to the automobile sections, the law also set national standards for air pollution, with the states being required to establish programs to meet the national standards within four to six years. The EPA was authorized to set both primary and secondary standards for pollutants. The primary ones were to promote human health with an added margin of safety for the most vulnerable, such as the elderly and infants. The secondary standards were to prevent damage to such things as crops, visibility, buildings, water, and materials.

The law also directed the EPA to determine maximum emission limits for plants and factories on an industry-by-industry basis. States could then use these as guidelines for more specific restrictions for individual factories. If any region violated any standards, the states there had to limit new construction of pollution sources until the air was brought up to federal standards. Any company wanting to build a plant there had to install equipment that limited pollution to the least amount emitted by any similar factory elsewhere in the country. The EPA is required to reevaluate its standards every five years.

The year 1970 also saw another Water Quality Act that extended federal control standards to oil and hazardous substance discharges from onshore and offshore vessel facilities. However, the big law affecting water was the 1972

Water Pollution Control Act, which amended the previous acts in that field. Included in the law is a requirement that manufacturers monitor discharges at point sources of pollution and keep records of the results of their efforts to reduce water pollution. Both the EPA and the state may inspect the records. The law also extended federal control to all navigable waters. When there is a violation, the EPA can issue an order requiring compliance or notifying the state of the problem. If the state does not begin appropriate enforcement within thirty days, the EPA can issue a compliance order requiring the violator to comply with a conditional or limited permit, or it can bring a civil action or begin criminal proceedings. Finally, the law (as did the Clean Air Act) gives citizens the right to bring suits to enforce standards in the U.S. district courts.

The year 1972 found the government finally passing a law in the field of noise pollution, realizing that noise can be a danger to the health and welfare of the population, particularly in urban areas. Human blood pressure and heartbeat can be adversely affected, and sustained noise can cause permanent injury. Accordingly, the Noise Control Act sets noise emission standards for a wide variety of product categories. Specifically, it targets aircraft noise, sonic booms, railroads, and motor carriers, as well as newly manufactured products that have been identified as being major sources of noise. These standards were to be established for all products identified as major noise sources within eighteen months of the law's passage, with public health, safety, and welfare as the goal.

As with both the Clean Air and Water Pollution Control Acts, criminal sanctions under this law range from fines of up to $25,000 per day of violation, or imprisonment for up to one year, or both, for the first offense. Subsequent offenders are liable for fines of up to $50,000 for each day of violation or for imprisonment of up to two years, or both. Each additional day of violation constitutes a separate offense.

As with the other two laws, citizens may sue in federal district courts. In addition, citizens may sue both the administrator of the EPA and the administrator of the FAA for alleged failure to perform their duties under the law.

The law provides for technical assistance to be given state and local governments to develop and enforce noise standards, and it also authorizes labeling requirements for any product that emits noise capable of adversely affecting the public health and welfare or that is sold on the basis of its effectiveness in reducing noise. When a product is labeled, purchasers or users must be informed of the level of noise the product emits or its effectiveness in reducing noise, whichever may be the case.

In 1975 Congress passed the Energy Policy and Conservation Act Amendments, setting corporate average fuel economy standards for new cars produced in the United States that required car companies to achieve a sales-weighted, fleet-average economy of 27.5 miles in the 1985 model year.

Congress followed this in 1976 with the Toxic Substances Control Act, which gave the EPA broad regulatory authority over chemical substances from before their manufacture to their disposal. The EPA had to make an inventory of approximately 55,000 chemical substances, and the EPA has to be notified before any new chemical substances are manufactured. In addition, companies were given recordkeeping, testing, and reporting requirements so that the EPA can assess the relative risks of chemicals and regulate them.

Another 1976 law was the Resource Conservation and Recovery Act, which requires the safe disposal of hazardous wastes. Regulations define hazardous waste and establish standards for their generation and transportation. Owners and operators of facilities that treat, store, or dispose of hazardous wastes must get a permit, and a waste generator has to prepare a manifest for hazardous wastes that tracks the movement of the wastes from the point of generation to the point of disposal. If a waste is hazardous, it must be properly packaged and labeled.

The Comprehensive Environmental Response, Compensation, and Liability Act was passed in 1980 and created a $1.6 billion fund (Superfund) for the cleanup of both spills of hazardous substances and inactive waste disposal sites. This was followed in 1984 by the Hazardous and Solid Waste Amendments to try to protect groundwater. The amendments place restrictions on the treatment, storage, and disposal of hazardous waste in land-management facilities. They provide new regulations for underground tanks that store liquid petroleum and chemical products. They also created new and more stringent requirements for land disposal facilities that existed then and that will be created. The EPA also had to develop standards before November 1986, governing the burning of hazardous waste fuel mixtures. Finally, the amendments require producers and distributors of hazardous waste fuels to place a warning label on the invoice or bill of sale.

In 1986 Congress passed the Emergency Planning and Community Right-to-Know Act. Under it there was created a Toxic Release Inventory, and industry must report on an annual release or off-site transfer of some three hundred toxic chemicals. Any company breaking the law can be sued. After that came the Clean Air Act Amendments of 1990 to update the 1970 Clean Air Act. Among other provisions, communities can not only sue polluters but they can seek a portion of the fines.

Congress next focused on drinking water and, in the 1992 Safe Water Drinking Act Amendments, made water suppliers monitor eighty-eight regulated contaminants, whereas in 1986 it was twenty-three. Then in 1996 Congress renewed the Safe Water Drinking Act. It set $7.6 billion in grants and low-interest loans over a seven-year period to help communities upgrade drinking water systems, plus it gave state and local officials more leeway in regulating contaminants. However, consumers must be given more information about any significant contaminants in their local supply.

Also in 1996, Congress passed a new Magnuson Fishery Conservation and Management Act. It defines overfishing and it gave the Secretary of Commerce one year to determine which fisheries are overfished or nearly so. For those that are overfished, the relevant fishery management council must develop a plan to stop the overfishing and enact a plan to rebuild the fish stock in twelve months. Fishery managers can no longer use short-term financial considerations to legitimize setting exploitation rates above what scientists consider to be ecologically sustainable in the long run. The law defines "bycatch," setting a new national standard obligating councils to manage all fisheries so bycatch of nontarget species is minimized. It includes fish thrown overboard dead because they were the wrong size or species to be of economic value to the fisher. The North Pacific Council must reduce these annually for four straight years. Finally, in order to halt the privatization of fisheries, there were to be no individual transferable quota programs for the next four years.

Since pollution is global, there have been many international agreements, especially with regard to ocean pollutants. The following is a list of international environmental agreements:

1. London Dumping Convention
2. Barcelona Convention
3. Cartagena Convention
4. Antarctic Treaty plus Convention of 1982 plus Environmental Protocol
5. Rio de Janeiro Earth Summit
6. Kyoto Conference on Climate Change
7. Buenos Aires Conference on Implementing the Kyoto Pact

The London Dumping Convention came into force in 1975 and regulates wastes loaded on ships with the express intent of dumping them at sea. The agreement prohibits the dumping of certain substances, such as mercury, DDT, PCBs, oil, and certain plastics, and requires special permits for certain other wastes, such as low-level radioactive waste. The Regional Seas Program of the United Nations Environmental Program encourages countries to develop regional action plans. One example is the Barcelona Convention, which prohibits the dumping of certain substances, such as mercury and radioactive wastes, into the Mediterranean. Another would be the Cartagena Convention, to which the United States belongs, and which is designed to reduce petroleum contamination of the Caribbean Sea and to control land-based sources of marine pollution.

There are also international agreements pertaining to the Antarctic seas. The Antarctic Treaty of 1959 prohibits use of the continent for nuclear explosion, and the Convention of 1982 requires a comprehensive ecosystems approach to controlling the use of living marine resources. Restrictions on harvests must protect the species being harvested and other species that depend on the harvested species for food. In 1996 the United States ratified the environmental protocol that had been signed in 1991 by 26 nations. It provides for more vigorous treatment for sewage, an end to incineration of waste and to open disposal, increased mandates for removal of waste altogether, and a fifty-year ban on mining for oil, gas, or any other mineral.

COSTS OF POLLUTION

Because pollution control is costly, sometimes a cost-benefit analysis is used to see if the benefits outweigh the costs. This is a point at which environmentalists and businesses often disagree. The EPA, conscious of the problem, has introduced the "bubble concept," which is based on the idea that it is often possible to reduce emissions of a given pollutant from one source far less expensively than from another. Thus, a "bubble" is placed over a plant or geographic area, and private decision makers are allowed to decide the standard for the area at the lowest cost.

Businesses will try to shift the cost of pollution control forward to consumers in the form of price increases, backward to stockholders in the form of lower dividends, or to the workers in the form of lower wages. If the demand for a product is inelastic, meaning there are few, if any, close substitutes and the product is inexpensive, the consumer will pay the higher price. On the other hand, if the demand for a product is elastic, the consumer will not pay the higher price and revenue will fall. Also, the more competitive a market is, the more difficult it will be for firms to pass pollution abatement costs on to consumers. In an oligopoly, however, a firm can move in concert with other oligopolistic firms or follow a price leader. A monopolist has more leverage and more opportunity to push the cost of pollution control onto the consumer by simply readjusting output on the demand curve for the product and by charging a higher price. In the case of natural monopolies, such as power companies, pollution control costs are reflected in higher rates to consumers.

Although jobs are created in the pollution abatement industry, that increased employment may be offset by the closing down of plants that cannot comply with the cost of cleaning up the environment. Businesses also find a problem with the regulatory infrastructure that has been built up in the federal and state levels of government to administer pollution control laws. In addition, government is making an effort to control other areas that are in some way related to environmental pollution, such as land use, energy, and urban transportation. All directly affect business operations. At times the conflict over the environment ends up in the courts, even in the Supreme Court.

THE SUPREME COURT AND POLLUTION

In the 1992 case of *New York v. United States*[2] Justice O'Connor, in a 6–3 decision, upheld parts of a 1985 federal law that provided financial incentives to states to find places to store low-level radioactive waste. However, the part that made the state the legal owner of all such waste within its borders if it had not met its disposal needs by January 1, 1996, was struck down. Along with the ownership, the state would assume all legal liability for any harm caused by the material. O'Connor thought it was a violation of the Tenth Amendment, which gives the states and their people the power over anything not expressly given the federal government in the Constitution nor prohibited to the states. She felt that Congress may not simply commandeer the legislative processes of the states. The federal government may not conscript state governments as its agents.

In 1994 the case of *Oregon Waste Systems, Inc. v. Department of Environmental Quality of the State of Oregon*[3] found the Court looking at the touchy issue of solid waste disposal. Oregon decided to charge $2.50 per ton on in-state disposal of solid waste generated in other states, but only 85¢ on that generated within Oregon. A 7–2 decision by Justice Thomas said that what Oregon was doing was unconstitutional because it discriminated against interstate commerce and did not advance a legitimate local purpose that could not be adequately served by reasonable nondiscriminatory alternatives.

Another 1994 case, *Chicago v. Environmental Defense Fund*,[4] involved the important issue of what can be dumped in ordinary landfills. The 1976 Resource Conservation and Recovery Act states that any toxic residue created by burning household and industrial waste in municipal incinerators must be treated as hazardous waste and not be dumped in ordinary landfills. Instead, it requires storage in specially constructed leak-proof sites and other handling that can be more expensive than conventional waste disposal. Chicago was charged with breaking the law by using landfills not licensed to accept hazardous wastes as disposal sites for the ash left after the incinerator. However, the city cited a 1984 amendment entitled *Clarification of Household Waste Exclusion* and said it should be exempt from the law because, in addition to household waste, it also burned nonhazardous industrial waste. Justice Scalia, however, in a 7–2 opinion, ruled against Chicago, saying that Congress had not created an exemption for the ash. He cited the plain meaning of the law rather than the law's history or the EPA's view of the law to support his conclusion (the EPA was supporting Chicago).

Still another 1994 case, *C. & A. Carbone, Inc. v. Clarkstown*,[5] involved a town that had a solid waste transfer station. In order to finance its cost, the town guaranteed a minimum waste flow, and then passed an ordinance requiring all nonhazardous solid waste within the town to be deposited at the station. That meant that a recycler had to bring nonrecyclable residue to the transfer station and pay a fee. Rather than do that, Carbone shipped it out of state. In a 6–3 opinion, Justice Kennedy said the ordinance violated the commerce clause because it regulated interstate commerce. It drove up the cost for out-of-state interests to dispose of their solid waste, and it deprived out-of-state businesses of access to the local market. It also discriminated against interstate commerce by favoring a single local proprietor. He said the town could still do uniform safety regulations, and it could still subsidize the facility through general taxes or municipal bonds. The decision was important in that more than half the states had some type of flow control.

Also in 1994 came *Jefferson County Public Utility District v. Ecology Department of Washington.*[6] The law involved was the 1972 Clean Water Act, and the issue was whether the state could impose a minimum stream flow requirement in order to protect a river's fishery when it gave permission to build a hydro-electric project. Justice O'Connor, for a 7–2 Court, upheld the state, saying that a state may impose conditions necessary to enforce a designated use in its water quality standard, and it is not limited to discharges. In this case it was necessary to enforce the designated use of the river as a fish habitat. A project must be consistent with the designated use and the water quality criteria, and a sufficient lowering of the quantity of water could destroy all of a river's designated uses. Also, a reduced stream flow can constitute water pollution. Any difference between water quality and quantity is artificial because, in many cases such as this, they are related. She also said this is consistent with EPA regulations.

In an important environmental case in 2000, *Friends of the Earth v. Laidlaw,*[7] Justice Ginsburg in a 7–2 opinion upheld the ability of private plaintiffs to invoke the citizen suit provisions of the Federal Environmental Laws to bring lawsuits to stop pollution.

Although not relating directly to pollution, the Court has also decided a couple cases dealing with the 1973 Endangered Species Act, a law passed by Congress to try to make the environment safe for wildlife. In the 1992 case of *Lujan v. Defenders of Wildlife,*[8] the group went to court over the Interior Department's interpretation of the law as being limited to domestic projects only. Justice Scalia, 6–3, said the group lacked standing to bring the case, but then 7–2 upheld the Department's interpretation of the law. Then in 1995, in *Babbitt v. Sweet Home Chapter of Communities for a Greater Oregon,*[9] Justice Stevens in a 6–3 decision upheld regulations issued under the law that prohibited modifying any habitat when it would impair an endangered species' ability to breed, feed, or find shelter, even on private land. This particular case involved loggers and the spotted owl. Stevens felt the Secretary of the Interior's actions were reasonable, given Congress's clear expression in the law to protect endangered and threatened wildlife. The word "harm" as used in the law naturally encompasses habitat modification that results in actual injury or death, and he would defer to Congress in this matter.

SUMMARY

As can readily be seen, environmental protection is a complex problem of the utmost magnitude. That pollution is a problem is a given, and most persons are highly supportive of regulations to assure a safer environment. Differences do exist as to the magnitude of some of the problems, as well as how best to solve the problems. It would seem best to err on the side of believing a problem is serious and imminent rather than believing the problem is more trivial and far in the future. The damage done by pollution is difficult to undo, so to catch it before it reaches a catastrophic level makes sense indeed. The government has done a lot in this area, but there is more that needs to be done both at the national and international levels.

QUESTIONS FOR DISCUSSION

1. Has the issue of environmental protection become overstated?
2. Which environmental problem is the most pressing?
3. Are our laws adequate to handle the pollution problem?
4. Should polluters be made to pay emission charges?
5. Should taxpayers bear some of the burden of protecting the environment?
6. Has the Supreme Court generally been supportive of environmental protection?

NOTES

1. For a comprehensive look at global warming, the *New York Times* of December 1, 1997, Section F, is helpful. The date was the opening of the Kyoto Conference.
2. 112 S. Ct. 2408 (1992).
3. 128 L. Ed. 2d 89 (1994).
4. 128 L. Ed. 2d 302 (1994).
5. 128 L. Ed. 2d 399 (1994).
6. 128 L. Ed. 2d 716 (1994).
7. 528 U.S. _____ (2000).
8. 112 S. Ct. 2130 (1992).
9. 115 S. Ct. 2407 (1995).

RECOMMENDED READING

O'Leary, Rosemary. *Environmental Change: Federal Courts and the EPA*. Philadelphia, PA: Temple University Press, 1993.
Rosenbaum, Walter. *Environmental Politics and Policy*. Washington, D.C.: CQ Press, 1998.
Schnitzer, Martin. *Contemporary Government and Business Relations*. 4th ed. Boston, MA: Houghton Mifflin Company, 1990. Chapter 13.
New York Times, December 1, 1997, Section F.
The World Bank, *1999 World Development Indicators*. Washington, D.C.: The World Bank, 1999.

DEREGULATION OF TRANSPORTATION

There has been a noticeable trend since the mid- to late 1970s toward getting the government out of the area of regulating business. In order to understand this trend, one must first examine the reasons behind regulation and whether or not those reasons were accomplished. As previously noted, the government first regulated a business when, in 1887, the Interstate Commerce Act created the Interstate Commerce Commission to regulate railroads. The railroads had brought regulation upon themselves with such practices as rate discrimination, including charging more for short hauls than for long hauls, and deviating from published tariffs. Since it was the farmers and small businesspersons who were most adversely affected, they organized into the Grange movement and took control of the legislatures of several midwestern states, passing laws regulating rates. The problem was, however, that most of the railroads engaged in these practices were interstate in nature, and the Supreme Court in the 1886 case of *Wabash, St. Louis, and Pacific Railway Company v. Illinois*[1] invalidated an Illinois law that had forbidden railroads to charge more for a short haul than for a long haul. Since the law affected all railroads, including those in interstate commerce, Justice Miller thought it unconstitutional as our Constitution gives Congress the power to regulate interstate commerce, not the states—thus, the creation the following year of the ICC.

GOVERNMENT REGULATION

RAILROADS

The Interstate Commerce Act made it unlawful for railroads to charge a higher rate for short hauls on shipments on the same line in the same direction. Schedules of freight rates and passenger rates had to be made public to prevent discrimination against shippers, and rate increases could be made only after advance public notice of ten days had been given. In 1906 the Hepburn Act gave the ICC jurisdiction over pipelines and express companies, and in 1910 the Mann-Elkins Act gave the ICC jurisdiction over telephone, telegraph, and cable and wireless companies engaged in interstate commerce.

Despite this promising beginning, the ICC had a rocky early few years, thanks to a highly conservative, probusiness Supreme Court. In the 1896 case of *Cincinnati, New Orleans, and Texas Pacific Railway Company v. Interstate Commerce Commission*,[2] the Court, speaking through Justice Shiras, held that the ICC was not given any authority in the law creating it to fix rates. It could only fact-find. The following year, in *Interstate Commerce Commission v. Cincinnati, New Orleans, and Texas Pacific Railway Company*,[3] Justice Brewer held that the ICC had no power over rates whatsoever. Rate-making is a legislative matter and Congress could not delegate it to an agency in the executive branch. Also in 1897, in *Interstate Commerce Commission v. Alabama Midland Railway Company*,[4] the Court held that when federal circuit courts heard appeals from ICC rulings, they need not accept the facts as presented by the ICC. This voided a provision in a law that held that the courts were limited to the facts as presented by the ICC. The rationale was that when a court hears a case in equity, as in these appeals, it must always be able to investigate facts anew. The reason this decision was detrimental to the ICC was that railroads would withhold key facts at the ICC hearing, then when the decision went against them they would present these facts at the circuit court. Based on these new facts, the ICC decision would look foolish and would be overturned by the Court, lowering the esteem of the ICC in the minds of the general public.

The Court finally changed its attitude toward the ICC with its 1907 decision in *Illinois Central Railroad Company v. Interstate Commerce Commission*[5] in which it said it would not investigate the facts anew in an appeal. Whatever the facts were as presented by the record in the case, that was what the Court would use. That was followed by the 1910 case of *Interstate Commerce Commission v. Illinois Central Railroad Company*,[6] in which Justice White ruled that the Court would defer to the policymaking power of the ICC. As long as the ICC had the power to rule the way it did, the Court would not overturn the ruling just because it disagreed with the wisdom of the policy.

In the 1914 *Shreveport Rate Cases*,[7] Justice Hughes even allowed the ICC to change the allowable rate charged by an intrastate train and set by that state's railroad commission. The state was Texas, and the reason the ICC became involved was that an interstate railroad (Louisiana to Texas) and the Texas railroad were serving the same region in east Texas. However, their rates were different. The ICC was allowing the interstate railroad to charge a higher rate. Since that hurt the interstate railroad's ability to attract riders, the ICC had two alternatives. It could lower the rate of the intestate railroad, which it would not do because it was convinced the rate was fair, or it could raise the rate of the Texas railroad. It did just that, and the Court upheld the ICC, saying that the ICC could regulate those intrastate rates which, as in the case at point, directly affected interstate commerce. Congress, in 1920, passed the Transportation Act that reaffirmed that decision, and in the 1922 case of *Railroad Commission of Wisconsin v. Chicago, Burlington & Quincy Railroad*,[8] Chief Justice Taft for a unanimous Court upheld it. He said that the Commission is supposed to see that a national railway system is achieved, and it is also supposed to assure that the railroads get a fair return. Therefore, the law was constitutional.

TRUCKS, BUSES, AND AIRLINES

In 1935 Congress passed the Motor Carrier Act that gave the ICC jurisdiction over trucks and buses engaged in interstate commerce. These common carriers could operate only under a certificate from the ICC, and rates and fares had to be published and not be discriminatory. These were minimum rates that had to be filed with the ICC, which could prescribe minimum (but not maximum) rates. The ICC also enforced safety standards. Private carriers were only under the ICC for such matters as hours of service for employees, safety, and equipment. Brokers for motor carrier routes had to be licensed by the ICC. However, Congress took away much of the ICC's regulatory power with the 1980 Motor Carrier Reform Act, the 1980 Staggers Rail Act, and the 1982 Bus Regulatory Reform Act. The ICC itself was abolished during the administration of President Clinton.

Meanwhile, in 1938 Congress decided to regulate the airline industry. It had already, in 1934 and 1935, given the postmaster general the power to regulate schedule frequencies, departure times, stops, speed, load capacities, etc., for airmail. But the Civil Aeronautics Act created the Civil Aeronautics Board and gave it regulatory authority over entry, routes, rates, airmail payments, and subsidies of common carriers. The CAB would issue a certificate of convenience and necessity for an air carrier to serve a particular route. Rates had to be approved and published by the Board, which also had control over pooling, combinations, intercorporate relations, and abandonment of service, although it had no control over security issues. Two years later an executive order by President Roosevelt created the Civil Aeronautics Authority to maintain the national airway system, to plan and administer the airport program, and to enforce safety, licensing, and traffic control regulations. However, Congress, in 1978, passed the Airline Deregulation Act eliminating the CAB by 1985 and ending economic regulation by then. The hope was to allow existing interstate carriers to enter new markets, and to make it easier for new firms to enter the air transportation industry. In addition, domestic airlines were allowed to cut or raise fares in single markets until, on January 1, 1983, all regulations on fares were eliminated.

The government did not get out of the airline business altogether. The Federal Aviation Administration, successor to the Civil Aeronautics Authority, can order design changes in airplanes, and the National Transportation Safety Board can recommend safety improvements. The intent of deregulation was to promote competition among air carriers, so that consumers would be better served.

TABLE 10-1   MAJOR FEDERAL TRANSPORTATION LAWS

1887	Interstate Commerce Act
1906	Hepburn Act
1910	Mann-Elkins Act
1935	Motor Carrier Act
1938	Civil Aeronautics Act
1978	Airline Deregulation Act
1980	Motor Carrier Reform Act
1982	Bus Regulatory Reform Act

CHARACTERISTICS OF REGULATION

In order to better understand the movement to deregulate, which was not confined to the transportation industry, one must first understand the mechanics of regulation. Regulation began with the transportation industry and later spread to such industries as communications and electric and gas services, all classified under the general category of public utilities. The rationale was that these industries must charge fair, nondiscriminatory rates and render on demand satisfactory service to the public. On the other hand, the utility generally is free from direct competition and is permitted, although not assured, a fair return on its investment. The reasoning behind singling out utilities for regulation is because they are considered to be natural monopolies (i.e., they offer a single service or a limited number of services, they are localized, and direct competition would be uneconomical). They are usually very capital intensive as there is a high ratio of fixed assets to total assets, and their fixed costs do not vary with output. The expenses of many utility companies, particularly those in the gas and electric fields, decrease as the size of the plant increases, although there is a minimum beyond which the average total costs would begin to increase should the plant grow larger. A relatively small plant would have higher average costs than a larger plant. When the government regulates the price charged by a utility, it is greater than the marginal cost, as it is equal to the average total cost. In other words, the utility is allowed to cover all its costs and earn a normal profit. The marginal cost price would be the socially optimum one, the one that maximizes society's welfare. However, that is not used because the utility might not be able to cover average costs and thus it would lose money, or it might make too much money if the demand increases.

Critics of regulation had several points to make. One was that the regulatory agencies began to act more in the interest of the firms they were regulating than in the public interest. Another was that there was too much regulation by the commissions. Still another was that there was a blurring of the principle of separation of powers, as the same people in the agencies made the rules, brought action against offenders, and served as judges. On the other hand, some commissioners were thought to be too far removed from actual fact-finding, with the result that they never heard testimony even though they had to make the decisions. A final criticism related to prices because, if the price allowed to be charged was below the market price, those who were not able to buy from the regulated firm would be paying more for the substitute product. Also, since firms that are regulated do not compete on the basis of price, the only thing that distinguished one company from another was service, a criticism particularly levied at the airline industry. Perhaps surprisingly, it was the more liberal element in our society that, for the previously discussed reasons, began openly to call for deregulation in the mid-1970s. When the conservative element joined in, the deregulation movement was assured of success. The only questions remaining were which industries to deregulate and to what extent. A general distrust of big government was reflected in this movement, and it was to extend into the 1980s and beyond. One area especially hit by deregulation in the early 1980s was the banking industry, and another one that is ongoing is the communications industry.

DEREGULATION

RAILROADS

What has the effect of deregulation been in the transportation industry? In 1998 Laidlaw, Inc., of Canada, bought Greyhound Lines, Inc. for $470 million in a merger of bus companies, and in 2000 Volvo got the truck division of Renault (which includes Mack Trucks in the United States) for $1.5 billion, making it the second biggest maker of trucks in the world, behind Chrysler Daimler. Both trucking and railroad rates have dropped between 30 and 50 percent, and railroad employment has dropped in half, although for those who remain, salaries and fringe benefits have risen. In 1995 the average salary per railroad worker was $48,000. The biggest impact of deregulation in the railroad industry, however, as with industry in general lately, has been the number and size of the mergers that have taken place. The end result is that in just a forty-year period, from 1955–1995, the number of railroads in the United States, excluding local lines, fell from 126 to 11. In fact, the Surface Transportation Board was created in 1996 to review railroad mergers. Among the larger mergers were the joining of the Union Pacific and Southern Pacific railroads into one, the Union Pacific, for $3.9 billion (they also have the Chicago Northwestern railroad), and the joining of the Burlington Northern and Santa Fe railroads. In 1999, the latter announced plans to merge with the Canadian National Railway Co. in a $6 billion deal which would create the largest railroad in North America and would be called North American Railways. Other big railroads are the Soo Line and the Illinois Central. However, the biggest completed merger was the 1997 acquisition of Conrail by CSX and Norfolk Southern railroads for $9 billion. A background study as to how these railroads evolved is illuminating.

CSX railroad traces its origins to the first American railroad, the Baltimore and Ohio, started in 1827. It was bought in 1962 by the Chesapeake and Ohio railroad, which had begun as Virginia's Louisa railroad in 1836. The B&O and the C&O got the Western Maryland railroad in the late 1960s, and all three became subsidiaries of the Chessie System in 1973. Meanwhile, the Seaboard Coast Line had been formed by combining Virginia's Portsmouth and Roanoke railroad, started in 1832, with the Atlantic Coast Line railroad, formed in the late 1800s from several southern railroads. In 1980, the Chessie System and the Seaboard Coast Line merged to form CSX. Besides being a railroad, CSX owns Sea-Land Services, Inc., which is an international container-cargo carrier with some 100 ships; American Commercial Lines, Inc., which has 3,200 barges and 116 towboats that navigate our inland rivers; an intermodal services company; a logistics company; and the Greenbrier resort.

Norfolk Southern railroad can trace its origins to the Norfolk railroad, an eight-mile Virginia line formed in 1838 which later became part of the Atlantic, Mississippi, and Ohio railroad, which in 1881 became the Norfolk and Western Railway Company. That railroad bought the Virginian Railway in 1959 and the New York, Chicago, and St. Louis Railway in 1964. Meanwhile, the Southern Railway Company, begun in 1827 as the South Carolina Canal and Railroad, started our first regularly scheduled passenger train in 1830. In 1982 it merged with Norfolk and Western to form the Norfolk Southern. The latter also owns North American Van Lines (a major moving van company), and Pocahontas Land Corporation (an owner of coalfields).

Conrail owes its beginnings to an 1831 railroad, the Mohawk and Hudson, which joined with nine others in 1853 to form the New York Central Railroad. Its major competitor for years was the Pennsylvania Railroad, formed in 1846. When railroads started having financial difficulties because of competition, the two giants merged in 1968 to form the Penn Central Transportation Company, which went bankrupt in 1972. The federal government set up Conrail in 1973 to take over the freight operations of the Penn Central and five other railroads; it began operations in 1976. The federal government sold its holdings in it in 1987. It was the largest freight railroad in the eastern part of the United States. One can easily see why CSX and Norfolk Southern both wanted Conrail, and why they thought it best to buy it jointly rather than engage in a price war. One other point of note is that the federal government in 1971 also created a corporation to handle the passenger service of Penn Central, namely Amtrak, and that is still a government corporation. However, under the 1997 Amtrak Reform and Accountability Act, the railroad cannot use government funds (which has totaled some $22.7 billion in operating and capital subsidies) to cover operating expenses after 2002. In 1999 it said that, beginning in the year 2002, it will give passengers free rides when its service falls below national standards for customer treatment, late trains, and the condition of railcars.

Has deregulation accomplished its objectives in the railroad industry? Since rates are lower, one would think so. However, because of the many mergers there are very few railroads remaining, thus not as much competition as critics of regulation had sought to achieve. Perhaps many of the merged railroads would have failed but for the mergers. Then too, there are always local railroads to give interstate railroads competition. Nevertheless, it seems the mergers have gone beyond what is optimum for the economy and for the consumers, and that corporate greed is the controlling factor. In other words, the rich get richer. The ones who benefit the most are the directors and officers of the merged companies, together with the stockholders. Too many workers lose their jobs or are urged to take early retirement, and with fewer and fewer railroads there is less competition, and less competition, in the long run, usually means higher rates. Perhaps the railroad industry is an anomaly. A look at the result of airline deregulation should help provide an answer.

AIRLINES

When airlines were deregulated, the major airlines were at a severe cost disadvantage. New entrants were able to use nonunion and smaller crews on their aircraft, which gave them a cost advantage over the major airlines with union contracts. Despite this advantage, most of the new entrants went broke: some 150 in the 1978–1986 period. The ones that survived generally took advantage of the opportunities now available to them and radically changed their routes and prices in order to attract passengers.

One method used to change route structure was the creation of hubbing, when airlines create hubs at one or more airports. They then schedule flights from these airports in banks, meaning that a number of flights come into an airport within a short period of time and a number leave a short time later. There are many gates at an airport that are utilized by the hub airlines; passengers enjoy the comfort of nonstop flights to their destinations and they accumulate frequent-flier miles with those airlines. In 1978, 14 percent of all passengers had to change airlines to reach their destinations, and in 1995 that figure was down to 1 percent. This is an efficient use of facilities and enables an airline to provide service on routes that were previously unserved. In addition, these hub airlines sometimes affiliate with commuter carriers in order to serve smaller markets. Some have developed multiple hub systems and have become regional and even national in scope. Besides not having to change airlines in the middle of a journey, there is less layover time with hubbing because airlines no longer stop at several cities to fill planes. In addition, since planes now fly with a higher percentage of seats filled, fares as a whole are lower. However, as with most things, there is a downside—if one or two airlines dominate a particular hub, there is the potential of a monopoly with resultant higher fares. In fact, hub airlines dominate in the fifteen cities where passengers pay the highest air fares. The Department of Transportation has made a study and concluded that ticket prices at seven airports dominated by one or two carriers outstripped average fares at airports served by many airlines. As was mentioned earlier, the Justice Department in May, 1999, filed an antitrust suit against American Airlines. It was for predatory pricing at the Dallas-Fort Worth airport, charging it with utilizing the scheme to drive Vanguard, Sun Jet, and Western Pacific from that airport. These discount carriers have been making inroads and, according to the Department of Transportation, air travelers save more than $6 billion a year by using them.

Since deregulation took effect, on the average, ticket prices have fallen thirty-six percent, particularly for long-distance flights and in the big-city markets. They have increased, however, in short-distance markets, and the number of passengers for short-distance flights has decreased. They have the alternatives of automobiles, trains, buses, and smaller planes. Those who do fly short distances, even though their fares have risen, are usually paying for the true cost of the service.

Since deregulation, most of the complaints that arise are about service. Now that air transportation has become so affordable that most people can fly, terminals have become crowded. The number of passengers flying has increased so much since deregulation (it has more than doubled) that there is a burden on terminal facilities and on the use of airplanes. The number of airline departures increased by two-thirds in the two decades after deregulation. This, in turn, has resulted in delays because, to accommodate travelers, airlines offer more flights at the peak periods. This puts a strain not only on the services supplied by the airports, but also on the services provided by one or more of the Federal Aviation Administration control centers who guide the aircraft through the sectors under their control. Other reasons for delay are weather and mechanical problems. Weather, indeed, is responsible for the majority of airplane delays. In 1999 the major airlines issued guidelines for better service. They will now tell customers of the lowest fare available, notify them of known delays, support an increase in the baggage liability limit (the Department of Transportation said it was doubling to $2,500 the minimum liability on lost, damaged, or delayed baggage), allow reservations to be held without payment for twenty-four hours, give prompt refunds, accommodate disabled passengers, and meet customer needs during long aircraft delays. There was much pressure on the airlines to take such steps as the previous winter, during a storm, passengers were forced to sit seven or more hours in planes on runways without food and other services. If the airlines had not issued the guidelines, Congress might have imposed some regulation on them.

Another factor to consider in airline deregulation is safety, and airline fatality rates have fallen since deregulation. That could be the result of many factors, including better technology. One area in which there are more near-accidents since deregulation, however, involves small private planes or military planes. Near-collisions involving only commercial airlines are a vary small percent of the total. In examining our traffic control system, the problems, rather than being due to deregulation, are due to federal budgetary constraints.

These have slowed FAA regulatory processes and procurement, have eliminated many expert technical personnel (who take more rewarding jobs in industry), and have prevented modernization of traffic control equipment.

This brings one to the final factor to be considered in airline deregulation and, as with railroads, it is the great increase in mergers. With several airlines going bankrupt and with the increase in mergers, the airline industry has become an oligopoly. Airlines do have to have the approval of the Department of Transportation in order to merge. The 1985 revision of the Federal Aviation Act sets two standards for DOT when it evaluates proposed mergers. One is the antitrust standard, which holds that any merger that would violate Section 7 of the Clayton Act by substantially lessening competition in any region of the United States must not be approved unless DOT finds the anticompetitive effects are outweighed by the public interest due to benefits accrued from meeting increased transportation needs. The second is the public interest standard, which holds that DOT must determine whether or not a merger is in the public interest. In addition to DOT approval, the Antitrust Division of the Justice Department must be notified of proposed mergers, and usually participates in airline merger hearings. However, the final say belongs to DOT, and it has approved mergers to which the Justice Department was opposed.

Some of the mergers consummated in the mid-1980s include U.S. Airways getting Piedmont Aviation, Northwest getting Republic, Delta getting Western, Texas Air getting Eastern, Frontier, and People's Express, and TWA getting Ozark. In 1991 Delta got most of Pan American. Five of the biggest ten carriers have disappeared. Today's ten biggest airlines, in terms of revenue passenger miles (one paying passenger flown one mile) as well as passengers, include United, American, Delta, Northwest, Continental, U.S. Airways, Southwest, Trans World, America West, and Alaska. In terms of operating revenue, America West and Alaska are replaced by two airlines that haul freight, Federal Express and United Parcel Service. In 1998, Northwest bought a controlling stake in Continental for $519 million. They merged their flight schedules and frequent-flier programs, but maintained separate identities and managements. The Justice Department treated it as a merger and initiated a suit to stop it. In 2000, United Airlines announced plans to buy U.S. Airways for $11.6 billion, which would make it the largest carrier in the United States by far.

In addition to mergers, several airlines have entered into alliances with other airlines, mostly foreign ones. For example, United is allied (Star Alliance) with Lufthansa (German), Thai Airways, SAS (Scandinavian), Air Canada, Varig (Brazil), Singapore Airlines, Air New Zealand, and ANA (Japan). American is in an alliance (One World) with Canadian, Japan Airlines, British Airways, and Quantas. Northwest and Continental entered into an alliance (Wings Alliance) with KLM Royal Dutch Airlines and Alitalia. Delta is allied with Swissair, Sabena Belgian, and Austrian Airlines, and in 2000 announced an alliance (Sky Team) with Air France, Aeromexico, and Korean Air. These alliances have an immunity from the antitrust laws that allows them to set rates, schedules, and fares together; pool frequent-flier programs; share employees and airport space, and jointly purchase food, fuel, etc. They also code-share all flights, which means they appear in travel agency computers as if they were operated by just one airline, which in turn helps to market their connecting services. Passengers need to book only one ticket and check in baggage once, regardless of how many times they change carriers.

The major carriers have increased their market share since deregulation, and ease of market entry is not present in the industry except for short-distance hauls in low-density markets. For the denser markets, air carriers require time and must absorb sunken costs to obtain gate space and establish patronage. The problem of airport access is crucial, whether it be gates, slots, ticket counterspace, or restricted access to an airport in the form of noise regulation, because the increase in the problem means that new airlines are hampered in their ability to enter markets. As for establishing patronage, that can be difficult when competing against carriers that offer frequent-flier programs that effectively increase the cost of switching carriers. One result is that in several major cities the bulk of the traffic is controlled by one or two airlines.

The Supreme Court did render an interesting decision in 1995 concerning frequent-flier programs. The case was *American Airlines, Inc. v. Wolens,*[9] and the airline had modified its frequent-flier program retroactively. The state of Illinois challenged this as both breach of contract and consumer fraud. A 6–2 decision written by Justice Ginsburg held that the breach of contract law could be used since that simply holds parties to their agreements which, in turn, advances the market efficiency that the Airline Deregulation Act was designed to promote. However, in a 7–1 split, she disallowed the use of the consumer fraud law as that controls the primary conduct of those fully under it, which is not the case with airlines. Breach of contract, on the other hand, deals with private obligations; thus the difference between the two laws.

SUMMARY

Has airline deregulation worked? The Federal Trade Commission's study concludes that it has been a success. Fares have fallen; air safety, particularly with the major airlines, has improved; more people are traveling by air, and congestion could be reduced if less flights were put at peak times; profits are up. But there is a downside, and that is the reduction in airlines due, in part, to so many mergers. If the antitrust laws were vigorously enforced, and if authority to administer them were transferred from the Department of Transportation to the Justice Department, airline deregulation would indeed be a success. Now, however, with an oligopolistic industry, one must be concerned with the fact that it is very difficult for new carriers to enter the market and compete effectively, which in turn makes it easier for the established carriers to act in concert on fares, with competition, as in days of regulation, mainly in services rendered to passengers. More competition would make deregulation truly a success.

All in all, deregulation of transportation, whether it be trucks, buses, railroads, or airlines, has been a mixed bag. The lowering of rates is impressive, but the number of mergers is disturbing, especially in the railroad and airline industries. With less and less competition come the dangers associated with oligopolies, not the least of which is higher prices. The government should be more vigilant with the antitrust laws and not so quick to approve mergers. Not everything big is bad, but competition is healthy and the transportation industry, since deregulation, has become less competitive.

QUESTIONS FOR DISCUSSION

1. What are the major arguments for regulating transportation?
2. What are the major arguments for deregulating transportation?
3. Has railroad deregulation worked?
4. Has airline deregulation worked?
5. Do you agree with the elimination of the ICC?
6. Are the many mergers in the railroad and airline industries good for the economy?

NOTES

1. 118 U.S. 557 (1886).
2. 162 U.S. 184 (1896).
3. 167 U.S. 479 (1897).
4. 168 U.S. 144 (1897).
5. 206 U.S. 441 (1907).
6. 216 U.S. 452 (1910).
7. 234 U.S. 342 (1914).
8. 257 U.S. 563 (1922).
9. 513 U.S. 219 (1995).

RECOMMENDED READING

Brown, Anthony. *The Politics of Airline Deregulation.* Knoxville, TN: University of Tennessee Press, 1987.

Cohen, Jeffrey. *Politics and Economic Policy in the United States.* Boston, MA: Houghton Mifflin Company, 1997. Chapters 10 and 11.

Eisner, Marc. *Regulatory Policies in Transition.* Baltimore, MD: Johns Hopkins University Press, 1993.

Gerston, Larry, Cynthia Fraleigh, and Robert Schwab. *The Deregulated Society.* Pacific Grove, CA: Brooks/Cole, 1988.

Reagan, Michael. *Regulation: The Politics of Policy.* Boston, MA: Little, Brown, 1987.

Schnitzer, Martin. *Contemporary Government and Business Relations.* 4th ed. Boston, MA: Houghton Mifflin Company, 1990. Chapter 14.

CHAPTER 11

DEREGULATION
OF FINANCIAL INSTITUTIONS

One of the major industries to be affected by the movement to deregulate is that of financial institutions, especially banks. This is a field that had been highly regulated, and for good reason. Alexander Hamilton, our first secretary of the treasury, thought it would be in this country's best interest for Congress to charter a Bank of the United States. The national government would transact business through this bank and therefore avoid dealing with state banks, some of which were not that sympathetic with what the national government was doing. The problem was that chartering a bank was not one of the powers expressly given to Congress in Article 1, Section 8, of the Constitution, which lists what Congress can do. Hamilton, however, argued that the final clause of that section says that Congress can make all laws "which shall be necessary and proper for carrying into Execution the foregoing powers," and since Congress was expressly given the powers to tax, regulate commerce, and coin money, surely it could charter a bank to help facilitate those powers. Although such luminaries as James Madison and Thomas Jefferson disagreed with that interpretation, Congress passed the bill and President Washington signed it into law in 1791. The Bank had a twenty-year charter and, when it expired, Congress waited five years before chartering the second Bank of the United States, also for twenty years. Since it was competition for state banks, some states passed laws restricting branches of the Bank in their states.

One such state was Maryland, and it imposed a tax on the branch in Baltimore. McCulloch, the cashier, would not pay, and a case ensued that eventually reached the Supreme Court. Chief Justice Marshall wrote the unanimous opinion in the 1819 case of *McCulloch v. Maryland*[1] upholding the law creating the Bank and echoing Hamilton's old arguments concerning the necessary and proper clause. He also said that states could not tax the Bank because it would be useless to allow Congress to charter a bank if a state could negate that power by a destructive tax. Marshall reiterated that decision five years later in another unanimous decision, *Osborn v. Bank of the United States*.[2] Here he also allowed an Ohio state official to be sued for damages, as he had collected the tax there despite knowing that it was unconstitutional.

The second Bank ran into opposition from President Jackson, who vetoed a bill to extend its charter and, upon winning reelection in 1832, proceeded to take all the federal money out of the Bank and put it in various state banks. We went without a national bank until the Civil War, when Congress passed the 1864 National Banking Act enabling the national government to charter national banks. These banks issued notes that circulated as currency. Since state banks had their own notes, Congress, in 1866, decided to impose a 10 percent tax on them, which effectively drove that competition out of existence. The Supreme Court had already said, in the 1837 case of *Briscoe v. Bank of Kentucky*,[3] that state banks were different from the state itself; this enabled them to issue notes that circulated as currency (states themselves are prohibited by Article 1, Section 10 of the Constitution from issuing bills of credit). Thus, it had no problem in the 1869 case, *Veazie Bank v. Fenno*,[4] upholding the tax, since it was not on the state itself but on a bank. It said also that a tax is not invalid simply because it is too high, and that it would not look into the motive behind a statute. It would only look to see if the statute is consistent with the Constitution. The Court said that the statute might not even be considered as a tax, but rather part of Congress's power to control the currency.

The power to control the currency was also the basis for the Court upholding the right of Congress during the Civil War to pass three Legal Tender Acts authorizing greenbacks to be used as money for all purposes, even for debts incurred prior to the passage of the Acts. The Court had at first said no, in the 1870 case of *Hepburn v. Griswold*,[5] as it felt the law took away property without due process, a Fifth Amendment violation. But the next year, in the *Second Legal Tender Cases*,[6] the Court reversed itself due to the addition of two justices to the Court.

REGULATION OF BANKS

The system of national banks seemed to work for a while, but soon much of the power in the banking business fell into the hands of a few large banks, especially in the eastern part of the country. When President Wilson took office he wanted to change that and, as a result, Congress in 1913 passed the Federal Reserve Act, creating our present structure. It divided the country into twelve districts; each one having a Federal Reserve Bank. All national banks had to become members of the system; state banks had the option of joining it. The notes issued by the Federal Reserve Banks were to circulate as currency and a Federal Reserve Board was created to oversee the operation. Again, this seemed to work, but along came the Depression and with it the failures of many banks. When Franklin

Roosevelt was elected president in 1932, one of the first actions he took upon being inaugurated the next year was to declare a moratorium on bank operations. Congress then passed an Emergency Banking Act providing for the inspection of banks and the reopening of licensed solvent banks.

In order to try to stimulate inflation, Roosevelt took the country off the gold standard. Congress then passed a joint resolution that canceled any clause in any private contracts or government bonds that called for payment in gold. The Supreme Court, in the 1935 case of *Norman v. Baltimore and Ohio Railroad Company*,[7] upheld the section of the Resolution regarding private contracts, as Congress has the power to regulate the currency and thus can say what is legal tender. However, in the companion case of *Perry v. United States*,[8] the Court felt that Congress could not do the same with government bonds as the government had pledged its word to pay in gold when people bought the bonds. After saying this, the Court turned around and refused to allow the suit, holding that the difference between the amount Perry would have received in gold and the amount he actually would receive from the bond was so negligible that he suffered no real damages and thus had no standing to bring a suit.

Roosevelt now got Congress to further regulate the banking industry. The 1933 Glass-Steagall Act created the Federal Deposit Insurance Corporation to guarantee bank deposits in all banks in the Federal Reserve system, originally up to $2,500 and now up to $100,000. Commercial banks had to give up their securities affiliates and to abstain from investment banking, and a limit was placed on the investment securities that member banks could have in their investment portfolios. Federal Reserve Banks were required to supervise the member banks' use of credit, and an Open Market Committee was created to control commercial bank policies. In 1935 Congress further regulated the industry with the passage of the Banking Act, by which the old Federal Reserve Board was dissolved. It was replaced by a Board of Governors, composed of seven members appointed by the president, with Senate approval, for fourteen-year terms. The president also designates who will be the chair and the vice-chair, with Senate approval, for four-year terms. The Board was given broader power over the discount rate, which is the interest rate it charges when it loans money to banks, and over the reserve requirements of banks, which are assets a bank must hold and not lend out. Each Reserve Bank must restate its discount rate every two weeks with the approval of the Board.

Since the FDIC insures deposits for its member banks as well as for any other mutual savings or commercial banks who want to participate, it needs to finance itself with semiannual assessments on each insured bank, based on the volume of the bank's deposits. It also receives income from investing the fund's balances.

One power the FDIC does not have is to close a bank. That can only be done by a chartering authority, which would be a state banking commission for a state bank or the Office of the Comptroller of the Currency for a national bank. Once a bank is closed, however, the FDIC is appointed receiver and is responsible for settling the affairs of the bank. The FDIC seldom had to worry about bank failures until the 1980s came along, but at that time the number of failures and their cost became significant enough to cause concern. In fact, one part of the 1982 Garn-St. Germain Act expanded the authority of the FDIC to arrange mergers between healthy and failing banks, and the 1987 Competitive Equality Banking Act expanded the options available to the FDIC to deal with failed banks.

The option employed most by the FDIC to deal with failed banks is called a purchase and assumption contract. Under it, a buyer comes forth to purchase all or some of the failed bank's assets and to assume its liabilities. This is usually done by having the FDIC invite a number of possible buyers to a bidder's meeting, with the highest bidder getting the bank.

There are other options available to the FDIC. One is a deposit payoff, with the FDIC paying depositors the full amount of their insured claims and beginning to liquidate the assets of the failed bank. Those whose deposits are not insured, as well as other creditors, get receiver's certificates under which they get a proportionate share of the collections received on the bank's assets.

Another option is a bridge bank, by which the FDIC keeps the bank open briefly until prospective purchasers have had enough time to assess the bank and make a reasonable offer for it. The bank retains much of its value and there is less community disruption.

Yet another option is the insured deposit transfer; the insured deposits and secured liabilities are transferred to another bank and the FDIC pays that bank sufficient cash to cover those liabilities. The acquiring bank, in turn, generally purchases some of the failed bank's assets.

Finally, there is open-market assistance, wherein the FDIC gives the bank money before it closes. The amount covers the difference between the estimated market value of the bank's assets and its liabilities. New capital is then provided by private investors.

The reason the FDIC does mostly purchase and assumption is that it does not disrupt the community too much when another bank moves right in for those who had been doing business with the failed bank. There might not even be a delay as the one bank will close at the end of a business day and the new bank will open the next day, with just a new name on the building.

When banks were first regulated, they were not allowed to conduct interstate business. However, in 1970 Congress changed that, except for deposit taking, and at the same time narrowed the definition of a bank to include only those institutions that both accepted deposits and made commercial loans. That enabled bank holding companies and others to establish an interstate network of consumer financing corporations, mortgage companies, etc., that were not regulated because they either did not accept deposits or they did not make loans. The 1982 Garn-St. Germain Act allowed bank regulatory agencies to permit the acquisition of failing banks across state lines. In 1994 federal limits on interstate banking were repealed.

With the movement to deregulate picking up steam in the late 1970s, with consumer groups complaining that interest ceilings placed by the government were discriminatory against small savers, such as the elderly, and with technological changes occurring that banks could not install due to regulatory constraints, the time was right to deregulate banking. With interest rates fluctuating wildly at that time, people were turning to other institutions to invest their money at higher rates, such as money market funds.

BANKING DEREGULATION

The result of the previously discussed events was the 1980 Depository Institutions Deregulation and Monetary Control Act. The law provided for the gradual elimination of interest rate limitations, although it also put all banks under the reserve requirements of the Federal Reserve system, even though the amount that had to be kept in reserve was lowered. All banks were allowed to offer checking services, negotiable order of withdrawal (NOW) accounts, and automatic transfer systems (ATS) accounts. Mutual savings banks could transact deals with business customers, and state usury laws could not be used to hinder agricultural, business, and mortgage loans (at that time, the prime rate was above the usury rate that many states allowed). At the same time Congress was easing restrictions, states were doing the same. For example, Pennsylvania in 1982 allowed banks to merge with each other.

Once deregulation occurred, there was a substantial increase in the level of interstate banking, and computer advances such as the electronic funds transfer system (EFTS) were adopted, especially by bigger banks. However, nonbank institutions expanded into the financial services industry, with services such as consumer, business, and commercial mortgage loans. Money market funds were there for deposits. There were virtually no limitations anymore on entry and expansion into the field, the scope, and the nature of the activities, or on geographic expansion. As a result, in 1996, for the first time, the amount of money deposited at federally insured commercial banks was less than the $3 trillion invested in mutual funds.

Unfortunately, banks began to fail in large numbers. There were many reasons for it. One of the most important was the depressed economic conditions in a particular region of the country. When the price of oil dropped precipitously, real estate prices dropped in the oil-producing states. Banks that had loaned money on real estate could not recoup their losses by selling real estate. The same thing happened in the agricultural states. When an agricultural recession hit in the early 1980s, farm prices dropped, farmers could not pay off their loans, their mortgages were foreclosed, and the banks, which now had the farms, could not sell them.

Other banks failed when they made loans to less-developed countries, such as Mexico; when oil prices dropped, Mexico had all it could do to pay the interest on the loans, much less the capital.

Yet another factor was fraud and insider abuse, including outright criminal conduct. The FDIC has published a list of warning signs to be used as aids to examiners and auditors to try to spot these, and some FDIC examiners receive special training focusing on criminal motivation and early detection in spotting these things.

Deregulation has also played a part. The banking system has had to adjust to dramatic changes, and the increased level of competition has placed new pressures on bank management. The more sophisticated and complicated the decisions become, the more chance there is for a wrong choice, which adversely affects the safety and soundness of the bank. The technological changes have also added pressures to the industry, as the advances in the delivery of services have increased competition. There are startup and maintenance costs, which are a fixed cost that smaller banks find difficult to cover, and if those banks are in depressed agricultural areas, as so many are, the result can be failures.

One tactic banks have used to try to get more money is to increase their fees. In the period from 1965–1995, the percentage of revenue received by commercial banks from fees rose from 18 percent to 35 percent. The rest of their income is from loans.

THE CASE OF SAVINGS AND LOANS

The savings and loan industry somewhat parallels the commercial banking industry. In 1932 Congress passed the Federal Home Loan Bank Act to improve the mortgage system and provide home-financing institutions better able to serve borrowers. Twelve federal Home Loan Banks were created; they raise money by issuing debentures or bonds guaranteed by the United States. They then make loans to member institutions on the security of mortgages. All federal savings and loan associations must be members, and others may join on the purchase of bank stock and by conforming to the system's regulations. The member institutions make mortgage loans to homeowners.

The Federal Savings and Loan Insurance Corporation insures the deposits of those in the system, up to $100,000 per deposit for individual accounts, as does the FDIC for commercial banks. However, when savings and loan institutions failed at comparatively high rates in the 1980s, Congress decided to recapitalize the FSLIC with the passage of the 1987 Competitive Equality Banking Act that created the Financial Corporation capitalized from the earnings of the Federal Home Loan Banks. The Financial Corporation then raises funds in the long-term credit markets, which it invests in FSLIC stock. The FSLIC, in turn, can use the proceeds, in addition to its other income, to close insolvent savings and loans. It can also use cash to try to prevent closing or to restore normal operations.

The savings and loan industry was deregulated with the same laws that deregulated the commercial banking industry. One was the 1980 Depository Institutions Deregulation and Monetary Control Act, which gradually eliminated limitations on interest payments and which expanded the authority of the savings and loan associations into the consumer loan business. The other was the 1982 Garn-St. Germain Act that permitted savings and loan associations to have a much greater access to commercial loans by allowing them to invest up to 55 percent of their assets in such loans. States were passing similar deregulatory legislation because, as in the commercial bank field, inflation was running in double digits in the 1970s and the savings and loans were stuck with old 5 and 6 percent mortgages at a time it cost them more to borrow. Depositors looked elsewhere because they could earn higher interest in money market accounts.

Why did so many savings and loans fail? One reason was poor management; with deregulation the banks were able to do almost anything with their money. Managers loaned money for practically any purpose, and not all of the loans were fiscally sound. Also, there was some evidence of corruption on the part of certain managers. Another factor was economic in nature, in that many of the failed banks were in the Southwest, particularly in the oil-producing states. Yet another factor was loose state regulation. Laws were passed to attract deposits that were used to fund high-risk and poorly underwritten investment schemes. The end result was a lot of repossessed real estate from failed savings and loans, and electronic runs by which wealthy investors transferred their funds by computers from a problem savings and loan to other areas of investment.

The upshot of all this was the creation of the Office of Thrift Supervision to try to coordinate the bailout effort, and the creation of the Resolution Trust Corporation to auction off the assets of any remaining insolvent savings and loans. It has auctioned off billions of dollars worth of real estate and loans

TABLE 11-1　MAJOR FEDERAL FINANCIAL INSTITUTIONS LAWS

1791 and 1816	Laws creating the first and second Banks of the United States
Civil War years	Three Legal Tender Acts
1864	National Banking Act
1866	Tax on state bank notes
1913	Federal Reserve Act
1932	Federal Home Loan Banking Act
1933	Emergency Banking Act
1933	Joint Resolution canceling gold payments
1933	Glass-Steagall Act
1935	Banking Act
1980	Depository Institutions Deregulation and Monetary Control Act
1982	Garn-St. Germain Act
1987	Competitive Equality Banking Act
1989	Financial Institutions Reform, Recovery, and Enforcement Act
1999	Repeal of Glass-Steagall
1999	Gramm-Leach-Bliley Act

backed by real estate, but it has also cost into the billions for the government to do this, which means, in turn, that the taxpayers are footing the bill. In order not to have so many failures again, the government now requires banks to keep 4 percent of their assets, and if the assets drop to less than 2 percent the bank is taken over by the government.

Mergers

It is apparent that the partial deregulation of the banking industry is only one of several factors that helped cause so many bank failures in the 1980s. However, one more recent phenomenon needs to be examined and, as with transportation deregulation, it is the great number of large mergers that have taken place in the 1990s. Some 4,500 banks have been eliminated since 1990. Banks feel they have to do it, as they now account for only 15 percent of the loans made in the United States. Mergers are facilitated by branch banking, as large banks can create branches by mergers with smaller banks. Also, if a bank wishes to offer a new form of service, a merger can be the easiest way to acquire the facilities. Then too, economies of scale are a motive, as spreading overhead costs over a larger volume of business reduces unit costs. Finally, mergers allow banks to increase their capital base, which allows them to make larger loans. Of course this is not a one-way street; small banks might want to merge to avoid failure and because they sometimes are at a disadvantage in attracting skilled management personnel.

Bank holding companies are very important, as they control not only a high percentage of commercial banks but they dominate branch banks. In the period from 1980–1993, the number of banking companies in this country dropped from 12,300 to 8,300, yet the number of branches rose from 38,000 to 54,000, and the number of automated teller machines (ATMs) rose from 19,000 to 95,000.

An example of the enormity of some mergers in the 1990s is the 1991 merger of Chemical Banking Corporation with Manufacturers Hanover Corporation, with combined assets of $135.5 billion. This was followed by the 1995 merger of Chase Manhattan Bank with Chemical for $10 billion, making Chase Manhattan the country's largest bank (although, due to subsequent mergers by other banks, it has dropped to number three), but costing 12,000 jobs. In 1997 NationsBank, one of the country's largest, announced it would buy Barnett Banks, the largest in Florida, for $15 billion. Also in 1997, Banc One and First USA merged, with a value of $7.9 billion. It moved Banc One from number eleven to number three among credit card issuers. The year 1998 saw the then two biggest bank mergers in the United States announced the same day. NationsBank, the third largest bank, merged with BankAmerica, the fifth largest bank, to become the country's second-largest bank—BankAmerica. The price for the merger was some $60 billion. NationsBank had started as NCNB (North Carolina National Bank) and had become one of the country's biggest; it had even gotten into investment banking with its 1997 purchase of Montgomery Securities. BankAmerica had also gone into investment banking in 1997 with its purchase of Robertson Stephens.

Not to be outdone, Banc One, the eighth largest, merged with First Chicago, the ninth largest, to become the country's fourth-largest bank, just ahead of J.P. Morgan. The price for the merger was some $30 billion. It is called Banc One, and it moved from number three to number two among credit card issuers.

Later in that year, Wells Fargo and Norwest, the then eighth and ninth largest, agreed to merge for some $34 billion, making Wells Fargo the country's seventh-largest bank.

In 1999 there were still more mergers. Fleet Financial Group acquired Bank-Boston Corporation for $16 billion, creating the eighth-largest bank in the country and preeminent in New England. It is called FleetBoston Corporation.

Next came the largest takeover of a U.S. institution thus far by a foreign financial concern. Deutsche Bank of Germany paid $10.1 billion for Bankers Trust, creating the world's largest commercial financial institution, with assets of about $1.55 trillion (Deutsche is Germany's biggest bank, and Bankers Trust is this country's ninth after the previously mentioned Fleet deal). It surpassed UBS AG of Switzerland, currently the largest bank, and the recently formed Citigroup, Inc., about which more will be said later. Rounding out the top ten U.S. banks is Sun Trust.

One of the best case studies of bank mergers would be to examine what has happened in the Philadelphia area, where commercial banking in the United States began in 1782. Since Pennsylvania allowed banks to merge, there are no longer any good-sized banks based in Philadelphia. They have all been acquired by out-of-city-based and, in one case, out-of-state-based banks, and the end result is that three banks now dominate the nine-county Philadelphia area. The largest, with approximately one-third of the market, is First Union, based in Charlotte, North Carolina. It traces its Philadelphia connection to 1986, when Industrial Valley Bank was sold to Fidelcor, which two years later was sold to First Fidelity, which in 1996 was sold to First Union, a combination worth about $5.4 billion. That, by itself, only made First Union number four in the region. What made them number one was their 1997 acquisition of the previous number one, CoreStates, the last remaining Philadelphia-based big bank. At $16.1 billion, the largest-ever bank merger, that makes First Union the sixth-largest bank in the nation.

CoreStates had been number one in the region due to mergers of its own. It had been known as Philadelphia National Bank, and changed its name to CoreStates in 1983. In that same year, a bank called Central Penn was sold to Meridian. Then in 1990 CoreStates bought First Pennsylvania Corporation, and in 1996 bought Meridian, a $3 billion value.

The two remaining big banks, even if looked at together, do not have the same share of the market as First Union, but they are large enough to be competitive. One is PNC Bank, based in Pittsburgh. It can trace its roots in the Philadelphia area to 1983 when Provident merged with Pittsburgh National Bank, and the result was PNC Bank. That same year Continental Bancorp, Inc. was sold to Midlantic, which in 1996 was sold to PNC Bank.

The other bank is Mellon Bank, also based in Pittsburgh. In 1983 it bought the Girard Company, and in the period from 1989–1992 it bought the bank PSFS.

Beyond those three banks, the rest of the over one hundred banks in the Philadelphia area have approximately one-third of the region's market. This situation is largely a result of the deregulation of financial institutions, and does not make for a great deal of banking competition in the Philadelphia area. What is even more disconcerting is the fact that there is not one Philadelphia-based bank left among the big banks, whereas there were at least eight or nine of them when the decade of the 1980s began. One other point worthy of note is that these large banks do not stop with acquiring other banks. They also acquire other kinds of financial companies. For instance, Mellon Bank has the Boston Company, which is a large investment bank, and in 1993 it acquired the Dreyfuss Corporation, one of the largest mutual fund companies in the country. First Union, in turn, purchased the Evergreen fund group in 1995.

The large number of mergers does not end with banks acquiring other banks and other financial institutions, because banks themselves might be bought by nonbanks. In the mid-1990s, for example, Wells Fargo and Company acquired First Interstate Bancorp for $11.6 billion, with some 7,200 people losing their jobs. Furthermore, with banks making inroads into the mutual funds market, other mergers are taking place there. An example is the Travelers Group, best known for insurance, which has Smith Barney as a subsidiary, and which, in 1997, acquired Salomon, Inc., known mostly for bond investments, for $9 billion. Travelers Group then merged the two into one company, Salomon Smith Barney. That same year Morgan Stanley, which does investment banking, combined with Dean Witter, Discovery and Company, which does retail stocks, to form the country's largest securities firm, worth $9.7 billion.

In 1998, the largest merger in terms of the amount of money involved took place in the financial services field. The two companies were Travelers Group and Citicorp, and the amount was some $70 billion. It became the country's biggest bank. Citicorp was, at the time, the country's second-largest bank and owned Citibank, the world's largest issuer of credit cards. Travelers is a multifaceted company that sells life insurance and annuities through the Primerica Financial Services and through Travelers Life and Annuity; sells property and casualty insurance through Travelers Property Casualty Corporation; does consumer loans, commercial credit, and credit cards; and does investing services through Salomon Smith Barney. It is the third-largest stock underwriter in the United States and fourth biggest in the world. It is number one in underwriting municipal bonds and number two in underwriting American and international debt offerings. The new company is called Citigroup.

Repeal of Glass-Steagall

Late in 1999 Congress repealed the Glass-Steagall Act, under the premise that American companies will be enabled to compete better in the new economy. Under the new law, banks will be able to affiliate with insurance companies and securities concerns with far fewer restrictions. It will also be more difficult for industrial companies to control a bank, as prior to the new law a number of commercial enterprises had been permitted to open savings associations known as unitary thrifts. One controversial provision in the new law allows mutual insurance companies to move to other states to avoid payments they would otherwise owe policyholders as they reorganize their corporate structure. This preempts the laws of many states which required the state's consent before such relocations. These companies can now simply move to states with more permissive laws and set up a mutual holding company.

What is the bottom line for the deregulation of financial institutions? Surely there are more financial services available than ever, only some of which are banks. This is a positive result. On the other hand, the decrease in the number of banks is alarming. Many failed, and many have been taken over by big banks through mergers, which decreases the amount of choice available to consumers. Banks have even been helped by some Supreme Court decisions.

Banks and the Supreme Court

In the 1978 case of *First National Bank of Boston v. Bellotti*,[9] a 5–4 opinion by Justice Powell struck down a Massachusetts law that had banned banks and businesses from trying to influence the outcomes of political referenda. He thought it an abridgement of free speech. In that same year, in *Marquette National Bank of Minneapolis v. First of Omaha Service Corporation*,[10] Justice Brennan wrote the unanimous decision that a national bank can charge out-of-state credit-card customers an interest rate allowed by the bank's home state, even if it was higher than that permitted by the state where the cardholder resides. Then in 1994, in *Central Bank v. First Interstate Bank*,[11] Justice Kennedy, in a 5–4 opinion, said that banks cannot be sued just because they had, as had the bank in this case, delayed in conducting an independent review of the property securing some bonds while serving as a trustee, and the bonds had defaulted. He thought the 1934 Securities Exchange Act did not permit such suits. In 1996, in *Smiley v. Citibank*,[12] a unanimous opinion written by Justice Scalia held that national banks could charge any late-payment fee permitted by their home state, regardless of whether the fee violates the law of the state where a cardholder lives. Citibank does its credit card operations from South Dakota, which has no cap. Since the Comptroller of the Currency said that the late fee is a form of interest, the Court, in light of the *Marquette* decision, accepted that interpretation as reasonable and thus ruled for the bank.

Also in 1996, the government found itself taken to task by the Court in the case of *United States v. Winstar Corporation*.[13] At issue was the $120 billion taxpayer bailout of the failed savings and loans through the passage of the 1989 Financial Institutions Reform, Recovery, and Enforcement Act. Under the act, paper assets of banks were converted into liabilities. Unfortunately, that caused two of three savings and loans to fail because the three had been induced by regulators to assume huge liabilities to salvage other savings and loans. Justice Souter, in a 7–2 opinion, held that the government knowingly went back on its word through accounting changes that made the savings and loans insolvent. He felt that the three contracts promised that the government, not the savings and loans, would assume the financial risk of any regulatory changes that might deprive the savings and loans of favorable accounting treatment. The bottom line was that the savings and loans could not meet the minimum capital requirements. The government's contention was that the contracts did not provide insurance against a legislative change, but Souter said that position was fundamentally implausible. He stated that it would have been madness to enter into them without that guarantee, for their very existence would have been in jeopardy from the moment the agreements were signed. He thought that this was a case of ordinary contract law, and that the government's arguments were at odds with its own long-term interest as a reliable trading partner. When the savings and loans were failing, the government urged the good ones to take the others over, stating that the liabilities would be carried on the books as good will that would be amortized over 35–40 years. These paper assets allowed the banks to make more loans. However, the 1989 law removed intangible assets, such as good will, from those that could be counted toward a savings and loan's minimum capital requirements. The consequences were swift and severe. The government had assumed the risk of paying damages for any financial injury from changes. The law was not a public and general one, but one for government self-relief.

PRIVACY

Congress, concerned that banks and other financial institutions, including tax-preparers, travel agents, and some department stores, had been giving information about consumers in an indiscriminate way, passed a law in 1999 to attempt to impose a remedy. It is the Gramm-Leach-Bliley Act, and under it these institutions must tell consumers how they are using their information, and it bars the institutions from sharing some of that information with outside companies but permits information-sharing among affiliated companies.

SUMMARY

In conclusion, one must be concerned about the rise in bank mergers because with a lessening of competition come all the dangers associated with oligopolies. One can sense that already, with the number of banks that are not only raising their existing fees but starting to impose fees for services that previously were free, such as having an in-person transaction at the bank rather than doing it by automation. If that is a portent of things to come, one must indeed worry that banking deregulation has unleashed a potential problem for consumers, especially those of limited means.

An illustration of how countries, including the United States, are concerned about global banking is an agreement reached by 102 countries in 1997, which took effect March 1, 1999. They decided to knock down barriers to financial firms, namely banks, securities firms, and insurance companies. The amount covered is $17.8 trillion in global securities assets, $38 trillion in global bank lending, and $2.2 trillion in worldwide insurance premiums. The point should be clear that financial markets are global in scope, and since the United States is such a key player, what we do in this country affects the world. Therefore, our deregulation of financial institutions affects people all over the world, not just our own consumers, and hopefully deregulation will prove effective. This agreement, in any event, is a positive step toward international cooperation.

QUESTIONS FOR DISCUSSION

1. Do you believe that Congress ought to be able to do things, such as chartering banks, when not expressly given the power in the Constitution?
2. Do you think that state banks should be able to issue notes that circulate as currency?
3. Do you think it proper that Congress taxed state banknotes out of existence?
4. Why has the Supreme Court consistently favored banks in its decisions?
5. Is it good that the government has substantially deregulated banking?
6. Do you see any problems with the megamergers in the financial institutions field?

NOTES

1. 4 Wheat. 316 (1819).
2. 9 Wheat. 738 (1824).
3. 11 Pet. 257 (1837).
4. 8 Wall. 533 (1869).
5. 8 Wall. 603 (1870).
6. 12 Wall. 457 (1871).
7. 294 U.S. 240 (1935).
8. 294 U.S. 330 (1935).
9. 435 U.S. 765 (1978).
10. 439 U.S. 299 (1978).
11. 511 U.S. 164 (1994).
12. 517 U.S. 735 (1996).
13. 518 U.S. 839 (1996).

Recommended Reading

Cohen, Jeffrey. *Politics and Economic Policy in the United States.* Boston, MA: Houghton Mifflin Company, 1997. Chapter 2.

Gerston, Larry, Cynthia Fraleigh, and Robert Schwab. *The Deregulated Society.* Pacific Grove, CA: Brooks/Cole, 1988.

Meier, Kenneth. *Regulation: Politics, Bureaucracy, and Economics.* New York: St. Martin's, 1985.

Schnitzer, Martin. *Contemporary Government and Business Relations.* 4th ed. Boston, MA: Houghton Mifflin Company, 1990. Chapter 15.

CHAPTER 12

DEREGULATION OF COMMUNICATIONS

The communications industry is one that has seen tremendous growth due to new technologies. The federal government first sought to regulate this field in 1910 when it placed telephone, telegraph, cable, and wireless companies engaged in interstate commerce under the jurisdiction of the Interstate Commerce Commission. However, radio proved to be such a perplexing problem that three conferences were held during the 1920s to try to bring order to an industry that was growing in a chaotic fashion. The result was the passage of the Radio Act of 1927 that established the Federal Radio Commission and placed it in the Department of Commerce. By assigning frequencies in an orderly manner, the FRC accomplished its task. However, when Franklin Roosevelt won the 1932 presidential election, he reorganized the executive branch. As a result Congress, in 1934, passed the Federal Communications Act, replacing the FRC with an independent regulatory commission called the Federal Communications Commission. The FCC was composed of five persons, appointed by the president with Senate approval, for five years each. The initial terms were staggered so that they would not expire simultaneously and, as is the practice for these kinds of agencies, no more than three of the five commissioners could come from the same political party. Besides regulating radio and later television, the FCC was also to regulate the telephone, telegraph, cable, and wireless companies that had been under the ICC. Whereas the FCC has power over such matters as services, accounts, interconnections, facilities, combinations, and finances, its power over rates is restricted as it has no control over broadcasting charges. That is left to the marketplace and the going rate can be high, as shown by what advertisers pay for spots on professional football's Super Bowl.

What the FCC does for radio and television is to assign frequencies and channels, grant them licenses to operate their stations, fix their hours of operation, and prevent interference among stations. Section 303 of the 1934 law charges the FCC with seeing that broadcasters serve the public convenience, interest, or necessity.

When it comes to rates, such as for the telephone and telegraph companies, they must file them with the FCC and make them available for public inspection. Notice must be given of rate changes. If a new rate is filed, the FCC may suspend it for a period not exceeding three months and hold hearings on its reasonableness. The burden of proving reasonableness is on the company.

TELECOMMUNICATIONS

The high point of government regulation of the telecommunications industry occurred in 1982 when the American Telephone and Telegraph Company, the largest in the world at that time, reached a settlement with the Justice Department in that agency's attempt to break up AT&T's monopoly of the telephone industry. AT&T divested itself of the local telephone services of its twenty-two Bell Operating Companies. They became part of seven independent holding companies: Ameritech, Bell Atlantic, Bell South, Nynex, Pacific Telesis, Southwestern Bell, and US West. AT&T also turned over to them its intrastate long-distance service. These companies, in turn, had to share their facilities with all long-distance telephone companies on the same terms, and could not discriminate against AT&T's competitors in buying equipment and planning new facilities.

On the other hand, AT&T was allowed to retain its equipment-manufacturing subsidiary, Western Electric; its research unit, Bell Laboratories; and its long-distance division (it still has about half the market for long-distance service in the United States). AT&T's stockholders retained their stock and were issued proportionate shares in the local companies. The divestiture, the largest in antitrust history, amounted to $87 billion.

Did the divestiture work? Because of new competition in the long-distance industry, prices have dropped about one-half for customers, and equipment prices have also dropped for phone companies. There has been growth in new technology, such as fiber-optic cable and fax machines. On the other hand, customers paid higher costs for equipment installation and service provided by the short-distance phone companies. Rates now seem stable, but there have been complaints about quality of service and there was, especially in the beginning, customer confusion over telephone bills.

Meanwhile, AT&T got larger in 1994 when it bought McCaw Cellular Communications for $11.5 billion, and in 1995 it split into three companies: one for long-distance and credit card operations, one for telecommunications equipment and systems, and one for its computer unit. It also won a big Supreme Court decision in the 1994 case of *MCI Telecommunications Corporation v. American Telephone and Telegraph Company.*[1] The FCC had relieved AT&T's competitors from the need to file a listing of their rates and services. Normally, rates must be posted 120 days before they take effect. However, the FCC decided that was only for dominant carriers, so it let the others negotiate customized service agreements with big companies. The FCC thought it could do so because the law does allow it to modify any requirement, but Justice Scalia, for a 5–3 Court, held that the provision in question connotes moderate change, not fundamental revision, and rate filings are the essential characteristics of a rate-regulated industry.

What about the seven "baby Bells"? They are not small, despite the nickname, and they are not even seven. Mergers have begun to permeate the field. One of the companies, Bell South, has stayed rather constant, while another, US West, bought Continental Cablevision in 1996 for $10.8 billion. US West Communications (renamed US West) was the regional Bell, with US West Media Group being the entity in the media field. The latter was renamed MediaOne Group and spun off as a separate company in 1997. In 1998 it sold its domestic wireless operation for $5.7 billion to Airtouch Communications, and in 1999, as we shall see later, MediaOne was bought by AT&T.

Vodaphone, a British wireless company, bought Airtouch in 1999, and later in 1999 Bell Atlantic and Vodaphone Airtouch (which is the world's largest wireless telephone operator) agreed to combine their U.S. wireless operations and create the nation's largest coast-to-coast network able to serve 21 million customers, covering about 90 percent of the population.

Bell Atlantic bought a stake in Metromedia and paid it to use its nationwide fiber optic data network for twenty years. It gives Bell Atlantic access to expensive equipment that allows it to directly connect its customers to points across the United States, instead of using outside companies to reach some areas, and it gives Metromedia money to accelerate the growth of its network, which can be used to transmit data, voice, video, and multimedia communications here and abroad.

Mergers have occurred with the other five. In 1997 Southwestern Bell and Pacific Telesis merged to form SBC. The price was $16.7 billion. The next year SBC Communications Inc. bought Ameritech for $72 billion. In 1999 it bought Comcast's cellular operations for $1.67 billion. In 2000, SBC, the nation's second largest local phone company, received FCC permission to offer long distance service in Texas. Not to be outdone, Bell Atlantic and Nynex merged for $22.7 billion in 1997, calling itself Bell Atlantic, and the next year Bell Atlantic merged with GTE for $65 billion. It is now called Verizon Communications. This created the nation's largest telephone company, as Bell Atlantic has local telephone service in thirteen states and GTE has local telephone service to rural areas in twenty-eight states. GTE started in 1935 as General Telephone, became General Telephone and Electric when it merged with Sylvania in 1955, and became GTE two decades later. GTE also brought to the merger long-distance service in all fifty states, regional computer networks, and World Wide Web services for businesses. Bell Atlantic folded GTE's wireless assets into its Vodaphone venture, creating one of the nation's largest mobile phone companies. GTE bought the long-distance company Sprint in the 1980s, but because the law required that Sprint stay a separate company (so that one company would not do both local and long distance), it decided to sell it in 1992. However, the 1996 Telecommunications Act dropped that provision, so GTE got back into it. Sprint, meanwhile, sold 10 percent each in 1996 to Deutsche Telekom of Germany and France

Telecom. Since Bell Atlantic's local calling region is thirteen states, it cannot start long-distance services in them without FCC permission. Thus far, permission was granted in 1999 to offer long-distance services in New York. Altogether, Verizon will control 63 million of the local phone lines (one-third of the nation's) plus 25 million cell-phone customers. It and SBC now control 69 percent of the nation's telephone lines.

Because the long-distance field is a multibillion dollar industry, companies are anxious to get into it. Metromedia entered the field in 1993 with a $2.5 billion merger with Resurgens Communications Group. In 1997 WorldCom purchased MCI for $37 billion. There were $24.1 billion worth of mergers in the telecommunications field in 1995 and $104 billion in 1996, including the four largest of the mergers that year in all areas. WorldCom Technologies merged with Williams Telecommunications for $2.5 billion and got 11,000 miles of fiber optic cable network. The following year, UUNET was acquired, as it was part of MFS Communications and MFS was bought by WorldCom for $14 billion. Once it had its Internet provider, the next year WorldCom bought CompuServe, an on-line service, from H&R Block for $1.2 billion. It then sold the consumer side of it (content, data bases, and subscribers) to America Online, to which it supplies the hardware network. An AOL competitor, Microsoft, in that same year bought Web TV, a net deliverer directly to television sets. There is much competition as to which company can have the leading site on the Internet. AOL in 1998 bought Netscape Communications Corporation for $4.21 billion, giving it the Netcenter web site in addition to its own (it also gets to distribute Netscape's Internet browser software). As part of the deal, Sun Microsystems, a maker of business software and computers, will distribute Netscape's corporate software for three years. As for the rest of the website competition, At Home Corporation, a high-speed Internet service, bought Excite, a web site (now known as Excite@Home and controlled by AT&T, which also has Worldnet). Walt Disney Company bought Infoseek and folded it into its new portal, the Go Network. Microsoft has its MSN portal, but in 1999 a big company became even bigger. Yahoo bought Geocities, another popular site, with the latter remaining as an independent unit. Yahoo bought Broadcast.com in 1999 for $5.7 billion. The latter is the Internet's leading supplier of radio and video programs. Lycos is another popular site, with its search services and information and online communications, as are Prodigy and Ebay. Later in 1999 Internet service providers Earthlink Network and MindSpring Enterprises merged in a $1.7 billion deal to create the number two provider in the United States, behind AOL.

As for making computers, Compaq Computer Corporation is the world's number one supplier for personal computers. It purchased Tandem Corporation, a maker of high-end mainframes used in retailing, banking, stock trading, and telecommunications, for $2.8 billion. Then in 1998 it purchased Digital Equipment Corporation, a maker of large corporate computers, for $9.6 billion. It also has the Alta Vista web site. Other big companies in the personal computer field are Dell, which has replaced Compaq as number one in the United States, Gateway, Hewlett-Packard, IBM, and Apple.

In the meantime, what is happening at AT&T? The world's largest telecommunications company bought, in 1998, Teleport Communications Group, which provided telecommunications services to businesses, and then bought Tele-Communications Inc., the nation's number two cable television company, including TCI's stake in At Home. By buying the former, it can bypass the wires of local phone companies, and by buying the latter, it can use those wires to offer local telephone and Internet services. It then entered into a global venture with British Telecom, Britain's biggest phone company, to sell $10 billion per year of telephone, Internet, and data services to big corporate customers around the globe by the formation of a new, jointly owned company. The next year the two companies agreed to spend $1.8 billion to buy 30 percent of Japan Telecom. Meanwhile, AT&T bought IBM's global network business for $5 billion. Again in 1999, AT&T struck a deal to offer telephone service over Time Warner's cable systems in thirty-three states, making it more involved in local phone service. It now has the potential to supply local phone service to 40 percent of U.S. households (35 million homes) over the next four to five years. AT&T will own slightly more than three-quarters of the joint venture. The hope of AT&T is that consumers will want the convenience of receiving phone service on the same cable TV circuits that deliver channels, Internet access (Worldnet is their service provider), and online banking. In response, MCI Worldcom (now just Worldcom) announced it would begin offering local phone service to residents in New York State by leasing the Bell Atlantic Corporation's local phone network. Then AT&T purchased cable TV's MediaOne for $58 billion (MediaOne owns a 25 percent stake in Time Warner Entertainment, which owns most of the cable systems of Time Warner). Meanwhile, Comcast, another cable company that had wanted MediaOne, got the right to buy as many as 2 million MediaOne customers from AT&T for up to $9 billion. Microsoft also got into the act, paying $5 billion for about a 3 percent stake in AT&T. Because of that, AT&T agreed to use Windows CE software in some of the cable TV set-top boxes it will use to put the Internet into homes. Microsoft also will buy MediaOne's 29.9 percent in a European cable operator.

The AT&T and MediaOne deal gives AT&T more than one-third of the nation's cable network for television, high-speed Internet access, and online telephone services, making it the nation's largest (the second largest is Time Warner). As previously mentioned, AT&T has a controlling interest in Excite@Home, the nation's largest cable Internet service, but since MediaOne has a substantial interest in the second largest, Road Runner (Time Warner also has an interest in it), the Justice Department wants Road Runner sold (federal regulations say that a company cannot own more than 30 percent of the nation's cable systems). Another factor to consider is that MediaOne and Time Warner have large interests in Time Warner Entertainment, a programming and cable operating company. The end result of this is that AT&T is involved with television, the Internet, and local, long-distance, and wireless telephone services. Its programming units include Liberty Media, Rainbow Media, and Sports Holidays, Inc. The FCC did approve the acquisition in 2000, subject to the companies selling some of their assets.

The year 1999 continued to be the year for megamergers with the announcement that WorldCom, the second largest U.S. long-distance company, would buy Sprint Corporation, the number three carrier, for $122 billion in stock, the then largest takeover ever. The combined company would be called WorldCom and would have about 30 percent of the country's long-distance market, second only to AT&T's approximately 45 percent. The deal would beat the previous high of Exxon purchasing Mobil for $80 billion and the SBC Communications-Ameritech deal for $72 billion. (The AOL-Time Warner $122 billion deal is still pending.) In 2000, due to opposition by the Justice Department and European regulators, the companies called off the proposed merger.

While all this was going on, one of the former "baby Bells" was keeping busy. US West announced a deal to merge with the telecommunications company Qwest Communications International for $44 million. The new entity will be called Qwest Communications. Qwest brought its broadband Internet data and video and voice communications capabilities to the deal, while US West brought its digital subscriber line and wireless and local phone service. At the same time, Global Crossing, a Bermuda local and long-distance phone company that had also wanted US West, acquired Frontier Corporation, a U.S.-based long-distance carrier, for $11 billion.

What are the implications of all these deals? For one, several of AT&T's competitors started a coalition in 1999 in the form of a nationwide lobbying effort to force AT&T to open its system to Internet competitors. The group calls itself Open Net. In 1999, AT&T said it would give its cable customers a choice of Internet service providers in June 2002, the expiration date for an exclusivity arrangement with Excite@Home, which it partly owns. In addition, the entrance of foreign companies into the U.S. telecommunications industry brings a provision of the Federal Communications Act into play, because it allows no more than 25 percent foreign ownership of a U.S. telecommunications company. However, the FCC can waive it if the country of the foreign company has liberalized its own market for U.S. companies, as has Great Britain, and/or if it would help a U.S. company compete more effectively. The 1996 Telecommunications Act further complicates the situation in that it prohibits the "baby Bells" from offering long-distance service in their home territories unless they are proved open to local competition. Once that opening is there and the long-distance companies want to offer local service, the FCC can set the pricing rules, according to the Supreme Court in the 1999 case of *AT&T v. Iowa Utilities Board.*[2]

The Court, in a 5–3 decision authored by Justice Scalia, said the 1996 Telecommunications Act allowed such power to the FCC to implement the act's local competition provisions. The Court also upheld most of the FCC's rules aimed at prohibiting local phone companies from separating parts of their network and then requiring a customer who leases those parts to pay the cost of reassembling them. It imposes unneeded costs on a competitor. The Court did strike down one FCC rule that required a local phone company to provide competitors with access to various local network elements. The Court also ruled that the FCC can impose a "pick and choose" rule on local phone companies, which allows competitors to buy or lease any service or network element under the same terms as they were provided under any previous agreement, without having to accept the entire agreement.

Another problem inherent in the communications explosion is the question of which companies will get the FCC licenses to provide mobile phone, paging, voice mail, and other services. The FCC decided that the fairest method would be to auction these specialized mobile radio service licenses, and it did just that in 1997. Nextel Communications was the biggest winner.

Then there is the emerging legal issue as to whether a search engine can sell banner ads linked to particular search keywords, including trademarked terms. Suits have already been filed against Excite, Webcrawler (owned by Excite), and Netscape for trademark infringement, unfair competition, and related offenses.

Another legal issue is whether some smut can be kept out of e-mails. A provision of the 1996 Telecommunications Act makes it a crime to transmit an obscene communication with intent to annoy, abuse, threaten, or harass another person. All e-mail was included, even messages sent from one friend to another. It was upheld by a three-judge federal court in 1998, and in 1999 the Supreme Court upheld the lower court's decision without issuing an opinion.

One more legal issue coming to the forefront is the practice of Internet advertising companies getting access to consumer data, raising the privacy issue. For example, in 1999 one of the advertising firms, DoubleClick, merged with Abacus Direct Corporation, a company that sells information about consumers' catalogue purchases. They use the DoubleClick name and are able to serve Internet "banner" ads to users based on what a person has purchased offline in the past. One of its chief rivals is already doing this; 24/7 Media has an agreement with Intelliquest, a marketing firm that processes product registrations for the approximately 85 percent of the companies who do not do it themselves. When a customer registers a product over the Internet with a company that works with Intelliquest and agrees to accept future marketing messages, a data file called a "cookie" is assigned to that person's browser. Intelliquest then provides 24/7 with the cookie number and the person's name and address. Even more startling is the amount of information that is available offline. Acxiom Corporation supplies customer information to marketing firms and has detailed data on 95 percent of the households in the United States, such as names, addresses, occupations, home values, and frequently hobbies, income investments, and cars. This complex issue is a long way from being resolved, and the industry is attempting self-regulation through its Online Privacy Alliance. One thing Congress has done was to pass the 1998 Children's On-Line Privacy Protection Act, under which web sites must obtain parental permission before collecting any personal information from children under thirteen. One other problem is copyright protection over the Internet, and the 1998 Digital Millennium Copyright Act makes it illegal to circumvent copyright-protection technologies.

The telecommunications industry, including the computer field with the Internet, has grown so fast that the government seems unable to keep up with it, hence the trend toward the megamergers. In fact, Congress, with the 1996 Telecommunications Act, deregulated the industry massively by letting each company engage in whatever activity it wants, such as phone companies providing television service, short-distance phone companies getting into long-distance, cable companies providing phone service, etc. Any venture one can imagine seems legal, which means that there will probably be more mergers than before, with companies buying others in order to enter a new field.

There was one area, however, that the Telecommunications Act tried to regulate, but to no avail. Title V is the Communications Decency Act, which established a number of content-based restrictions on what could appear on the Internet. Among them were things deemed obscene, indecent, child pornography, and the availability of abortion services. When the American Civil Liberties Union challenged the law, the government did not try to defend the part dealing with abortion services, and the ACLU did not challenge the parts dealing with obscenity and child pornography. The case centered around indecency, namely, sending sexual communications to minors, which in the law were defined as those under the age of eighteen. Anyone convicted under the law faced a fine plus a prison sentence of up to two years. The case, *Reno v. ACLU*,[3] was decided in 1997, and in a 7–2 opinion (unanimous in part), Justice Stevens held the law to be an unconstitutional infringement of free speech. The law censored speech that was protected for adults under the First Amendment, and was both vague and overly broad.

Even though the law was struck down, online information services said they would try to keep this type of material off the Internet. Even before the law was passed, CompuServe blocked access to some discussion groups, and America Online blocked the use of certain prohibited words it deemed vulgar. Both the industry and civil libertarians would rather the industry police itself than the government step in with censorship. Whether that approach will work is something only the future will tell. In 1999, the Internet Corporation for Assigned Names and Numbers (ICANN), a nonprofit corporation for international governance of the Internet, was created.

THE MEDIA

The FCC currently licenses a radio or television station for a period of eight years, which means that there must be an available frequency in order to even be granted an initial license. The Mass Media Bureau of the FCC will issue the construction permit if the applicant meets the conditions, such as U.S. citizenship, good character, and the financial ability to do it. Once the license is granted, the 1996 Telecommunications Act allows broadcasters to renew them automatically without competition as long as they have served the public interest and not seriously broken any FCC rules or federal laws. They do not have to worry about competing applications, although the FCC could renew it for less than eight years if it felt the station had a problem that would be corrected during that time.

The FCC's licensing policies were upheld by the Supreme Court in the 1943 case of *National Broadcasting Company v. United States*[4] NBC and the other networks with chains of stations challenged some regulations that restricted their control over local stations, but the Court, speaking through Justice Frankfurter, upheld the regulations as well as the licensing policies. He felt that because there are only so many frequencies available, the FCC had to determine who should get them through licensing, and a denial of one was not a denial of free speech. The Court also upheld the FCC rule of only one radio station per owner in a particular community, a rule meant to try to prevent monopolies.

The FCC was concerned over the years with cross-ownership, meaning how many radio and television stations could be owned by the same company. For many years it limited companies to seven AM radio stations, seven FM radio stations, and seven television stations, but in 1984 it decided to gradually eliminate the restrictions, first going to twelve each and in 1994 to twenty each. Under the 1996 Telecommunications Act, there are almost no limits. The following limits are in the law: If a community has fourteen or less commercial radio stations, no one party can control more than half, and no one party's television stations can reach more than 35 percent of the households in the country. The law ordered the FCC to reconsider the rule regarding one television station per market. The FCC was also ordered to allow all but the biggest television networks (ABC, CBS, NBC, and Fox) to own more than one network, and all television networks were allowed to own cable systems, unless that would discriminate against broadcasters affiliated with that network. The law against a cable company owning a television station in its service area was repealed; the FCC can grant it on a case-by-case basis. The deregulation in this law will lead to an expansion of companies engaging in areas that were previously barred to them, and might also lead to even more mergers in a field in which megamergers have become commonplace.

The FCC issued rules regarding cable first in 1962 and again in 1966, but the latter was restrictive to cable in that the FCC tried to protect existing television stations from competition. The Court upheld the rules in the 1968 case of *United States v. Southwestern Cable*.[5] It felt that cable, like radio and television, should be subject to FCC rules. But the FCC soon realized that television was not being hurt by cable and began to deregulate it. Congress then passed the 1984 Cable Communications Policy Act, which put cable into the 1934 Federal Communications Act but which also allowed for local governments to handle the awarding of franchises. Congress later passed the 1992 Cable Television Consumer Protection and Competition Act. One part of that law concerned the so-called "must-carry" controversy that started in 1966 when the FCC said cable systems had to carry the signals of all local television channels viewed by a significant portion of a community. This was an attempt to help educational TV as well as UHF stations that were not as strong as the VHF ones. After a lower court ruled the provisions unconstitutional, the FCC revised them, but again a lower court ruled them unconstitutional. Then Congress said in the 1992 law that cable systems had to use some of their channels for local television stations. This time a lower court upheld it, the Supreme Court sent the case back for further hearings, the lower court again upheld it, and finally, in the 1997 case of *Turner Broadcasting System v. FCC,*[6] the Supreme Court in a 5–4 decision authored by Justice Kennedy upheld the rule. He felt that since some 40 percent of households in this country do not have cable, they must depend upon local broadcasters, but many of those broadcasters would go off the air if cable did not pick them up. He said that the rule preserved free television broadcasting, promoted a wide dissemination of information from many sources, and promoted fair competition in the television market. There was no free speech violation because it burdened no more speech than necessary to accomplish the above interests.

One of the most controversial areas involving the relationship of government and the media is in regard to the content of what goes out over television, radio, and cable stations. Back in 1941 the FCC said that radio stations could not do editorials, but then in 1949 it came up with the fairness doctrine that allowed stations to editorialize as long as other points of view were also aired. Stations also had to allow the right of reply to personal attacks. In the 1969 case of *Red Lion Broadcasting Company v. FCC,*[7] a unanimous Court upheld the doctrine. Justice White felt the doctrine promoted free speech because there were only so many licenses for broadcasters, and that scarcity meant that those without licenses must be able to have some access. This is how matters stood until 1985 when the FCC itself became critical of it; two years later a lower court told the FCC to reexamine its doctrine. The FCC then said it would not enforce the balanced programming part of it, but would enforce the personal-attack rules. This was accepted by the lower court. Congress attempted to restore the doctrine, but a veto by President Reagan was not overridden.

Another area of content restriction is the equal-opportunities part of the 1934 Federal Communications Act, which says that stations who allow a candidate running for office air time must allow all other candidates for that office equal opportunities, and the stations have no power over censoring the material. However, when the FCC ruled that short radio and television news clips of a candidate required reply time, Congress amended the law to exclude bona fide newscasts, news interviews, news documentaries, and on-the-spot coverage of news events. That amendment was in 1959. The following year Congress made a one-time exemption so that John F. Kennedy and Richard Nixon could debate in their quest for the presidency without any minor candidates taking part. The FCC in 1975 ruled that presidential debates could be broadcast as news events if they were sponsored by a nonpartisan group, then in 1984 said that a nonpartisan sponsor would not be required for them.

Meanwhile, Congress, in 1971, amended the 1934 law to require broadcasters to allow candidates for federal elections to purchase reasonable amounts of time for campaign purposes. When, in 1979, the three major networks refused to sell time because it was too early for the 1980 campaign for the presidency, the FCC agreed with those who were denied that time, and in 1981 the Supreme Court, in *CBS v. FCC,*[8] upheld the FCC. Chief Justice Burger felt the law properly balanced the First Amendment rights of all concerned: candidates, public, and broadcasters.

One problem faced by the FCC in the late 1970s was format change, with stations changing their programming to some other type. The FCC decided to allow the stations to do this, and the Supreme Court sustained the FCC in the 1981 case of *FCC v. WNCN Listeners Guild.*[9] Justice White saw no First Amendment problem.

In the 1934 law Congress did prohibit the broadcasting of lottery information, and in 1948 moved the prohibition to the Criminal Code, which provides for a fine of up to $1,000 or imprisonment up to one year. With the advent of state-run lotteries in many states, Congress in 1988 amended the law to allow broadcasting of information about state lotteries and Indian reservations' lotteries. However, the station doing the broadcasting must be in the same state as the lottery. In the 1993 case of *United States v. Edge Broadcasting Company,*[10] the Supreme Court, in a 7–2 opinion authored by Justice White, upheld the law being used against a radio station in North Carolina near the Virginia border that broadcast ads for the Virginia lottery (North Carolina did not have a lottery). Even though 90 percent of the station's listeners were in Virginia, the Court felt that the government had an interest in substantially reducing lottery ads, and that the First Amendment affords only a limited protection of commercial speech.

Another part of the 1934 law prohibited the broadcast of profane, indecent, or obscene material, and that was also switched to the Criminal Code in 1948. The penalty can be up to a $10,000 fine and up to two years in prison. The 1996 Telecommunications Act puts the fine up to a maximum of $500,000 for corporations that knowingly permit their television facilities to be used for illegal programming. The issue came before the Supreme Court in 1978 in the case of *FCC v. Pacifica Foundation*[11] that concerned the recording called "Filthy Words" being played over the radio; in it several words regarded as objectionable by many people were repeated over and over again. The FCC banned the record, and the Court, speaking through Justice Stevens, upheld the ban. Even though those words did not meet the Court's definition of obscenity, they still were explicit enough to be regulated by the FCC because the use of the air waves is not totally without restriction. The FCC has the obligation to protect the listeners of radio stations, especially children, from material deemed offensive by society.

The FCC, for the next few years, only took action against excessive indecency, as in this case, and actually allowed this type of material between 10 P.M. and 6 A.M. However, in 1987 it made the ban a twenty-four hour one and broadened what was considered indecent. A lower court agreed with the expanded definition but asked the FCC to reconsider the total ban. Congress then passed a law in 1988 making the ban twenty-four hours, but the lower court suspended it until the FCC rendered its report in 1990, again endorsing the total ban. The next year the court rejected the total ban, so Congress in 1992 passed another law, this one allowing the material to be broadcast between midnight and 6 A.M. The FCC adopted a rule to that effect. The court agreed with it but moved the starting time to 10 P.M., since the 1992 law allowed public stations that finished at midnight to use the 10 P.M. to midnight period for material that was considered indecent.

When Congress passed the 1984 Cable Communications Policy Act, it placed cable systems under the same content restrictions as broadcasters, such as equal opportunity for political candidates, right of reply for personal attacks, no lottery information (later amended as previously mentioned), and no obscenity and indecency. State and local governments also banned obscene and indecent material, but the Miami, Florida, ordinance was struck down by two lower federal courts for the indecency part, and the same thing happened to the Utah law. The Supreme Court affirmed without comment. Congress, therefore, decided to enter the fray again in the 1992 Cable Television Consumer Protection and Competition Act. There were three major parts in the law concerning censorship, and the Supreme Court considered them in the 1996 case of *Denver Area Educational Telecommunications Consortium v. FCC*.[12] Justice Breyer, in a 7–2 opinion, upheld the provision allowing cable operators to decide whether or not to transmit indecent programming. It was private censorship, not governmental, and society has the right to keep this material away from children. However, he struck down in a 5–4 vote the second provision that allowed cable operators to censor public access channels because those channels were already closely scrutinized by the educational and governmental institutions that use them. Two others agreed with that rationale; the final two votes supported the view that public access channels are like a public forum and similar First Amendment rules should prevail. As for the final provision, Breyer struck it down 6–3. It required cable operators that allowed indecent programming to place it all on one channel and block access to it unless a viewer requested access in advance and in writing. He thought it too broad and that there were less restrictive means to protect children from seeing this material. Also, those who requested access might fear for their reputations if the list were made public.

The Supreme Court gave a victory to radio and television in the 1999 case of *Greater New Orleans Broadcasting Association v. United States*.[13] Justice Stevens, for a unanimous Court, struck down a law that banned broadcast advertising for lotteries, gift enterprises, or similar schemes offering prizes dependent upon lot or chance. The problem was that Congress had amended it to allow ads for casinos on Indian reservations, state-run lotteries, or any gambling sponsored by nonprofit promoters for charitable purposes. The Court decided that the law had too many exemptions and inconsistencies and therefore could not be enforced in those states in which casino gambling is legal. It was a violation of free speech that did not sufficiently advance the government's stated interest in protecting compulsive gamblers and did not do it in the least intrusive way.

Newspapers are much freer with regard to governmental regulation. For example, two lower federal courts said that newspapers are free to decide what advertising they wish to accept and what they do not. To see what the Supreme Court has said, one can look at the 1974 case of *Miami Herald Publishing Co. v. Tornillo*.[14] A Florida law required newspapers to print replies to stories that were critical in nature, and Chief Justice Burger, for a unanimous Court, struck it down as a violation of freedom of the press.

TABLE 12-1   MAJOR FEDERAL COMMUNICATIONS LAWS

1927	Radio Act
1934	Federal Communications Act
1984	Cable Communications Policy Act
1988 and 1992	Laws against indecent broadcasting
1992	Cable Television Consumer Protection and Competition Act
1996	Telecommunications Act

Although the 1996 Telecommunications Act allowed for massive deregulation of the communications field as far as structure is concerned, such as various types of companies now being permitted into other areas of communication, there still remains some content regulation for broadcasters. Admittedly, the Court will step in if the regulation oversteps its bounds, but broadcasters still must abide by some regulation. On a continuum, the printed media is the freest, followed by cable, and then by radio and television. With the public at large feeling that not everything should go out over the air waves, the chances of much change in the situation seem remote.[15]

MERGERS

As with the field of telecommunications, there have been so many mergers of such giant proportions in the last several years as to boggle the mind. An examination of them is enlightening and also frightening because it means there is less and less competition, thus people are less and less able to receive various points of view. For example, virtually all city newspapers have the same owner, and almost all the daily newspaper circulation is controlled by companies that publish two or more dailies. Newspaper companies own commercial radio and television stations. There is a trend toward concentration in the publishing industry, largely due to high advertising and publishing costs. As an example, in 1998 Bertelsmann, the fifth largest media company in the world by revenue, bought Random House. At the time, Random House was number four and Bertelsmann number eight in North American book sales. Bertelsmann already owned Bantam Doubleday Dell publishing, as well as the BMG record label and *McCalls* and *Family Circle* magazines. Random House, in turn, also owned Knopf, Ballantine, Pantheon, and Fodor's travel guides.

Congress made an attempt at preserving competition in the newspaper industry by passing the 1970 Newspaper Preservation Act. It allows competing newspapers to share certain costs, such as printing and distribution, and to split certain revenues, such as advertising and circulation dollars. However, newsrooms and editorial pages would remain separate, ideally to provide diverse viewpoints. Despite this, many newspapers disappeared, mostly due to mergers.

Illustrative of these mergers is the one in 2000 in which Tribune Company bought Times Mirror for $8 billion. Tribune Company owns the *Chicago Tribune*, the *Sun Sentinel* (South Florida), the *Orlando Sentinel*, twenty-two television stations, four radio stations, the Chicago Cubs baseball team, and investments in AOL and in the WB network. Times Mirror owned seven newspapers, including the *Los Angeles Times*, *Newsday* (Long Island), *The Sun* (Baltimore), and the *Hartford Courant*, plus twenty magazines, including *Field & Stream*, *Popular Science*, *Golf*, *Ski*, *Skiing*, and *Yachting*. By all estimates this megamerger is an indicator of what is to happen in the future as newspapers struggle for survival in this increasingly electronic age.

In the movie theater industry, mergers have led to theaters showing many movies under the same roof. It is difficult to find an old-fashioned theater that has only one screen. In the music business, Seagram Co. has become a dominant factor. It purchased 80 percent of MCA in 1995 for $5.7 billion and renamed it Seagram Universal Studios. Its Universal Music Group included the record labels Universal Records, MCA Records Nashville, MCA Records, GRP Recording Company, and Geffen Records. Then in 1998 the Group acquired PolyGram (which was 75 percent owned by a Dutch firm and which it merged with its music division) for $10.2 billion, a sale that included the record labels Mercury Records (since 1960), Def Jam (60 percent), Island Records (since 1989), A&M Records (since 1990), and Motown Records (since 1993). It has since merged Island Records and Mercury Records, one called Verve (from PolyGram) with GRP jazz labels, Motown and Universal, and its unit called Interscope along with Geffen and A&M became units of Universal's West Coast music group. Besides MCA records, MCA had Universal Pictures, theme parks, ODEON Corporation (a television production unit), and 40 percent of CINEPLEX. Seagram was concentrating its efforts in the music business in order to compete with its rivals, Warner Music, Bertelsmann, and SONY Music, in terms of newly released albums. However, in 2000 Time Warner announced that Warner Music would merge with EMIGroup of Britain to create the world's largest record company valued at $20 billion and called Warner EMI Music. EMI and Warner are also the two largest companies in music publishing. Not to be outdone, Seagram Co. was purchased in June 2000 by the French company Vivendi for $34 billion. The new name will be Vivendi Universal.

Meanwhile, Bertelsmann, which is the world's largest book publisher (Bertelsmann owns Random House, among other publishing houses), is attempting to become bigger in the record industry through its global music company, BMG. BMG has RCA Records, BMG Direct (a music club), Windham Hill Group, and Arista Records. It has an alliance with AOL, which gives owners of CDs from BMG artists access to the Internet, and it has joined with AT&T to create a secure system for selling digital downloads (online sales).

In 2000, Time Warner, Sony Corporation of America, Bertelsmann Music Group, EMI Music Distributors, and Universal Music and Video Distributors, all of which control 85 percent of the $15 billion CD market, agreed to a consent order with the FTC to stop marketing agreements that had been used to end a price war, inflate the prices of CDs, and sharply restrict the ability of retailers to offer discounts. Specifically, they cannot link any future financing of advertising with prices for CDs for seven years, and for thirteen years after that they cannot impose price conditions in advertisements that are paid for by the retailers.

Bookstores are also falling prey to mergers, as well as to online sellers such as Amazon.com. Barnes and Noble is the nation's number one bookseller, aided by its acquisition of Dalton in 1986 and Doubleday in 1990. Its proposed merger with Ingram Book Group, the nation's leading book distributor, was called off in 1999 due to the opposition of the staff of the FTC. Borders is also big, helped by its purchase of Waldenbooks. Bookstores have actually increased by 329 percent in this country since 1975, although they have fallen by 3 percent in the 1990s. But just try to find the independent bookstore—it is hard to do. Newsdealers and newsstands have increased 82 percent in this country since 1970, including a 3 percent gain from 1995–1996. Therefore the reading material is plentiful but the source is not.

The trend toward mergers in the media began in 1985 when ABC network was bought by Capital Cities. ABC also owns movie theaters and publishing companies and publishes newspapers in various cities, as well as trade publications such as *Institutional Investor* and *Women's Wear Daily*. Ten years later, Disney bought Capital Cities-ABC for $19 billion, making it the second biggest media company by revenue and giving it control over ten television stations, thirty radio stations, a film library, theme parks, the Disney Channel, ESPN, History Channel, and movies made by MIRAMAX, Hollywood Pictures, Touchstone, and Disney. Publishing now includes Fairchild (magazines), Hyperion (books), and Disney Publishing Worldwide. Music includes Walt Disney Music Publishing and Buena Vista Music Group.

Not to be outdone, in 1986 NBC network was bought by General Electric, and in 1996 MSNBC (owned by Microsoft) and NBC went together in a joint venture television channel. It also has a stake in Snap, a small portal, and has cable channel CNBC for business news.

That left CBS alone, until in 1995 it was bought by Westinghouse for $5.4 billion, and in 1997 Westinghouse Electric Corporation became CBS Corporation and got out of its industrial side. CBS has CBS Television, CBS New Media, CBS Entertainment, fifteen television stations and its cable television networks, and has purchased the Nashville Network and Country Music Television. In 1999 it bought King World Productions, television's biggest program syndicator, for $2.5 billion. It also owns Eyemark Entertainment for syndication. But its biggest push was in the radio field. Since Congress, in the 1996 Telecommunications Act, eased restrictions on ownership, more than one-fourth of the more than 10,000 radio stations have changed hands. In 1996 Westinghouse/CBS bought Infinity Broadcasting Company with its over 160 stations for $4.7 billion, and in 1997 it bought American Radio Systems for $1.6 billion. In 1998 Chancellor Media merged with Capstar Broadcasting, creating a company (Chancellor Media) with 463 stations in 105 markets. In 2000, Clear Channel (the nation's largest radio company) plans to merge with AMFM (the nation's second largest) for about $16.6 billion, which will give it 874 radio stations (plus nineteen television stations). Other large radio operators are Jacor and ABC/Disney.

During the time the three networks were involved in these transactions, other companies were also expanding in the media field. In 1989 SONY purchased Columbia Pictures and Tristar Pictures for $4.8 billion, and in that same year two giants, Time and Warner, merged for $14.9 billion. That put the following into its hands: Warner Brothers film and television studios; post-1948 Warner Brothers cartoons and movies; HBO; Cinemax; Warner Brothers Network; interests in Court TV and Comedy Central; cable systems; *Time*; *People*; *Entertainment Weekly*; *Fortune*; *Money*; *Sports Illustrated*; DC Comics; Little, Brown, and Company Book Publishers; Warner Books; Book-of-the-Month Club; fifty record labels in its Warner Music Group, including Warner Brothers, Atlantic, and Elektra; Six Flags theme parks; Warner Brothers retail stores; and home videos. Time-Warner and SONY jointly own Columbia House.

Time-Warner solidified its position as number one media company by revenue with its 1996 merger with Turner, a $7.5 billion stock deal. This brought the following into the company: Castle Rock Entertainment; New Line Cinema; Turner Pictures (which it has since closed); Hanna Barbera cartoons; pre-1948 Warner Brothers cartoons and movies; MGM/United Artists movies (which in 1997 got Orion Pictures); Cable News Network; CNN International; Headline News; TNT; WTBS; the Cartoon Network; Turner Classic Movies; the Atlanta Braves baseball team; 96 percent of the Atlanta Hawks basketball team; World Championship Wrestling; and CNN Airport Network. In 1999 MGM regained broadcast rights to more than 800 old MGM and United Artists films, and in 2000 made a deal with Blockbuster to try to show them on the Internet.

Meanwhile, in 1993, Paramount merged with Macmillan, a publishing company, for $553 million, making it the second largest book publisher. The following year it merged with Viacom for $9.6 billion, and the year after that they formed the United Paramount television network (Viacom owns half of it). Viacom owns several Internet properties designed for children and music fans, six theme parks, several cable networks, such as MTV, VH1, NIK, SHO, and TMC, the TV production companies Spelling Entertainment and Viacom Productions, nineteen television stations, and an interest in Comedy Central. Viacom also bought Blockbuster video rental chain in 1994 for $8.4 billion, but is now planning to spin it off. Paramount, meanwhile, brought to the merger Paramount Pictures, a movie studio, Paramount Domestic Television for syndication, Paramount Television, half of USA (which it sold to Seagram in 1997 for $1.7 billion, giving Seagram the entire network), Simon & Schuster publishers (minus the educational unit it recently sold, as mentioned previously), five amusement parks as well as the New York Knicks basketball team, the New York Rangers hockey team, and the part of Madison Square Garden where they play. It decided to sell those last three in 1994 to Cablevision Systems Corporation and ITT-Sheraton for $1.075 billion. Cablevision then bought all but 11.5 percent of them from ITT-Sheraton in 1997 for $650 million.

As mentioned previously, Seagram wanted to concentrate in the music field, so in 1998 it sold a majority of USA to an emerging player in the field, Barry Diller. The next year Seagram sold Diller the film studios October Films,

Gramercy Pictures, and what remained from Polygram Filmed Entertainment. In 1997, USA had merged with Ticketmaster in a deal valued at $800 million, and later merged online operations with CitySearch, an online city guide. It is now called Ticketmaster Online CitySearch. In 1999, USA expanded CitySearch by acquiring the Sidewalk online entertainment guide from Microsoft Corporation. USA Networks has other companies selling goods online: Home Shopping Network, Hotel Reservations Network, and Internet Shopping Network. In addition, it has Universal Television, the Sci-Fi Channel, and USA broadcasting, the latter being sixteen local television stations out of the top twenty-two markets. This makes USA Networks a force in the media world.

Another major player in the field is Gannett, which owns *USA Today*, television and radio stations, and cable franchises, and has bought Multimedia. Then there is Murdoch's News Corporation, which has Fox Entertainment and is the fourth largest media company by revenue. Included in its holdings are Fox Television Network, the Family Channel (which it got for $1 billion), Fox News, Fox Kids Network, Asian and European satellite television networks, Twentieth Century Fox movie studios, Fox Animation Studios, *TV Guide*, HarperCollins publishers, newspapers (such as the *New York Post*), News America Digital (which runs Internet services for Fox News and Fox Sports), and the use of Primestar satellite television. In 1996, Fox and Liberty Networks went in on a joint venture. Liberty Media Group is controlled by AT&T Corporation and has interests in BET, CNN, and Court TV, and a large stake in Liberty Digital. Fox/Liberty Networks own *Outdoor Life* and Speedvision cable networks, and in 1997 bought, for $850 million, 40 percent of Rainbow Programming, a unit of Cablevision that controlled the Knicks, Rangers, and the part of Madison Square Garden where they play, plus one-third ownership of the Golf Channel. Murdoch wants to be a major player in the sports field, so the News Corporation paid Liberty $1.4 billion to take control of the 40 percent interest in Rainbow, as well as Fox Sports Network and FX. Liberty will still keep 50 percent of the venture's International Sports Programming. Liberty sold Murdoch its 40 percent stake in the Staples Center, the new arena for the Los Angeles Kings hockey team, and in 1998 Murdoch purchased the Los Angeles Dodgers baseball team.

After the aforementioned mergers came the richest merger in media history, when, in 1999, Viacom bought CBS Corporation for $36.75 billion, making Viacom the third largest media company by revenue. The new company will carry the Viacom name, although the CBS name will continue to identify the TV network. By virtue of the deal, CBS gets a TV and film studio to provide shows for its network, and Viacom gets major advertising outlets to promote its films and TV shows. Some TV stations might have to be sold off due to federal ownership rules, and the UPN network might be sold or else become part of CBS because of the federal rule that forbids a company to own more than one TV network. One reason the merger took place was a 1999 FCC ruling that allowed companies to own more than one TV station in the same city, as long as that city had at least eight independently owned TV stations.

The new century brought with it the inevitable merger, announced in

January 2000, of the nation's largest online company, AOL, with the world's leading media and entertainment company, Time Warner. AOL paid $122 billion in the biggest corporate merger ever, and the combined company will be called AOL Time Warner. Time Warner will therefore be able to reach people online with its movies, music, and magazines.

These examples of the mergers taking place in the media field should make one worry that deregulation plus antitrust laxness is creating an industry in which a few players dominate; therefore, the public is not being exposed to various viewpoints, but only to the ones preferred by those dominating the field. An interesting example of individuals attempting to get away from a concentrated field and starting a company themselves is the 1995 creation of Dream Works SKG movie studio by Spielberg, Geffen, and Katzenberg. The extra competition they give is good, although one wonders if another dominant player has simply entered the arena. Nevertheless, having an addition to the industry rather than a deletion is a positive step. As can be seen by this examination of mergers, in 1996 alone they amounted to more than $37 billion in the communications industry, and the years since then have shown a continuation of that. Where it will end is unclear, but the industry has become a highly oligopolistic one.

There is one other point to look at, and that is the relative lack of minorities in the broadcasting industry. The FCC has a policy giving special, favorable consideration for minority ownership and participation in management for television stations, as well as a distress-sale policy in which a broadcaster faced with the loss of a license may sell to a minority-owned business at 75 percent of the station's market value, as long as that minority-owned business meets certain requirements. These were challenged in court, but the Supreme Court, in the 1990 case of *Metro Broadcasting, Inc. v. FCC*[16] upheld them in a 5–4 decision authored by Justice Brennan. He stated that the policy did not violate equal protection but instead had congressional support and served the important governmental objective of broadcast diversity. This decision, however, marked the end of the Supreme Court's looking favorably upon affirmative action programs. Although the Court has not reversed this decision, its other decisions show that affirmative action programs must be narrowly tailored to meet specific problems. The future of the FCC's minority preference policy is uncertain.

SUMMARY

The field of communications affects almost everybody in the United States, whether one is speaking of telecommunications or the media. The electronic age is here to stay, and the government has had a difficult time keeping up with new technology. The 1996 Telecommunications Act saw the government retreat from its regulation of the field, although it still keeps some regulation, especially through the FCC. Nevertheless, the field has opened up and companies are taking advantage of the opening. Whether the public is best served by this approach remains to be seen, but there is no denying that fewer and fewer companies are left to serve the public in this age of communications.

QUESTIONS FOR DISCUSSION

1. Why did the radio industry ask for regulation?
2. Do you approve of the FCC having no control over broadcasting charges?
3. Are telephone company mergers good for the economy?
4. Has the deregulation of the telecommunications industry led to more competition?
5. Do you agree with the invalidation of the Communications Decency Act?
6. Are the megamergers in the media field good for the public?

NOTES

1. 512 U.S. 218 (1994).
2. 119 S.Ct. 721 (1999).
3. 117 S.Ct. 2329 (1997).
4. 319 U.S. 190 (1943).
5. 392 U.S. 157 (1968).
6. 117 S.Ct. 1174 (1997).
7. 395 U.S. 367 (1969).
8. 453 U.S. 367 (1981).
9. 450 U.S. 582 (1981).
10. 509 U.S. 418 (1993).
11. 438 U.S. 726 (1978).
12. 518 U.S. 727 (1996).
13. 119 S.Ct. 1923 (1999).
14. 418 U.S. 241 (1974).
15. For a more detailed study of the media, see Thomas L. Tedford's excellent book, *Freedom of Speech in the United States*, 3rd ed. (State College, PA: Strata Publishing, 1997), especially Chapter 13 on "Broadcasting, Cable, the Internet, and Access Theory" from which much of the factual material in this section was obtained.
16. 497 U.S. 547 (1990).

RECOMMENDED READING

Carter, T. Barton, Marc Franklin, and Jay Wright. *The First Amendment and the Fourth Estate*. 7th ed. New York: Foundation Press, 1998.
———, *The First Amendment and the Fifth Estate*. 4th ed. New York: Foundation Press, 1997.
Franklin, Marc, and David Anderson. *Mass Media Law*. 5th ed. New York: Foundation Press, 1997.
Lively, Donald, Allen Hammond IV, Blake Morant, and Russell Weaver. *Communications Law*. Cincinnati, OH: Anderson Publishing Company, 1997.
Schnitzer, Martin. *Contemporary Government and Business Relations*. 4th ed. Boston, MA: Houghton Mifflin Company, 1990. Chapters 5 and 7.
Teeter, Dwight, Jr., Don LeDuc, and Bill Loving. *Law of Mass Communications*. 9th ed. New York: Foundation Press, 1998.
Telford, Thomas. *Freedom of Speech in the United States*. 3rd ed. State College, PA: Strata Publishing, 1997.

CHAPTER 13

INTERNATIONAL TRADE

The importance of international trade has been recognized by nations for thousands of years. The Phoenicians controlled the seaborne commerce of the Mediterranean 4,000 years ago, and the goods they secured from Babylon and Egypt or produced in their own shops they carried throughout the Mediterranean to Africa and southern Europe. Foreign trade flourished during the Roman Empire, and Rome itself depended on the grain it imported from Egypt and Africa. Roman traders penetrated Germany as far as the Baltic Sea, and others sought the markets of Turkestan to buy Chinese goods.[1] The Chinese were engaged in international trade even before the Romans.[2] In the fourteenth and fifteenth centuries, the Italian trading centers of Genoa and Venice carried on trade with Asia, exchanging woolen cloth and raw materials for spices.

At the beginning of the twentieth century, the United Kingdom was the world's leading trading nation and the pound was the most important currency unit in the world. Its many colonies served as markets for British goods, and it was able to import goods that were unavailable or too expensive to produce at home. But times have changed, and it is now the United States that is the world's leading trading nation, while the United Kingdom has slipped to the fifth position. Japan, which was not even in the top twenty leading trading nations in 1900, ranks third.[3] Germany, which was second in 1900, still ranks second. The United States, Germany, and Japan were responsible for 30 percent of the world's international trade in 1999.

THE RATIONALE FOR INTERNATIONAL TRADE

The basic rationale for international trade between nations is that it maximizes the interest of consumers throughout the world by giving them a wider variety of goods from which to choose. Differences in the efficiency of land, labor, and capital make it profitable for nations to specialize in the production of goods and services in which their resource situation is the most advantageous, and exchange them for the goods and services of other nations with different resource advantages. If there were no restraints placed on the movement of goods and services from one region to another, or from one nation to another, the welfare of consumers would be maximized.

Certain trade theories have been developed over a period of time to explain why the exchange of goods and services between nations is beneficial. Mercantilism was the dominant trading policy for the European countries between 1500 and 1800. To the mercantilists the important question was: What is the right policy for a government to pursue in order to increase the national wealth and the national power? The answer was a strong central government with the acquisition of colonies that would serve as markets and provide it with wealth. This theory of international trade was replaced with a new theory of international trade based on the writings of Adam Smith and David Ricardo.[4] They believed society benefited from a division of labor and commerce. Each country would do that which it did best, and free trade benefited consumers in all nations.

MERCANTILISM

The United States is a direct result of the policy of mercantilism pursued by the British. England hoped to replicate what Spain found in its conquest of Mexico and Peru in the early 1500s—gold and silver. Although it did not find gold and silver, it found other natural resources that were brought back to London.[5] The United States became a colony of England. It served as a market for British goods and exported to England goods that could not be produced there. Trade between England and its colony was regulated. American goods had to be shipped only on British ships, and British goods had to be purchased by Americans. Moreover, there was taxation without representation. England would send over its representatives to govern the colonies based on instructions of the British government.

ABSOLUTE ADVANTAGE

The theory of absolute advantage was based on Adam Smith's book, *The Wealth of Nations*.[6] His writings and those of Ricardo and others dominated Western economic thought for 150 years. Absolute advantage states that there is a basis for trade when one nation can produce a good or service more efficiently than another nation, in which case the latter should buy from the former. To put it simply, if Brazil has the resources to produce coffee more cheaply and of better quality than the United States, we should buy their coffee. Conversely, if the United States can produce automobiles more cheaply and of better quality than Brazil, they should buy our cars. Each country gains by concentrating on what it does best. Resources are allocated to those areas in which they can be used most efficiently.

COMPARATIVE ADVANTAGE

The theory of comparative advantage is associated with David Ricardo, who was an important economist during the early part of the nineteenth century.[7] It holds that if one country has an advantage over another country in the production of several goods, it should produce the good in which it has the greatest comparative advantage and buy the good in which it has the least advantage from the other country. Assume that Brazil has an advantage over the United States in the production of coffee and sugar. Brazil can produce five units of coffee for every unit of coffee produced by the United States, and it can only produce two units of sugar for every unit produced in the United States. As the example below indicates, a ratio of 5 to 1 is better than a ratio of 2 to 1, so Brazil should produce coffee, and the United States has only a 1 to 2 disadvantage in producing sugar. The exchange between the countries should be coffee for sugar.

	Brazil	**United States**
Coffee	5 units	1 unit
Sugar	2 units	1 unit

FACTOR ENDOWMENT THEORY

The factor endowment theory, which was developed by Bertil Ohlin, a Swedish economist, simply states that each nation is best equipped to produce the goods that are best related to the factors—land, labor, or capital—that are most abundant.[8] For example, Argentina and Australia, which have an abundance of land relative to labor and capital, should and do specialize in the production of agricultural and meat products. Countries that have a large amount of labor relative to land and capital should specialize in labor-intensive industries, such as clothing. China is a case in point.[9] Countries that are capital intensive should specialize in the production of goods that require a great deal of capital. Germany and Japan, with their automobile industries, would be examples of countries that are capital intensive.

NATIONAL COMPETITIVE ADVANTAGE

The most recent contribution to international trade theory is the book *The Competitive Advantage of Nations*, written by Michael Porter, a management professor at Harvard, and published in 1990.[10] He proposes a paradigm to explain the dynamic relationship among a country's industries, institutions, and people that is pivotal to achieving economic advantage over other nations. He contends that the theories of absolute advantage and comparative advantage are obsolete because their emphasis on only natural resources and other factors was obsolete. Instead, his approach takes the form of a dynamic diamond whose parts push each other forward or backward. It is competition—the fiercer the better—that is likely to produce a country's success. As Figure 13-1 shows, the dynamic diamond is divided into four parts, one at each point of the diamond.

1. Company Strategy, Structure, and Rivalry—the dominant environment in which firms compete shapes their ability to compete internationally. To survive competitively in their home country, firms must strive to reduce costs, boost product quality, raise productivity, and develop innovative products. Firms that have been tested this way in the home market are better able to compete internationally. Further, many of the investments they have made in the home market for research and development and quality control, are transferable to other countries.

2. Demand Conditions—This includes the size of the market, sophistication of consumers, and media exposure of product. Consumer demand for convenience, utility, and affordability made the United States the first mass-market, mass-production society, and put its industry in a strong position to capitalize on subsequent demand all over the world for goods that have that quality.

3. Related and Supporting Industries—Firms that are located close to their suppliers will enjoy better communications and the exchange of ideas and inventions with them than firms that are not located close to their suppliers. Competition among these suppliers will lead to lower prices, higher quality products, and technological innovation in their inputs, in turn reinforcing firms' competitive advantage in world markets.

4. Factor Conditions—This would not only include the basic factors of land, labor, and capital but more advanced factors such as the educational level of the workforce and the quality of a nation's infrastructure. The possession of natural resources, such as oil and coal, are no longer considered the determinants of national success that they once were. The training of its work force, innovation, and research will give a nation a competitive advantage over other nations.

FIGURE 13-1   PORTER'S DIAMOND OF NATIONAL COMPETITIVE ADVANTAGE

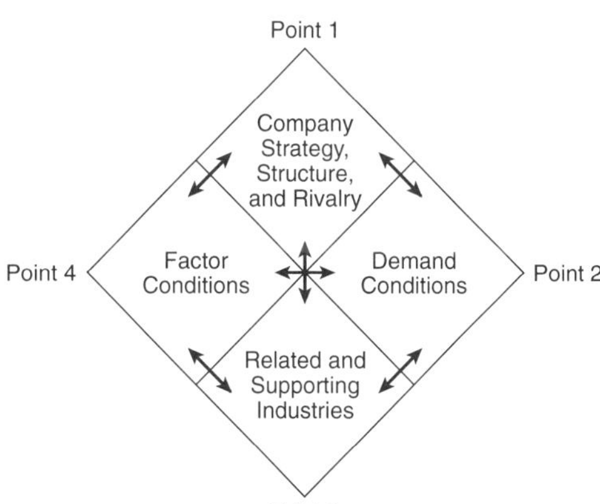

Source: Michael Porter, *The Competitive Advantage of Nations*. (New York: Free Press, 1990), p. 72. Reprinted with permission.

Two other factors, chance and government, can also play an important role in developing a nation's competitive advantage. Chance events are occurrences that have little to do with circumstances in a nation and are outside the power of a government to influence. Wars, oil shocks, natural disasters, and political decisions by governments are examples of chance. The decision of the Japanese to bomb Pearl Harbor caused the United States to enter World War II, which benefited American industry by spurring research and development financed by government. Many products were produced during the postwar period long before they would have been produced were it not for the war. Government is another factor. Japan and South Korea are cited as examples of government policies being responsible for their economic success.

THE INTERNATIONAL TRADE AND INVESTMENTS OF THE UNITED STATES

The international trade of the United States consists of two categories—the export and import of goods and the export and import of services. The export and import of goods is called the merchandise trade account and the export and import of services is called the invisible account. Merchandise trade covers exports and imports of automobiles, machinery, food and beverages, agricultural products, and other tangible goods. Services include health care, travel, financial services, telecommunications, transportation, and other intangibles. In 1998 U.S. exports of goods amounted to $682 billion and imports of goods amounted to $913 billion, for a deficit of $231 billion.

THE MERCHANDISE TRADE ACCOUNT

The United States is the world's largest trading nation. The total value of its exports and imports for 1998 was around $1.6 trillion, Germany was second with a total of $1.2 trillion, and Japan was third with a total of $900 billion. As Table 13-1 indicates, the bulk of U.S. merchandise trade is with three major regions of the world—the NAFTA countries of Canada and Mexico, the European Union consisting of fifteen European countries, and East Asia, which includes China, Japan, and the Newly Industrialized Countries (NICs) of South Korea, Singapore, Malaysia and Hong Kong, and Taiwan.[11]

One thing that is faithfully reported each month in the newspapers and on the national news is the U.S. trade deficit with other countries. It has been many years since it has been positive, and 1998 was no exception. The deficit for the year was $231 billion, most of which was with Japan, China, and East Asia. The trade deficit with Japan was $54 billion and with China $57 billion. The United States also has a trade deficit with Canada and Mexico and with the European Union, but the combined total is less than that for Japan. An explanation for the trade deficit with Japan is that the United States imports automobiles and automotive parts from Japan. In the case of China, which has cheap labor, the United States imports a wide variety of consumer goods from them.

SERVICE ACCOUNTS

Services are another important component of international trade. They are different from merchandise trade in several ways. First, they are intangible and are referred to as invisibles in the U.S. current account. Second, they are usually

TABLE 13-1   U.S. EXPORTS AND IMPORTS, 1998 (BILLIONS OF DOLLARS)

	EXPORTS	IMPORTS
World	682,997	913,828
Europe	170,493	202,838
European Union	163,019	176,367
Austria	2,506	2,558
Belgium-Luxembourg	14,524	8,796
Denmark	1,874	2,382
Finland	1,915	2,595
France	17,728	24,077
Germany	26,642	49,824
Greece	1,355	467
Ireland	5,653	8,385
Italy	9,027	21,013
Netherlands	19,004	7,591
Portugal	888	1,266
Spain	5,465	4,784
Sweden	3,819	7,837
United Kingdom	39,070	34,793
Western Hemisphere	298,762	319,971
NAFTA		
Canada	156,308	174,844
Mexico	79,010	94,709
South America	41,887	33,007
Argentina	5,885	2,252
Brazil	15,157	10,123
Venezuela	6,520	9,282
Asia	187,590	367,871
China	14,258	71,156
Japan	57,888	121,982
East Asia NICs	63,292	85,955
Hong Kong	12,924	10,538
South Korea	16,538	23,937
Singapore	15,674	18,357
Taiwan	18,157	33,123
Middle East	20,928	18,874
Africa	11,158	15,838
Australia and Oceania	14,226	7,368

Source: http://www.ito.doc.gov/industry/otea/usfth/aggregate

not storable and are wasted if not used. An example would be an empty airline seat. Third, they usually require consumer participation. Payments received from tourists measure the services that American hotels and shops provide to visitors from other countries. Financial and shipping charges to foreigners measure the fees that American banks, airlines, and shipowners charge for services provided. It also works in reverse. Foreign countries receive payments from American tourists flying foreign airlines, staying at foreign hotels, and eating at foreign restaurants. The United States gains from an inflow of income from the provision of various forms of services to foreign countries, and loses from an outflow of income from the provision of various forms of services performed by other countries.

The service sector and service exports are increasing in importance in the American economy. Service jobs are expected to account for virtually the entire net gain in U.S. employment in the first decade of the twenty-first century. In 1998 service exports of $239 billion exceeded service imports of $155 billion, a surplus of $84 billion, which offset about 40 percent of the deficit in the merchandise trade account. Travel at $75 billion and passenger fares at $22 billion accounted for 40 percent of the total. Travel expenditures consisted primarily of the local expenditures of foreign visitors. Passenger fares and other forms of transportation services consisted of foreign purchases from U.S. firms. Royalties and license fees and a wide variety of financial, professional, and technical services amounted to $83 billion.[12]

BALANCE OF PAYMENTS

Just as a country's gross domestic product is an account of all the goods and services produced within a country, its balance of payments is an account of goods and services, capital loans, gold, and other items flowing into and out of a country. A balance of payments (BOP) is similar to a business balance sheet in that each is a summary of the monetary results of economic and business activity over a period of time. In the balance of payments account, a credit (+) is any transaction that results in a monetary inflow from other countries, while a debit (–) is any transaction that results in a monetary outflow to other nations. Double entry bookkeeping assures in principle that total credits equal total debits. Table 13-2 presents an example of a BOP account. There are four categories—current account, capital account, official reserve account, and statistical discrepancy.

CURRENT ACCOUNTS

The current account consists of four categories—the merchandise trade account, the service account, income from U.S. assets abroad and foreign income from U.S. assets in the United States, and unilateral transfers. As previously noted, the merchandise trade account was negative for 1998, because U.S. consumers bought more goods from abroad than foreign consumers bought from the United States. The service account was positive because the United States exported more services than it imported. The third category, income from U.S. assets abroad and foreign income from assets in the United States, is also of importance. Income takes the form of dividends, interest, and profits that are repatriated back to the United States or, if earned in the United States, sent to the home countries. The final category, unilateral transfers, involves money sent to other countries in the form of foreign aid, dividends, and other forms of income. An example would be an American living in Mexico who receives U.S. Social Security checks.

TABLE 13-2 BALANCE OF PAYMENTS ACCOUNT

CURRENT ACCOUNT

EXPORTS +	*IMPORTS −*
Merchandise Trade	Merchandise Trade
Services	Services
Travel	Travel
Financial	Financial
Royalties	Royalties
Other	Other
Income from U.S. Assets Abroad	Income from Foreign Assets in U.S.
	Gifts

CAPITAL ACCOUNT

EXPORTS +	*IMPORTS −*
Foreign Assets in the United States +	U.S. Assets Abroad −
Portfolio Investment	Portfolio Investment
Short-term[1]	Short-term[1]
Long-term[2]	Long-term[2]
Direct Investment	Direct Investment

OFFICIAL RESERVE ACCOUNT

EXPORTS +	*IMPORTS −*
Gold Inflows	Gold Outflows
SDRs[3]	SDRs[3]
Foreign Currencies	U.S. Currencies

STATISTICAL DISCREPANCY

[1]Securities with a maturity date of one year or less—a U.S. Treasury bill.

[2]Securities with a date of more than one year—a U.S. Treasury six-month bond.

[3]Special Drawing Rights (SDRs) are credits granted by the International Monetary Fund that can be used to settle transactions between central banks.

THE CAPITAL ACCOUNT

The capital account consists of investment inflows and outflows into and out of a country. Inflows into a country are a + item in its capital account, while outflows from a country are a deficit (–) in its capital account. There are two major types of investment—direct investment and portfolio investment. Direct investment occurs when assets are acquired for the purpose of controlling them.[13] This can be done through the acquisition of an existing plant or other tangible asset, the construction of a plant or other tangible assets, or through joint ventures with other firms or countries. An example of direct investment in the United States is the construction of a plant in Alabama by the German auto firm Daimler Benz to produce the Mercedes-Benz car. This is a plus item in the American capital account because German money flows into the United States and a minus item in the German BOP.

The second major type of investment is portfolio investment, which involves holdings of intangible assets such as stocks and bonds. There are two types of portfolio investment—short-term and long-term. Short-term portfolio investment involves holdings of liquid assets with a maturity date of one year or less. Examples would be a U.S. Treasury bill, with a three months' maturity date, checking and savings accounts, and commercial paper. Long-term portfolio investments include those that have a maturity date of more than one year. Examples would involve corporate stocks and bonds, and government bonds and notes. Individuals, mutual funds, banks, corporations, and companies can own portfolio investments. The purchase of a U.S. government bond by a foreign investor is a plus item in the U.S. current account because money comes into the United States. It is also a liability in that there is foreign ownership of the bond. The foreign owner is a creditor; the U.S. Treasury is the debtor. Conversely, the American investor who buys French government bonds is a creditor and the French government is a debtor.

Tables 13-3 and 13-4 present a breakdown of direct investment flows into the United States by countries and areas of the world, and U.S. direct investment flows to countries and areas abroad for 1998. As the table indicates, investment flows are like trade flows in that both are from developed countries to developed countries. Europe is the main area of U.S. direct investments and the main supplier of foreign direct investment to the United States. The United Kingdom and Japan account for around 33 percent of FDI in the United States. The greatest imbalance is in the Latin American and Caribbean area, where U.S. investment exceeds the area's investment in the United States by $9 billion. Bermuda is a popular resort area, so U.S. money has been invested in the construction of hotels and condominiums. The poorer areas of the world are bypassed by world trade and investment. The entire continent of Africa, with a population of 800 million people, had less investment than Panama, with a population of less than three million people.[14]

TABLE 13-3	U.S. DIRECT INVESTMENT ABROAD 1998 (MILLIONS OF DOLLARS)		
Canada	8,311	Caribbean	5,156
Europe	50,833	Bermuda	3,376
European Union	43,978	South America	5,538
Austria	478	Argentina	638
Belgium	2,637	Brazil	2,602
Denmark	339	Chile	796
Finland	350	Africa	1,648
France	2,552	Nigeria	709
Germany	4,410	Middle East	924
Greece	72	Asia and Pacific	12,274
Ireland	2,231	Australia	2,026
Italy	1,953	Hong Kong	1,518
Luxembourg	1,667	Japan	1,613
Netherlands	12,387	Singapore	2,440
Portugal	331	World Total	90,792
Spain	1,593	NAFTA	11,592
Sweden	929	European Union	43,049
United Kingdom	12,049		
Central America	5,462		
Mexico	3,281		
Panama	1,660		

Source: U.S. Department of Commerce, International Trade Administration, Bureau of Economic Analysis International Investment Data. "U.S. Direct Investment Abroad." March 11, 1999.

TABLE 13-4 FOREIGN DIRECT INVESTMENT IN THE UNITED STATES, 1998 (MILLIONS OF DOLLARS)			
Canada	3,683	Latin America and Caribbean	2,078
Europe	30,242		
European Union	27,898	Africa	–101
Austria	166	Middle East	548
Belgium	353	Asia and Pacific	5,483
Denmark	246	Japan	5,436
Finland	390	Total FDI in United States	41,924
France	3,567		
Germany	3,965		
Ireland	1,001		
Italy	227		
Luxembourg	495		
Netherlands	6,367		
Spain	56		
Sweden	1,720		
United Kingdom	9,345		

Source: U.S. Department of Commerce, International Trade Administration, Bureau of Economic Analysis. "Foreign Direct Investment in the United States." March 11, 1999.

THE OFFICIAL RESERVE ACCOUNT

The official reserve account reflects in part gold flows and the claims to gold among governments, for it is an accepted medium of international payment among governments. Gold movements are like short-term capital movements; they serve primarily to make up the difference in payments and receipts resulting from other international transactions. A second item included in the reserve account is convertible foreign exchange, which is exchange freely convertible into currencies such as the U.S. dollar. A third item is Special Drawing Rights (SDRs), which are credits granted by the IMF for the purpose of selling transactions among banks to settle accounts. An SDR has a value that is currently calculated daily as a weighted average of five major currencies—the dollar, mark, yen, franc, and pound. U.S. outflows of reserves represent a negative item in the official reserve account; U.S. inflows of reserves represent a positive item in the reserve account.

STATISTICAL DISCREPANCY

Statistical discrepancy, or errors and omission, is the last account in the BOP accounting system. It is the balancing item that is supposed to make credit and debits equal. Its purpose is that information about offsetting debit and credit items may come from different sources. Because data from these sources differ in coverage, accuracy, and timing, the balance of payments seldom balance as they are supposed to in accounting.

INTERNATIONAL MONETARY SYSTEMS

International trade involves the use of different national currencies, which are linked together by foreign exchange rates. An exchange rate is the number of units of one currency that must be given up to acquire one unit of another currency. For example, on a particular day, $1.00 may exchange for 6.6 Mexican pesos, conversely 1 peso would exchange for $.156. These exchange rates fluctuate daily and are determined by supply and demand factors that would affect the dollar and the peso.[15] There have been three types of international exchange rate systems, ranging from a fixed exchange rate system called the gold standard, to a mixed gold and paper standard, to the exchange rate system of today, by which some currencies are allowed to fluctuate based on supply and demand, while other currencies are either pegged or managed.

THE GOLD STANDARD

The gold standard lasted roughly from 1821 to 1931. It was a fixed-exchange rate system, by which each country defined the value of its currency in terms of a fixed amount of gold, thereby establishing fixed exchange rates among the countries on the gold standard. The key currency was the British pound sterling. For example, the U.S. Treasury was required by law to pay $20.67 for an ounce of gold, and the Bank of England was required to buy and sell gold for 4.25 pounds for an ounce of gold. The exchange rate between the dollar and the pound was $4.8665 = 1 pound, or 1 pound = 113.22 grams of gold, and $1 = 23.22 grams of gold. Dollars in paper and gold were interchangeable. Debts could be paid in either one. International trade could be financed in dollars or gold, and payments between countries could be settled either way.

The most important point about the gold standard was that the amount of money in circulation was tied to the amount of gold in circulation. Governments could only print money that was backed by gold, so basically the money supply was equal to the gold supply. A nation on the gold standard had two responsibilities. First, it had to buy and sell gold to the public in exchange for paper money at a fixed exchange rate, and second, it had to permit gold to be exported and imported without restriction. An outflow of gold from the United States to France increased the money supply in France, but decreased it in the United States. Prices would rise in France and fall in the United States. French exports to the United States would be more expensive and U.S. exports to France would be cheaper. France would buy more U.S. goods and the United States would buy fewer French goods, and gold would flow back to the United States.

The gold standard began its collapse in World War I when countries had to suspend their pledge to buy gold and sell gold at a fixed rate. After World War I, most countries readopted the gold standard in the 1920s. However, the Depression of the 1930s finished the gold standard. Countries would no longer pledge to buy and sell gold at a fixed price. Currencies were devalued so that each nation could try to make its goods cheaper in world markets, thereby stimulating its exports and reducing its imports. But when one country devalued its currency, others would retaliate by devaluing theirs, so no one gained. International trade declined, and unemployment rates in the United States and other nations increased, creating economic conditions that helped bring about World War II.

THE BRETTON WOODS AGREEMENT AND THE GOLD AND PAPER STANDARD

The rationale for the Bretton Woods Agreement, which was held in 1944, was to prevent what had happened during the 1930s. Various forms of trade restrictions and currency devaluation used by nations to improve their trade position increased unemployment and prolonged the Depression. The Bretton Woods Agreement devised a new monetary system that would serve as a substitute for the gold standard. This system, which lasted from 1945 to 1973, did as follows:

1. The dollar, which was the world's strongest currency, was made convertible into gold at $35 an ounce. Other countries could convert their currencies into dollars and acquire gold.

2. Each country fixed an exchange rate for its currency in relation to the dollar. For example, the German mark exchanged at a rate of 4 marks = $1.00.

3. It created the International Monetary Fund, which was supposed to serve as a substitute for the gold standard in that all member countries were supposed to adhere to certain rules of the game. For example, they agreed to maintain stable exchange rates, to abstain from exchange controls, and to avoid competitive currency devaluation. The IMF had the authority to lend to countries that had a deficit in their balance of payments.

4. Countries wishing to become members of the IMF had to make an initial payment of gold (25 percent) and their currency (75 percent) to the IMF.

The Bretton Woods system began to decline when the United States no longer dominated world trade. Other countries had recovered from World War II and were competing in world markets. Accelerating inflation during the Vietnam War made dollars less attractive as a medium of exchange relative to other currencies, particularly the deutsche Mark (DM). In 1971, the German Central Bank revalued the DM against the dollar, and in the same year President Nixon announced that the United States would no longer buy gold at $35 an ounce. In December 1971, the Smithsonian Agreement among the central banks of ten major nations fixed the value of gold at $38 an ounce and allowed exchange rates to fluctuate + or − 2.25 percent around their new par values. The oil shock of 1973 destroyed the gold-paper standard. The oil-importing countries incurred deficits in their balance of payments and cut their ties to the dollar.

EXCHANGE RATES TODAY

The IMF currently classifies exchange rates into three categories: those that are pegged to a single currency or group of currencies, those with limited flexibility, and those that float freely with minimum government intervention.

Pegged Exchange Rates Pegged exchange rates are usually used by small countries that tie their currencies to one of the major world currencies (e.g., the dollar). Some countries, which were formerly a part of the British or French empires, tie their currencies to the pound or franc, while others tie their currencies to the U.S. dollar. An example is Argentina, which has pegged its peso at an exchange rate of 1 peso = 1 dollar. Senegal, which was once a part of the French empire, ties its currency unit to the franc.

Limited Flexibility Currencies that have limited flexibility are commonly called managed float, which means that their currencies fluctuate within certain limits around the currency of another country. An example is the Mexican peso, which fluctuates within an upper or lower range against the value of the American dollar. Another example is the Polish zloty, which fluctuates within limits around the German mark. Managed float means that it is the responsibility of the central banks of Mexico and Poland to use monetary policy to keep their currencies within the ranges set above and below the dollar and the mark.

Free Float   Free-floating exchange rates are determined by the forces of supply and demand. Each day the exchange rate between the U.S. dollar and the German mark can fluctuate based on supply and demand factors. Travel expenditures by American tourists in Germany would increase the demand for German marks; conversely, travel expenditures by German tourists in the United States would increase the demand for dollars. Factors affecting the supply and demand of German marks in the determination of the dollar/mark exchange rate can be presented as follows:

<u>Supply</u>	<u>Demand</u>
U.S. exports to Germany	U.S. imports from Germany
Travel expenditures by Germans in the United States	Travel expenditures by Americans
German investment in the United States	U.S. investment in Germany

THE U.S. DOLLAR

The U.S. dollar is the world's leading currency. Other currencies, such as the Argentine peso, are pegged to it. It is the dominant currency in the Eurocurrency market. Eurocurrencies are currencies deposited outside the country of issue. A Eurodollar is simply a dollar held by any bank outside of the United States, including foreign branches of U.S. banks. Eurodollars consist of 65 to 80 percent of the Eurocurrency market. The Eurodollar is heavily used for the following reasons:

1. It eliminates the cost risks of converting from one currency to another. In a trade between an American exporter and a European importer, the terms of payment are usually set at a rate in the future. The exchange rate between the dollar and the mark will change before the date is reached, either to the advantage of the American exporter or the German importer. A Eurodollar can be transferred from importer to exporter through a bank.

2. The largest volume of Eurobonds are denominated in U.S. dollars. Eurobonds are a way to raise long-term capital. They are sold outside the borrower's country. For example, a U.S. company can sell bonds in England in pounds, francs, marks, or dollars.

The dollar has been the world's strongest currency unit during the last half of the decade of the 1990s. This has been beneficial for the U.S. economy by reducing import prices and thus reducing the chance of inflation. A combination of interrelated factors has been responsible for the strength of the U.S. dollar relative to other currencies, but particularly the mark and yen. One reason was the unsettled state of the Japanese and other East Asian economies in 1997 and 1998, which caused investors to find a safe haven for their funds. Second, the United States is regarded as the leader and most politically and economically stable of the world market economies. In order to buy U.S. assets, they must first buy U.S. dollars. The increase in demand for dollars drives up their value relative to other currencies.

THE FINANCIAL COLLAPSE OF JAPAN AND SOUTHEAST ASIA

In 1997 Japan and the countries of southeast Asia were affected by a currency crisis of the first magnitude. Their currencies collapsed against the dollar, creating social tensions. The ouster of Suharto, the leader of Indonesia for thirty-six years, in May 1998, was a direct result of the country's financial crisis. The rupiah, the Indonesian currency unit that exchanged at a rate of 2,710 = $1.00 on August 25, 1997, was devalued against the dollar and on February 24, 1998, exchanged at a rate of 9,300 = $1.00. This created hardship in Indonesia, particularly among the poor, as Indonesian imports from other countries cost more. Attempts by the Indonesian government to reduce spending to curb inflation only made matters worse, and street riots that increased daily eventually led to the resignation of Suharto. Corruption was also a major factor, in that Suharto and his family had enriched themselves at the expense of the poor.[16]

The Japanese Financial Crisis At the beginning of the decade of the 1990s, the Japanese economy was the envy of the world, and its financial markets were the source of great wealth. It was predicted by many experts that Japan would be the dominant world power of the twenty-first century. Japanese firms were studied as role models of efficiency and innovation and their ideas of employee involvement, quality control, and product design were put to work around the world. The Japanese culture was held to be superior to other cultures. They were group-oriented as opposed to the self-centered individualism of the United States. Their people worked harder and saved more than Americans, and their schools were better. But in a few years, their economy and their currency collapsed as Table 13-5 indicates.

TABLE 13-5   REAL GDP FOR JAPAN FOR 1980–1989 AND 1990–2000

AVERAGE PERCENTAGE CHANGE	
YEARS	*REAL GDP*
1981–1990 (ten-year average)	4.0
1990	5.1
1991	3.8
1992	1.0
1993	0.3
1994	0.6
1995	1.5
1996	5.0
1997	–1.6
1998	–2.5
1999	0.3
2000	0.9

Source: International Monetary Fund, *World Economic Outlook* (Washington, D.C.: IMF, May 2000), p. 104.

What contributed to the collapse of the Japanese economy in the 1990s? One of the main reasons was the collapse of the "bubble economy," which was based on unregulated real estate loans to Japanese borrowers who speculated not only in Japan, but also in the United States and other countries. Money was also borrowed to speculate in the Japanese stock market.[17] When the real estate and stock markets collapsed in the early 1990s, Japanese banks were stuck with bad debts. The problem was exacerbated by a fall in the world value of the yen because Japanese banks measured the value of their capital in yen. Banks also counted their stockholdings as capital and the Japanese stock market declined in value during the 1990s.[18] Another major problem in Japan was widespread corruption in business and government, which resulted in inefficient resource allocation.

The declining value of the yen against the dollar has had a negative effect on trade between the United States and Japan. In June 1998 the exchange rate between Japan and the United States was around 140 yen = $1.00. This made Japanese exports to the United States cheaper and U.S. exports to Japan more expensive for Japan. The May 1998 U.S. merchandise trade deficit with Japan was $14 billion. American companies operating in Japan were adversely affected by the falling value of the yen because they had to convert yen into more expensive dollars. But the major problem facing Japan is that other East Asian countries have had serious financial problems, thus limiting their ability to buy from and sell more goods to Japan, their most important trading partner.

The East Asian Financial Crisis   Southeast Asia and Korea were a part of the East Asian miracle. All, with the exception of Thailand, were a part of the British, Dutch, and Japanese empires. As Table 13-6 (on page 250) indicates, their growth rates have been impressive. Seven of the top ten fastest growing economies over the last thirty years were East Asian. But the East Asian currency crisis began in mid-1997 and its repercussions are being felt all over the world. The countries that have been most affected are South Korea, Thailand, and Indonesia.

There were three major causes of the East Asian currency crisis, as follows:

1. Most of the countries kept their currencies pegged to the U.S. dollar. This policy worked when the dollar was weak because their exports could sell cheaply in the world markets. But as the dollar strengthened in world markets, Asian exports became less competitive in price.

2. There was rampant corruption at the top levels of government.

3. The financial and banking systems were weak and unregulated. There were no equivalents of the U.S. Securities and Exchange Commission and the Federal Reserve System. Loans were often unsecured and went to finance investments in local real estate and stock markets. As the economies of these countries weakened, businesses could not pay debts and banks were saddled with bad loans. There were runs on banks in Thailand, Indonesia, Malaysia, and the Philippines.

TABLE 13-6   LONG-TERM AVERAGE ANNUAL GROWTH RATES FOR EAST ASIAN COUNTRIES, 1965–1996 (REAL PER CAPITA GNP)

COUNTRY*	PERCENT ANNUAL AVERAGE GROWTH
China	6.8
Hong Kong, China**	5.7
Indonesia	4.8
Korea	6.7
Malaysia	4.1
Singapore	6.3
Thailand	5.1
Japan	3.6

*Taiwan is not included because it is not recognized as a country. Its growth rate during the period 1965–1996 was about the same as South Korea's.

**Hong Kong is now a part of China, but is kept as a separate entity.

Source: The World Bank, *1999 World Development Indicators* (Washington, D.C.: The World Bank, 1999), pp. 24–26.

The East Asian currency crisis had an adverse effect on the American economy in three ways:

1. U.S. multinationals, such as Coca Cola and IBM, had to transfer their earnings into dollars at lower exchange rates because East Asian currencies were devalued against the dollar.
2. This, in turn, created a ripple effect that caused instability in the U.S. and European stock markets.
3. East Asian stock markets declined by as much as 50 percent. Mutual funds that specialized in East Asian markets lost money.

INTERNATIONAL MONETARY INSTITUTIONS

The two most important international monetary institutions are the International Monetary Fund and the World Bank. Both were a result of the Bretton Woods Agreement of July 1944, which reorganized the world monetary system. As mentioned previously, it was a system of fixed exchange rates based on a modified gold standard. The agreement created the IMF to prevent the use of exchange rate devaluations, which had contributed to prolonging the Depression of the 1930s. The IMF was created to oversee the functioning of the new monetary system by promoting international monetary cooperation and by promoting a stable exchange rate system. The World Bank was created to help finance the reconstruction of Europe after World War II.[19] Its mission has expanded over time to help the economies of the less-developed countries through loans.

INTERNATIONAL MONETARY FUND

As of November 1999, 184 countries were members of the IMF. To belong, a country has to pay a quota consisting of 25 percent gold and 75 percent in the country's currency. The amount of the quota is based on the relative economic importance of the country in the world economy. Each country has voting rights based on the amount of its quota.[20] The borrowing power of each member country is based on the size of its quota. It has the right to borrow up to 25 percent of its quota, and additional amounts are subject to IMF-imposed restrictions. These restrictions would include the elimination of export subsidies, reductions in a country's money supply, and higher interest rates. A country's quota is a part of its official reserves in its balance of payments account.

Special Drawing Rights (SDRs)   Special Drawing Rights (SDRs) constitute an international reserve asset that can be used when countries incur balance of payments deficits. They were created by the IMF in 1969 and are used as a unit of account. In addition, several countries peg their currencies to the SDR. All member countries of the IMF may use SDRs to acquire foreign exchange when they have short-term balance of payments problems. For example, if Argentina has a balance of payments problem with the United States, it can use its SDRs to acquire dollars. SDRs have a value determined by the weighted value of five currencies: the U.S. dollar, the German mark, the French franc, the Japanese yen, and the British pound sterling.[21] They have a value that fluctuates daily, and they are part of a country's unilateral transfer account in its balance of payments.[22]

THE WORLD BANK GROUP

The World Bank, or World Bank Group as it is more commonly called, was created in 1945 as the International Bank for Reconstruction and Development (IBRD). Its original purpose was to help rebuild the war-torn economies of Europe. In recent decades emphasis has been placed on loans to less-developed countries to improve their infrastructures. Examples would be the financing of engineering and agricultural projects. Service and educational projects are also eligible for loans. Capital is provided by the countries that are members of the IBRD. Loans are made only to governments or to organizations having a government guarantee. Private business firms can bid on contracts for development projects, such as building roads, and can act as suppliers and engineers.

Other institutions that are a part of the World Bank Group include the following:

1. The International Finance Corporation (IFC): The IFC provides loans to individual business firms, with the criteria that the projects benefit the economies of the developing countries, and that they have a reasonable chance of making a profit. The IFC can make loans at conventional interest rates for a period of up to twelve years and can also purchase stock shares.

2. The International Development Association (IDA): The primary purpose of IDA is to help the poorest countries among the World Bank Group members. It, too, provides loans for development purposes at low rates of interest, or even on an interest-free basis. Loans can also be made for a period of time of up to fifty years. An example of this type of loan would be a loan to Ethiopia to improve rural water supplies.

3. The Multilateral Investment Guarantee Agency (MIGA): The purpose of MIGA is to provide political risk insurance for firms doing business in countries with a high degree of political risk.[23] It was created in 1988 to encourage direct investment in less-developed countries by offering private investors insurance against noncommercial risks, such as wars and government expropriation of property.

THE UNITED STATES AS A DEBTOR NATION

The United States has had a deficit in its merchandise trade account for the period 1986–1999. The deficit reached a high of $231 billion in 1998 and was even higher in 1999.[24] Regardless of whether the dollar has been weak or strong against other world currencies, the trade deficit persists. During this period the United States imported around $2.5 trillion more of goods than it exported. Approximately 30 percent of the deficit has been with Japan, which has created trade tensions between the two countries. At the same time that the United States has been running a deficit in its trade account, Japan has been running a surplus in its trade account, largely because of the sales of its automobiles to the United States. The U.S. trade deficit for 1998 was $231 billion, whereas the Japanese surplus in its trade account was $72 billion for 1998.

Today, the United States is the world's leading debtor nation and Japan is the world's leading creditor nation. A part of the debt increase can be attributed to the fact that the American dollar increased in value relative to European and Japanese currencies, making U.S. assets abroad worth less. The U.S. merchandise trade deficit has been a contributory cause of the deficit. Countries with trade surpluses can use the amounts to invest in the United States. U.S. Treasury securities are of particular importance to foreign investors because they represent one of the safest forms of investment in the world. Much of the rise in U.S. stock market prices can also be attributed to foreign investors who find U.S. stocks an attractive vehicle for investment.

SUMMARY

The balance of payments accounts of any country are a systematic record of its transactions with the rest of the world over a given period of time. The accounts include trade, services, capital movements, and unilateral transfers. Trade includes merchandise exports and imports such as machinery and foodstuffs.

Services are also an important export and import. The United States has a deficit in its merchandise trade account, most of which can be attributed to an excess of imports from Japan and China over exports. Capital movements comprise the capital account and consist of direct investment and portfolio investment. International payments between countries can be made in gold and convertible foreign exchange. These payments come under the balance of payments category of official reserve accounts.

QUESTIONS FOR DISCUSSION

1. What is the purpose of the International Monetary Fund?
2. Discuss Michael Porter's theory of national competitive advantage.
3. The great bulk of American foreign trade is done with three major trading areas of the world. Discuss. Which area is the most important? Why?
4. What is a country's balance of payments? The United States usually has a negative balance of payments. Is that good or bad?
5. Discuss some of the factors that affect the supply of and the demand for American dollars.
6. The IMF currently classifies exchange rates into three categories. Discuss.

NOTES

1. Stewart C. Easton, *The Western Heritage* (New York: Holt, Rinehart, and Winston, 1961), p. 112.
2. David Landes, *The Wealth and Poverty of Nations* (New York: W. W. Norton, 1998).
3. Angus Maddison, *The World Economy in the 20th Century* (Development Center for the Organization for Economic Cooperation and Development, Paris: 1989), p. 29.
4. The building of classical economic theory can be attributed to the writings of Adam Smith and David Ricardo. It dominated economic thought of the Western world from the late eighteenth century until the 1930s.
5. Mercantilism was also used in Holland, France, and Spain. Colonial empires were built by each of these nations.
6. Adam Smith, *The Wealth of Nations* (Indianapolis: Liberty Classics, 1981).
7. David Ricardo, *The Principles of Political Economy and Taxation* (New York: E. P. Dulton and Co., 1948), pp. 82–83.
8. Bertil Ohlin, *Interregional and International Trade* (Cambridge, MA: Harvard University Press), 1933.
9. Although China is a large country, much of its land is not suitable for agriculture. Labor is plentiful, so the cultivation of rice and other agricultural products is labor intensive.
10. Michael Porter, *The Competitive Advantage of Nations* (New York: Free Press, 1990).
11. Taiwan is not recognized as a nation because of the objection of China, which considers it to be a Chinese province.
12. Also included would be royalties from American music sold abroad.
13. A minimum of 10 percent stock ownership is the basic requisite for a direct investment.

14. Total U.S. direct investment in Africa in 1998 amounted to $1.6 billion compared to U.S. direct investment in Panama of $1.7 billion.
15. For example, American college students going to Cancun for a vacation would increase the demand for pesos.
16. Suharto and his family are reputed to hold assets in excess of $5 billion in Indonesian companies and real estate.
17. In the United States, the Securities and Exchange Commission is responsible for regulating the U.S. stock market. There is no equivalent regulatory agency in Japan.
18. In the United States, banks cannot claim stocks as capital assets.
19. The World Bank and the Marshall Plan aid were responsible to a considerable degree for European recovery.
20. The International Monetary Fund has a pool of funds amounting to around $200 billion, coming mostly from the rich nations. The biggest givers are as follows: (1) United States, $36.0 billion; (2) Germany, $11.2 billion; (3) Japan, $11.2 billion; (4) United Kingdom, $10.1 billion; (5) France, $10.1 billion; (6) Saudi Arabia, $7.0 billion.
21. The U.S. dollar accounts for around 40 percent of the value of an SDR.
22. On March 14, 2000, 1 SDR = $1.36.
23. However, there are some countries that are not covered by risk insurance. An example would be Rwanda.
24. The 1999 deficit was $330 billion.

RECOMMENDED READING

Brademas, John, and Fritz Herrmann. "Tackling International Corruption." *Foreign Affairs*. Vol. 77, No. 5 (September/October 1998), pp. 17–22.

Burtless, Gary, Robert Z. Lawrence, and Robert Litan. *Globaphobia: Confronting Fears About Open Trade*. Washington, D.C.: Brookings Institution/Twentieth Century Fund, and Progressive Policy Institute, 1998.

Lawrence, Robert Z., ed. *Brookings Trade Forum*. Vol. 1. Washington, D.C.: Brookings Institution, 1998. Forum deals with unfair trade practices.

CHAPTER 14

GOVERNMENT AND INTERNATIONAL TRADE

Almost everyone is in favor of trade between nations as long as the results are of equal benefit to all concerned. However, this is not usually the case. Although to consumers, trade between nations clearly contributes to higher living standards, some producer groups may be adversely affected by it. Those whose sales are reduced by foreign competition and those whose incomes are reduced when foreign goods are made available to domestic consumers will want protection against foreign imports. When imports of Japanese cars began to threaten the profitability of the American automobile industry, the companies and the UAW went to Congress and asked that restraints be placed on the number of Japanese cars that could be brought into the United States. French farmers are subsidized by their government even though their farm products cost more than imports.

Since its inception, the United States has generally followed a policy of trade protection designed to protect domestic consumers against foreign competition. At first, the rationale for trade protection was based on the "infant industry" argument. American industries that were just getting started were in no position to compete against the established industries of Europe, so protective tariffs were used. Then tariffs were lowered at the request of farmers who could import farm equipment from abroad more cheaply than it could be purchased in the United States.[1] Trade protection hit its peak during the Depression of the 1930s when the Smoot-Hawley tariff was passed. The raising of the tariff against foreign goods provoked retaliation from abroad as other countries raised their tariffs on American goods, increasing unemployment here and abroad.

Governments are very much involved in international trade. In the United States, federal, state, and local governments promote international trade and investment. The federal government promotes foreign trade through the Department of Commerce and through agencies like the Export-Import Bank

(Eximbank). State governments promote international trade through their development offices and trade missions. They offer various forms of subsidies to attract foreign investments. Local governments create Free Trade Zones (FTZs) to attract companies. In general, government trade policies can be divided into two types—those that are designed to promote exports and investment and those that are designed to discourage imports.

GOVERNMENT POLICIES TO PROMOTE EXPORTS

Several types of government policies can be used to promote exports. Of these, tax policies are probably the most important. A government can manipulate its tax system to grant exemptions and rates to various forms of activities, corporations, and people. Japan, for example, has exempted income earned from its exports from the corporate income tax. Favorable tax treatments of certain types of income can influence shifts in economic behavior. Governments can also promote exports through loans financed out of budget revenues or other sources. The U.S. Export-Import Bank (Eximbank) is an example. Subsidies can also be used to aid export industries or to attract foreign investment. Favorable tax treatment is one form of a subsidy.[2] Another would be rebates to exporters.

EXPORT-IMPORT BANK (EXIMBANK)

The Export-Import Bank (Eximbank) is a federally owned enterprise that receives its financial support from the federal budget. Its mission is to promote U.S. exports. It does this by making direct loans to exporters and by insuring and guaranteeing loans made by private lenders. Since it concentrates on areas where private financing is not available and on meeting foreign competition, its programs are generally intended to supplement private sources of credit. Direct loans extended by Eximbank are dollar credits made to borrowers outside the United States for the purchase of U.S. goods and services. Disbursements under the loan agreements are made in the United States to the suppliers of the goods and services, and the loans plus interest must be repaid in dollars by the borrowers. The purposes for which the loans can be used are the following:

1. To supplement private sources of financing when the lenders are unable or unwilling to assume the political and financial risks involved.
2. To extend credit on terms longer than those private lenders can provide.
3. To match the special terms that foreign governments provide to their exporters.

In addition, Eximbank has financial guarantee programs under which it can guarantee, backed by the full faith and credit of the United States, the repayment of credits extended by private lenders to foreign purchasers of U.S. goods and services. In this respect, the bank's role is comparable to that of the many foreign institutions that provide guarantees and insurance to help their country's exporters and safeguard them from undue risks from overseas sales. Under the financial loan authority, Eximbank can guarantee repayment by a borrower of up to 100 percent of the outstanding principal due on such loans, plus interest equal to the U.S. Treasury rate for similar debt obligations.

OVERSEAS PRIVATE INVESTMENT CORPORATION (OPIC)

Political and financial risks are facts of life in the world marketplace. Political risk can apply to wars, revolutions, riots, and terrorism.[3] It can also cover default on debt payments by governments, increased taxes, and currency controls.[4] There are a number of areas of the world in which political risk is high, for example, Bosnia, Iran, Iraq, Nigeria, Rwanda, Russia, and many other countries. Financial risk refers to nonpayment of debts and currency instability. A foreign importer may default on debts owed to an American exporter.[5] Currency instability also has an adverse affect on trade. Using the East Asian currency crisis as an example, U.S. exporters doing business in Indonesia or Thailand were hurt because the values of their currencies declined in value against the dollar, making imports of American goods more expensive.

The Overseas Private Investment Corporation (OPIC) provides insurance for U.S. direct investment in less-developed countries. It is an agency of the U.S. government, and is financed out of the federal budget.[6] It provides loan guarantees and political risk insurance. It can also make direct loans and some equity investments. The types of projects assisted are those that promote economic development, such as manufacturing, fishing, mining, agriculture, and tourism. Loans are usually made to firms with sales of less than $142 million annually.

1. Direct loans are made for amounts ranging from $500,000 to $6 million. Proceeds may be used to acquire goods and services in the United States or in a foreign country.

2. Guaranteed loans can be provided to lenders, including banks and insurance companies. If, for example, an American bank lends money for a development project in Nigeria, OPIC will guarantee the loan against potential loss.

3. Equity participation on the part of OPIC can occur. It can purchase up to 30 percent of stock or bonds in U.S. companies, local companies, or joint ventures.[7]

4. Risk insurance is the largest and most important of OPIC's activities and covers expropriation, currency inconvertibility, and any form of political violence.

FOREIGN TRADE ZONES (FTZS)

In order to encourage foreign trade, many countries, including the United States, set up foreign trade zones that allow business firms to store, assemble, and display goods from abroad without first having to pay a tariff. FTZs are widely used by local governments in the United States to promote trade and create jobs. New Orleans is an example. Goods may be brought into the FTZ of the city tariff-free. Once they are assembled and leave the zone, a tariff must be paid, but not on the cost of assembly or profit. For example, a furniture maker would pay a duty only on the raw materials brought into the zone, but not on the cost of assembling the final product or on profits. A foreign automaker can bring parts to New Orleans FTZ, assemble them, and not pay a tariff until the finished product is delivered to a U.S. showroom.[8]

FOREIGN SALES CORPORATION ACT (FSCA)

The FSCA was passed in 1984 for the purpose of encouraging small business firms to go into the exporting business. It allows small firms to form into foreign sales corporations (FSCs) in order to stimulate exports. There are specific benefits to be derived from the formation of an FSC. It can get a tax exemption on income earned from foreign trade. It can get a tax exemption on a portion of foreign trade income earned from the sale or lease of export property, and the performance of engineering and managerial services. There is an exemption from U.S. income taxes of up to 50 percent of earnings by small firms. To be incorporated, an FSC must conform to the following requirements:

1. It has to incorporate under the laws of a foreign country with which the United States has an agreement for the exchange of tax information, or of any U.S. possession with the exception of Puerto Rico.
2. It has to maintain an office outside of the U.S. customs territory.
3. It cannot have more than twenty-five stockholders.

TRADE PROTECTION

Government policies to promote the development of their home industries go back to mercantilism. The mercantilist nations believed that the value of exports should always exceed the value of imports. In this way, the wealth of each nation would be increased. To accomplish this objective, trade was regulated between these nations and their colonies. England would not allow its American colonies to produce steel because it would compete against British steelmakers. Only raw materials of lesser value could be sent to England; in return, the British would export finished products of more value to America, thus always having a favorable trade balance with its colonies.[9]

It can be said that Japan's economic development after the end of World War II was based on mercantilist policies. Its development was based on an export-driven strategy, by which the Ministry of International Trade and Industry promoted an industrial policy based on picking and promoting industries that could export successfully throughout the world. An example is the Japanese automobile industry that grew from the production of 32,000 cars in 1950 to becoming the world's largest automobile producers by 1980.[10] The automobile industry was helped through the provision of low-cost loans by the Japanese banks. During the early stages of its development, the automobile industry received subsidies from the government, and was protected from foreign competition by tariffs and quotas.[11]

TARIFFS

The tariff is probably the most common device used by other nations to restrict foreign trade. It is simply a tax levied on foreign goods coming into a country. The result is to make imported goods more expensive than comparable domestic goods which, of course, are not subject to the tax. The main effect of a tariff is that it raised the prices of the goods protected by it; if it did not raise prices, it would afford no protection. The sugar beet industry of the United States provides a good example of tariff protection. It is much more expensive to produce sugar made from beets than it is to import cane sugar made in Cuba and elsewhere. The end result is that American consumers pay more for sugar than they would have to in the absence of the tariff.

IMPORT QUOTAS

Compared with tariffs, which have been used by countries since the days of mercantilism, import quotas are relatively new. Introduced in France in the 1930s as an antidepression measure, the import quota has become a significant part of most countries' international commercial policy. As the name implies, a quota places limits, numerical or other, on the amount of a product that can be imported. For example, one country decides to restrict its auto imports from another country to two million cars a year. An import quota is generally considered more restrictive than a tariff. With a tariff, there is still the option of buying the foreign product, albeit at a higher price, but the import quota limits even this option. Prices cannot be forced by a tariff to rise by more than the amount of the tariff, but there is no upper limit to the price increase that can result from a quota. The prices to consumers are raised, and the restrictions placed on imports take away the incentive of domestic producers to innovate and promote efficiency.

The Automobile Industry and Import Quotas   In 1981, the U.S. auto companies asked Congress and the Reagan administration for quotas against the Japanese automobile industry. At stake, the U.S. auto industry claimed, was the survival of the industry and the necessity of preserving jobs. Import quotas would provide a time-out or respite, so to speak, while the auto industry could recuperate, retool, and develop new cars that could compete successfully against Japanese cars. Precedents for import quotas had already been established. Beef quotas have assisted cattle raisers, sugar quotas have kept high-cost domestic sugar cane and sugar beet growers in business, and quotas and other forms of support have been used to protect domestic steel producers from further losses to Asian and European steel producers. The Reagan administration made a compromise to reach an agreement with Japan whereby Japanese auto companies would voluntarily limit their exports to the United States. These quotas, set at 1,680,000 cars a year over a three-year period, ended in March 1984. A new quota, which raised the number of cars the Japanese could ship to the United States to 1,850,000 cars, was applied from April 1, 1984, to March 31, 1985. The allocation of import shares among Japanese automobile manufacturers was determined by the Japanese government on the basis of each company's shares of the U.S. market before the quota was imposed. The breakdown of the market was as follows:[12]

Toyota	31%
Nissan	27
Honda	21
Mazda	9
Mitsubishi	7
Subaru	4
Isuzu	1

Results of the Import Quota on Japanese Cars   The import quota had a number of results, few of which were of benefit to U.S. consumers. As the market allocation indicates, the quota benefited those Japanese auto firms that had already established a market for their cars in the United States. Toyota was assured of a market share of around one-third of the quota. Conversely, Japanese car companies that had not established a market share before the quota were virtually shut out of the U.S. car market. U.S. consumer choice was limited to a choice of the cars produced by Toyota, Nissan, or Honda, or the U.S. cars, or the cars of countries to which the import quota did not apply. However, the import quota on Japanese cars also had other effects on U.S. consumers:[13]

1. It raised the prices of both American and Japanese cars to U.S. consumers. One estimate was that the price of Japanese imports increased an average of $920 to $960 per car in the 1981–1983 period. Since restrictions were placed on Japanese cars, the companies shipped their top-of-the-line models. It was estimated that Japanese producers and their dealers benefited by as much as $2 billion a year during the quota.
2. The prices of U.S. automobiles also increased by an estimated $1,300 for each new U.S. car sold during the period 1981–1983. The estimated additional costs to consumers for new U.S. and Japanese cars was $4.3 billion in 1983.
3. One benefit of the import quota was to protect U.S. jobs. An estimated 20,000 to 25,000 jobs were saved in the automobile industry, at a cost to consumers of $160,000 a year per job.

4. Another purpose of the import quota was to enable the U.S. car companies to improve the quality of their cars. There is little evidence that such improvement were made.

5. The U.S. automobile companies increased their market shares and made record profits. In 1984, Chrysler's profits were the highest in its history. Automobile industry profits were $6.3 billion for 1983 and close to $10 billion in 1984.

6. With such profits, the automobile companies paid their executives and some employees substantial bonuses. Chairman Philip Caldwell of Ford Motor Company received a 1983 salary and bonus of $1.4 million plus $5.9 million in long-term compensation. Chrysler Chairman Lee A. Iacocca received stock options valued at $17 million.

DUMPING

Dumping is simply selling a product in another country at a cost lower than its production cost. The loss is often made up by a subsidy from the government. An example is the development of the Korean automobile industry. Three Korean conglomerates were picked to produce cars for exports, and targets were set for each of them. Export prices for cars were set low, often below cost, and the government made up the difference. For example, one Hyundai model that cost $3,700 to produce was sold for $5,000 in Korea and $2,200 overseas.[14] The car was overpriced in Korea and underpriced in Southeast Asia and Latin America. The intent was to establish a market for the car in these areas by selling below cost, with the Korean government covering the loss. Hyundai was also supported by the state-owned Korean banks, which provided low-cost interest loans.

EXCHANGE CONTROLS

Exchange controls have been used by many countries. All importers needing foreign exchange to pay for imports can be required to obtain it from a government agency. Before approving such a request, the agency will want to know what is to be imported, whether the import competes against domestic producers, and from what country the import comes. India provides an example. Many imports were excluded from India to protect certain industries. The government set different exchange rates, depending on the importance of the import. If it were necessary for the economy, the exchange rate the government offered to importers might be 5 rupees = $1.00; if it was not important, the exchange rate might be 50 rupees = $1.00.[15] The government, not the free market, decided what was important and what was not important.

THE OMNIBUS TRADE AND COMPETITIVENESS ACT, 1988

The Omnibus Trade and Competitiveness Act joined the Bible and *Gone With the Wind* as one of the longest publications ever written.[16] It is 1,115 pages long and contains something for everyone. The purpose of the act is to develop coherent trade policy in dealing with countries with whom the United States has an unfavorable trade deficit, thus preventing future declines in the U.S. economy. In the past, U.S. presidents have preferred to handle trade on an ad hoc basis, with each issue left to the political and economic circumstances of the moment. But no trade dispute can be separable from many other kinds of issues. Congress wanted future presidents, beginning with President Bush, to give more weight to trade in their foreign policy and to make their performance more consistent. However, nearly all the provisions in the act give the president the right to do nothing when he (or she) considers that to be in the country's best interest.

The most important provision of the act is Section 1102, which states that the president, on finding that import restrictions of other countries have an adverse effect on the foreign trade of the United States, is to negotiate to reduce them.[17] The principal negotiation objective is to improve the provisions of GATT and nontariff measure agreements in order to define, deter, and discourage the use of unfair trade practices, including subsidies, dumping, and export targeting practices. Agreements entered into by the president are valid only if he (or she) informs Congress of his (or her) intent to enter into them. The president must also inform Congress if the United States provides reciprocal benefits under a trade agreement. Other purposes of the act are to provide increased cash assistance and job training for U.S. workers who lose their jobs as a result of foreign competition; restrictions against certain imports that threaten national security; and increased funding to improve foreign language teaching in the United States.

The General Agreement on Tariffs and Trade (GATT)

The General Agreement on Tariffs and Trade (GATT), like the World Bank and the International Monetary Fund, is a by-product of the Depression of the 1930s when the world economy collapsed. It was created in Geneva, Switzerland, in 1947, and had as its major purpose the reduction of trade barriers that had contributed to the prolongation of the Depression. To do this, member countries agreed to uphold the following principles:

1. Nondiscrimination in trade through adherence to Most Favored Nations (MFN) treatment, which means that any preferential treatment given to one country be given to all member countries. However, to assist less-developed countries in their economic development, wealthier countries may lower tariffs to these countries without lowering them for other countries.
2. Reduction of tariffs through negotiation.
3. Elimination of import quotas.
4. Resolution of differences between member countries by negotiation.

A series of negotiations called "rounds" have occurred since GATT's inception in 1947. The first rounds were concerned, for the most part, with reducing tariffs. Beginning in the 1960s, however, the focus shifted as countries began to rely less on tariffs and more on import quotas and subsidies. GATT rules had little influence over government investment policies that affected international trade or on policies concerning the protection of intellectual property rights such as patents, trademarks, and copyrights. Agricultural trade, which usually involved the use of subsidies, was another area in which GATT rules did not apply. So the eighth round of negotiations, called the Uruguay Round, began in 1986 and was concluded in 1995.

THE URUGUAY ROUND

The Uruguay Round involved a series of discussions among member nations that lasted from 1986 to 1995. A number of issues ranging from agricultural policy to intellectual property were discussed. Agricultural subsidies and restrictions on the import of agricultural products were a major bone of contention among nations. Japan is an inefficient producer of rice. The availability of land for the production of rice in Japan is limited, so there are a large number of rice farmers cultivating small rice fields. The supply of rice to Japanese consumers is limited and expensive. It would be far cheaper to import rice from the United States but Japanese farmers, like U.S. farmers including those who produce tobacco, have political clout.[18] Japanese restrictions on the import of American rice discriminates against American rice producers and Japanese consumers who pay on the average five times as much for Japanese rice than for American rice. One of the objectives of the Uruguay Round, summarized below, is to reduce subsidies on agricultural products.

1. Agricultural liberalization: A major accomplishment of the Uruguay Round was to convert various types of subsidies into tariffs to be reduced by 36 percent over a period of time. The rice markets of Japan and South Korea, which are closed to imports, will gradually be opened over a period of time, thus providing better market opportunities for foreign suppliers. Domestic farm supports are to be reduced by 20 percent, and subsidized exports are to be reduced 36 percent in value and 21 percent in volume.[19] Countries were treated differently based on their income levels. In industrial countries, import tariffs on agriculture were to be reduced by 36 percent over a six-year period. Developing countries committed themselves to reducing their tariffs over twenty years, and less-developed countries were exempted from any commitment.

2. Services: The export of services is an area in which the United States has a trade surplus. Of particular importance is the export of such services as finance, telecommunication, and transportation. There are no international trade rules covering services, so countries protect their service industries from foreign competition. Some countries may require that their exports and imports be carried only on their own ships. Other countries may place restrictions on the provision of financial services by foreign banks.[20] The Uruguay Round sets basic fair-play principles involving nondiscrimination against services, with each country pledging openings in areas ranging from banking to entertainment. Part of the Uruguay Round was the creation of the General Agreement on Trade in Services (GATS) that will establish rules for services that aim for nondiscrimination and market access.

3. Intellectual Property: Intellectual property rights are very important to the foreign trade of the United States because American movies, television programs, music, and various other forms of entertainment are popular overseas. When copyrights and other forms of intellectual property are infringed upon, as they are in a number of countries, income is lost to their owners. The Uruguay Round strengthened the protection granted to the owners of intellectual property. The TRIPS (Trade-Related Intellectual Property Rights) agreement was a part of the Uruguay Round. It covers such intellectual property rights as patents, copyrights, trademarks, and designs. It covers all the 123 signatory countries of the Uruguay Round. Much of TRIPS simply extends the international agreements of intellectual property that are discussed in the next section.

4. Manufacturing: The export of manufacturing is the most important item in the U.S. merchandise trade account and so is the import of manufacturing from the rest of the world. Contributing to the deficit in the merchandise trade count is the fact that we import more automobiles from Japan than we export to Japan. Tariffs, import quotas, and other devices are used to protect domestic manufacturing industries. Successive rounds have had as their objectives the reduction of these trade restraints. The Uruguay Round aims at cutting tariffs on manufactured goods from rich countries by more than one-third. Over 40 percent of imports will enter duty-free. Tariff reductions were also set for such countries as South Korea, Thailand, and other East Asian countries. The reduction of import quotas was also a major objective of the Uruguay Round.

THE WORLD TRADE ORGANIZATION (WTO)

The World Trade Organization (WTO), the successor to GATT, was created by the Uruguay Round and entered into existence on January 1, 1995. It is a permanent forum for 134 member governments to address issues affecting their multilateral trade relations as well as to supervise the implementation of the trade agreements negotiated in the Uruguay Round. The WTO operates in much the same manner as GATT, while overseeing a wider variety of trade agreements.[21] It also creates a stronger dispute settlement process by having an appellate court to review interpretations of trade agreements. There are some fifteen agreements that are the responsibility of WTO. The WTO financial services agreement signed on December 13, 1997, covers countries representing 95 percent of the global financial services market. The WTO is based in Geneva, Switzerland, and an organization chart of its operations is presented in Figure 14-1.

INTELLECTUAL PROPERTY

Patents, trademarks, and copyrights convey intellectual property rights to their owners. These rights date back a long time. With the rise of strong nation-states in Europe at the close of the Middle Ages, kings began the practice of granting patents as a reward for developing new inventions. Patents were granted to

FIGURE 14-1 WTO ORGANIZATION CHART

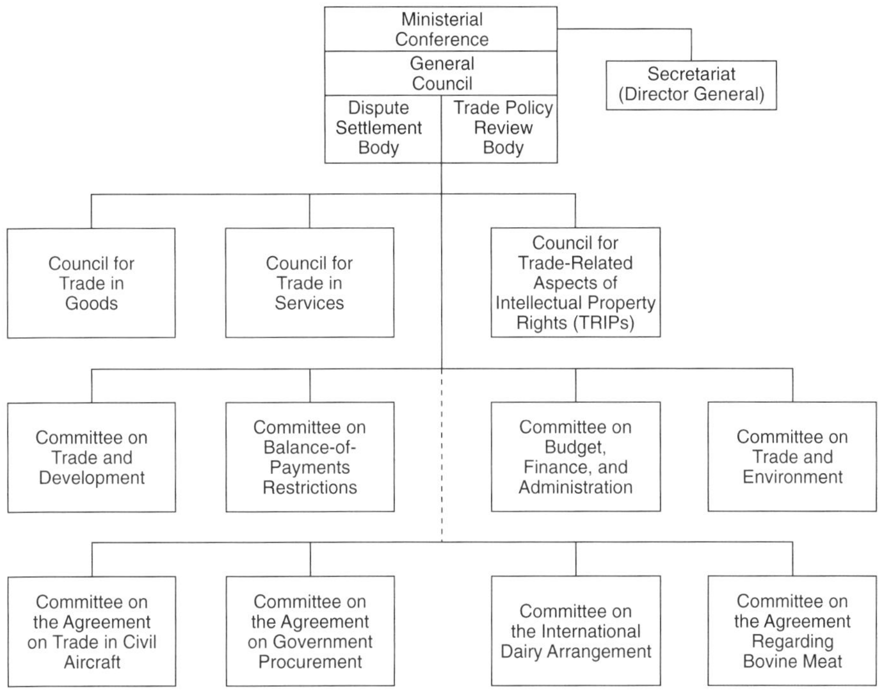

------ The four committees provided for in the plurilateral trade agreements do not report to the General Council, but are required to keep the General Council informed of their activities. However, their members use the WTO dispute settlement mechanism and are subject to the decisions of the Dispute Settlement Body.

inventors, giving them the right to exclude others from making or using the invention for a number of years. Patent rights are recognized in the U.S. Constitution, which specifies that Congress has power to protect the progress of science by securing for limited times to inventors the exclusive right of discovery. This provision of exclusive rights was implemented by statutes. Patents in the United States are protected for seventeen years.

A trademark is a name or symbol used to indicate the source or origin of certain goods. It may be used in a variety of ways. It may be used in advertising that relates to a particular product. An example would be the clown, Ronald McDonald, who is immediately identified with the hamburger restaurants of the same name. It may be used on product packaging, company letterheads, and on company buildings. An example would be the Holiday Inn star. Because of the variety of users and uses possible, effective control of trademark use, particularly in other countries, is difficult. Nevertheless, control is vital to ensure that usage is consistent with a company's image and that its legal rights are protected. Trademarks are registered at the U.S. Patent and Trademark Office and are issued for a period of twenty years.

TABLE 14-1   DURATION OF PATENTS FOR SELECTED COUNTRIES

Country	Years
Australia	16
Brazil	15
Canada	17
Germany	18
France	20
India	16
Italy	15
Japan	15
Mexico	15
Peru	10
Russia	15
Spain	20
United Kingdom	16
United States	17

Source: Ray August, *International Business Law* (Englewood Cliffs, NJ: Prentice Hall, 1993), p. 611.

Copyrights are particularly important to the publishing and entertainment industries. They vest rights in authors and entertainers that prevent others from using their works without permission. The entertainment industry is of particular importance in U.S. foreign trade. American movies, music, and TV programs are popular in other countries and often are easy to replicate. Copyrights are protected by the U.S. Copyright Act of 1976, are administered by the Copyright Office of the Library of Congress, and are protected for the life of the author or entertainer plus fifty years.

INTERNATIONAL PROTECTION OF INTELLECTUAL PROPERTY

On the international level, there is no formal machinery for the making of laws because there is no world government. The international equivalents of legislation are treaties and conventions. Treaties are agreements between one or more nations. Conventions are sponsored by international organizations such as the United Nations. An example of a convention was the Geneva Convention, which was sponsored by the League of Nations for the purpose of outlawing the use of poison gas in future wars.[22] Both treaties and conventions are binding on signatory nations because of a shared sense of commitment, and because one nation fears that if it does not respect its promises, other nations will not respect their promises. Typically, conventions are used to protect international intellectual property rights.

Patent Protection   There are two important conventions that apply to patents. The first is the Paris Convention of 1883, which now has more than one hundred signatory countries. It requires national treatment, so that a patent applicant from France will be treated in the U.S. patent system the same way the United States treats its nationals. It also establishes a right of priority for patent filings. An inventor who files for a patent in the home country will have twelve months to file for patents in the other countries, with the filing date in all countries being the original date.

The Patent Cooperation Treaty of 1978   The PCT is administered by the World Intellectual Property Organization (WIPO) and has the United States and a number of other countries as members. The treaty provides for centralized filing procedures and a standardized international application format. U.S. companies and individuals may file an international patent application at the U.S. Patent and Trade Office and designate the member countries in which patent protection is desired.

Trademarks   There are several international agreements on trademark rights. The first is the Paris Convention, mentioned previously, which also applies to trademarks. It established the principle of same national treatment, and allows a six-month priority from the date of registration. The Madrid Agreement allows trademarks, once granted in a home country, to have an international filing at WIPO. These and other conventions covering trademarks embody the national treatment principle and provide certain rights for companies seeking trademark protection abroad. One is a right of priority, created by filing a first application in the United States or another nation, followed by one or more corresponding applications in other member countries.

Copyright Law   Copyright laws cover artistic property whereas patent and trademark laws cover industrial property. Artistic property covers artistic, literary, and musical works. Holders of copyrights have three legal rights—pecuniary, reproduction, and distribution. There are two major international copyright conventions. The first is the Berne Convention of 1887, which established the national treatment principle requiring member countries to honor copyrights of individuals who are nationals of their countries. Copyright laws apply for the author's life plus fifty years. The Universal Copyright Convention, which was signed in 1952 and revised in 1971, also follows the principle of national treatment. Any work must bear the symbol, the date of first publication, and the name of the copyright owner. The copyright lasts for the length of life of the holder plus twenty-five years.

CORRUPTION

Corruption, which usually involves some sort of bribe, is a way of life in many countries of the world, rich and poor. In fact, there are specific words for bribery. In Latin America it is called *la mordita*, "the bite"; in the Middle East countries it is called *baksheesh*, which can be translated as "rake-off"; and in the Russian

Federation it is called *blat,* which means "under the table." Bribery can be divided into two forms. The first, which is commonly called grease, is a minor payment to a minor government official to get something done. An example would be a payment to a police officer to tear up a traffic ticket. The second involves a payment of a large sum of money to an elected official or high-level administrator to influence the outcome of an election or get a government contract.

Bribery makes the international headlines so often that it has almost become passé. In South Korea, two former presidents were sent to jail for taking bribes. In France, cabinet ministers and mayors resigned amid kickback probes. In Japan, officials of the Ministry of Finance had to resign because they accepted bribes from Japanese business firms. A former president of Brazil had to resign while he was in office because he took bribes. In the post-Communist countries of the Ukraine and the Russian Federation, bribery is so rampant that many foreign companies have given up and gone home. In Kenya, senior government officials gave subsidies to a local businessman to export gold and diamonds to Switzerland even though Kenya produces no gold or diamonds.

CRITICISMS OF BRIBERY

The main criticism of bribery is that it distorts efficient resource allocation by preventing competition in the market between firms for government contracts. The contract goes to the firm or individual that pays the most money to get it, not to the firm or firms that are more efficient and would do the job at a lower price. Bribery also acts as a tax on an investment or transaction. A 20 percent bribe on a contract of $1 million is a tax, but it does not go to the people in the form of government expenditures, it goes to government officials. Moreover, it makes a mockery out of any attempt to create a democratic society because elected officials who presumably are the servants of the people enrich themselves at the public's expense. Bribery can corrupt the process of law so vital to the functioning of democracy.

Table 14-2 presents a corruption index ranking for 85 countries ranging from those countries that are the least corrupt to those countries that are the most corrupt. Some 85 countries out of more than 200 countries were ranked. Most of the countries that are the most corrupt are located in three areas of the world—Africa, East Asia, and Latin America. The Scandinavian countries rank the highest, and the United States, which prides itself on telling the rest of the world how to live, ranked seventeenth. The Russian Federation, which has had many problems, ranked seventy-sixth. It was also corrupt when it was a part of the Soviet Union.

THE FOREIGN CORRUPT PRACTICES ACT (FCPA)

The Foreign Corrupt Practices Act (FCPA) was passed in 1977 in response to scandals arising from the revelation of large payments made by U.S. corporations to foreign government officials. An example was the Lockheed Aircraft

TABLE 14-2   1998 CORRUPTION INDEX FOR SELECTED COUNTRIES

Country	Rank	Score
Denmark	1	10.0
Finland	2	9.6
Sweden	3	9.5
Canada	6	9.2
Germany	15	7.9
United States	17	7.5
France	21	6.7
Japan	25	5.8
Italy	39	4.6
Brazil	46	4.0
China	52	3.5
Mexico	55	3.3
India	66	2.9
Russia	76	2.4
Venezuela	77	2.3
Colombia	79	2.2
Nigeria	81	1.9

Source: Transparency International 1999.

Corporation, which was found guilty of payments of $22 million over a period of five years to government officials in Japan, Italy, and the Netherlands to win contracts for its aircraft. The disclosures revealed the involvement of such high personages as Prime Minister Tanaka of Japan, who eventually went to prison, and Prince Bernhard of the Netherlands. This case drew worldwide attention. The Securities and Exchange Commission (SEC) began to bring action against some American companies under the disclosure provisions of the Securities and Exchange Act of 1934. In all, about 400 American companies admitted making payments to officials in foreign countries to obtain contracts.

Provisions of FCPA   The FCPA was an amendment to the Securities and Exchange Act of 1934. It comes under the jurisdiction of the Securities and Exchange Commission, and it has the following provisions:

1. The SEC sets accounting standards by requiring business firms to keep accurate books and records and to devise and maintain a system of internal accounting controls.
2. It prohibits the corrupt use of the mails or any means of commerce to offer, pay, or promise to pay an authorized or unauthorized payment or gift to any foreign official, foreign political party, officer, candidate, or third party who might have influence with foreign officials or politicians when the objective is to influence a decision favorable to the business firm giving the payment.

3. It is a criminal offense to offer a bribe to a foreign official. For unlawful acts, companies may be fined $1 million and individuals may face fines of $10,000 and five years in prison.
4. The law does not apply to "grease" payments that are intended only to expedite normal business affairs. Hence, "grease" payments for work permits, visas, police protection, or phone service are legal because they are routine costs of doing business in most countries.

Criticism of FCPA   American firms have been opposed to the FCPA on the grounds that it has tilted the playing field against them in the world marketplace. Their main contention has been that they are placed at a disadvantage in doing overseas business, because foreign firms have been allowed to offer bribes whereas they cannot. The major competitors of the United States are France, Germany, Japan, and the United Kingdom, and all have allowed their firms to deduct bribes as a legal cost of doing business. British firms resorting to bribery in overseas business need only report it to Inland Revenue as a business cost. Multinationals of other countries have played by different game rules, with the resultant loss to American multinationals. The opening of new major markets in China and India, where bribery is very common, has also caused concern.

Enforcement of the FCPA has been rather lax during most of its history. From 1977 to 1995, only sixteen bribery prosecutions have been brought against American firms. However, enforcement activity has begun to pick up. In 1995 Lockheed Martin Corp. pleaded guilty to conspiring to violate the FCPA, admitting that an executive had paid an Egyptian official to assure the purchase of three C-130 cargo planes. It incurred a criminal fine of $21.8 million and entered a civil settlement for $3 million. Two Lockheed executives also pleaded guilty in connection with the violations, and one of them is serving a prison sentence. In 1997, IBM came under investigation for activities in Argentina. It is alleged to have paid bribes through an Argentine subcontractor to obtain a contract to modernize the computer system of a large Argentine bank.

OECD CONVENTION ON COMBATING BRIBERY OF FOREIGN PUBLIC OFFICIALS

In December 1997, thirty-three leading developed nations signed the Organization for Economic Cooperation and Developments Convention on Combating Bribery of Foreign Public Officials. Each signatory country has agreed to take measures necessary under its own law to punish any person who offers a bribe to influence an official of another country for the purpose of influencing favorable treatment. Bribery will be punishable by criminal penalties based on the laws of the signatory country whose citizens were involved in the bribery. Each signatory country can also apply civil sanctions against a person who has bribed a foreign official. The treaty does not ban payments to political parties or candidates, but once it is ratified by the thirty-three nations, including the United States, it will criminalize bribery. It remains to be seen whether or not the convention will be successful in eliminating bribery, particularly in such countries as China, India, the Russian Federation, Nigeria, and others.

SUMMARY

There are a variety of national and international laws that apply to foreign trade. One set of laws covers the use of tariffs, import quotas, and other devices designed to restrict the free flow of goods and services among nations. The General Agreement on Tariffs and Trade, created after the end of World War II, was designed to reduce trade barriers between countries through negotiation. A series of international conventions have been created to protect owners from the misuse of these forms of intellectual property. Finally, there are laws designed to prohibit bribery as a way of doing business throughout the world. An example is the Foreign Corrupt Practices Act.

QUESTIONS FOR DISCUSSION

1. In what ways do governments promote exports? How is it financed?
2. What are the functions of Eximbank?
3. Compare the impact of tariff and import quotas on foreign trade.
4. What is intellectual property? Why is it necessary to have laws to protect its owners?
5. In what areas of the world is corruption most prevalent? Is there anything that can be done about it?
6. What are grease payments?

NOTES

1. This was one of the causes of the Civil War. The South felt that the North was discriminating against it because the tariff compelled it to buy more manufactured goods from the North.
2. Favorable tax treatment of foreign trade takes many forms. An example would be export exemption from income taxes.
3. Kidnapping is one form of terrorism. It has been on the increase in some Latin American countries. Assassination is another form of terrorism.
4. Currency controls refers to the amount of money that can be taken into or out of a country.
5. This occurrence would involve dispute resolution that is normally covered in the contract between exporter and importer.
6. The governments of all major exporting nations would have similar arrangements.
7. A joint venture is an arrangement between two or more firms or with firms and a government to produce and sell a particular product. The partners provide capital and management expertise and share in the profits.

8. FTZs have increased in importance in the United States. They have increased from around 25 in the 1970s to around 300 in 1998.
9. See the discussion of mercantilism in Chapter 13.
10. The Japanese automobile industry dates back to the early part of the twentieth century.
11. This is also true of the South Korean automobile industry.
12. Robert W. Crandall, "Import Quotas and the Automobile Industry: The Costs of Protection," *The Brookings Review*, Vol. 2, No. 4 (September 1984): 11.
13. *Ibid.*, 11–16.
14. Congress of the United States, Office of Technology Assessment, *Competing Economies: America, Europe, and the Pacific Rim* (Washington, D.C.: U.S. Government Printing Office, October 1991), pp. 329–331.
15. Since the 1990s, India has relaxed many of its trade restrictions, but still maintains some exchange controls.
16. H.R. 3, 100th Congress, 2nd session, April 20, 1988.
17. *Ibid.*, 23–27.
18. A very good example was the failure of Congress to pass legislation that would have raised the tax on a package of cigarettes and would have made the tobacco companies responsible for reducing teenage smoking. The tobacco lobby cited lost jobs if the law were passed.
19. These are guidelines, not categorical goals.
20. Mexico has restricted U.S. banks operating in Mexico from providing various services not offered by Mexican banks.
21. Jim Sanford, "World Trade Organization Opens Global Markets, Protects U.S. Rights," *Business America* (Washington, D.C.: U.S. Government Printing Office, January 1995): 4–7.
22. Poison gas was used by the Germans and the Allies in World War I. It was a particularly painful way to die, and those who recovered were affected by it for the rest of their lives. It was alleged that American troops used poison gas during the Vietnam War, but the allegation was proven false.

RECOMMENDED READING

Brademas, John, and Fritz Herrmann. "Tackling International Corruption." *Foreign Affairs*. Vol. 77, No. 5 (September/October 1998): 17–22.

Burtless, Gary, Robert Z. Lawrence, and Robert Litan. *Globaphobia: Confronting Fears About Open Trade*. Washington, D.C.: Brookings Institution/Twentieth Century Fund, and Progressive Policy Institute, 1998.

Lawrence, Robert Z., ed. *Brookings Trade Forum*. Vol. 1. Washington, D.C.: Brookings Institution, 1998. Forum deals with unfair trade practices.

CHAPTER 15

REGIONAL TRADING BLOCS

Globalism and regionalism are two main currents in the world today. Technological innovation is a driving force in the world economy and has no distinctive nationality. As technology has developed, it has increasingly become an internationally marketable commodity. A globalized market for goods and services has also resulted from rapid technological developments that have greatly diminished the costs of international transportation and communication, and international trade in manufacturing products has been boosted by the trend toward convergence in per capita incomes and demand patterns of industrial countries. There has also been a globalization of financial markets in that the pool of savings is worldwide and financial intermediaries know no international boundaries. Finally, American companies increasingly think in terms of the advantages of international plant location.

At the same time, as a counter to globalization, there are also increasing trends toward regionalism. Three major economic spheres have been formed or are in the process of being formed. The first is the European Union, consisting of fifteen member countries. Its major objectives are the free movement of people, services, and capital from one country to another; the free movement of goods through the elimination of tariffs; and the creation of a common currency, the euro. The second is the North American Free Trade Agreement (NAFTA), which includes the United States, Canada, and Mexico, with the objective of eliminating tariff barriers among the three countries. Finally, there is the Asia-Pacific Economic Cooperation (APEC), which was created in 1989. Its purpose is to remove all trade and investment barriers in the Asia Pacific area by 2020.

Other trading blocs are regional in nature. An example is MERCOSUR, which consists of the countries of Brazil, Argentina, Paraguay, and Uruguay. Its purpose is to promote freer trade among these countries by lowering tariff barriers. A similar regional trading bloc is the Andean Community, consisting of the countries of Bolivia, Colombia, Ecuador, Peru, and Venezuela. Its goal is to set a common external tariff among the five countries. Then there is the Caribbean Community (Caricom), which consists of fourteen small, formerly British colonies in the Caribbean and South and Central America. It started out as a free trade area and later became a customs union. Another example of a regional trading bloc is the Asian Free Trade Area, which includes Brunei, Indonesia, Malaysia, Philippines, Singapore, Thailand, and Vietnam. ASEAN started out as a preferential trade arrangement, granting preference margins on certain commodities. It became a free trade area in 1992.

Regional trading arrangements cover a spectrum ranging from preferential trade agreements, with GATT as an example, to economic union, with the European Union (EU) as an example. These arrangements are as follows:

1. Preferential Trade Arrangements (PTA): Preferential Trade Arrangements can range from giving trade preferences to a set of trading partners to all countries covered in an agreement.

2. Free Trade Area (FTA): The North American Free Trade Agreement (NAFTA), which includes Canada, Mexico, and the United States, is an example. Its objective is the eventual removal of tariffs and other trade barriers among the three countries; however, each country may establish its own trade policies with nonmember countries.

3. Customs Union (CU): A customs union is a higher level of integration. It occurs when the members of an FTA go beyond removing trade barriers among themselves and set a common level of trade barriers against outsiders. This could entail a common tariff on goods coming from other countries. It would set all trade policies for its members as a unified whole.

4. Common Market: A common market involves a higher stage of trade integration. It would not only include the free exchange of goods and services among members, but also the free movement of factors of production: labor and capital.

5. Economic Union (EU): It goes far beyond the free movement of goods, services, and the factors of production. It involves the creation of common national economic policies, including a common currency and taxes. The decision of the European Community (EC) in 1994 reflected the determination to proceed to this higher stage of integration. However, the full unification of economic policy, including the creation of a common currency, the euro, requires full political integration of all the countries involved in the economic union. Thus, the European Union involves both an economic union and a political union.

The European Union (EU)

The European Union (EU) is the largest regional trading bloc in the world. The fifteen countries comprising the EU have about 6 percent of the world's population, but account for 30 percent of the world's gross domestic product and 45 percent of the world's foreign trade. Table 15-1 presents the population, real per capita gross domestic product, and real gross domestic product

TABLE 15-1 POPULATION, REAL PER CAPITA GDP, AND REAL GDP FOR THE EUROPEAN UNION

COUNTRY	POPULATION (MILLIONS)	REAL PER CAPITA GDP (DOLLARS)	REAL GDP (MILLIONS OF DOLLARS)
Austria	8,072	22,010	177,665
Belgium	10,190	23,090	235,287
Denmark	5,284	23,450	123,910
Finland	5,140	19,660	101,052
France	58,607	22,210	1,301,075
Germany	82,071	21,170	1,737,443
Greece	10,522	12,540	131,946
Ireland	3,661	17,420	63,775
Italy	57,523	20,100	1,156,212
Luxembourg	422	—	—
Netherlands	15,807	21,300	336,689
Portugal	9,945	14,180	141,020
Spain	39,323	15,690	616,978
Sweden	8,849	19,010	168,219
United Kingdom	59,009	20,870	1,231,518
374,425			**7,522,789**

Source: The World Bank, *1999 World Bank Atlas* (Washington, D.C.: The World Bank, 1999), pp. 24, 25, 42, 43.

for each country. Germany and France are the two wealthiest countries, accounting for about 40 percent of the GDP of the European Union.

Members of the European Union have agreed to do five things. First, by combining both political and economic integration, the members have effectively transformed themselves into one country. Second, the members will integrate their economies by coordinating their economic policies through one central bank and one common currency, the euro. Third, the members will eliminate all barriers that restrict the movement of capital and labor among themselves. Fourth, the members will adopt a common trade policy toward nonmember countries. Finally, the member countries will create a free trade area by removing tariffs, import quotas and other barriers to international trade among themselves; however, each country can establish its own trade policies toward nonmember nations.[1]

HISTORY OF THE EUROPEAN UNION

The concept of a united Western Europe has been a major force since the end of World War II. The Benelux (Belgium, Netherlands, Luxembourg) customs union of 1944 was designed to remove tariffs on commodity trade among the countries. In 1950, Robert Schumann, French minister of foreign affairs, proposed that France and the Federal Republic of Germany[2] pool their coal and steel production under the auspices of a European organization that eventually became the European Coal and Steel Community (ECSC). It consisted of six countries—Belgium, France, the Federal Republic of Germany, Italy, Luxembourg, and the Netherlands—which in 1957 signed the Treaty of Rome establishing the European Economic Community (EEC) and the European Atomic Energy Commission (Euratom). The major reason for the creation of the EEC was to reduce tariff and other trade barriers among member countries. The Treaty of Rome together with the Treaty of Paris form the Constitution of the Economic Community.[3]

Between 1959 and 1979, a customs union was created. The first step was taken in 1959 when customs duties among the six countries were reduced.[4] The customs union was completed in 1968. It combined the elimination of internal barriers among the six countries with the adoption of common external trade policies toward nonmember countries. Thus, a firm from a nonmember country paid the same tariffs on exports to any member of the customs union. In 1969 at the Hague Summit, the leaders of the six countries called for an economic and monetary union and closer political ties. The European Economic Community became known as the European Community (EC), and in 1973 Denmark, Ireland, and the United Kingdom became members, raising the total to nine member countries. In 1974 the European Council was created, comprising the heads of state of each country, their foreign ministers, and key Community officials.

The European Monetary System   In 1979 a move toward an eventual monetary integration of the European Community was made through the creation of the European Monetary System (EMS), which was designed to coordinate the monetary policies of the member nations. It did two things, as follows:

1. It created the Exchange Rate Mechanism (ERM) that was designed to limit fluctuations among the EC currencies. For example, the franc could increase or decrease sharply in value against the mark. This worked to the disadvantage or advantage of the parties affected by the fluctuations of the currencies. Thus, most of the EMS members chose to participate in the ERM. They pledged to maintain fixed exchange rates among their currencies within a limit of ± 2.25 percent.[5] It was the responsibility of the central banks of the member countries to keep their currencies within the range of ± 2.25 percent. If German interest rates rose, then the interest rates of other countries had to rise; if German interest rates fell, the interest rates of the other countries also had to fall.[6]

2. It created the European Currency Unit (ECU). Its value was determined by a weighted "basket" of the currencies of the EC members based on the importance of their currencies in the world market. The German mark accounted for 32 percent of the value of the ECU, the French franc accounted for 20.4 percent, and the British pound accounted for 11 percent.[7] The ECU was a unit of account. It was important in international financial circles and had a value. It was used as a denomination for Eurobonds, traveler's checks, bank deposits, and loans. It also constituted bank reserves and could be moved from one bank to another. In 1992, the Maastricht Agreement created the ECU as a real currency designed eventually to replace the marks, francs, pounds, and pesos used by member nations. Eventually it became the euro.

Prelude to Maastricht   The period from 1979 to 1993 witnessed the expansion of the European Community beyond its original concept of a common market, where trade barriers would be lowered, toward a political and economic union. Greece was admitted to the EC in 1981 and Spain and Portugal were admitted in 1986. During this period, the European Commission, one of the governing bodies of the European Community, issued the White Paper on Completing the Internal Market. Its objective was to remove all trade barriers among member countries, and to promote the free movement of people, services, goods, and capital among countries. The Single European Act, confirming these objectives, was ratified in 1986 and set the goal for the creation of a single European market by December 31, 1992. Various trade barriers were removed, most passport controls were eliminated, and technical standards, which varied from country to country, were made uniform.

THE MAASTRICHT TREATY, 1991

In December 1991 leaders of the twelve EC member countries met in Maastricht, the Netherlands, to discuss the future of the EC. An agreement was worked out that would change the future of Europe. It was agreed that a common currency was required to cement a closer economic union similar to that of the United States. The advantage of a single currency would be the elimination of the exchange rate problems when the different currencies were exchanged for each other. This would benefit banking, business, and tourism. This new currency would go into effect on January 1, 1999. The treaty also laid down the framework of a future European government, with a common foreign and defense policy, a common parliament, and a common citizenship with the right to live, work, vote, and run for office anywhere within the EC. The treaty was ratified and became effective on November 1, 1993.

European Monetary Union (EMU)   The European Monetary Union is one part of the European Union. There are two major parts to the EMU which are as follows:

1. A new central bank called the European Central Bank (ECB) has replaced the central banks of the fifteen member countries and is based in Frankfurt, Germany. It has replaced the former German central bank (Deutsche Bundesbank), which to a large extent dictated monetary policies, not only for Germany but for Western Europe. The central banks of the EU member nations have lost their former autonomy and have come under the jurisdiction of the ECB. It is very similar to the U.S. monetary system in that the Federal Reserve is based in Washington and there are twelve Federal Reserve Banks located in major economic areas throughout the United States. The ECB coordinates monetary policy for the member nations.

2. On January 1, 1999, the euro became the official currency unit for eleven members of the European Union, thus providing the world with three major currencies—the dollar, the euro, and the yen. The old currencies of these countries will be no longer traded in international exchange markets around the world. European stocks and bonds are quoted in euros, and the

euro is increasingly used for bank transactions, business deals, and public finances. It also will be used for noncash transactions until the year 2002, when it will formally replace the old coins and notes of each of the eleven nations. Until that time, conversion rates of each currency into the euro has been set by the European Commission. For example, one euro = 1.95583 German marks, 6.5595 French francs and 1,936.27 Italian lira. The United Kingdom, Denmark, and Sweden opted out of accepting the euro because of public anxiety that dropping their national currencies would mean giving up too much independence. Greece did not meet the eligibility requirements.

The basic rationale for the euro was that it would eliminate the problem of currency conversion when transactions had to be made in different currencies. Tourists visiting Europe would have to exchange dollars for pounds when they were in England, pounds into marks if they visited Germany, and marks into lira if they visited Italy. These and other European currencies would fluctuate against each other daily. There was a cost in converting from one currency to another, and also a transactions risk. Contractual relationships between buyer and seller usually involve payment at some time in the future. An exporter in Germany would contract with an importer in France for payment in ninety days. By the time of payment, if the franc fell in value against the mark, the French importer would lose; if the mark fell in value against the franc, the German exporter would lose. By using the same currency unit, the euro, neither would lose.

It remains to be seen whether or not the euro and indeed the European Union will be successful. Supporters of the euro contend that a single currency will save Europeans $25 to $30 billion annually by eliminating exchange rate risks and the costs of exchanging different currencies. With the euro, foreign investors will have easier access to investment opportunities across a broad territory. And those investments will be priced in a single currency that is expected to be more stable than a number of different currencies. It represents the culmination of an effort that began after the end of World War II to promote peace by uniting the European economies. Finally, there are those analysts who predict that the euro will present the first serious challenge to the dollar since the dollar dethroned the British pound as the world's leading currency.

There are also critics of the euro who contend that it will not solve Europe's problems, which are a high unemployment rate and numerous rules and regulations that tend to stultify entrepreneurship. The euro has dropped 16.6 percent against the dollar since it was introduced on January 1, 1999. There is concern over the economic soundness of the European Union, in part attributable to the conflict in Kosovo. The euro is also supposed to facilitate a flow of investment from one European nation to another, but some nations may benefit while others may not. Finland, with an unemployment rate of 15 percent, should presumably benefit, but will not because it is expensive to hire Finnish labor. Under Finnish law, if a salary is $1,000 a month, an employer pays a tax payment of $900 to the Finnish government. Firing someone is very difficult, no matter the cause.

The Maastricht Treaty set up several financial criteria for membership into the European Union, as follows:

1. Budget deficits had to be below 3 percent of GDP.

2. The public ratio of debt to GDP had to be below 60 percent.

3. The inflation rate had to be no higher than 1.5 percentage points above the average of the three lowest-inflation countries in the union.

4. Long-term interest rates, as a measure of inflationary expectations, could not exceed by more than 2 percentage points those of the three best performing countries.

5. Candidates could not experience a devaluation in their currencies for at least two years. Austria, Finland, and Sweden were admitted as members to the EU in 1995, bringing the total to fifteen members. Norway was also accepted, but Norwegian voters voted against membership on two separate occasions. In 1997 the Treaty of Amsterdam was concluded. The treaty pledged that EU members would promote higher levels of employment, increase gender equality, achieve greater environmental protection, and strengthen consumer and social policies. Other measures included creating freer movement of persons in the EU and more effective ways of combating international crime.

FIGURE 15-1   EU MEMBERS

Figure 15-2   Eleven Nations Qualify for EURO

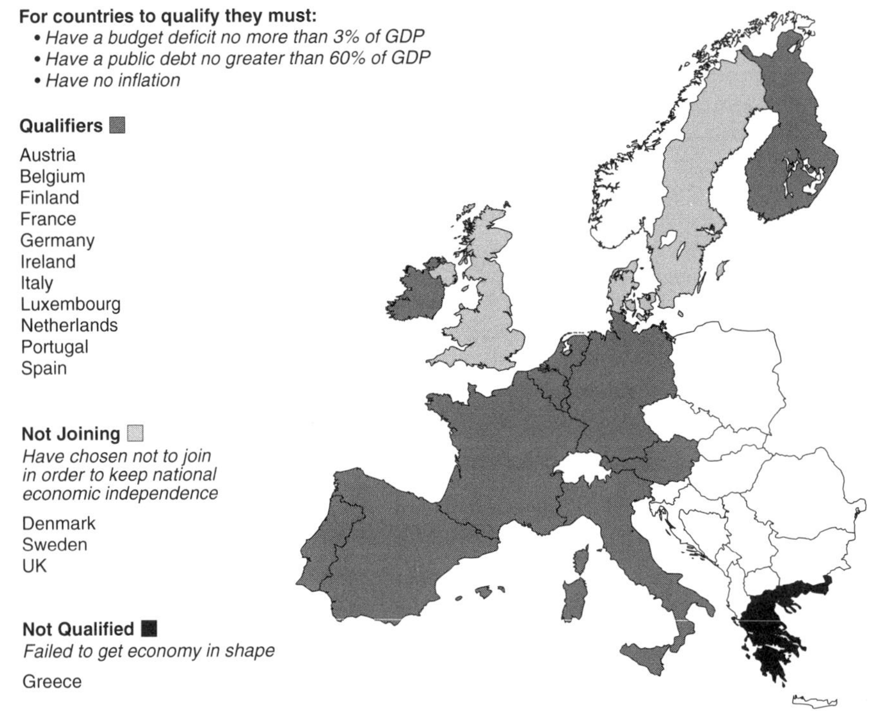

POLITICAL UNION

The political system of the European Union will become very much like that of the United States. It consists of the Council of the European Union, the European Commission, the European Parliament, and the European Court of Justice. There are now fifteen members. Austria, Sweden, and Finland became members in 1995, while Norway and Switzerland have opted out. Other countries, such as Poland, Hungary, and Slovenia have applied for membership in the EU, but their admission is unlikely in the immediate future. The functions of each component of the EU political system are as follows:

1. The European Council of Ministers: The European Council of Ministers is based in Brussels and consists of fifteen members who are selected by their home governments for a term of five years. Normally, a country's foreign minister represents his or her own country. The council presidency rotates among the members every six months. The council is the premier decision-making body of the EU but, unlike the United States where each state regardless of size has two senators, decision making in the EU is weighted toward those countries with the largest economies. In council decisions, France, Germany, Italy, and the United Kingdom have ten votes each, while Luxembourg, the country with the smallest economy, has two votes. Approval on proposals requires a unanimous or qualified vote, depending on the importance of the proposal.

2. The European Commission: Based in Brussels, the European Commission consists of twenty members selected to serve for five years. The larger countries get two members; the smaller countries get one. It has several major functions, which are as follows:

   a. It proposes legislation to be considered by the Council.

   b. It implements all EU treaties, including the Treaty of Rome.

   c. It has extensive legislative powers in implementing various internal agreements, such as the completion of the Common Agricultural Policy (CAP).

3. The European Parliament: The European Parliament is based in Strasbourg, France, and has 626 members who are directly elected by their respective countries, based on population size. Germany, the largest country, has 99 members, while the United Kingdom, France, and Italy have 87 each.[8] Members are elected for five-year terms. It is a consultative rather than a legislative body. It debates legislation proposed by the Commission and forwarded to it by the council. It can propose amendments to that legislation, but they are not binding on the Commission or the council.

4. The European Court of Justice: The European Court of Justice is based in Luxembourg and comprises one judge from each country. Like the Supreme Court of the United States, the Court of Justice is the supreme appeals court for EU law. It is also somewhat similar to the Supreme Court in that member nations' courts as well as our states' courts can refer their cases to it.

5. National Governments: The legislatures of each of the fifteen member nations implement approved proposals as their laws. They will collect taxes and commit revenues for state functions such as education and road building. The value-added tax, which is a tax levied on the value created at each stage of the production process, is the single most important tax used by the European countries.

THE TREATY OF ROME

The 1957 Treaty of Rome provides the legal base for the European Union. Its purpose is similar to that of the antitrust laws of the United States; namely, to provide rules of competition. The Commission enforces the Treaty. Its two major provisions are Article 85 and Article 86.

Article 85 prohibits agreements, contracts, cartels, and joint activities that intend to restrict or distort competition within the EU. Price-fixing, division of markets, tying arrangements, and price discrimination are all prohibited under Article 85. It does recognize the fact that some contracts benefit consumers by improving the production or distribution of goods or by promoting product improvement.

Article 86 bars one or more companies from using a dominant market position to restrict or distort trade. Prohibited abuses of dominant positions would include price-fixing and price discrimination. Either buyers or sellers can have dominant market positions. The Commission and the European Court of Justice have defined market dominance as the power to control suppliers and customers and the ability to prevent competition.

Most of the fifteen countries are civil law countries, using either the Napoleonic Code (France, Spain, Portugal) or the Germanic Code (Germany, Austria). These laws will remain intact.

THE IMPORTANCE OF THE EUROPEAN UNION TO THE UNITED STATES

The European Union is a major foreign trade rival of the United States. It forms the world's largest trading bloc, accounting for 30 percent of the value of world foreign trade. Table 15-2 provides a comparison of the monetary value of foreign trade to the European Union and its most important rival, NAFTA. The European Union is an important outlet for American goods and services, and an important supplier of the same to the United States. In terms of foreign investment, 40 percent of U.S. foreign direct investment is in the European Union countries, and over half of foreign direct investment in the United States comes from the European countries.

The United States, and for that matter Canada and Mexico, is bound to Europe by culture and history. The great majority of immigrants who came to this country during the latter part of the nineteenth century and the early part of the twentieth century came from Europe, and ties still remain. The Protestant and Catholic religions were exported from Europe to the United States. Democratic institutions exist in Europe and in the United States. Living standards in the United States and Europe are comparable, so there is a mass market for consumer goods that has promoted increased investment in Europe by U.S. business firms, and conversely by European business firms in the United States. As the European Union expands to take in more countries, its importance to the United States will increase.

For all practical purposes the world can be divided up into three major economic areas: the Euro Area, which consists of the eleven countries that have adopted the euro as their common currency, the United States, and Japan. The three most important currencies of the world are the euro, the dollar, and the yen. The combined population of the three areas is around 700 million, or about 12 percent of the world's population, and their combined share of GDP is around 65 percent. The three areas account for around one-third of the foreign trade of the world. Assuming that the United Kingdom, Denmark, and Sweden adopt the euro and Greece meets the eligibility requirements, the euro area and the European Union will be the same. Eventually, what you will have is a United Europe, the United States, and Japan accounting for the bulk of economic activity in the world.

THE NORTH AMERICAN FREE TRADE AGREEMENT (NAFTA)

The North American Free Trade Agreement (NAFTA) is not an economic union nor a political union as is the European Union. It has no common monetary unit, nor does it involve the complete economic and political integration of the

TABLE 15-2   U.S. EXPORTS TO THE EUROPEAN UNION AND IMPORTS FROM THE EUROPEAN UNION, 1998 (BILLIONS OF DOLLARS)

EXPORTS TO THE EUROPEAN UNION		IMPORTS FROM THE EUROPEAN UNION	
Belgium–Luxembourg	14.5	Belgium–Luxembourg	8.8
France	17.7	France	24.1
Germany	26.6	Germany	49.8
Ireland	5.6	Ireland	8.4
Italy	9.0	Italy	21.0
Netherlands	19.0	Netherlands	7.6
Spain	5.5	Spain	4.8
United Kingdom	39.1	United Kingdom	34.8
Other	12.5	Other	17.1
	149.5		**176.4**
Canada	156.3	Canada	174.8
Mexico	79.0	Mexico	94.7
NAFTA	**235.3**		**269.5**

Source: http://www.ita.doc/industry/otea/usfth/aggregate

three countries involved—the United States, Canada, and Mexico. It is simply a free trade area where the three countries have agreed to remove trade and other barriers to international trade among themselves. NAFTA was an extension of the Canada-U.S. Free Trade Agreement, which was signed in 1988 and entered into force in 1989. NAFTA was negotiated among the United States, Canada, and Mexico in 1992, ratified in 1993, and entered into force on January 1, 1994. It is an area that accounts for one-third of the world's GDP and 18 percent of world trade.

NAFTA is quite controversial in the United States. It passed in Congress by a fairly small margin after weeks of acrimonious debate. It was an issue in the presidential campaign of 1992 when Ross Perot gained much political capital by saying that the gigantic sucking sound you hear is the loss of American jobs to Mexico. It was also felt that America had little to gain by admitting Mexico into NAFTA. After all, it was argued, Mexico is a Third World country, with a standard of living much lower than ours or Canada's. Supporters of Mexico's admission to NAFTA argued that it would create jobs that were higher paying than those that were lost to Mexico. Tariffs would be lower and more manufactured goods would be sold to Mexico. Supporters also argued that American consumers would benefit from the import of lower-cost fruits and vegetables from Mexico.[9]

Tables 15-3, 15-4, and 15-5 (on page 284) present comparisons of NAFTA to the EU. Table 15-3 presents the population, real per capita GDP, and real GDP for the NAFTA countries compared to the EU. Table 15-4 presents U.S. direct investment in Canada and Mexico, and Canadian and Mexican direct investment in the United States for 1998. U.S. direct investment in the EU

TABLE 15-3   POPULATION, REAL PER CAPITA GDP, AND REAL GDP FOR NAFTA, 1998

COUNTRY	POPULATION (THOUSANDS)	REAL PER CAPITA INCOME (DOLLARS)	REAL GDP (MILLIONS OF DOLLARS)
United States	267,636	29,080	7,783,092
Canada	30,287	21,750	658,472
Mexico	94,349	8,110	765,170
	392,272		**9,206,734**
European Union	374,121		7,390,604

TABLE 15-4   U.S. DIRECT INVESTMENT IN CANADA AND MEXICO, AND CANADIAN AND MEXICAN DIRECT INVESTMENT IN THE UNITED STATES, 1998 (MILLIONS OF DOLLARS)

U.S. DIRECT INVESTMENT		DIRECT INVESTMENT OF CANADA AND MEXICO IN U.S.	
Canada	108,190	Canada	67,705
Mexico	28,676	Mexico	2,031
	136,866		**69,736**
European Union	423,812	European Union	411,008

Source: U.S. Department of Commerce, Bureau of Economic Analysis, "U.S. Direct Investment Abroad and Foreign Direct Investment in the U.S.," March 11, 1999.

TABLE 15-5   U.S. TRADE WITH CANADA AND MEXICO, 1998 (MILLIONS OF DOLLARS)

	EXPORTS	IMPORTS	TOTAL
Canada	156.3	174.8	331.1
Mexico	79.0	94.7	173.7
	235.3	**269.5**	**504.8**

Source: http://www.ita.doc/industry/oeta/usfth/aggregate

countries is much larger than it is in Canada and Mexico, and EU direct investment in the United States is much larger that Canadian and Mexican direct investment in the United States. Table 15-5 presents the foreign trade of the NAFTA countries for 1998. Canada is the most important U.S. trading partner, and U.S.-Canadian trade exceeds the entire amount of U.S.-EU trade. Mexico is the third most important U.S. trading partner. Furthermore, trade among the NAFTA countries is increasing at a more rapid rate than U.S. trade with the EU.

PROVISIONS OF NAFTA

There are several provisions to NAFTA, ranging from the elimination of tariffs and other barriers to the free flow of goods and services among the three countries, to cooperation on environmental problems. These provisions are presented as follows (starting on page 285):

Market Access

1. Within fifteen years after its implementation in 1994, all tariffs will be eliminated on North American products traded among Canada, Mexico, and the United States.
2. Within five years after its implementation, 65 percent of all U.S. exports of industrial goods to Mexico will enter tariff-free.
3. Mexico, once the treaty was implemented, would immediately eliminate tariffs on nearly 50 percent of all industrial goods imported from the United States.
4. Government procurement was to be opened up over ten years, with firms of the three countries able to bid on government contracts.[10]
5. Tariffs are to be removed on car imports over a period of ten years. Mexico's import quota on cars is also to be lifted during the same period.
6. Most tariffs between the United States and Mexico on agricultural products were eliminated immediately after implementation of the agreement in 1994.

Investment

1. NAFTA gives U.S. companies the right to establish firms in Mexico and Canada or acquire existing firms.
2. Investors have the right to repatriate profits and capital; the right to fair compensation in the event of expropriation;[11] and the right to international arbitration in disputes between investors and government that involve monetary damage.
3. NAFTA broadens investments to cover such areas as banking, real estate, legal services, consulting, publishing, and tourism.
4. Certain types of investments are restricted. Mexico prohibits foreign investment in petroleum and railroads;[12] Canada prohibits investment in its cultural media; and the United States excludes investments in aviation transport, maritime, and telecommunication.

Intellectual Property Rights

1. NAFTA requires each country to provide for the enforcement of the rights of authors, artists, and inventors against infringement and piracy.
2. It ensures protection for North American producers of computer programs, sound recordings, motion pictures, encrypted satellite signals, and other creations.
3. It locks in the availability of patent protection for most technologies in Mexico, allowing U.S. firms to patent a broad range of inventions in Mexico.

Environment   Environmentalist groups in the United States were opposed to NAFTA on the grounds that the Mexican government had done very little about controlling environmental problems. Major cities such as Mexico City, Guadalajara, and Monterrey had serious air pollution problems.[13] However, the main cause of environmental concern was the U.S.-Mexico border where maquiladora plants were operating from Matamoros to Tijuana.[14] These plants import unfinished goods or component parts from the United States, further process these goods or parts, and re-export them to the United States. The goods produced by maquiladoras enjoy preferential customs and tax treatments by both countries' governments. The plants by themselves create pollution, but they attract thousands of workers to such border cities as Matamoros, Juarez, and Tijuana, creating air and water pollution. To address this concern, the U.S. and Mexican governments created the Border Environmental Plan that covers air, water, hazardous materials, and ground pollution. Its objectives are as follows:

1. To strengthen existing environmental laws
2. To build waste water treatment systems
3. To create joint air pollution monitoring programs
4. To increase cooperative planning, training, and education

Protection for U.S. Workers

1. NAFTA provides a transition period of up to fifteen years for the elimination of U.S. tariffs on the most labor-sensitive U.S. products, such as household glassware, footwear, and some fruits and vegetables.
2. It provides safeguards that permit a temporary hike in U.S. tariff rates to pre-NAFTA levels to protect U.S. workers and farmers from being injured or threatened with injury by increased imports from Mexico.
3. It provides tough rules of origin to guarantee that the benefits of NAFTA tariff reductions go only to products made in North America.
4. It holds the three countries liable for penalties for nonenforcement of child labor, minimum wage, and health and safety laws.

Other Treaty Provisions

1. Any country can leave the treaty with six months' notice.
2. It allows for the inclusion of any additional country. Chile was to be invited to join in 1996, but there was little support for its membership.[15]

RESULTS OF NAFTA

The early years of NAFTA were affected by the Mexican currency crisis of December 1994. Mexico's trade deficit increased in 1993 and 1994 to the point that it was losing its foreign financial reserves. In December 1994, at a time when foreign exchange reserves held by the government had dropped from $26 billion to $7 billion, the peso, which had been tied to the dollar at an exchange rate of approximately 3.4 pesos to the dollar, was devalued by about 35 percent against the dollar. To shore up confidence in the Mexican financial system, the Clinton administration provided a $40 billion assistance package to guarantee the sale of Mexican government dollar-denominated Treasury bonds to foreign investors. The devaluation of the Mexican peso increased Mexican exports to the United States and Canada because they were cheaper than before. U.S. and Canadian exports to Mexico declined because they became more expensive.[16]

In general, criticisms of NAFTA have become rather subdued in the United States. The American economy has performed well, the unemployment rate

FIGURE 15-3 NAFTA—NORTH AMERICA

has fallen to its lowest level in twenty-five years, and the stock market is up, transforming many Americans into paper millionaires. U.S. exports to Mexico were up by 40 percent in 1998; conversely, Mexican exports to the United States increased by 19 percent in the same year. U.S. exports to Canada were up 16 percent and U.S. imports from Canada increased by 12 percent. Some U.S. jobs were lost to Mexico, but jobs were also created as a result of an increase in exports to Mexico and Canada. Typically, the jobs created by increased trade with Mexico are in the higher-paying, higher value-added industries, such as communications, and the jobs lost to Mexico have been in the lower-paying, lower value-added industries.

THE MERCADO COMUN DEL SUR (MERCOSUR)

On March 26, 1991, the Asuncion Treaty was signed by four South American countries—Argentina, Brazil, Uruguay, and Paraguay—to create a common market called the Mercado Comun del Sur. This market combines the two largest and most important countries in South America—Argentina and Brazil—with two of the smallest countries in South America—Paraguay and Uruguay. Two other countries, Bolivia and Chile, have also applied for admission to MERCOSUR. The common market encompasses over 60 percent of the population of South America, 60 percent of its land area, and 55 percent of its GDP. Table 15-6 (on page 288) presents the population, real per capita GDP, and the real GDP for these countries as of 1998.

REASONS FOR MERCOSUR

The performance of the Latin American countries, particularly when compared to the East Asian countries, was poor during the 1980s.[17] Inflation was high, economic growth rates were low, and currency instability was common.

TABLE 15-6   POPULATION, REAL PER CAPITA GDP, AND REAL GDP
OF THE MERCOSUR COUNTRIES, 1998

COUNTRY	POPULATION (THOUSANDS)	REAL PER CAPITA GDP (DOLLARS)	REAL GDP (MILLIONS OF DOLLARS)
Argentina	35,677	10,100	360,338
Brazil	163,689	6,350	1,039,425
Paraguay	5,085	3,860	19,628
Uruguay	3,266	9,110	29,753
Bolivia[1]	7,767	2,810	21,825
Chile[1]	14,622	12,240	178,973

[1]Associate members. They will join MERCOSUR in 2000.

Source: The World Bank, *1999 World Bank Atlas* (Washington, D.C.: The World Bank, 1999), pp. 24, 25, 42, 43.

Argentina had a negative growth rate during the 1980s. Its currency problems were so bad that the peso was replaced by a new currency called the astral. Brazil had borrowed heavily in the world capital markets, pledging future revenue from coffee as debt repayment, but the world price of coffee fell during the 1980s. Uruguay had its internal problems with urban terrorists, called the Tupumaros, who made a practice of kidnapping American businessmen. Paraguay was ruled by a military dictatorship and had one of the lowest living standards in South America.

PURPOSE OF MERCOSUR

The basic objective of MERCOSUR was to accomplish automatic tariff reductions to establish a common market by January 1, 1995. The countries agreed to give their firms preferential access to each other's markets and to cut internal tariffs over the period 1991–1995 on goods that accounted for 95 percent

FIGURE 15-4   MERCOSUR—SOUTH AMERICA

of intracountry trade. The formal customs union began on January 1, 1995. In that year, a common external tariff was introduced that would be phased in over a six-year period. At the same time, the four countries would have achieved the transition to a common market governed by the Common Market Council (CMC) and the Common Market Group (CMG).[18] A free trade agreement between Chile and MERCOSUR, with an eight-year phase-in on the majority of goods, was signed with Chile in June 1996 and with Bolivia in December 1996.

THE ASIA PACIFIC ECONOMIC COOPERATION (APEC)

The Asia Pacific Economic Cooperation (APEC) is the largest trade group in the world. It consists of 40 percent of the world's population, over half the world's GDP, and accounts for over half the world's foreign trade. As Table 15-7 indicates, it is a very diverse group, ranging from China, the largest country in the world, to Brunei with a population of 290,000. Using real GDP as a measurement of the size of an economy, it has the three largest economies in the world—the United States, China, and Japan. Unlike the EU, APEC covers an enormous amount of territory and distance. Geographically, Australia, Canada, China, and the United States are much larger in size than the EU. In terms of distance,

TABLE 15-7 POPULATION, REAL PER CAPITA GDP, AND REAL GDP FOR APEC COUNTRIES, 1998

COUNTRY	POPULATION (THOUSANDS)	REAL PER CAPITA GDP (DOLLARS)	REAL GDP (MILLIONS OF DOLLARS)
Australia	18,532	19,510	361,532
Brunei[1]	308	—	—
Canada	30,287	19,640	594,838
Chile	14,622	12,240	178,973
China	1,227,177	3,070	3,767,433
Hong Kong, China	6,502	24,350	158,324
Indonesia	200,390	3,390	679,322
Japan	126,091	24,400	3,077,629
Korea	45,991	13,430	617,659
Malaysia	21,667	7,730	167,659
Mexico	94,349	8,110	765,170
New Zealand	3,761	15,780	59,348
Papua New Guinea	4,501	2,820	12,693
Philippines	73,527	3,670	296,826
Singapore	3,104	29,230	90,729
Chinese Taipei[2]	—	—	—
Thailand	60,602	6,490	393,307
United States	267,636	29,080	7,782,855

[1]Brunei is an oil-rich country ruled by a sultanate.
[2]Taipei is the capital of Taiwan, which is not recognized as a country.
Source: The World Bank, *1999 World Bank Atlas* (Washington, D.C.: The World Bank, 1999), pp. 24, 25, 42, 43.

the EU is much more compact that APEC. Australia and Japan are more than half-way around the world from Canada and the United States. Most of the APEC countries are of little importance to the United States in terms of trade and investment.

So why, then, is APEC important enough for the United States to join? The answer is that, as both Presidents Bush and Clinton have said, the United States is a Pacific nation. As is shown in Table 15-8, the total value of U.S. foreign trade with China, Japan, Singapore, South Korea, and Taiwan was larger than that with the European Union. Also, until the Asian currency crisis, South Korea, Malaysia, Thailand, and Indonesia had much higher economic growth rates than most countries, and China had an average annual real growth rate of 10 percent during the period 1990–1999. Japan, before it developed serious economic problems, had outperformed the other major industrial countries. It can be assumed that the Asian countries will eventually rebound from their economic problems. Meanwhile, the fall in the value of the yen and other Asian currencies will increase U.S. imports, while adversely affecting the earnings of the U.S. companies in Asia.

CREATION OF APEC

APEC was formed in 1989 as an informal group of twelve countries, with the purpose of increasing economic cooperation in the Asian region. The first formal meeting of APEC was held in Seattle, Washington, in November 1993, and

TABLE 15-8 U.S. EXPORTS TO AND IMPORTS
FROM THE APEC COUNTRIES, 1998 (BILLIONS OF DOLLARS)

COUNTRY	EXPORTS	IMPORTS
Canada	156.3	174.5
Mexico	79.0	94.7
Japan	57.9	122.0
South Korea	16.5	23.9
Taiwan	18.2	33.1
Singapore	15.7	18.4
Hong Kong, China	12.4	10.5
China	14.3	71.1
Australia	11.9	5.4
Malaysia	9.0	19.0
Philippines	6.7	11.9
Thailand	5.2	13.4
Chile	4.0	2.5
	407.1	**600.4**
Total EU	149.5	176.4
Total Asian	187.6	367.9

Source: http://www.ita.doc.gov/industry/otea/usfth/aggregate/HI98t06,07.txt

was attended by President Clinton. The countries attending the meeting agreed to a broad vision of free trade and investment to be defined within a year. A second meeting was held in Bogor, Indonesia, in 1994, at which the countries agreed to a policy of free trade and investment by the year 2020. Subsequent meetings in Osaka, Japan, endorsed an action agenda that would provide a blueprint for the implementation of free trade. The agenda discussed at Osaka included customs standards, government procurement, rules of origin, mobility of workers, and the implementation of the Uruguay Round. At Subic, Philippines, in 1996, individual member countries published short- and medium-term plans that contained time frames for the elimination of trade and investment barriers by 2020. The 1997 APEC meeting in Vancouver, Canada, resulted in the liberalization of trade in fifteen key economic sectors, amounting to intra-APEC trade of $3 trillion. These sectors include chemicals, forest products, fish products, automotive, food, civil aircraft and others. Market-opening measures are to be implemented by 1999.

The Chinese Economic Area (CEA)   The CEA, composed of China, Hong Kong (now part of China), and Taiwan, all of which are separate members of APEC,[19] is the fastest economic growth area in the world. It is the second-largest economy of the world when measured by total real GDP, and the fifth-largest if measured by money GDP.[20] Real GDP for 1998 increased by 7.8 percent in China, 5.3 percent in Taiwan, and 3.2 percent in Hong Kong, compared to a world average of 1.4 percent. The combined trade of the CEA amounted to $900 billion in 1998, making it the fourth-largest trading area in the world.[21] As Table 15.8 indicated, the total value of U.S. trade with the CEA in 1998 was $159.6 billion, which made it the third most important trading partner of the United States. In terms of foreign direct investment, the United States had a total of $29 billion invested in the CEA in 1997, which is more than the combined total for Africa, Eastern Europe, and the Middle East.

CRITICISM OF REGIONAL TRADING BLOCS

Regional trading blocs have proliferated like dandelions. In addition to the EU, NAFTA, MERCOSUR, and APEC, there are others, including the following:

1. The Central American Common Market (CACM): CACM consists of the Central American countries of Costa Rica, El Salvador, Guatemala, Honduras, and Nicaragua, with a combined population of 32 million. It is a free trade area.

2. The Central European Free Trade Area (CEFTA): CEFTA consists of the countries of the Czech Republic, Hungary, Poland, Slovak Republic, and Slovenia, with a combined population of 66 million. With the exception of Slovenia, the other countries were formerly a part of the Council for Mutual Economic Assistance (CMEA), dominated by the former Soviet Union.[22] Free trade is to be phased in by the year 2000.

3. Southern Africa Development Community (SADC): SADC consists of twelve southern African countries, including South Africa, with a population of 145 million. Its objective is to eliminate tariff barriers in the region.

4. Common Market for Eastern and Southern Africa (COMESA): COMESA consists of twenty countries in Eastern and Southern Africa, with a population of 275 million. It began as a preferential trade area in 1981. Its goal is the creation of a common market by 2000 and eventually an economic union.

5. Australia-New Zealand Closer Economic Relations (ANZCERTA): ANZCERTA includes two countries with a combined population of 21 million and a GDP of $425 billion. Its purpose is to eliminate tariff and nontariff barriers, including subsidies and government procurement policies, on all trade between the two countries.

Regional trading blocs are criticized on the basis of their exclusivity. It is probably good for those countries who belong because it combines their interests toward achieving a common goal. However, by liberalizing trade only with their neighbors, countries are, by definition, discriminating against those not lucky enough to be asked to join the bloc. Some goods will be imported from other members of the free-trade area at the expense of producers elsewhere, and members will begin to specialize in areas in which they lack comparative advantage. Slow progress has also bedeviled regional trade integration. Despite much talk about expanding NAFTA to include every country in North America and South America by early in the twenty-first century, the membership in NAFTA remains stuck at three and will stay there for the foreseeable future. NAFTA also has complicated rules of origin requirements by stipulating how much of a car needs to be made in Mexico to qualify as NAFTA admissible.[23]

There are also arguments for regional trading blocs. The first argument is economic. Regions can achieve additional gains from the free flow of trade and investment among the member countries beyond those normally attainable through trade. They can specialize in the production of goods and services that they can produce most efficiently. Foreign direct investment can stimulate economic growth. In the case of NAFTA, investments in the three countries have increased since its inception in 1994. In that year U.S. direct investment in Canada was $72.8 billion; in 1998 it was $108.2 billion, a gain of 49 percent, while U.S. direct investment in Mexico increased from $16.4 billion in 1994 to $28.7 billion in 1998, a gain of 75 percent.[24] Conversely, Canadian investment in the United States increased from $43.2 billion in 1994 to $67.7 billion in 1998, a gain of 57 percent, while Mexican direct investment in the United States increased from $1.1 billion in 1994 to $2.0 billion in 1998, a gain of 83 percent.[25]

The second argument for regional trading blocs is political. A main argument for the creation of the European Union is that old enemies would be brought together as trading partners. Within a period of seventy years, France and Germany fought three major wars on French soil, with Germany as the invader. Italy and Austria have also been enemies and have gone to war over territorial claims. Political relationships between the United States and Mexico have been anything but smooth, and MERCOSUR brings together two old enemies, Argentina and Paraguay. Thus, by linking neighboring economies and making them more dependent on each other, incentives are created for political cooperation between the countries. In turn, the potential for violence between the countries is reduced.

SUMMARY

The world is rapidly merging into regional trading blocs. The most important one is the European Union, which is more than a trading bloc. Its goal is to achieve the complete economic and political integration of Western Europe. There is a common monetary currency called the euro. By January 2002 at the latest, the euro will become the currency of the European Union, and along with the dollar and the yen, will become a major world currency. It will also rival the United States and Japan as a world economic and political superpower. There will be the free movement of goods, services, and factors of production among the member countries. There will be one central bank, based in Frankfurt, Germany, which will coordinate monetary policy for the EU. Politically, there will be institutions somewhat similar to those of the United States. An example would be the Court of Justice, which is the supreme court of appeals for the EU.

The other regional trading blocs are not nearly as ambitious in their scope. NAFTA involves the regional integration of Canada, Mexico, and the United States into a free trade area. There is no common currency, no common political system, and no common central bank. NAFTA aims at the elimination of tariffs among its members, and the removal of most of the barriers on the cross-border flow of services. MERCOSUR is a customs union created by Argentina, Brazil, Uruguay, and Paraguay, and is to be expanded to include Chile and Bolivia. The Asia Pacific Economic Cooperation (APEC) involves the largest trading bloc in the world, and includes the United States, Japan, and China among its members. Its purpose is to lower tariffs and other trade barriers among its members. There are also a number of other regional trading blocs throughout the world.

QUESTIONS FOR DISCUSSION

1. Discuss the differences between NAFTA and the European Union.
2. Discuss the economic and political organization of the European Union.
3. What is the European Monetary Union? What is the euro and why was it created?
4. In what ways is the European Union of importance to the United States?

5. In terms of foreign trade, is the European Union or NAFTA more important to the United States?

6. In terms of foreign direct investment (FDI), is the European Union more important to the United States?

7. Has NAFTA been a success or a failure? Discuss.

8. What are the major provisions of NAFTA?

9. How does MERCOSUR differ from NAFTA?

10. Are regional trading blocs good or bad? Discuss.

NOTES

1. Many nonmember nations have preferential tariff agreements with member nations.

2. At that time, Germany became two independent nations: the Federal Republic of Germany (West Germany) and the German Democratic Republic (East Germany). After the end of World War II, Germany was split into four occupation zones controlled by the British, Americans, French, and Russians. The western part controlled by the British, Americans, and French became West Germany, a capitalist nation, and the Russian part became East Germany, a communist nation.

3. They also form the constitutional foundation of the European Union.

4. This was the first step toward the creation of a common external tariff.

5. In September 1992, the United Kingdom and Italy pulled out of the ERM. In August 1993, the 2.25 fluctuation band widened to 15 percent.

6. The Deutsche Bundesbank was the most powerful bank in Western Europe and the mark was the dominant currency.

7. As new members came in the weighting system was changed, but the mark remained the most important currency.

8. Luxembourg, the smallest country, has two.

9. This has occurred.

10. Some American firms have won bids in Mexico.

11. This has been an issue in Mexico and the United States since the Mexican government nationalized American and British oil companies in 1938.

12. Prohibition of foreign ownership of petroleum goes back to the Mexican constitution of 1917. The railroads, built by the Americans in the nineteenth century, were nationalized.

13. Mexico City is regarded as one of the most polluted cities in the world. The city has expanded its population from 3.2 million in 1950 to around 20 million in 1998. Air pollution is a serious problem.

14. Matamoros is at the entrance of the Rio Grande into the Gulf of Mexico, while Tijuana is across the border from San Diego. The distance between the two cities is about 2,000 miles.

15. Chile is a member of APEC and soon will be a member of MERCOSUR. It has the highest real per capita income of all the Latin American countries.

16. American and Canadian firms operating in Mexico lost money because they had to exchange cheaper pesos for more expensive dollars.

17. The growth rates of three of the four countries were negative for the decade. By contrast, the growth rate of South Korea was 8.8 percent for the decade.

18. The MERCOSUR countries have also committed themselves to the creation of the South American Free Trade Area (SAFTA), which will include the other South American countries.

19. Taiwan is claimed by China, and does not enjoy diplomatic recognition as a country.
20. The World Bank, World Development Report 1999/2000 (Washington, D.C.: The World Bank, 1999), pp. 230, 231.
21. International Monetary Fund, *World Economic and Financial Surveys, World Economic Outlook* (Washington, D.C.: International Monetary Fund, May 1999), pp. 173–177.
22. CMEA consisted of the Soviet Union and the Soviet-bloc countries of East Germany, Poland, Czechoslovakia, Hungary, Romania, and Bulgaria. Most foreign trade was among the members in the form of barter arrangements.
23. NAFTA specifies that, for an automobile to qualify as a North American product, 62.5 percent of its value must be produced in Canada, Mexico, or the United States.
24. U.S. Department of Commerce, Bureau of Economic Analysis. "U.S. Direct Investment Abroad, 1998."
25. U.S. Department of Commerce, Bureau of Economic Analysis, "Foreign Direct Investment in the U.S., 1998."

RECOMMENDED READING

The euro became the currency for eleven European countries in 1999. The following articles are recommended:

"Fanfare for the Euro." *The Economist*, May 2, 1998, pp. 45–46.

"Who Wants the Euro and Why." *The Economist*, May 2, 1998, pp. 52–53.

Not everyone is convinced that the European Union will succeed. For opposing views, see Dornbusch, Rudi. "Euro Fantasies." *Foreign Affairs*. Vol. 75, No. 5 (September–October 1996), pp. 110–124.

Soros, George. "Can Europe Work?" *Foreign Affairs*. Vol. 75, No. 5 (September/October 1996), pp. 8–14.

Books on the European Union and regional integration:

Kenen, Peter B. *Economic and Monetary Union in Europe*. Cambridge, England: Cambridge University Press, 1996.

Lipsey, Richard G. and Patricia Meller, eds. *Western Hemisphere Trade Integration*. New York: St. Martin's Press, 1997.

Criticisms of regional integration:

Nader, Ralph and Lori Wallack, "GATT, NAFTA, and the Subversion of the Democratic Process," *U.S. Trade Policy and Global Growth*, R. A. Blecker, ed. New York, Economic Policy Institute, pp. 93–96.

"Spoiling World Trade." *The Economist*. December 7, 1996, pp. 15–16.

Ferguson, Miall and Laurence J. Kotlikoff. "The Degeneration of the EMU" *Foreign Affairs* vol. 79, no. 7 (March–April 2000), pp. 110–121.

CHAPTER 16

THE AMERICAN ECONOMY

In 1999, the American economy was the healthiest it had been in three decades. The unemployment rate was the lowest it had been in twenty-five years, and the core inflation rate was the lowest it had been in thirty years. The rate of economic growth in 1997 was the highest it had been in almost a decade, and it continued to remain high through 1999. More than 14 million new jobs have been created since 1990, and the rate of poverty has declined. The stock market has kept hitting new highs month after month, making paper millionaires out of many Americans. Japan, the main competitor of the United States and picked by many experts to be the dominant world economic power in the twenty-first century, has developed serious economic problems that may take many years to resolve. Meanwhile, the European Union is in the process of becoming the United States of Europe, with a common currency and a common economic and political system.

A number of institutional arrangements characterize the American economic system. These arrangements reflect a set of basic beliefs that define how a society should be organized, how goods and services should be produced, and how income should be distributed. In the United States these beliefs are incorporated into the institutional arrangements that typify a capitalist market system—private enterprise, the profit motive, the price system, competition, individualism, and consumer sovereignty. Private enterprise is the linchpin of the American economy: It creates the great majority of jobs in the American economy. It involves the ownership of the factors of production—land, labor, and capital. And linked to private enterprise is the profit motive that drives production managers to produce goods that can be sold at prices that are higher than the costs of production.

PRIVATE ENTERPRISE

Private enterprise can range from large global enterprises, with thousands of employees, to a street vendor selling hot dogs. Many industries in the United States are dominated by a few large companies, for example, the soft drink industry that is dominated by Coca-Cola and PepsiCo. In other industries, there are a large number of small firms. There is freedom of ingress and egress in these industries. Anyone with an idea and capital is free to start his or her own business. There is the right to succeed and the right to fail, and many do fail.[1]

LARGE CORPORATIONS

The concentration of many industries in the hands of a few firms is a fact of life in the United States and other industrial nations. The trend toward industrial concentration in this country began in the last century, when many industries came to be dominated by large firms. In the 1920s corporate largeness was stimulated by changes that were occurring in the economy, in particular the mass production of automobiles. Size came to have an advantage from the standpoint of using modern management and marketing techniques. World War II also contributed to the trend toward largeness. Large corporations produced the airplanes and tanks used by the United States and its allies in the war. The trend toward largeness has continued unabated through the latter part of this century.[2]

Table 16-1 presents a comparison of the assets of large corporations to the total assets of the industries they represent. In the table, corporations with assets of $250 million or more are considered to be large corporations. In particular, manufacturing, transportation and public utilities, wholesale and retail trade, and finance, insurance, and real estate are the industries dominated by large companies.

TABLE 16-1   COMPARISON OF THE ASSETS OF LARGE CORPORATIONS TO TOTAL CORPORATE ASSETS BY INDUSTRIES, 1996 (MILLIONS OF DOLLARS)

INDUSTRY	TOTAL	250 MILLION AND OVER
Agriculture, forestry, and fishing	94,140	13,512
Mining	299,106	241,827
Construction	284,595	43,462
Manufacturing	5,425,185	4,669,946
Transportation and public utilities	2,069,953	1,895,800
Wholesale and retail trade	2,016,232	1,621,719
Finance, insurance, and real estate	17,360,053	15,722,111
Services	1,092,310	612,500

Source: U.S. Department of Commerce, Bureau of the Census, *Statistical Abstract of the United States, 1999* (Washington, D.C.: U.S. Government Printing Office, 1999), p. 551.

Moreover, most large American corporations are multinational, meaning they operate all over the world and have no geographical boundaries. Firms that have become multinationals tend to be engaged in certain kinds of business activities:[3] oil production, pharmaceuticals, chemicals, automobile production, electronic products, and prepared foods. Multinationals are also likely to exist in industries whose product market is often dominated by a relatively few firms, such as the world automobile industry, consisting of around a dozen major firms, all of which operate in global markets. Another example would be the U.S. pharmaceutical industry, dominated by such firms as Merck, Pfizer, Bristol-Myers, and Warner-Lambert, all of which operate in many foreign markets. Finance is another area in which multinationals abound. The large American banks have branches all over the world. Citicorp is an example.

But as Table 16-2 indicates, the United States has no monopoly on multinational corporations, because many are as likely to be Japanese as American. There are some very large German, British, Swiss, and French multinationals,

TABLE 16-2   REVENUES OF THE 15 LARGEST GLOBAL CORPORATIONS FOR 1997 (MILLIONS OF DOLLARS)

FIRM	COUNTRY	TOTAL REVENUES
General Motors	U.S.	178,174.0
Ford	U.S.	153,627.0
Mitsui[1]	Japan	142,688.3
Mitsubishi[1]	Japan	128,922.3
Royal Dutch Shell	British/Dutch	128,141.7
Itochi[1]	Japan	126,631.9
Exxon	U.S.	122,379.0
Wal-Mart	U.S.	119,299.0
Marubeni[1]	Japan	111,121.2
Sumitomo[1]	Japan	102,395.2
Toyota Motors	Japan	95,137.0
General Electric	U.S.	90,840.0
Nissho Iwai[1]	Japan	81,893.8
International Business Machines	U.S.	78,508.0
Nippon Telegraph and Telephone[2]	Japan	76,983.7

COUNTRY		MONEY GDP
Denmark		168,917.0
Norway		151,918.0
South Africa		132,455.0

[1]These companies are Japanese combines called keiretsu, or trading companies called Sogo Shosha.
[2]Nippon Telephone and Telegraph is state-owned.
Sources: *Fortune,* "The World's Largest Corporations," August 3, 1998, p. F-1; The World Bank, *1998 World Bank Atlas* (Washington, D.C.: The World Bank, 1998), pp. 42 and 43.

such as British Petroleum, Shell, Nestle (Swiss), Hoechst (German), Pechiney (French), Daimler-Benz (German [it is now Daimler-Chrysler due to a 1999 merger]), Volkswagen (German), Renault (French), Siemans (German), and Credit Suisse (Swiss). Many of these large corporations have a volume of sales larger than the GDP of most of the countries of the world. General Motors, with total sales of more than $189 billion in 1999, was larger than the GDP of 182 of the 205 countries of the world. Its sales were larger than the GDPs of Denmark and Norway, and four times as large as that of South Africa, the richest country in Africa.

SMALL ENTERPRISES

There are also millions of small and medium-sized firms that provide employment for the majority of American workers, as well as much of the innovation necessary for international competition. The number of small companies is increasing, in part as a result of downsizing by large corporations. Former employees create new companies that find a niche in areas once dominated by corporate giants. In addition, small family-owned companies use new technology to carve out market niches in many industries, exploiting the latest technology, employing highly skilled workers, and utilizing sophisticated managerial techniques. Moreover, as the United States becomes a more service-oriented economy, opportunities have increased for consulting firms. A breakdown of employees and payrolls by employment size is presented in Table 16-3.

TABLE 16-3 EMPLOYEES AND PAYROLLS BY EMPLOYMENT-SIZE FIRMS, 1996

EMPLOYMENT-SIZE EMPLOYEES	(THOUSANDS)
Under 20 employees	26,115
20 to 99 employees	29,697
100 to 499 employees	26,086
500 to 999 employees	7,274
1000 or more employees	13,026
Total employment	**102,199**
ANNUAL PAYROLLS	(BILLIONS OF DOLLARS)
Under 20 employees	647
20 to 99 employees	747
100 to 499 employees	730
500 to 999 employees	240
1000 or more employees	485
Total payroll	**2,849**

Source: U.S. Department of Commerce, Bureau of the Census, *Statistical Abstract of the United States, 1999* (Washington, D.C.: U.S. Government Printing Office, 1999), p. 555.

Unions

Workers in the United States and other countries have not been content to rely solely on market forces to determine their economic status. Instead, they have banded together to form labor unions for the purpose of bargaining collectively with employers. The workers' need for a job is not reduced, but under collective bargaining an employer must deal with labor as a unit, not as separate individuals. Labor unions vary in strength and importance in the world's major industrial nations. In Germany, they participate in their employers' decision-making process through the policy of codetermination, which allows labor representatives to sit on management boards.[4] On the other hand, labor unions in Japan are little more than company unions and have little to say in management decision making.

Unions in the United States hit their peak in terms of membership during the 1940s and 1950s and then began a slow decline as the country shifted from a goods-producing society to a service society. This shift represented a change in the type of work people do, from physically intensive labor to knowledge-intensive labor. In 1945 almost half the American labor force was employed in manufacturing jobs; by 1999 the number of manufacturing jobs had declined to 16 percent. Conversely, the number of persons employed in service-producing jobs have more than doubled since 1945. The majority of jobs today are knowledge-based white-collar jobs, not blue-collar jobs, and white-collar workers tend to identify more with management than with labor. Many union jobs were lost in the automobile and steel industries during the 1970s and 1980s as foreign competition began to erode U.S. markets.

The Increased Role of Government

The point has been made in earlier chapters that various elements have combined over time to transform pure laissez-faire capitalism into what can be referred to as "state-guided" capitalism. Various forms of regulation became necessary to correct certain flaws in the market system. Antitrust laws became necessary to protect the public against the abuse of monopoly power. Social regulation came into being because the market mechanism was not effective in eliminating certain social problems, such as employment discrimination. Social Security measures became necessary during the Depression of the 1930s to protect workers against the loss of income from unemployment and to provide older workers with income when they retired. But one area of government responsibility has not been discussed, and that is the responsibility for the maintenance of economic stability.

The Employment Act of 1946

The Employment Act of 1946 is a watershed act in that it gave congressional sanction to the idea that the federal government is responsible for the nation's level of income and employment. Prior to that time, it was held that it was the responsibility of the individual to look out for himself or herself. The mass un-employment of the Depression changed that attitude. The federal government created a number of employment projects to put people to work.[5] World War II ended but did not solve the problem of unemployment, and after the war was over, it was predicted that discharged veterans would be unemployed and there would be a reversion back to the mass unemployment of the Depression.[6] The solution to this problem would have to come from the federal government, and the federal budget would be the key instrument in solving the problem.

KEYNESIAN ECONOMICS

In 1936 the British economist John Maynard Keynes published *The General Theory of Employment, Interest, and Money*.[7] Only Adam Smith's *Wealth of Nations* and Karl Marx's *Das Kapital* have had as much impact on economic and polit-ical thinking as *The General Theory* did, but it was some years before its analy-sis was accepted by policymakers in the United States and Europe. Keynes took the position that there was nothing inherent in a market system that would as-sure a level of resource use consistent with full employment. The interaction of the forces of supply and demand would correct any failure to create the full use of resources, including labor.[8] The Depression proved otherwise because un-employment remained high for an extended period of time.

In Keynesian economic theory, the level of output is linked to an econo-my's total output of goods and services. The volume of output, in turn, de-pends on the level of income and aggregate demand. The catalyst in the Keynesian framework, at least in the short run, is aggregate demand. It is at one and the same time the source of total income and the basis on which the level of employment is determined. If demand is not sufficient to employ all avail-able resources, income will be lower than it need be. As demand falls, so will income, and as income falls, so will output and employment. The key to eco-nomic stability is to maintain income at a level consistent with high employ-ment of labor and resources.

Since income is derived from demand, what are the components of aggre-gate demand? There are two main components, consumption and investment. Consumption (C) is consumer demand for goods and services, and investment (I) is business firms' investment demand for capital goods. There is also a third component, government (G) demand for goods and services, and a fourth com-ponent, foreign trade (X–M), where X represents income from exports and M represents income going out of the country for imports. The Keynesian equa-tion can be expressed as follows:

Y = C + I + G + X–M

where Y = Total output of an economy

C = Consumption expenditures

I = Investment expenditures

G = Government expenditures

X–M = Exports minus imports

IMPLICATIONS FOR PUBLIC POLICY

Keynesian economic theory repudiated laissez-faire economics and accepted government intervention as the prime requisite for economic stability: There had to be more government intervention in life. The first objective was to reduce unemployment through the use of government fiscal and monetary policies that would stimulate consumption and investment. Prosperity could be achieved through a more equitable and less arbitrary distribution of income through progressive income taxation and various social welfare measures designed to increase consumption through an increase in consumer purchase power. The Keynesian view that inequality of income is a barrier to the creation of new wealth reversed the traditional notion that the accumulation of wealth depended on the savings of the rich. Progressive income taxes were to be used to redistribute wealth.

ACCEPTANCE OF KEYNESIAN ECONOMICS IN THE UNITED STATES

It is commonly believed that Keynesian economics, or the "new economics," as it was called by many, was introduced in the United States by the Kennedy administration. There was an intellectual revolution in economic policymaking at that time, based on the belief that a steadily growing, fully employed economy was both desirable and attainable, and that fiscal and monetary policies could contribute greatly to full employment and economic growth. Fiscal policy measures, as practiced by the Kennedy and Johnson administrations, were directed largely toward influencing the level of aggregate demand so as to bring it into line with the goal of stimulating economic growth. Of major concern in the early 1960s was the low rate of U.S. economic growth in comparison to that of the Soviet Union. The growth rate was an issue in the 1960 campaign, and the Democratic Party's national platform promised to raise it to 5 percent a year.

The Revenue Act of 1964   The Revenue Act of 1964 was a classic example of the application of Keynesian economic policy. The purpose of the act was to provide a stimulus to the American economy through the use of tax cuts. Income tax rates were reduced for all individuals and corporations. Personal income tax rates were cut by more than 20 percent and corporate income taxes by about 8 percent. Personal withholding rates were reduced by the full amount as early as March 1964. The Revenue Act was aimed at the demand side rather than the supply side of the American economy, and its main objective and achievement was to put productive capacity to work by raising the level of private aggregate demand. Effects on the productive capacity of the country were largely incidental, but nonetheless important.

REAGANOMICS

Reaganomics, or as it is commonly called "supply-side economics," was a reaction against the "demand-side" economics that had guided government stabilization policies in the United States and Europe. The Keynesian prescriptions—tax tinkering and government spending to stimulate aggregate demand—became an article of faith in the West. Everything was fine when demand was slack and unemployment was on the increase. But during the 1970s, stagflation—a term applied to low growth and inflation—was the problem. Supply-siders wanted to place more attention on the supply side of the economy to stimulate investment and economic growth. They wanted to reduce taxes, thus increasing the rate of saving and investment. Given the right incentives, they felt the free market would do a better job than government in stimulating economic growth.[9]

There were five components of Reaganomics—a large across-the-board tax cut, a cut in social welfare spending, an increase in defense expenditures, less government regulation, and restricted growth in the money supply. The tax cut reflected a belief in the efficacy of supply-side economics. The cuts were designed to favor people with incomes of $50,000 or more annually, because they provided the bulk of savings in the United States. Savings were supposed to increase and be channeled into investment.[10] This was supposed to create a tax cut from savings to investment to increased productivity. Increases in defense expenditures were not designed for economic reasons but had the effect of increasing the deficit in the federal budget because they were larger than cuts in civilian spending.

Results of Reaganomics   President Reagan will probably be regarded as one of the most popular and charismatic U.S. presidents of the twentieth century, but there is controversy concerning his performance as president. Those who think he was a good president point to the prosperity of the country and credit increased defense spending as being ultimately responsible for the collapse of the Soviet economy. His critics point to the massive increase in the federal debt, the Iran-Contra scandal, and increased inequality of income distribution. The truth, as in most controversies, lies somewhere in the middle.

Tables 16-4 and 16-5 (on page 304) summarize some of the economic results of Reaganomics. The average unemployment rate was higher during the Reagan years than it was during the 1970s, although it did start to fall after 1983. The average rate of economic growth was about the same for both periods; however, for the years 1983 through 1988, growth rates were higher than the average for 1970–1979. It is in the area of inflation that Reaganomics enjoyed its greatest success. When Reagan was first elected president in 1980, the most important problem confronting the American economy was the rate of inflation. The consumer price index increased at a rate of 13.3 percent in 1979 and 12.4 percent in 1980. The average rate of inflation was 4.2 percent compared to 7.1 percent for the period 1970–1979. Monetary policy was changed on several occasions. It was restrictive for the first year and inflation was reduced. Unemployment increased in 1982 and 1983, and the Federal Reserve eased the money supply and interest rates fell. Interest rates were later raised to prevent inflation and then lowered in the period from late 1984 to late 1988.

TABLE 16-4   COMPARISON OF ECONOMIC INDICATORS IN THE 1970S AND 1980S (PERCENT)

YEARS	UNEMPLOYMENT	ECONOMIC GROWTH	INFLATION
1970–1979	6.2	2.8	7.1
1980	7.1	0.0	12.5
REAGAN YEARS			
1981	7.6	2.5	8.9
1982	9.7	–1.9	3.8
1983	9.6	4.2	3.8
1984	7.5	7.3	3.9
1985	7.2	3.9	3.8
1986	7.0	3.4	1.1
1987	6.2	3.5	4.4
1988	5.5	4.2	4.4
Reagan average	**7.5**	**3.4**	**4.3**

Source: *Economic Report of the President 2000* (Washington, D.C.: U.S. Government Printing Office, 2000), pp. 309, 354, 378.

TABLE 16-5   INCREASE IN THE FEDERAL GOVERNMENT DEFICIT AND DEBT DURING THE REAGAN YEARS (BILLIONS OF DOLLARS)

FISCAL YEARS	DEFICIT	DEBT	DEBT AS A PERCENT OF GDP
1970	–2.8	380.9	36.7
1971	–23.0	408.2	36.3
1975	–53.2	541.9	33.3
1978	–59.2	776.6	33.9
1979	–40.7	829.5	32.4
1980	–73.8	909.1	32.6
REAGAN YEARS			
1981	–79.0	994.8	32.6
1982	–128.0	1,137.3	35.4
1983	–207.8	1,371.7	40.1
1984	–185.4	1,564.7	41.0
1985	–212.3	1,817.5	44.3
1986	–221.2	2,120.6	48.5
1987	–149.8	2,346.1	50.1
1988	–155.2	2,601.3	52.5
Increase during Reagan years		**1,606.5**	**261.5**

Source: *Economic Report of the President 2000* (Washington, D.C.: U.S. Government Printing Office, 2000), p. 397.

The premise on which supply-side economics was based was that a tax cut favoring the upper-income groups would increase saving that would flow into investment and increase spending. The increase in spending would raise tax revenue back to the level it was before the tax cut. However, as Table 16-5 indicated, things did not work out the way they were supposed to. The federal debt, which was $909.4 billion in 1980, increased to $2,601.3 trillion in 1988. Deficits increased in the budget because expenditures were larger than expected tax revenues. Much of the increase in spending was on national defense. Spending was supported by deficit financing, which involved the sales of U.S. Treasury securities to Americans and foreigners. There was also a negative trade balance, as U.S. imports exceeded U.S. exports. The United States became a debtor nation in 1986, the first time since 1914. Conversely, Japan became the world's leading creditor nation.

THE PERFORMANCE OF THE AMERICAN ECONOMY IN THE 1990s

In many respects, the last decade of this century was comparable to the decade of the 1920s, in that both were affluent. The prosperity of the 1920s was based on the automobile industry that created the development of related industries such as steel, glass, rubber, and chemicals. The stock market was the vehicle to riches in the 1920s as it has been in the 1990s; however, the stock market of the 1920s collapsed, ushering in the Depression of the 1930s. The 1980s ended with the prediction that Japan would replace the United States as the world's leading superpower in the twenty-first century. American industry was held to be uncompetitive, particularly against Japanese industry. But all this changed rather dramatically in less than a decade. Financial crises have created serious problems in Japan and in other East Asian countries.

THE BUSH ADMINISTRATION, 1989–1992

In November 1988, George Bush was elected president of the United States. His record during his one term in office was mixed. He initiated certain regulatory reforms. The Energy Policy Act of 1992 encouraged competition among firms that generated electricity, and the Federal Communications Commission was given new authority to stimulate competition in the communications industry. The Americans with Disabilities Act (ADA), passed in 1990, was designed to prevent discrimination against individuals with disabilities and to provide them with equal access to public services. The Civil Rights Act of 1991 was passed and it broadened the scope of antidiscrimination law by expanding civil rights protection for employees. In particular, the law made it possible for women to obtain more damages for various discriminatory practices, including sexual harassment.

There was the feeling during this time that the United States was losing its competitive edge in world markets and was in danger of being replaced by Japan as the world economic leader. A Council on Competitiveness was created for the purpose of ascertaining how American firms could be made more competitive in international markets. Among various issues that were discussed was whether or not to adopt an industrial policy similar to the one used in Japan to achieve success in world markets. Industrial policy involves the choosing of a particular industry or industries to emphasize at a point in time. It outlines the basic strategy a nation intends to follow to achieve economic growth and meet foreign competition. The council had overall authority to review all new rules proposed by regulatory agencies to determine their cost effectiveness.

Table 16-6 compares the economic performance of the Bush and Clinton administrations as measured by inflation, unemployment, and the rate of increase in real GDP. Bush economic policy did not deviate much from Reagan economic policy. The inflation rate, which was 4.6 percent in 1989, was reduced to 2.7 percent in 1992. Conversely, the unemployment rate increased from 5.3 percent in 1989 to 7.5 percent in 1993. The real rate of growth in GDP ranged from a high of 3.4 percent in 1989 to a low of –.9 percent in 1992. In that year it was the highest of all the industrial countries. The stock market was in the beginning of a bull market that continued through the decade.

THE CLINTON ADMINISTRATION

President Clinton will be remembered as one of the most controversial presidents of the twentieth century. His achievements were significant. He was responsible for the ratification of the agreement that made the United States a member of NAFTA. He revised the tax system and antitrust enforcement

TABLE 16-6   FEDERAL GOVERNMENT DEFICIT AND DEBT DURING THE BUSH AND CLINTON YEARS (BILLIONS OF DOLLARS)

FISCAL YEARS	DEFICIT	DEBT	DEBT AS A PERCENT OF GDP
BUSH YEARS			
1989	–152.5	2,868.0	53.6
1990	–221.2	3,206.6	56.4
1991	–269.4	3,598.5	61.4
1992	–290.4	4,002.1	65.2
CLINTON YEARS THROUGH FISCAL 2000			
1993	–255.0	4,351.4	67.2
1994	–203.1	4,643.7	67.8
1995	–163.9	4,921.0	68.3
1996	–107.5	5,181.9	68.8
1997	–21.9	5,369.7	67.4
1998	69.2	5,478.7	67.5
1999	124.4	5,606.1	66.2
2000	166.7	5,686.3	65.8

Source: *Economic Report of the President 2000* (Washington, D.C.: U.S. Government Printing Office, 2000), p. 397.

increased significantly during his terms in office. The American economy prospered while he was in office. Inflation and unemployment have been reduced to thirty-year lows and the stock market has reached record highs.[11] In comparison to Europe and Japan, the American economy performed very well. While unemployment declined in the United States, it increased in Europe, but particularly in France and Germany. In March 2000, the American unemployment rate was 4.1 percent compared to 10.5 percent in France and 10.0 percent in Germany.[12] In terms of industrial production and consumer price stability, the United States outperformed both the European Union and Japan.

Clinton did not get a majority of the popular vote in the national elections of 1992 and 1996, and the Democrats lost control of the House of Representatives and the Senate in 1994. One of his failures during the first two years of his administration involved health care, which has become increasingly expensive. General Motors, for example, estimated that it costs about $1,000 per car to pay its health care bill, compared to about $200 per car for Japanese car companies. Such high health care costs caused many large businesses to lobby for health care reform. President Clinton's proposed national health care system with the creation of new federal programs met opposition from small businesses, who contended that the cost would put many of them out of business, and eventually national health insurance was dropped from his agenda.

However, President Clinton's greatest accomplishment may be the balancing of the federal budget. Ever since the deficit soared in the 1980s, successive presidents and Congress have tried to cut it, but have had little success. In 1985, Congress enacted the Balanced Budget and Emergency Deficit Control Act, better known as Gramm-Rudman-Hollings. It set annual deficit targets for five years, declining to a balanced budget by 1991. However, faced with the prospect of huge spending cuts in 1987, President Reagan and Congress amended the law, postponing a balanced budget until 1993. This revised goal was never achieved, in part because of the high cost of bailing out the savings and loan industry. In 1990, President Bush and Congress enacted spending cuts and tax increases designed to cut the accumulated deficits by about $500 billion over five years.[13] They also enacted the Budget Enforcement Act (BEA).

The BEA set annual limits on total discretionary spending for defense, international affairs, and domestic spending. Second, it created pay-as-you-go rules for entitlements and taxes: Those who proposed new spending on entitlements or lower taxes were forced to offset the costs by cutting other entitlements or raising other taxes. It did in fact limit discretionary spending and force proponents of new entitlements and tax cuts to find ways to finance them. But the deficit continued to rise because federal health care spending grew rapidly.[14] In 1993, President Clinton and Congress made another effort to cut the deficit. They enacted a five-year deficit reduction package of spending cuts and higher revenues. The law was designed to cut the accumulated deficits from 1994 to 1998 by $500 billion. As Table 16-6 indicated, the deficit has been reduced, and a surplus is projected for fiscal 1999.

INCOME, WEALTH, AND POVERTY

President John F. Kennedy once said, "A rising tide lifts all boats." The decade preceding his presidency and the decade thereafter supported his optimism. Contrary to expectations, the American economy did expand after World War II. Many veterans went to college or trade school under the GI bill, and were absorbed into an expanding labor force. Economic growth continued in the 1950s and income was raised for American families at all levels, including the poor, and income inequality fell dramatically. The economic prosperity of the nation continued through the 1960s. Beginning in the 1970s, however, income inequality began to increase. The gap between rich and poor continued to widen through the 1980s and 1990s, regardless of economic conditions. As income inequality increased, so did an increase in wealth inequality. Most of the gains in income have gone to the highest-earning 20 percent of U.S. households, while little or no gain was made by the bottom 40 percent.

INCOME INEQUALITY

The primary rationale for income inequality is based on motivation, which means that individuals are usually motivated by the desire for monetary gain in their economic activities. Individuals attempt to follow their economic self-interest and try to acquire as many goods as possible for themselves, without much regard for the effect of their actions on other people. The desire for material gain is supposed to motivate people to work harder and longer than any other motive that could be substituted for it. Monetary gain can also be tied to such factors as the desire for power and prestige, which can be reflected in private property ownership and freedom of enterprise. Income inequality is also supposed to result in efficient resource allocation in that people are attracted to those occupations for which the demand and rewards are the greatest.

Table 16-7 presents the share of aggregate income received by each fifth and top 5 percent of families for selected time periods from 1970 to 1997. As the table indicates, the only significant gain in aggregate income, as measured in constant CPI adjusted dollars, is that of those families in the top 20 percent and 5 percent of all family incomes. If anything, income inequality widened during the latter part of the 1990s, based on the rise in stock prices.

The Winner-Take-All Society — One explanation of rising income inequality in America was provided in a book written by Robert H. Frank and Philip J. Cook called *The Winner-Take-All Society*.[15] The authors contend that a growing number of markets have come to resemble the entertainment industry, where a few superstars command very high incomes. It is relative, not absolute, performance that is rewarded. A tiny difference in talent, skill, or just plain luck can result in vastly greater rewards for a few people. Although the competition for top people in winner-take-all markets attracts talented workers, it generates two kinds of waste. First, it attracts too many contestants. Second, it gives rise to unproductive patterns of consumption and investment.

TABLE 16-7   PERCENTAGE DISTRIBUTION OF AGGREGATE INCOME BY QUINTILES
AND TOP 5 PERCENT OF AMERICAN HOUSEHOLDS FOR SELECTED YEARS, 1970–1995

YEARS	Q1	Q2	Q3	Q4	Q5	TOP 5
1970	5.4	12.2	17.6	23.8	40.9	15.6
1975	5.6	11.9	17.7	24.2	40.7	14.9
1980	5.3	11.6	17.6	24.4	41.1	14.6
1985	4.8	11.0	16.9	24.3	43.1	16.1
1990	4.6	10.8	16.6	23.8	44.3	17.4
1991	4.5	10.7	16.6	24.1	44.2	17.1
1992	4.3	10.5	16.5	24.0	44.7	17.6
1993	4.1	9.9	15.7	23.3	47.0	20.3
1994	4.2	10.1	15.7	23.3	46.9	20.1
1995	4.4	10.1	15.8	23.2	46.5	20.0
1997	4.2	9.9	15.7	23.0	47.2	20.7

Source: U.S. Department of Commerce, Bureau of the Census, *Statistical Abstract of the United States 1999* (Washington, D.C.: U.S. Government Printing Office, 1999), p. 479.

The growth of the winner-take-all society can be attributed to the development of communication technologies, in particular electronic communication and data processing. This has had two mutually reinforcing effects. One is that a huge increase in the demand for the works of a particular author or singer can be satisfied without any corresponding increase in supply. The other is called the "network" effect: The value to people throughout the world of listening to a particular singer or watching a particular movie is reinforced by the thought that all their friends are watching the same program. This helps to explain why a limited number of actors, authors, movie producers, and sports stars do very well. Coupled with the development of communications technologies is the emergence of English as the universal language, which furthers the expansion of winner-take-all markets.

WEALTH

At the beginning of the twentieth century, John D. Rockefeller was the richest man in the world. He was worth $2 billion and his fortune was made in oil. He put together the Standard Oil Trust, the most powerful business combine ever to exist in the United States. It was eventually dissolved by the Supreme Court in 1911. Bill Gates, the founder of Microsoft, begins the twenty-first century as the richest man in the United States and the world. His fortune is around $100 billion.[16] Even after allowing for purchasing power parity between the two fortunes, Bill Gates is still wealthier. Microsoft was charged by the Justice Department with violation of the Sherman Antitrust Act. Rockefeller was pilloried during his time as being the consummate epitome of the plutocrat, and was referred to by President Theodore Roosevelt as a "malefactor of great wealth." He was in part the cause of the passage of the personal income tax in 1913.

Inequality in the distribution of wealth increased during the last twenty years of the twentieth century. In 1989 the top 1 percent of wealth-holders held 39 percent of total wealth as measured by net worth, while the bottom 80 percent of wealth-holders received 15 percent.[17] The distribution of wealth in 1989 was the most unequal since the 1920s when the top 1 percent of wealth-holders held 45 percent of total wealth. Over the next fifty years, inequality in the distribution of wealth began to decline, and by 1970 the top 1 percent of wealth-holders owned 20 percent of total wealth. Inequality in wealth distribution grew rapidly in the 1980s and continued through the 1990s. During this time, equities began to increase in importance as a part of wealth. The rise in stock prices during the 1990s enriched many CEOs who were able to utilize stock options.

Bill Gates and Warren Buffett are two of the richest men in the world. Their combined net worth in 1999 was $136 billion.[18] Bill Gates alone is wealthier than half the American people put together. Their combined wealth is probably greater than half the countries of Africa. Gates is the consummate epitome of an American entrepreneur, and Buffett is a superinvestor whose holdings in Coca-Cola alone have made him a billionaire many times over. Their success tends to be typical of the 1990s, but they were not alone. Other fortunes were made, particularly in the technology sector where in 1999 Amazon and Yahoo! were selling for more than $100 a share even though neither company had earned a cent. Many individual investors also became rich to the point that a popular book was called *The Millionaire Next Door*.[19]

Table 16-8 presents a distribution of wealth in the United States based on the mean and median net worth of families in 1995. The median net worth of families in constant U.S. dollars in 1995 was $56,400, up slightly from 1992 but unchanged from 1989.

POVERTY

Poverty is at the opposite end of the spectrum from wealth and income. In 1997 the number of persons living in poverty was 35.6 million, representing 13.3 percent of the American population.[20] Neither was significantly different from the corresponding 1995 figures of 36.5 million poor and a poverty rate of 13.7 percent. From 1960 to 1973 the national poverty rate decreased from 22 percent of the population to 11 percent. It rose to highs of 15 percent in 1982, 1983, and 1993. The poverty rate differs dramatically by sex, race, and family structure. The most likely to be poor are families headed by single mothers. The poverty rate in households headed by a single female is 46 percent. Many females raising children alone are high school dropouts and lack the necessary skills to compete in a workplace that demands ever-increasing skills.

Poverty is often a revolving door. Over a three-year span, 30.3 percent of the American population lived below the poverty line for at least two months. But just 5.3 percent of them stayed poor for two full years. In 1994, on average 15.3 percent of Americans were poor each month, and about 22 percent were poor for at least two months. About 13 percent of Americans were poor for more than two years. Single mothers were eight times more likely to live in poverty for two years than married couples. On average people were likely to be poor for four and one half months. Blacks, Hispanics, and children are among the poorest groups in the nation. Children are most likely to be poor, no matter what the measure. And the elderly, once the poorest of Americans, are the least likely to live in poverty, thanks to Social Security, Medicare, and the AARP.

Table 16-9 presents a breakdown of poverty in the United States by various categories. The majority of those persons who are classified as poor are white; however, Hispanic female heads of households are more likely to be poor than white female heads of households.

TABLE 16-8   FAMILY NET WORTH—MEAN AND MEDIAN IN CONSTANT 1995 DOLLARS (THOUSANDS OF DOLLARS)

	1989			1995		
	PERCENT OF FAMILIES	*MEAN*	*MEDIAN*	*PERCENT OF FAMILIES*	*MEAN*	*MEDIAN*
Less than $10,000	15.5	29.0	1.6	16.1	43.6	4.7
10,000–24,999	24.5	70.0	24.0	26.9	77.2	30.0
25,000–49,999	29.8	127.3	56.0	30.6	117.7	53.4
50,000–99,999	22.0	247.2	129.5	19.8	256.0	121.1
100,000 and more	8.3	1,350.4	547.1	6.5	1,435.3	482.0

Source: U.S. Department of Commerce, Bureau of the Census, *Statistical Abstract of the United States 1999* (Washington, D.C.: U.S. Government Printing Office, 1999), p. 488.

TABLE 16-9   PERSONS AND FAMILIES IN POVERTY BY SELECTED CHARACTERISTICS (THOUSANDS)

	NUMBER	PERCENT
Total	35.6	13.3
Family Status		
In families	25.2	11.6
Unrelated families	0.7	0.4
Unrelated individuals	8.7	20.8
Male	3.4	17.4
Female	5.2	24.0
Race		
White	24.4	11.0
Black	9.1	26.5
Asian	1.4	14.0
Hispanic	8.3	27.1
Children below Poverty Level		
All races	13.4	19.2
White	8.4	15.4
Black	4.1	36.8
Hispanic	3.9	36.4

Source: U.S. Department of Commerce, Bureau of the Census, *Statistical Abstract of the United States, 1999* (Washington, D.C.: U.S. Government Printing Office, 1999), pp. 482–483.

SUMMARY

The United States possesses many strengths as it enters the twenty-first century. Its standard of living, as measured by real per capita GDP, is the highest in the world. Its unemployment rate, as of April 2000, was the lowest of all major industrial nations, with the exception of Japan. The rate of inflation is also low. The dollar is the world's strongest currency unit, and the average productivity of U.S. industries and workers as a whole is at the top or near the top compared to other nations. As is discussed in the final chapter, there are those scholars who are already predicting that the United States will dominate the world of the twenty-first century. However, it is important to remember that, quite recently, there were those scholars who predicted that Japan would dominate the twenty-first century.

QUESTIONS FOR DISCUSSION

1. Income and wealth inequalities have increased in the United States over the last twenty years. Why has this happened? Is it good or bad, and if bad, what should be done about it?
2. What are some of the factors responsible for poverty in the United States?
3. What are the strengths and weaknesses of the American economy?
4. Do Microsoft and other large American corporations have too much power, and if so, what should be done about it?
5. In comparison to other major countries, the United States has the most unequal distribution of income. Is this good or bad?
6. Bill Gates and Warren Buffett are probably the two richest men in the world. Is their wealth compatible with a democratic society?

NOTES

1. It is estimated that fully 50 percent of all new small business firms fail during their first year of operations. The main reason is a lack of capital.
2. If anything, mergers have grown larger. In 1999 two major world automobile firms, Daimler-Benz and Chrysler, merged.
3. Multinationals are also called global corporations or transnational corporations.
4. Codetermination, or Mitbestimmung as it is called in Germany, takes place at two levels—supervisory boards and workers' councils. Supervisory boards must have one-third worker representation in firms with 500 to 2,000 employees and one-half worker representation for firms with 2000 or more employees. Workers' councils exist at the factory level.
5. An example would be the Civilian Conservation Corps (CCC) that employed more than a million youths between the ages of seventeen and twenty-one. They built state parks, firebreaks, and the Blue Ridge Parkway and were paid $30 a month, of which $25 was sent home.
6. This did not happen. Pent-up demand for goods that were in short supply during the war stimulated spending. Many GIs went to college. The beginning of the Cold War in 1947 stimulated defense spending.

7. John Maynard Keynes, *The General Theory of Employment, Interest, and Money* (New York: Harcourt, Brace, and Co., 1951).
8. If the supply of labor increased, wages would fall; if it decreased, wages would rise. There would always be a level reached at which workers would be put to work. Changes in supply and demand would always create an equilibrium wage at which workers would be hired.
9. The growth rate was beginning to slow down in the United States and Europe. In Europe governments through taxation were taking an ever larger share of GDP. In the United States the economist Arthur Laffer developed the Laffer curve, which purported to show that after a certain level of taxation was reached, a country's level of economic growth would decline.
10. This did not happen. Those who received tax cuts spent their money.
11. The DOW reached a level of 11,000 in 1999 and has fluctuated below it in 2000. It was above the level as of April 6, 2000. The NASDAC hit an all-time high of 4880 in March 2000, as people have bought the idea that the quickest way to get rich is to buy technology stocks. It dropped some 800 points in April.
12. *The Economist*, April 1, 2000, p. 98.
13. This probably cost Bush the 1992 presidential election. His famous promise "read my lips; no new taxes" during the 1988 election was broken even though he did right by raising taxes.
14. Medicare-Medicaid expenditures are growing rapidly in the United States as its population is getting older. There is a redistribution of income from workers to retirees. The same is true in other developed countries.
15. Robert H. Frank and Philip J. Cook, *The Winner-Take-All Society* (New York: Free Press, 1995).
16. The paper value of his stockholdings decreased by $11 billion on April 4 when the Justice Department announced that it would prosecute Microsoft as a monopoly. This $11 billion was larger than the GDP's of 90 of the world's 205 countries.
17. U.S. Government Printing Office, Bureau of the Census, Statistical Abstract of the United States (Washington, D.C.: U.S. Government Printing Office, 1999).
18. Warren Buffett's wealth has declined in value, particularly since the stock value of two of his major holdings, Coca Cola and Gillette, have declined in value.
19. Thomas J. Stanley, *The Millionaire Next Door* (Marietta, GA: Longstreet, 1996).
20. U.S. Department of Commerce, Bureau of the Census, Statistical Abstract of the United States, 1999 (Washington, D.C.: U.S. Government Printing Office, 1999), pp. 483–485.

RECOMMENDED READING

Bernstein, Jared, Elizabeth C. McNichols, Lawrence Mishel, and Robert Zahrandnik. *Pulling Apart.* Washington, D.C.: Center on Budget and Policy Priorities, January 2000.

Economic Report of the President 2000. Washington, D.C.: U.S. Government Printing Office, 2000.

Frank, Robert H. *Luxury Fever: The New Middle Class Luxury Boom.* New York: Free Press, 1998.

Landes, David and S. Landes. *The Competitive Advantage of Nations.* New York: W.W. Norton, 1998, Chapter 19.

Schor, Juliet B. *The Overspent American.* New York: Basic Books, 1998.

Walt, Stephen. "Two Cheers for Clinton's Legacy." *Foreign Affairs.* Vol. 79, No. 2, March–April 2000, pp. 63–79.

CHAPTER 17

TOWARD THE NEXT AMERICAN CENTURY

To thee belongs the rural reign,
Thy cities shall with commerce shine:
All thine shall be the subject main,
And every shore it circles thine.[1]
Rule Britannia, Britannia rule the waves

At the beginning of the twentieth century, England did rule. Queen Victoria celebrated her diamond jubilee in 1900. She had been queen for sixty-three years and ruled over the largest empire ever known, on which it was said "the sun never set." Representatives from every colony in the British empire came to pay her homage. Kings, including her cousin, Kaiser Wilhelm of Germany, were also in attendance. Never at any one time in history had there been so much pomp and ceremony bestowed on a monarch. The parade in her honor was six miles long and took seven hours to complete. Britain was the world's leading seapower and the pound sterling was the world's strongest currency and the foundation of the gold standard. A year later she was dead, and in 1914 World War I began, marking the beginning of the end of the British empire.

The United States entered the twenty-first century in the same position that England was in at the beginning of the twentieth century. Its economy is the largest in the world, and the dollar has replaced the pound as the most important currency in the world. It is the leading military power and enforces a Pax Americana throughout the world. Its culture is well on its way to becoming, for better or for worse, a world culture, and there are those who loudly trumpet its praise. Alan Greenspan, chairman of the Federal Reserve, concluded that "only free-market systems [i.e., the American model] exhibit the flexibility and robustness to accommodate human nature and harness technology to ever high living standards."[2] Mortimer Zuckerman, editor-in-chief of *U.S. News & World Report*, wrote an essay called "A Second American Century."[3] It begins by proclaiming "Why We Will Remain Number One," and ends by suggesting the twenty-first century will belong to America.[4]

How then did we get to this happy state of events? The answers are, in part, location and luck. Location spared the United States the devastation that occurred in Europe and Japan as a result of the two major world wars of the twentieth century. The luck factor is that the United States was able to develop new technologies that were put to use after the wars were over. But there were other factors at work. Immigration provided new waves of citizens that contributed to economic development. The country is endowed with climate and natural resources. Then there is the entrepreneurial spirit that the country seems to possess in abundance. We are a nation of risk-takers.

THE TWENTIETH CENTURY

At the beginning of the twentieth century, Americans inhabited a world in which household electricity was a luxury, an automobile an object of curiosity, and recreation represented a trip to a band concert in the park or to a vaudeville show. The population of the United States in 1900 was 76 million people, many of whom were immigrants from Europe. Americans did not live that long, because many died of communicable diseases such as malaria, pneumonia, tuberculosis, and typhoid fever. Most Americans did not have a high school education; few went to college. The majority of Americans lived in rural areas and were employed in agriculture. But as the century progressed, people witnessed an unparalleled progression of advances. Mass production of the automobile created millions of industrial jobs, stimulated highway construction, and ended rural isolation. Relief from diseases arrived with the development of a number of wonder drugs that increased the longevity of people.

As Figure 17-1 (on page 316), Figure 17-2 (on page 316), Figure 17-3 (on page 317), and Table 17-1 (on page 317) indicate, the United States has changed drastically since the beginning of the twentieth century. Changes in technology, transportation, and communication have created a world where anything can be made anywhere on the face of the earth and sold everywhere else in the world. National boundaries are no longer as important as they used to be because we have entered an era of globalization. Education has become far more important than it was at the beginning or even the middle of the twentieth century, because technology has increased the need for skilled workers. Americans, but particularly those who are older, have become far more affluent during the twentieth century than they were at its beginning.

FIGURE 17-1   AVERAGE INCOME LEVELS (U.S. PER-CAPITA GDP IN 1998 DOLLARS)

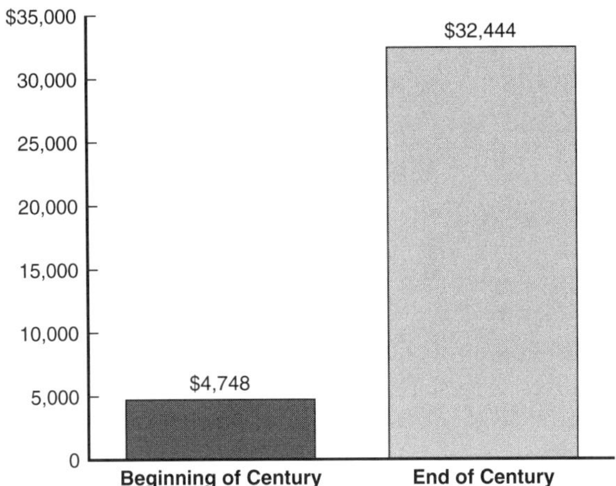

Note: Exact years in the figure are 1900 and 1998.

Sources: Beginning of the century estimated by JEC based on Bureau of the Census data. End of century based on Bureau of Economic Analysis (BEA) data for 1998.

FIGURE 17-2   THE TOP TEN CAUSES OF DEATH (DEATH RATES PER 100,000 POPULATION)

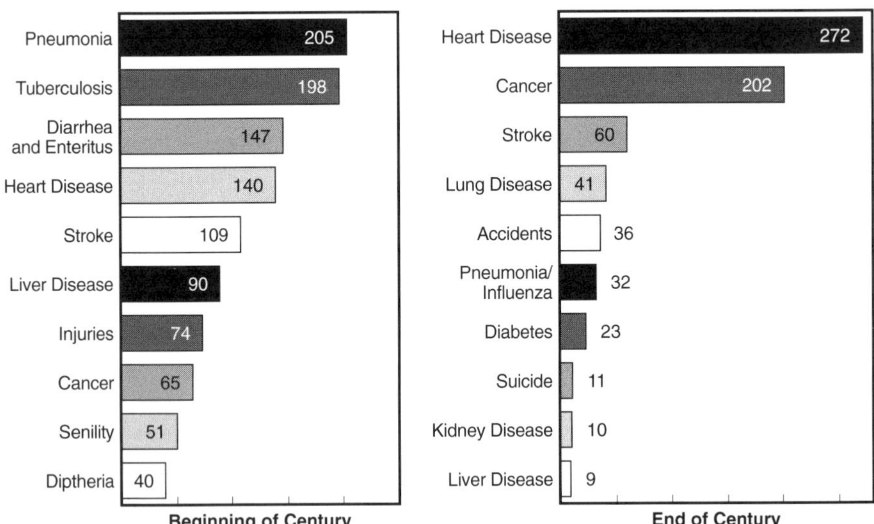

Note: Exact years in the figure are 1900 and 1997.

Source: Beginning and end of the century based on Centers for Disease Control data received by fax and CDC Web page at <www.cdc.gov>.

FIGURE 17-3 AVERAGE LIFE EXPECTANCY AT BIRTH

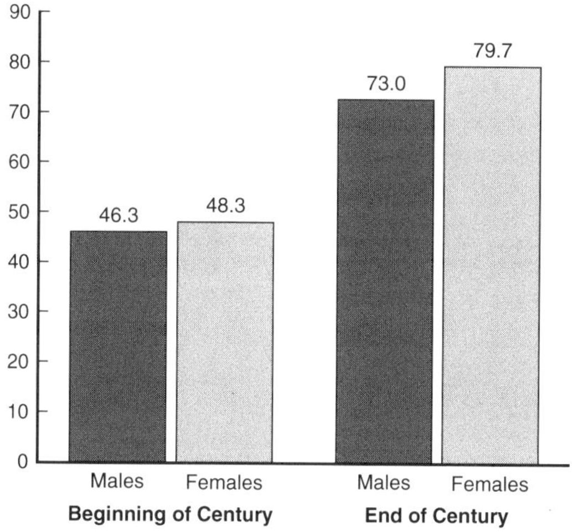

Note: Exact years in the figure are 1900 and 2000 (projected).
Source: Beginning and end of the century from Bureau of the Census data.

TABLE 17-1 WORK TIME NEEDED FOR THE AVERAGE WORKER TO BUY SELECTED PRODUCTS

PRODUCT	BEGINNING OF CENTURY	END OF CENTURY
Half gallon of milk	56 minutes	7 minutes
One-pound loaf of bread	16 minutes	3.5 minutes
Hershey chocolate bar	20 minutes	2.1 minutes
Three-pound chicken	2 hours 40 minutes	14 minutes
Pair of Levis jeans	9 hours 42 minutes	3 hours 24 minutes
100 kilowatt hours of electricity	107 hours 17 minutes	38 minutes
3-minute coast-to-coast phone call	90 hours 40 minutes	2 minutes

Note: Items are for various years near the beginning and end of the century.
Source: Michael Cox and Richard Alm, *Myths of Rich and Poor*, 1999.

POPULATION

The population of the United States increased from 76 million at the beginning of the century to 274 million at the end of the century. There were three major shifts in the population. The first was immigration. As Figure 17-4 (on page 318) indicates, the great majority of immigrants at the beginning of the last century came from Europe; by the end of the century, 42 percent of immigrants came from Latin America. Second, as Figure 17-5 (on page 318) shows, there has been a shift of population away from such regions as the Northeast

FIGURE 17-4   U.S. POPULATION BY REGION

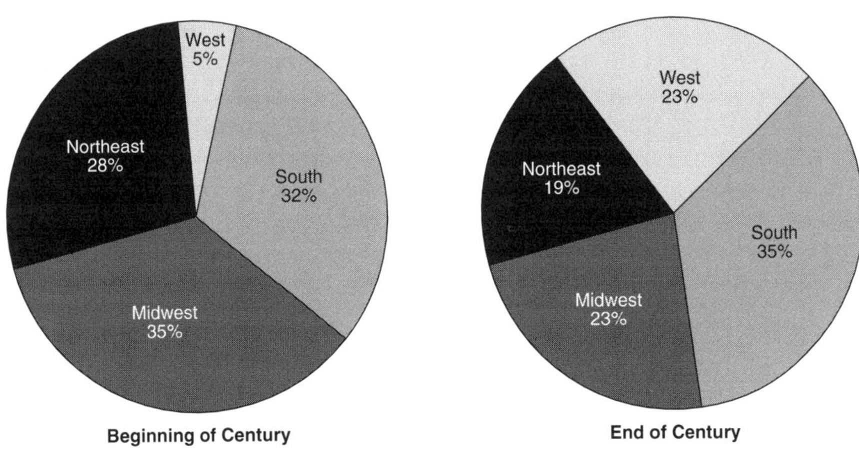

Note: Exact years in the figure are 1900 and 1998.
Source: Beginning and end of the century from Bureau of the Census data.

FIGURE 17-5   U.S. IMMIGRATION BY REGION OF ORIGIN

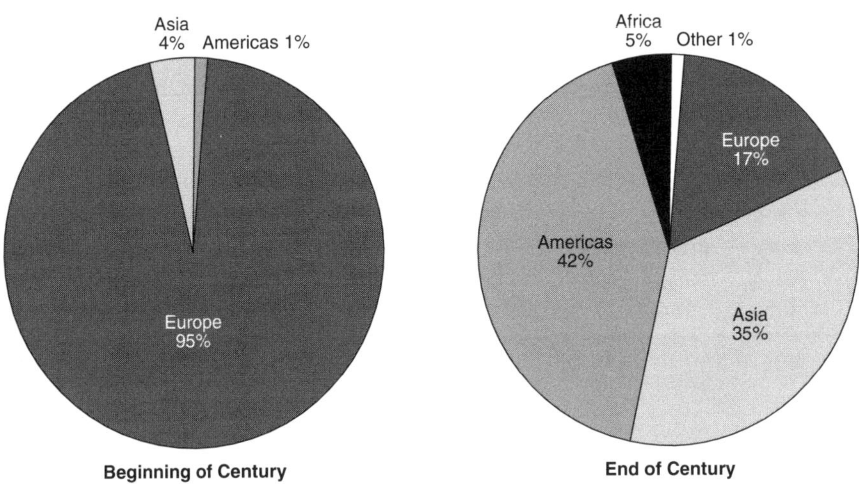

Note: JEC calculations based on five-year average of 1900–1904 and 1994–1998.
Sources: Beginning of the century from Bureau of the Census data. End of the century from INS Web Page.

and Midwest to the South and West. Accompanying the shift was a lessening of income inequality by regions. The third population shift involved the aging of the population. In 1900, only 4 percent of the population was 65 and over; by the end of the century 12.6 percent of a much larger population was 65 and over. The aging of the population has resulted in an increased role on the part of the federal government.

GOVERNMENT AND THE AMERICAN ECONOMY

At the beginning of the last century, over half of government spending was done at the local level. By the end of the century, the federal government accounted for over two-thirds of government spending. Total government expenditures increased from 7.6 percent of GNP at the beginning of the century to 28.1 percent at the end. The level and composition of taxes also changed. In 1900 the two most important sources of revenue were alcohol and tobacco excise taxes and customs duties. Taxes that were not in existence at that time accounted for the great bulk of federal government revenue by the end of the century. In 2000, personal income and Social Security taxes accounted for 83 percent of revenue. Entitlement expenditures that were zero in 1900 amounted to 56 percent of total expenditures by 2000. Figure 17-6 (below) and Figure 17-7 (on page 320) present changes in expenditures and taxes during the last century.

THE UNITED STATES AND THE WORLD

In 1900 the population of the world was around 1.6 billion people, one-third of whom lived in China and India. The leading powers were the United States, England, France, Italy, the Austro-Hungarian empire, Russia, and Japan. With the exception of the United States and France, all were ruled by monarchs. The total GDP of the world was around $1.6 trillion. There were around sixty countries in existence, and international currency exchange was governed by the gold standard.[5] Most of the world was a part of the British, Dutch, French,

FIGURE 17-6 GOVERNMENT EXPENDITURES BY LEVEL

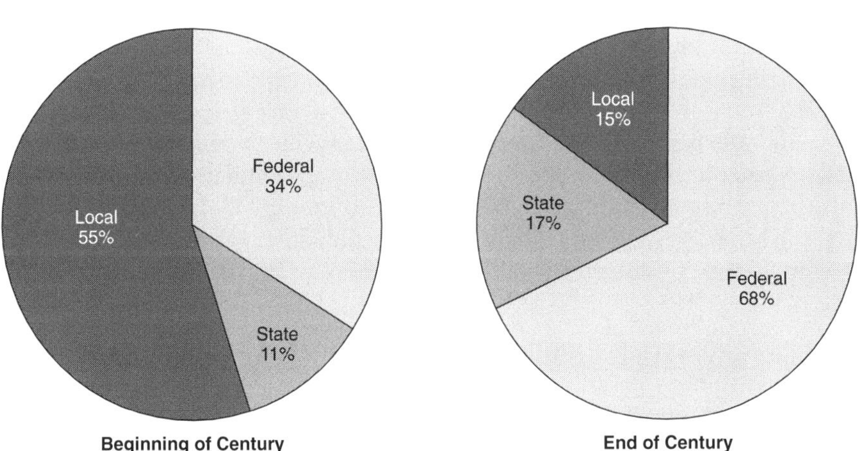

Note: Intergovernmental flows are treated as expenditures of the disbursing level of government. Exact years in the figure are 1902 and 1998.

Sources: JEC estimates based on BEA and Census data.

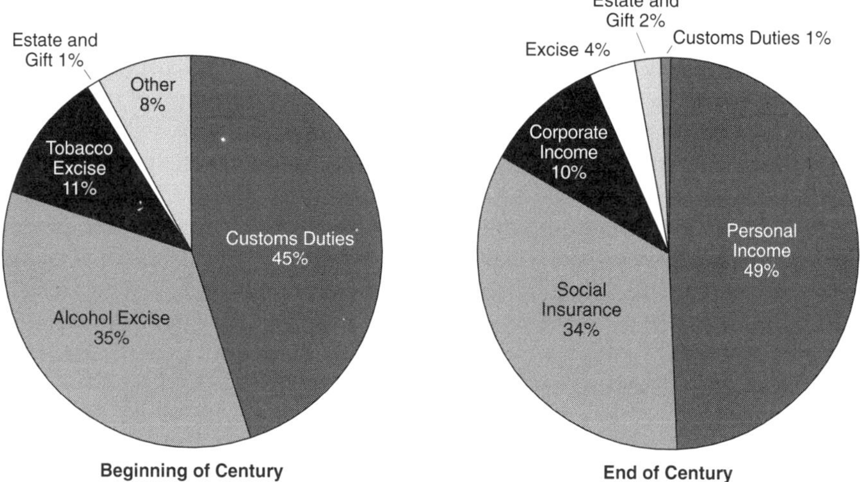

FIGURE 17-7   FEDERAL TAXES BY TYPE

Note: Exact years in the figure are 1900 and 1999.

Sources: Beginning of the century from Bureau of the Census data. End of the century from Senate Budget Committee data.

and German empires. The leading export nations were the United States, England, and Germany. Foreign direct investment by the major world powers amounted to $108 billion and was mostly concentrated in the mineral resources of Latin America. Three-fourths of the foreign investment was made by England, the United States, Germany, and France.

As Figures 17-8 and 17-9 indicate, the world changed enormously during the twentieth century. One change was the rise of Japan as a world economic power, and another change was the decline of Britain as a world economic power. The population increased from 1.6 billion in 1900 to 6.0 billion at the end of the century, with China and India contributing almost half of the increase. Living standards increased for most people, but income inequality between rich nations and poor nations also increased. Foreign trade and investment are dominated by the same countries today that were dominant at the beginning of the century, but trade is no longer based on the exploitation of natural resources; instead it is based on the production of high value-added products.

EVENTS THAT SHAPED THE TWENTIETH CENTURY

Five events had an enormous impact on the world of the twentieth century, and they were all interrelated. World War I was the catalyst; without it the other events would not have happened. The Russian Revolution of 1917 was one result of the war; the current problems in the Balkans another. World War I led to World War II. One result of this second world war was the establishment of

FIGURE 17-8   U.S. GDP AS A SHARE OF WORLD GDP

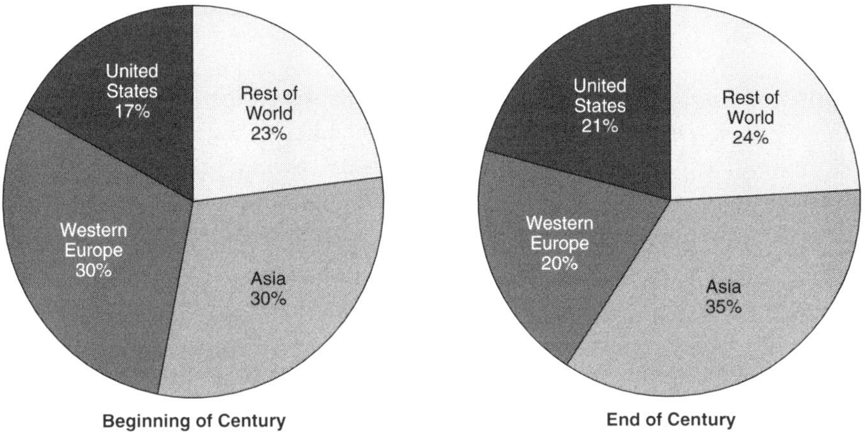

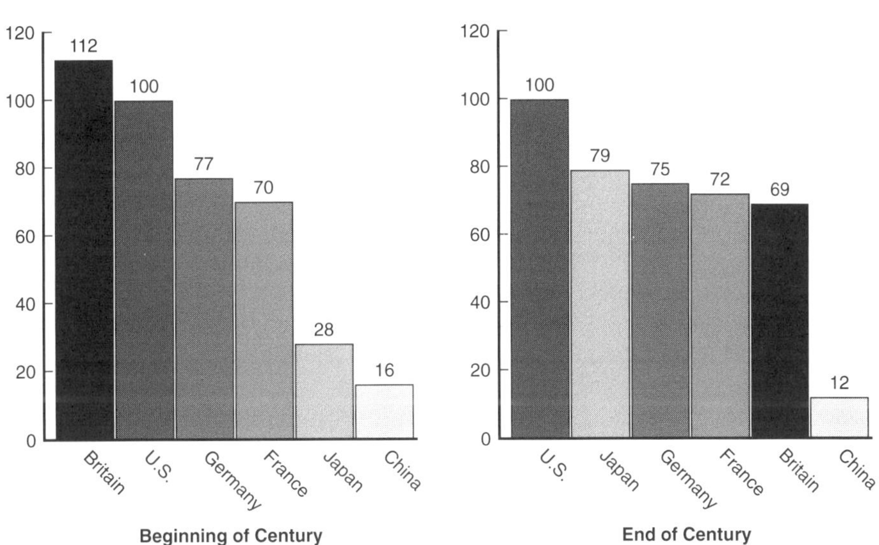

Note: Western Europe includes twelve countries; Asia includes eleven countries. Exact years in the figure are 1900 and 1992.

Sources: JEC calculations based on *Monitoring the World Economy 1820–1992*; Angus Maddison for the OECD, 1995.

FIGURE 17-9   RELATIVE INCOME LEVELS OF MAJOR COUNTRIES (PER-CAPITA GDP RELATIVE TO THE UNITED STATES)

Note: All figures at purchasing power parities scaled to the U.S. value. Exact years in the figure are 1900 and 1998.

Sources: JEC calculations based on *Monitoring the World Economy 1820–1992*; Angus Maddison, 1995 (beginning of the century); and OECD (end of the century), except China, which is sourced from the *CIA World Factbook 1999*.

the Soviet Union as one of the two major world superpowers that dominated the world for more than forty years. The end of colonialism was a direct result of World War II. No longer did England, France, and other countries have the resources to control their colonies. The rise and fall of communism is considered by many as the most important event of the century. For much of the century, there was a clash between two totally different approaches to resource allocation. The final event was the technological revolution of the latter part of the century, which has created a global economy.

WORLD WAR I

World War I lasted from 1914 to 1918. It involved all the major powers of the world. Germany and the Austro-Hungarian Empire were on one side, and France, England, Russia, Italy, Japan, and the United States were on the other. Casualties were heavy on both sides—some eight million soldiers were killed and twenty million wounded. World War I destroyed the old political order. The Austro-Hungarian empire disappeared and with it the Hapsburg Monarchy. In Russia, the Bolshevik Revolution of 1917 deposed the czar and ushered in a communist regime that was to last for seventy-four years. In Germany, the monarchy collapsed when Kaiser Wilhelm fled to the Netherlands, and the Weimar Republic was created. The United States was the main winner. It began the war as the leading debtor nation and ended it as the leading creditor nation.

The Treaty of Versailles ending World War I imposed harsh measures on Germany, including the loss of much of its territory and the payment of war reparations to the victors, measures that led to the rise of fascism in Germany and to World War II. The Treaty of Versailles also broke up the old Austro-Hungarian empire, with the creation of Austria, Hungary, Czechoslovakia, Poland, and Yugoslavia. On the assumption that Slavs were Slavs, little attention was paid to ethnic divisions. Yugoslavia was created to include Bosnians, Croats, Slovenes, Serbs, Albanians, Macedonians, and other ethnic groups, none of whom had much in common. Ethnic and religious animosities have existed for centuries.

WORLD WAR II

World War II ended the Depression, destroyed fascism, reshaped Europe, and ended colonialism. It also created two superpowers that were to dominate the world for most of the remainder of the century—the United States and the Soviet Union. Western Europe, helped to a considerable degree by Marshall Plan aid from the United States, was recovering from the devastation caused by the war. The Bretton Woods agreement of 1944 created a new international monetary exchange system. The dollar became the major world currency unit and the currencies of other countries were pegged to it.[6] The World Bank was created to provide financial assistance to those countries with balance of payments problems. Finally, the war was instrumental in initiating the development of regional cooperation, which eventually led to the creation of the European Union.[7]

THE END OF COLONIALISM

The race to acquire colonies, particularly in Africa, began in the nineteenth century. At the Treaty of Berlin in 1885, five countries decided to divide Africa into economic enclaves. Belgium got that area known as the Congo, which became one of the largest copper-producing areas in the world. England, which was already established in Egypt and the Cape of Africa, acquired the Sudan, southern Africa, and part of southwest Africa. France, which already had Algeria, was given west Africa. Germany was given parts of east Africa and southwest Africa, and Portugal was given what was left, including the areas that are now the countries of Angola and Mozambique. Two world wars changed all this, and in the 1950s and 1960s most of these colonies became independent nations. Some fifty new countries were created.

Colonialism also ended in Asia. Laos, Cambodia, and Vietnam, former French colonies, became independent countries. Singapore, Malaysia, Burma, and India, which split into Pakistan, India, and Bangladesh, became independent from England. The countries of North Korea and South Korea were once Japanese colonial possessions. The United States lost the Philippines, and the Dutch lost Indonesia. China, which had been dominated by foreign powers for more than a hundred years, became a communist country in 1949. The East Asian countries—Japan, South Korea, Singapore, and Hong Kong—and Taiwan developed as one of the major trading areas in the world. East Asia relied on an export-driven policy to promote economic development.

THE RISE AND FALL OF COMMUNISM

Like the French and American Revolutions, the Russian Revolution was in the making for many years before it actually broke out. No one could understand the success of communism in Russia, which was a backward country in comparison to England and Germany, without some knowledge of the factors that made the revolution possible. One factor was the defeat of Russia by the Germans during the war, which caused widespread discontent. A second factor was the existence of an autocratic government in which one person, the czar, was the supreme ruler. A third factor was poor labor conditions. Wages were low and paid irregularly, hours were long, and working conditions were unsafe. Strikes were put down and labor unions were illegal. Finally, peasants, who constituted 70 percent of the population, lived in poverty.

The Soviet Union lasted seventy-four years. During much of that time, it and the United States were the dominant world military powers. The world was divided into two spheres of influence—the communist sphere dominated by the Soviet Union and the capitalist sphere dominated by the United States. The collapse of the Soviet Union in 1991 represented the greatest social disaster of the twentieth century. In its beginning, it offered hope for the creation of a Utopian society, but that never came close to reality. Constant coercion held the country together, but coercion could not last forever. Its centrally planned economy could no longer compete in a highly complex and dynamic industrial world. The communist world was pretty much isolated from the rest of the world and its insularity cost it dearly.

TECHNOLOGICAL CHANGE

At the beginning of the twentieth century, manufacturing companies dominated the American economy. Most were natural-resource–based companies. U.S. Steel was located near sources of coal and iron; Standard Oil located its production facilities near sources of oil in Mexico and the United States; Armour and Swift were located in Chicago where their meatpacking plants were near supplies of beef and pork; American Tobacco was located in North Carolina where tobacco was produced; and Anaconda Copper based its operations in Chile where copper was in abundance. Countries that had natural resources were better off than those that did not. Thus, the resource-rich countries of Argentina, Brazil, and Mexico had much higher real per capita incomes at the beginning of the century than Japan, which had no natural resources. Comparative advantage favored those countries that had natural resources over those that did not.[8]

But times have changed. Skill and knowledge stand alone as the only source of comparative advantage. High-value brainpower industries are now important, and investments are now made in knowledge and skills instead of natural resources. A global economy exists and corporations can base their operations anyplace in the world. Success or failure depends on whether or not a country can make a transition to the human-made brainpower industries of the future. The international transfer of technology means that anything can be produced anywhere and sold everywhere. Transportation and communication costs have fallen dramatically and the speed with which each can be done has risen exponentially. Research and design can be coordinated in different parts of the world, and components can be made wherever it is cheapest to do so and shipped to assembly points that minimize total cost. Technology has created world capital markets, where firms can borrow in New York, Frankfurt, Paris, or Tokyo.

THE TWENTY-FIRST CENTURY

One thing is for certain, the world of the twenty-first century will be totally different from the world of the twentieth century. Knowledge rather than natural resources will be the required need for economic and human development. New communications technologies are shrinking distances and eroding borders and time. But it is entirely possible that the information revolution will bypass the poorest countries of the world, making them worse off than they were in the twentieth century when at least some of the countries had raw materials to export. There are slums and villages without telephones, electricity, and running water, much less fax machines and computers. Few people go on to college or even finish secondary schools, so they lack the knowledge to be assimilated into an ever-more complicated world.

POPULATION

In 1798 the English clergyman Thomas Malthus published a book called *An Essay in the Principles of Population*, which made him famous and earned for economics the title of the "dismal" science. He asserted that population grew exponentially, doubling every twenty-five years, while food supplies tended to increase in an arithmetic progress. An example is provided in Table 17-2.

This proposition was based on two assumptions: Technological change could not increase food supply faster than population, and population growth would not be limited by fewer births, only by more deaths. Although both assumptions have proved to be wrong, there is an element of truth in his prediction. The world population doubled from around 250 million two thousand years ago to 500 million by the sixteenth century. The population then doubled to 1 billion by 1830 and to 2 billion around 1930. The next doubling to 4 billion took only forty-four years. It took more than four thousand years of recorded history for China to have its first 500 million people, but only a little more than three decades to double its population to a billion. India's population doubled between 1820 and 1949 and doubled again between 1949 and 1982.

Several factors will affect population growth during the twenty-first century. There has been a reduction in childbearing rates in both the rich and poor countries of the world. However, in the poor countries, where the majority of the world's population live, there has also been a reduction in the death rate.[9] Many of the diseases that once would carry off millions of people have been eradicated and improved health standards have reduced the infant mortality

TABLE 17-2   MALTHUSIAN PROGRESSIONS FOR POPULATION AND FOOD SUPPLY

YEAR	POPULATION SIZE	FOOD SUPPLY
0	1	1
25	2	2
50	4	3
75	8	4
100	16	5
125	32	6
150	64	7
175	128	8
200	256	9

rates in the poor countries. Thus, a lower death rate relative to the birth rate will continue to create population pressure in most of the poor countries, with India being a case in point. As Table 17-3 indicates, in many of the poorest countries of the world, their population will double in a relatively short period of time, which will continue to create problems of poverty, malnutrition and illiteracy.

The rich countries of the world have 15 percent of the world's population, but receive 80 percent of the world's GDP.[10] They possess two important demographic characteristics that separate them from the poor countries. First, their population is aging, and second, their birth rates are falling to the point where in some countries the population is not reproducing itself. As Table 17-3 indicates, the population of the countries used in it will actually show a decline during the twenty-first century. Only the United States will show an appreciable gain. The aging of the population in these countries will cause a major financial problem with respect to pensions and medical care that will be difficult to resolve. Even the United States, with its dynamic economy, is having problems with the future funding of Social Security.

TABLE 17-3 WORLD POPULATION, BIRTH RATES, DEATH RATES, AND DOUBLING TIME, MID–1999

	POPULATION (MILLIONS)	BIRTH RATES (PER 1,000)	DEATH RATES (PER 1,000)	DOUBLING TIME (IN YEARS)
World	5,982	23	9	49
Africa	771	39	14	28
Nigeria	114	43	13	23
Ethiopia	60	46	21	28
Asia	3,637	23	8	46
Bangladesh	126	27	8	38
China	1,254	16	7	73
India	987	28	9	37
Pakistan	146	39	11	25
North America	303	14	8	119
United States	272	15	9	116
Latin America	512	24	6	38
Mexico	100	27	5	32
Brazil	168	21	6	45
Europe	728	10	11	—
Russia	146	9	14	—
Germany	82	10	10	—
France	59	12	9	210

Source: Population Reference Bureau, *1999 World Population Data Sheet* (Washington, D.C.: PRB, 1999).

Table 17-4 presents the distribution of world population among economies grouped by GNP per capita for 1998. Sixty percent of the world's population lives in countries that are considered poor, meaning they have a per capita income of $760 or less. Conversely, 15 percent of the world's population lies in countries with a per capita GNP of $9,631 or more. The United States has less than 5 percent of the world's population, but its per capita GNP in 1998 was approximately 60 times larger than the average per capita income of the same sixty countries that are considered poor. The average per capita GNP of the rich countries was 50 times as large as the average per capita GNP of the poor countries.

POVERTY, ILLITERACY, AND GENDER DISPARITY

Half of the world's population lives on less than the international poverty standard of less than $2 a day. As Table 17-5 (on page 328) indicates, the majority of these people live in Asia and Africa. Approximately 800 million of them live in Africa. At the other end of the spectrum, the United States, Japan, and Germany account for one-half of the world's GNP. Illiteracy is a result of poverty. Some 275 million children throughout the world are illiterate because they live in poor countries that cannot afford to build schools to educate them. Close to one-third of the world's population is illiterate. As Table 17-6 (on page 328) indicates, in India nearly 50 percent of the adult population is illiterate; in Pakistan 62 percent of the adult population is illiterate. The majority of those who are illiterate are women, as far fewer women receive an education than men. Table 17-6 presents the illiteracy rates for selected countries for 1997.

GLOBALIZATION

In an event somewhat similar to the storming of the Bastile in 1789 by French peasants and shopkeepers, thousands of Americans, representing diverse groups ranging from those who wanted to save sea turtles to those who wanted to repeal NAFTA, went to Washington to storm the hallowed halls of the International Monetary Fund and the World Bank. The French mob wanted the hide of Marie Antoinette (who is noted for the quote "let them eat cake") and various other aristocrats. The American mob wanted the hides of international bankers whom they held responsible for getting poor countries into debts they could not pay. Multinational corporations also came under heavy

TABLE 17-4   DISTRIBUTION OF WORLD POPULATION GROUPED BY GNP PER CAPITA, 1998

PER CAPITA GNP	PERCENT OF WORLD POPULATION
Low $760 or less	60
Lower-middle $761–$3,030	15
Upper-middle $3,031–$9,360	10
High $9,361 and more	15

Source: The World Bank, *World Bank Atlas 2000* (Washington, D.C.: The World Bank, 2000), p. 38.

TABLE 17-5 COUNTRY POPULATION AND PERCENTAGE OF PEOPLE LIVING BELOW THE INTERNATIONAL POVERTY LINES

COUNTRY	POPULATION (MILLIONS)	POPULATION BELOW 1PP A DAY (PERCENT)	POPULATION BELOW 2PP A DAY (PERCENT)
Brazil	166	24	44
China	1,239	22	58
Ecuador	12	30	66
Ethiopia	61	46	89
Honduras	6	47	76
India	980	47	88
Lesotho	2	49	74
Mexico	96	15	40
Nepal	23	50	87
Niger	10	62	92
Nigeria	121	31	60
Pakistan	132	12	57
Philippines	75	27	63
Senegal	9	54	80
Uganda	21	69	92
Zambia	10	84	98
Zimbabwe	12	41	68

Source: The World Bank, *Entering the 21st Century* (New York: Oxford University Press, 2000), pp. 236–237.

TABLE 17-6 THE ADULT ILLITERACY RATE FOR SELECTED COUNTRIES

COUNTRY	PERCENT
India	54
Pakistan	41
Nigeria	41
Bangladesh	61
Ethiopia	65
Sudan	47
Morocco	44
Iraq	42
Algeria	40
Egypt	47
Iran	27
Haiti	55
Nepal	62

Source: United Nations Development Program, *Human Development Report 1999* (New York: Oxford University Press, 1999), pp. 136–137.

criticism. They were held responsible for many of the world's problems, including despoliation of the world's rain forests.

Globalization has come to mean the increased international mobility of information, goods, capital, and people. Proponents say it will help the poor nations of Africa, Asia, and Latin America become part of the world economy and improve the lives of their citizens. Protesters deride globalization, saying only elites and corporations benefit. Regardless of who is right, globalization is a *fait accompli*. As modern technology has increased, it has become an internationally marketable commodity, because it is readily transferable through the operations of global corporations. This has resulted in the globalization of production. For example, a General Motors car may have parts assembled in South Korea by Korean workers, engines built by Japan, styling and design done by German engineers, advertising done by a British advertising agency, and so forth. Cross-border linkages comprise most international trade among advanced industrial countries.

DEBT

In June of 1999, a human chain of more than one million people formed a line extending for miles along the Thames River in England to protest the debt of the poor countries that is held by international banks. In the United States the bishops of the Catholic and Episcopal churches have requested that the international banks forgive the debts of the poor countries. But it isn't as simple as it may seem. Many countries, including some that are not poor, have incurred debt management problems because of poor political leadership and corruption. Politicians have spent borrowed money on high living or on projects that have little value to the poor. There are other factors that have created debt problems. In many countries, export earnings fluctuate wildly because the prices of raw materials are more volatile in world markets than the prices of manufactured goods. Oil, which is important to the economy of Nigeria, has fluctuated in price from $35 a barrel to $9 a barrel over the last twenty years.

Table 17-7 (on page 330) presents the external, or foreign, debt of selected countries. They range from Argentina and Brazil, which are classified as upper-middle–income countries, to some of the poorest countries in the world. Ethiopia is an example; its money per capita income of $110 is the lowest for any country in the world. Its external debt is almost twice the size of its GNP and eight times as large as its export earnings. The prospects for much improvement in the Ethiopian economy are not good. Its exports are basically low value-added raw materials. The Sudan is even worse off than Ethiopia.

POLITICAL INSTABILITY

In May 1998 India and then Pakistan conducted nuclear tests that threatened the political stability of the world and highlighted a problem that could very well destabilize the world in the twenty-first century. The problem is religion.

TABLE 17-7   TOTAL EXTERNAL DEBT OF SELECTED COUNTRIES (MILLIONS OF DOLLARS)

COUNTRY	EXTERNAL DEBT	PERCENT OF EXPORTS
Argentina	123.2	352
Brazil	193.6	277
Cameroon	9.3	315
Congo; Democratic Republic	12.3	783
Ethiopia	10.8	791
Ghana	6.0	229
Guinea	3.5	330
Haiti	1.1	272
Madagascar	4.1	370
Mali	2.9	240
Mozambique	6.0	785
Myanmar	5.1	289
Nicaragua	5.7	441
Niger	1.6	329
Rwanda	1.1	373
Sierra Leone	1.1	779
Sudan	16.3	2,421
Tanzania	7.2	427
Uganda	3.7	239
Zambia	6.8	374

Source: The World Bank, *1999 World Development Indicators* (Washington, D.C.: The World Bank, 1999), pp. 254, 255, 256, 258, 259, 260.

Pakistan is a Moslem nation and India is a Hindu nation, and religious tolerance is not a natural by-product of the culture of either nation. During the first three days of India's independence in 1947, 750,000 people were killed in riots between Hindus and Moslems, and property damage was enormous. The Moslem area of western India became Pakistan. At least 12 million people left their ancestral homes and migrated to one or the other of the newly independent countries, and factories and other business establishments were vacated, causing unemployment for both Hindu and Moslem workers.

But religion is not the only problem in the contretemps between India and Pakistan. A major cause of both World War I and World War II was territorial disputes. In World War I, France wanted the return of Alsace-Lorraine, which it had lost to Germany after the Franco-Prussian War of 1870. In World War II, Germany wanted the return of Silesia and other territory it had lost after World War I. In the case of India and Pakistan, the territory is the Kashmir, and three wars have been fought over it. A part of Kashmir, which is mostly Moslem, was ceded to Pakistan. A plebiscite was then supposed to be held in order to determine the future status of the Kashmir, but it has not occurred. India contends that the Kashmir is vital to its national interest because it serves as a buffer between India and China.

The problems between India and Pakistan can be replicated in other parts of the world, although on a somewhat smaller scale. Certainly a major trouble spot in the world is the Middle East, where friction between the Arabs and Israelis exists and will continue to exist in the twenty-first century. Iran and Iraq were at war with each other during the 1980s, and both have created problems during the 1990s. There has been much bloodshed in Africa with tribal rivalries responsible for the genocide in Rwanda and Zaire. Political instability is high in African countries, and the world has become a far more difficult place to police. It is no longer possible to send gunboats and Marines in to put down disorders as the United States did in Latin America during the early part of the twentieth century.[11]

WHY SOME NATIONS ARE RICH AND OTHERS ARE POOR

Professor David Landes of Harvard has written a book called *The Wealth and Poverty of Nations*, in which he attempts to explain why some nations are rich and others are poor.[12] It begins with a discussion of geography, which he believes determines a nation's destiny. His premise is that a nation's natural endowments, including a temperate climate, have given certain areas of the world, such as Europe and the United States, an advantage over other areas. The Industrial Revolution occurred in Europe because its mild summers permitted intensive economic activity, unlike the tropics, where heat and humidity limited economic activity. The agricultural revolution of the nineteenth and twentieth centuries also occurred in nations with favorable climates and rainfall and raised their living standards. This may be contrasted to a tropical climate, where jungles and rainforests have inhibited the growth of agriculture.

CLIMATE AND POLITICAL SYSTEMS

Western democracy is a product of geography and climate, which supported a more independent way of life. In countries with less benign climates, state control of the individual was inevitable. In China and India, flood and drought made the control of water flow essential to survival. This involved the construction of large-scale hydraulic projects by forced labor. Only a centralized state could provide enough labor to work on these projects. Private property and individual initiative were luxuries the state couldn't afford because they were regarded as a threat to the ruling political and religious elites. Religion was also a product of climate and geography. It was often harsh and uncompromising in its tenets, and denigrated the role of women.

CULTURE AND ECONOMIC SUCCESS

The success of Europe and the United States can be attributed to the fact that geography created a culture conducive to economic growth. It was Protestantism, as epitomized by John Calvin and Martin Luther, that promoted the rise of modern capitalism by sanctioning a mode of behavior—rational, ordered, and hard-working—that led to business success. It gave encouragement to the belief that man could master his environment. Culture and geography also determined Japan's success. Buddhism also encouraged a similar work ethic.

But before *te deums* are sung proclaiming the reign of the United States as the leader of the twenty-first century, a caveat is in order. It was only a few years ago that many experts were proclaiming the twenty-first century as the Japanese century. In 1992 Lester Thurow, one of the most respected economists in America, confidently predicted that Europe would dominate the twenty-first century because of its superior type of capitalism. It can be argued that economic growth in the United States during the decade of the 1990s was not particularly spectacular; it is just that other countries had done worse. The current sense that the United States is on top of the world is based on an exaggeration of the implications of a few good years here and a few bad years elsewhere. It will certainly begin the twenty-first century with a headstart over Europe and Japan, both of which have major problems.

In 1992 *Time* published a special issue called *Beyond the Year 2000*. One of the articles in it was called "How the World Will Look in Fifty Years." One of its predictions was that Japan would weaken, Europe would triumph, and the United States would swallow some bitter cures. Its batting average at the end of the century was one out of three. Japan has weakened. It posed the question that was relevant at the time the article was written, "Is the United States in an irreversible decline as the world's premier economic power?" At that time it appeared to be so, but it is no longer true. However, there is no guarantee that this will continue to be true in the twenty-first century.

SUMMARY

Each century is progressively better-off than the preceding century, and the twentieth century was an improvement over the nineteenth century. People lived longer, were healthier, and had higher living standards than their counterparts in the previous century. Of course, two major world wars probably killed off more people than all of the previous wars in history combined. Assuming there is no nuclear holocaust caused by nations that don't like each other, certain predictions can be made. There is an astonishing increase in the rate of technological innovation that may move the world toward an improved quality of life. The economic environment is changing rapidly, where liberalized trade and investment could benefit all people and eradicate much of the poverty in the world. There is an urgent need to deal effectively with issues such as greenhouse gas emissions, megacity evolution, and demands on fresh water. International cooperation is of paramount importance.

Questions for Discussion

1. Is it inevitable that the United States will dominate the twenty-first century? What events could cause this not to happen?
2. What factors caused the end of colonialism?
3. Will the gap between rich nations and poor nations widen during the twenty-first century? What can be done about it?
4. Demographics will create problems for both rich and poor countries in the twenty-first century. Discuss.

Notes

1. "Rule Britannia" was written by James Thomson in 1740.
2. *The Economist*, April 25, 1998, p. 29.
3. Mortimer B. Zuckerman, "A Second American Century." *Foreign Affairs*. Vol 77, No. 3 (May–June 1998), pp. 18–31.
4. *Ibid.*, p. 31.
5. The gold standard lasted from 1821 to 1931. An ounce of gold was equal to $20.67 and 4.85 British pounds. Currency exchange rates between the United States and England were $4.85 = 1 pound.
6. The United States could buy gold for $35 an ounce. It provided backing for the dollar. The new international monetary standard lasted from 1945 to 1973.
7. See Chapter 15.
8. Argentina produced cattle and wheat, Brazil produced coffee, and Mexico produced oil.
9. Sixty percent of the world's population live in poor countries.
10. World Bank, *World Bank Atlas 2000* (Washington, D.C.: World Bank, 2000), p. 43.
11. During the early part of the twentieth century, the U.S. Marines occupied Haiti, Honduras, and Nicaragua. The United States invaded Mexico and had a Mexican president assassinated.
12. David S. Landes, *The Wealth and Poverty of Nations* (New York: Norton, 1998).

Recommended Reading

Haase, Richard, and Robert Litan. "Globalization and Its Disconnects." *Foreign Affairs*. Vol. 77, No. 3 (May/June 1998), pp. 2–6.

Landes, David L. *The Wealth and Poverty of Nations*. New York: W.W. Norton, 1998.

Longman, Philip J. "How Global Aging Will Challenge the World's Economic Well-Being." *U.S. News and World Report*. March 1, 1999, pp. 30–35.

United Nations Development Program. *Human Development Report, 1999*. New York: Oxford University Press, 1999.

World Bank, *Entering the 21st Century*. New York: Oxford University Press, 2000.

World Bank, *World Bank Atlas 2000*. Washington, D.C.: World Bank 2000.

INDEX